RESEARCH STORIES FOR INTRODUCTORY PSYCHOLOGY

RESEARCH STORIES FOR INTRODUCTORY PSYCHOLOGY

LARY SHAFFER

State University of New York at Plattsburgh

MATTHEW R. MERRENS

State University of New York at Plattsburgh

Allyn and Bacon

Boston ■ London ■ Toronto ■ Sydney ■ Tokyo ■ Singapore

Executive Editor: *Carolyn Merrill*
Editorial Assistant: *Lara Zeises*
Senior Marketing Manager: *Caroline Croley*
Production Editor: *Christopher H. Rawlings*
Editorial-Production Service: *Omegatype Typography, Inc.*
Composition and Prepress Buyer: *Linda Cox*
Manufacturing Buyer: *Megan Cochran*
Cover Administrator: *Jennifer Hart*
Electronic Composition: *Omegatype Typography, Inc.*

Library of Congress Cataloging-in-Publication Data

Shaffer, Lary.
    Research stories for introductory psychology / Lary Shaffer, Matthew R. Merrens.
        p.   cm.
    Includes bibliographical references and index.
    ISBN 0-205-29929-6 (alk. paper)
    1. Psychology—Research—Methodology.   2. Psychology.   I. Merrens, Matthew R. II.
Title.

BF76.5 .S43   2001
150′.7′2—dc21

                                                                              00-025330

Printed in the United States of America

10 9 8 7 6 5 4 3 2 1   05 04 03 02 01 00

To our wives, children, and grandchildren

CONTENTS

PART VIII   STRESS AND HEALTH   230

PREFACE

The goal of this book is to help you to see psychological studies in a larger scientific context and to understand the reasoning that underpins the structures of these studies. We do not believe that introductory students need to be protected from the procedures of scientific psychology. Our approach is to explain research methods as important parts of the stories of contemporary research studies. In order to think critically, you need to know that the findings of psychology are tightly laced to the methods: it makes little sense to talk about one without the other. By reading about both scientific methodology and the findings derived from it, you can come to appreciate what scientific psychology is really about. You will see that the results of studies discussed in this book may contradict the kinds of commonsense guesses about behavior that permeate the pop psychology of television, the Internet, magazines, and newspapers.

Although the research stories in this book have been retold, they have not been dumbed down. You will find appropriate levels of challenge as you master the material. Some details have been eliminated. Other detailed notions, required for understanding by the beginning student, have been introduced or expanded. Moreover, scientifically terse introductions and procedures have been more fully explicated, and statistical analyses have been reduced to understandable dimensions.

Sometime when you have a few minutes, you should go to the library and look at one or more of the original research articles that have been discussed in this book. Each primary reference is found in a footnote on the first page of the chapter. It might interest you to know how much editing and rewriting have been done in bringing this material to you.

While reading these chapters, you will see the gears and wheels of the process that generates knowledge about behavior. You must understand the methodological processes in order to be able to critically assess the validity of assertions about behavior. The kind of critical thinking you will develop with this book is a set of highly transferable skills. Critical thinking is essential for you in the job market or as a graduate school applicant.

Psychology is unique among the disciplines in the broad applicability of the skills you should learn. It is probably safe to say that all of you will be required to evaluate assertions about human behavior as part of your adult lives. Particularly in the age of the Internet, professional advancement will go to the person who can evaluate information. The World Wide Web is packed with information about human behavior. That information is only as good as the research methods that underlie it. The winning skill in the next century will be the ability to sort information along a continuum of quality or accuracy.

At the very least, when you are finished with these readings we hope that you will critically challenge assertions about behavior. Your first question should be, "Who found that out and what methods did they use?" Once you have answers, you can use your knowledge of methods to assess the validity of claims about behavior. The tool kit of skills you will get from this book can go with you not only to other courses, but also, more importantly, out into the world. The studies in this book are examples of good, contemporary psychological science. Because these stories are real science, they have flaws, limitations, and shortcomings. No study is perfect. Any study can be criticized, and one of our goals for an introductory course is to take you along with us while studies are critically examined for strong and weak points. Our experience suggests that this activity will leave you with a mature and practical grasp of psychology. We do not want you to accept findings uncritically. Instead, we want you to understand that a well-designed study is a powerful way to gather knowledge, even if there are practical limitations within the methods. The "facts" in any science are certain to change over time, but the ability to evaluate these facts is of lasting value.

You should be aware that this book consistently offers a scientific viewpoint about psychology. We believe that science is the most powerful method yet developed for establishing a confident understanding of behavior. We think a great disservice would be done to you if we were not steadfast in our commitment to science.

ACKNOWLEDGMENTS

This project would not have been possible without the tireless assistance of Ms. Mary Turner, Ms. Cheryl Lafountain, and Ms. Cynthia Pratt of the Feinberg Library at SUNY. They showed endless patience with requests for interlibrary loan and document copying. Bryan Kieser kindly helped us with Latin translation. Additionally, we gratefully acknowledge several of our undergraduate students for help with earlier versions of this material. Alan Morrison has been with us from the start of the project. We told him not to be shy about tearing chapters apart, and he took us at our word. He read the chapters multiple times and made insightful suggestions. Carrie Shapiro worked hard on the teaching materials that are used with the book. When Jen Edmonds laughed at our attempts to draw a few apparatus pictures, we challenged her to do better and she did. Introductory psychology students Lori Christopherson, Lachlan Chambliss, Surjit Chandhoke, Michael Harrington, and Sharon Clarke voluntarily made detailed corrections to each chapter while reading it as course material. Psychology department secretary Judy Dashnaw also volunteered to read the chapters and have made numerous improvements. The keen intelligence, detailed work, and generosity of these people have made this a better book.

While we have been working on the book, several of our colleagues have been willing to adopt it for use in their classes. Dr. Renee Bator, at SUNY Plattsburgh, as well as Dr. G. Terry Bergen, Dr. John Klein, and Ms. Julie Volkens, at Castleton State College, Castleton, Vermont, have used it in duplicated draft form since the beginning. In the past year it was also adopted by the Psych 1 staff at the University of Vermont: Dr. Justin Joffee, Dr. James Rosen, Mr. Joshua Cooper, Ms. Julianne Krulewitz, and Mr. David S. Henehan. The experience and comments of these supportive and enthusiastic scholars have made this a better book and we are very grateful to them. We are also grateful to Gordon D. Atlas, Alfred University; George T. Bergen, Castleton State College; Terry D. Blumenthal, Wake Forest University; James F. Calhoun, University of Georgia; Dianne Friedman, Radford University; Paul Greene, Iona College; R. Steven Schiavo, Wellesley College; Linda J. Skinner, Middle Tennessee State University; and Fred Whitford, Montana State University who offered helpful suggestions and comments that have strengthened the book.

We are eager to have your reactions so that we may continue to improve the book. Please feel free to write, phone, or email us at any time: Lary Shaffer: Department of Psychology, SUNY—Plattsburgh, 101 Broad Street, Plattsburgh, NY 12901, 518-564-3383, lawrence.shaffer@plattsburgh.edu; Matthew Merrens: Department of Psychology, SUNY—Plattsburgh, 101 Broad Street, Plattsburgh, NY 12901, 518-564-3379, matthew.merrens@plattsburgh.edu.

ABOUT THE AUTHORS

Lary Shaffer (D. Phil., Oxford University) is a State University of New York Distinguished Teaching Professor at SUNY—Plattsburgh. He is a recipient of the SUNY Chancellor's Award for Excellence in Teaching and has taught courses in introductory psychology, developmental psychology, and animal behavior since 1975. He is currently working on a new book of research stories that will be used to teach life span development.

Matthew R. Merrens (Ph.D., University of Montana) is professor of psychology at SUNY—Plattsburgh. He formerly served as chair of the psychology department at SUNY—Plattsburgh and is a recipient of the SUNY Chancellor's Award for Excellence in Teaching. He has edited four books on introductory psychology, developmental psychology, social psychology, and personality.

RESEARCH STORIES FOR INTRODUCTORY PSYCHOLOGY

CHAPTER 1

OH RATS!

If you ask most people, they will tell you that a psychology course is supposed to teach you to analyze peoples' minds. As a demonstration we are going to try to analyze your mind. This reading describes an experiment about rats. Now, here is what is on your mind:

> "Rats! *Rats?* Let's see, (flip, flip, flip) how long *is* this chapter, anyway?"

> or

> "Rats! *Rats?* I wonder if the bookstore would still give me all my money back if I sold this stupid book and dropped this course. After all, the book has hardly been used."

> or

> "Rats! *Rats?* This is probably just some junk they put in the first chapter. The rest of the book must be about the unconscious and interesting stuff like that."

> or

> "Rats! *Rats?* Damn! I thought that this was going to be a cool course and now, one page into it, I am reading about **RATS.**"

Did we read your mind? If we did, it was because we have common sense, rather than because we know about psychology. If we didn't, it shows that psychologists cannot read minds. Either way, there is no evidence here for mind reading. Hold that thought. You have only been reading this book for two minutes and you already may have learned something: people who tell you that they can read your mind are not psychologists. Psychologists know better than to say things like that.

Psychologists study behavior. Sometimes a lot can be learned about behavior from the study of rats. This chapter is really about behavior, not rats. Okay, so we lied when we implied that this chapter was about rats. If you were inclined to believe everything found in textbooks, then you have learned something else: textbooks sometimes lie. We will not lie to you (again) on purpose, but we may well lie accidentally. Psychology is a vital discipline and, as such, it is changing all the time. Although we intend to describe psychology as it is today, new research may alter current concepts, theories, or beliefs at any time.

Incorporating the research of C. Kim, L. Kalynchuk, T. Kornecook, D. Mumby, N. Dadgar, J. Pinel, and J. Weinberg, "Object-Recognition and Spatial Learning and Memory in Rats Prenatally Exposed to Ethanol," 1997, *Behavioral Neuroscience, 111*, pp. 985–995.

STUDYING RATS

Because psychologists usually study behavior, rather than a particular organism, not all research in psychology involves the study of human beings. Sometimes other animals are used because the researcher really wants to know about the behavior of that animal, often to answer questions about its evolution or ecology. In other cases, nonhuman animals are used as participants because they are more convenient. Many studies of learning have used rats because they were economical to maintain in large animal colonies that have rows and rows of drawerlike cages. The researcher who could use rats as participants had easy access to research participants from the animal colonies that used to be part of psychology departments in most universities. The behavior under investigation in basic studies of learning can sometimes be so similar from species to species that it does not matter what type of animal is studied. Nonhuman animals have also been the participants of choice when researchers believed that a study was too dangerous for human participants. In this case, the researchers may want to know about humans, but believe that other animals are sufficiently similar to permit their findings to be applied to humans. The experiment with rats to be discussed below was one of these important investigations in which humans could not be used as research participants.

AN EXPERIMENT

In this book, we will use the word *experiment* in a very restricted and special sense. When most people speak of an experiment, they are talking about unsystematically trying something, as in: "I'm going to do an experiment to see if dogs like carrots." You toss the dog a piece of carrot. If he eats it, dogs are presumed to like carrots and if he spits it out, they dislike them. *One* dog in *one* state of hunger with *one* piece of carrot does not tell us much of anything about dogs and carrots. Alternatively, someone might say "I am going to do an experiment to see what will happen if I go to bed early tonight." Aside from all the problems of drawing conclusions based on one person doing something on one day, there is the additional problem that no particular outcome has been anticipated. In a real experiment, there is a clear statement about what is expected to happen as a result of the procedures. The experiment is a test of the correctness of this statement, called the *hypothesis*. In the example of going to bed early, there is no hypothesis. Nothing is being tested, so nothing important is likely to be learned. Going to bed early might be accompanied by a variety of outcomes, such as getting more sleep and feeling rested or waking up earlier and feeling tired the next day. In any event, there is little basis for the conclusion that going to bed early caused either of these—they might easily have happened regardless of bedtime.

C. Kwon Kim and a number of colleagues (Kim et al., 1997) did an experiment to demonstrate the effects of learning in rats that had been exposed to alcohol. We have chosen to discuss this particular study because of the importance of the question. In addition, it has the structural characteristics of a well-conducted experiment. First, we are going to do an overview of this experiment and then we will go back and highlight the features that permit this study to belong to the rarefied and elite class of research called the experiment. As with other studies discussed in this book, this one is important for its findings, but it is also important for its methods. For reasons that will become clear, not every scientific study can have all the procedural elements that are part of the experiment reported by Kim et al. (1997). Each of these elements is important to ensure that the conclusions drawn from the study are accurate.

THIS EXPERIMENT

Kim and coworkers obtained both female and male rats of a well-known genetic strain from a breeder. Because rats from the same strain are genetically quite similar, the differences found in the experiment were not likely to be the result of some genetic differences among the sample of rats in the study. The rats were all maintained in cages in a room that had controlled temperature and lighting. Here, again, an effort was made to avoid differences that might affect the outcome of the study. The males and females were housed together until the females became pregnant. Pregnancy in rats is indicated by the loss of a mucous vaginal plug. When the females lost this plug, it was known that they were on Day 1 of their pregnancy, and they were moved to individual cages.

At this point, each female was randomly assigned to one of three groups. Group E was fed a totally liquid diet—a sort of liquid rat chow—which contained adequate food but derived 36 percent of the calories from ethanol. Ethanol is the same kind of alcohol that is in beer, wine, and other alcohol-containing drinks. There were 21 rats in group E. A second group was called the *pair-fed*, or PF, group. This group was fed throughout pregnancy on a liquid diet that was the same as that of Group E, except that a sugarlike substance, maltose-dextrin, was substituted for the alcohol in their diets. This group was called pair-fed because each rat in this group was fed the same amount of liquid food (in grams per kilogram of body weight) as one of the Group E animals. Through its own consumption, each Group E animal determined how much a Group PF animal would be allowed to eat. In this way these two groups were directly comparable except that one group had alcohol as part of every meal and one did not. A third group of 21 pregnant females, Group C, for *control*, was fed usual rat food and water. The special diets of Group E and Group PF were replaced with standard rat chow and water on Day 22 of gestation. The rat pups were born on about Day 23.

There were no differences among the three groups of rats in the number of live or stillborn offspring. On the day following birth, Group E and PF pups weighed less than Group C pups, but they caught up on subsequent days. By the time of birth, Group PF mothers weighed less than Group E or C mothers, but not alarmingly less. The weights of these mothers caught up and they were not different by Day 15 after birth. Their mothers raised all the pups until they were weaned at 22 days old. Then the pups were group housed by litter and sex until testing began. One male rat from each litter was randomly selected for testing. These rats were called the *participants*. When the participants were 16 months old, their learning was tested in a maze task.

The Test Situation

Two different tests were conducted on these rats. One of these involved a visual discrimination task that we will not discuss further because it showed no significant differences among any of the participants. The other was a maze learning task called the Morris water maze. The Morris water maze was a large (180-cm-diameter × 60-cm-high) tank that was filled to the 22-cm level with water made opaque with nontoxic white paint. This opaque water was a maze because somewhere in it, 3–4 cm below the surface, there was a 12-cm-diameter circular platform. From trial to trial the platform remained in the same place within the maze. The other features of the research room also remained the same and could act as visual-orienting cues to help the rat in finding the invisible submerged platform on successive trials.

The rat was put in the maze and would swim around until it found the platform. Finding the platform was rewarding for the rats because they could stop swimming and climb up on it. The rat could not see the submerged platform; it had to find the platform in space. Once the rat had found it, learning was measured by putting the rat back in the water and timing how long it took to find the platform again. This measure is called *latency*. It is the amount of time it takes to perform a specific task. As learning progresses, we would expect the latency to get less and less as the rats learned the exact location of the platform and found it faster.

The researchers would place the rat in the maze and then retreat behind a screen so that the rat could no longer see them. While concealed behind the screen, the researchers watched the rats by means of a video monitor. The video monitor was connected to a video camera directly above the maze, permitting observations to be made without interfering with the swimming rat. Researchers watched the rat on the monitor and timed the latency for finding the platform. The experimenters who worked with the rats in the maze did not know which group the rats belonged to: Group E, PF, or C. Each trial in the maze began when a single rat was placed in one of four equally spaced positions around the rim of the pool. The start position was randomly selected from one of these four. Once started, the rat would swim until it found the platform. If it did not find the platform in 90 seconds, the trial was over and the rat was removed from the pool. Each rat was tested by giving it six trials a day on each of 10 days in a row. This kind of procedure is often called testing the animal in "blocks of six trials over 10 consecutive days."

The last two trials were different. On the 59th trial, the platform was raised up to the point where it was visible. On the 60th trial, the platform was removed, and the rat was allowed to search for it for one minute. On this trial, the data consisted of the number of times the rat swam directly over the area where the platform had been located. The researchers used a clever way to make a permanent record of the swimming path of the rat: they secured a piece of thin paper over the screen of the video monitor and traced the image of the moving rat with a marker as it swam about. The result was a tracing of the route taken by the swimming rat. The measure of success was called *annulus crossing*. An annulus is a ring. The rats were scored correct for each crossing of a ring drawn on the paper around the location where the platform used to be. The 59th trial was conducted to test whether some rats failed to find the platform in earlier trials because they were merely unable to respond to visual stimuli within the maze. The researchers believed that rats who had been exposed to prenatal alcohol had complex cognitive disabilities, not merely visual deficits. If they were correct, then all groups of rats would be expected to do well on Trial 59. The 60th trial was a test of the persistence of the rat in seeking the approximate location of the platform. *Persistence* was another behavioral outcome that might have been affected by prenatal exposure to alcohol, and Trial 60 was designed to investigate this possibility. The researchers did not expect to find differences among the rats in persistence at the task, but conducted Trial 60 to confirm this belief.

Results

Although all rats improved, the rats from the ethanol group had significantly longer latencies when the task was to find the hidden platform (see Figure 1.1, top).

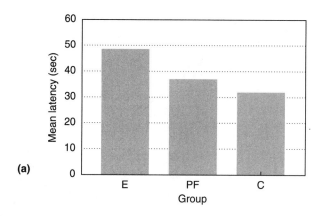

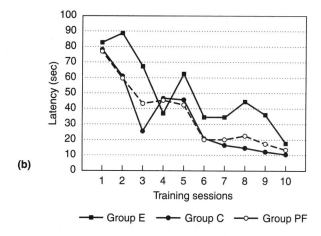

FIGURE 1.1   (a) **Mean Latency to Find the Platform by Group**   (b) **Latency to Find the Platform across Sessions**

As always when behavior is measured, there was some variability. Looking at the bottom graph in Figure 1.1, for example, you can see that on Day 4, the ethanol group had shorter latencies than the other groups. Statistical analyses can help to determine if this particular data point is sufficiently important to be considered more than chance variation. Something accounted for this difference, and it might be interesting to know what it was, but, in the absence of that information, the overall trend is clearly one of longer latencies for the ethanol group.

Figure 1.2 shows what happened on Trial 59, in which the platform was visible, and on Trial 60, in which the platform was missing and the rats were swimming across the area where it had previously been found.

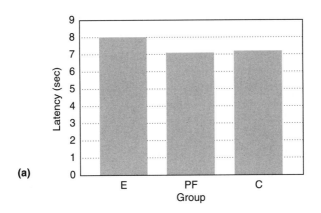

(a)

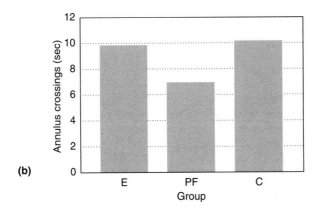

(b)

FIGURE 1.2   (a) Latency to Find the Visible Platform (b) Annulus Crossings at Site of the Missing Platform. Latency (in seconds) to find the visible platform in Trial 59 (a) and annulus crossings in searching for the missing platform in Trial 60 (b). None of the differences shown are statistically significant.

Although there might appear to be differences in latency making the ethanol group appear to be slower, these differences were so small that they were not statistically significant. Likewise, the numbers of annulus crossings when the platform was missing were also determined statistically to be no different from random or chance fluctuations in behavior. When differences are very small, statistical tests can help to determine if they are meaningful. In contrast, differences might merely be the result of small, ordinary, and unsystematic variations in behavior.

Discussion

Kim et al. (1997) concluded that prenatal exposure to alcohol could negatively influence the ability of rats to learn tasks involving the position of objects in space. Spatial learning may be different from some other kinds of learning that has been found to be less susceptible to the influence of prenatal alcohol exposure. This study supported the findings of a number of other studies of spatial learning and prenatal ethanol exposure. In contrast to the public perception, no one study "proves" anything for most scientists. Instead, it is recognized that all studies could have been more complete in some way. However, when a number of different studies by different researchers all point in the same direction, we may begin to have confidence in the overall findings. People who have training in science rarely talk about "proven" facts. That is the jargon used in advertisements and the news media. In contrast, when research outcomes are discussed, scientists acknowledge possible shortcomings by choosing words such as the findings *demonstrated* or *supported* the hypothesis that was being tested. The hypothesis in this study was that prenatal ethanol would affect later spatial learning in rats. It was supported.

These findings join an enormous body of research indicating the danger that maternal alcohol consumption poses to developing organisms. In humans, this is so well documented that it has a name: fetal alcohol syndrome, or FAS. This syndrome includes some superficial characteristics, such as widely spaced eyes and a thin upper lip. However, it can also include permanent mental retardation and brain damage. Devastating effects such as low intelligence and poor judgment have been linked to FAS (Streissguth, Barr, Sampson, & Bookstein, 1994). How much alcohol is safe for a woman to consume during pregnancy? None (Astley, Clarren, Little, Sampson, & Daling, 1992). In thinking about this, it is important to remember that early in pregnancy women probably do not even know they are pregnant. The woman who stops drinking alcohol as soon as she knows she is pregnant is probably too late.

This study was an experiment and, as we noted, experiments contain a number of features that give us particular confidence in their findings. Because this is the first study in this book, we are going to dissect it and discuss these important components. In the rest of the book, we will be using these concepts to describe other studies, so you would be well advised to learn them now.

THE HYPOTHESIS

The hypothesis is the notion that the research is designed to test. In this case, it was that prenatal exposure to ethanol results in spatial learning deficits. Outside of science, *hypothesis* is often used to describe a wild guess about how something works. In scientific terms, a hypothesis is more serious than that. A scientist usually has a number of reasons to believe a hypothesis is correct before it is carefully tested. Past research or informal, less-structured observations may suggest correct hypotheses. Sometimes researchers will do pilot tests, which are incomplete versions of research that can be quickly done, to suggest the correctness of a hypothesis. Following pilot testing, a formal study may be undertaken. Usually scientists believe their hypotheses are correct, and they are trying to convince others by doing careful research to test their beliefs.

THE INDEPENDENT VARIABLE

The independent variable is the *difference* that is directly created or arranged by the experimenter. In this study, the independent variable was the difference in diet of the rat mothers: ethanol, maltose-dextrin, or rat chow. It is often said that the experimenter *manipulates* the independent variable. This literally means that the experimenters *handle* that part of the study. Conceptually, the researcher is trying to create one or a few differences to see what effects they will have on outcomes. In this study, researchers were as careful as possible to eliminate any differences other than the ones they wished to study, the differences in diet. Perhaps a good way to think about a variable is to consider its opposite, a constant. In an experiment, most things are held constant, so that differences in outcomes can be seen to be the result of the independent variable.

THE DEPENDENT VARIABLE

The dependent variable is the important measured outcome of the study. It is the measure of the particular behavior that is being studied. This name is easy to remember because it *depends* on the independent variable. In this study, a dependent variable was the latency for finding the platform. Dependent variables are also sometimes called dependent *measures* or dependent *outcomes*. In some studies there may be several independent variables or several dependent variables. In this study, prenatal diet was the independent variable but there were several dependent variables. Latency to find the submerged platform was one. Latency to find the platform when it was raised was another dependent measure. Annulus crossing was a third dependent outcome.

Usually a two-sentence description of a study can be constructed if you identify the independent and dependent variable. Identification of the variables in a study is the first step to understanding it. For example, in research about the effects of loud music on studying, the loud music would be the independent variable and some measure of study effectiveness—maybe a nice little quiz—would be the dependent variable. Once you have found the variables, you can begin to ask if these particular variables constitute an adequate test of the hypothesis.

OPERATIONAL DEFINITION

An operational definition is the definition of some psychological characteristic in terms of the way it is measured. For example, an IQ test result might be the operational definition of intelligence. In the study we have discussed in this chapter, latency was an operational definition of learning and the number of annulus crossings was the operational definition of persistence. One way to critically evaluate studies is to examine the operational definitions to see if they are adequate. For example, intelligence might be operationalized by asking people how smart they are. For most purposes, that operational definition would probably not be adequate.

RANDOM ASSIGNMENT

In this study, rat mothers were randomly assigned to Groups E, PF, and C. This means that any rat had an equal chance of ending up in any group. There was also another random process at work because among the litters of rat pups, one animal was randomly selected to be in the study. Any other method of assigning rats to groups might result in some other characteristic of the rats playing a role in the dependent measure. The differences observed in the dependent variable are supposed to be the result of the differences the experimenter has manipulated. Random assignment to groups was the best way to ensure that the groups were not different before the independent variable was presented. For example, instead of random assignment, if the largest rat mothers were placed in Group C, the next largest in Group PF and the smallest in Group E, there would be no way to be sure that latencies observed in their pups were a result of alcohol exposure. Latencies might also be the result of maternal size.

No researcher would purposely assign all the big rats to one group, unless size was going to be studied as a variable. Nevertheless, the researcher wants to eliminate all systematic differences among animals in the groups to ensure that the only systematic difference remaining is the independent variable. The best way to achieve this is through random assignment to groups. Unless assignment is random, it is easy for an investigator to unknowingly introduce some kind of systematic differences into groups of participants. In a study like this, imagine that the rat parents arrived from the breeder in five crates, stacked one on top of another. Further imagine that the experimenters removed rats from the top crate, assigning them to Group E until Group E was full, then to Group PF, and last to Group C. This might be fine, but it might not. These rats were born and grew up in a rat colony. These colonies are racks of cages, usually five or six cages high and six or eight cages wide. Viewed from the front, the rat colony has the appearance of a rat apartment house, with each rat, or rat family, in its own little space. We do not know how the breeder decided which rat to put in which crate. The breeder might have loaded the crates by emptying cages in the top row of the rat colony first. Rats who had grown up in bottom cages might be behaviorally different than rats who grew up in top cages. You think this is far-fetched? Imagine growing up only being able to see people's knees. Unless this difference was to be the independent variable, a way to overcome it is to randomly assign rats to groups upon arrival at the lab where the experiment is to be conducted. Even if researchers think that such early experiences would make no difference, every effort is made to see that the only systematic difference between groups is the one created by the researcher: the independent variable.

Random assignment is not always possible. Nevertheless, part of thinking critically about research is being able to ask the right questions. If you were to read a study in which participants were not randomly assigned to groups, you should immediately begin to ask yourself about factors other than the independent variable, accidentally introduced into groups, that might have effects upon the dependent measures. Sometimes research articles do not say whether assignment to groups was random. When this happens, it is probably safest to conclude that they were not and to adjust your confidence in the findings accordingly.

Randomization may also appear in other aspects of a study. In this study, the swimming began at randomly assigned places in the pool. Something like a lottery was conducted ahead of time to determine where each rat would start. This was an additional attempt to remove bias. Imagine that two or three different experimenters are actually working with the rats in the pool. If one of them always starts the rats at the same location around the edge of the maze, this might influence the latency measure for these animals. If it also happened that this particular researcher started most of the rats from Group C, then the observed latencies might be merely a result of starting position, not the independent variable of alcohol exposure. This is another instance in which you can ask critical questions about studies. If some procedure was not randomized when you think it should have been, you might have less confidence in the findings.

"BLIND" STUDIES

Usually, if the participants in research did not know details, such as what group they were in or what the independent variable was, they were said to be *blind*. A study in which this is part of the procedure is sometimes called a *single-blind* study. If the participants were told what was going on in a study, there was an increased chance that their responses would be different, even unintentionally. In this study, the rat pups were not aware that other groups had been prenatally exposed to different things, so we somewhat facetiously suggest that this study qualifies to be thought of as single blind.

The term *blind experimenters* is used to indicate that the experimenters who actually worked with the participants did not know the group assignment of any particular participant. It is usually desirable that both the participants and the researchers who work with them in the experiment be prevented from discovering the details of group assignment or the nature of the independent variable. In a famous study, Robert Rosenthal (1973) gave students the task of teaching a rat to run a maze. The rats were randomly selected from a large group and given to individual students. However, some students were told that they had a smart rat and some were told that their rat was not very smart. Although the rats were really randomly assigned to student experimenters, the students who believed that their rats were smart ended up with rats who did better in the maze-learning task. Further study indicated that these students, without being aware of it, treated their rats differently. For example, they handled the rats more often, and this was associated with better maze performance. If experimenters can transmit their expectations to rats, it is probably even easier to do so with humans. For this reason, whenever possible, neither participants nor researchers should have knowledge that would allow them to react differently to the independent variable. When this is done a study is called *double blind*.

The American Psychological Association now discourages the use of the term *blind* because it considers this to be an insensitive label that is often easy to avoid. New studies in psychology are more likely to say that participants were *unaware* rather than *blind*. Nevertheless, the concepts of *single blind* and *double blind* are used in many other scientific fields and universally in older studies, so it is important that you understand what this means. There is a large section in the *Publication Manual* of the American Psychological Association that offers guidelines designed to help authors to reduce bias in the language of research reports (American Psychological Association, 1994).

CONTROL GROUPS

You know by now that the independent variable is the difference that the experimenter handles, or manipulates. In order to see the effect of prenatal ethanol, it was essential to compare the behavior of some rats who were exposed to prenatal alcohol with some who were not exposed to it. The rats who were exposed to prenatal alcohol were called the experimental group, and any rats who were not exposed to prenatal alcohol were said to belong to *control groups*. Sometimes there are two or more control groups. In other research designs, people can serve as their own control group by receiving one version of the independent variable at one time and another one later. In this study, both Group PF and Group C were control groups. The reason why there were two control groups may have been obvious to you as you read about the study. The experimental group had a liquid diet with alcohol as a component. If they had been compared only to Group C, the researchers would not know if the effects observed had been a result of alcohol compared to no alcohol, a solid diet compared to a liquid diet, or both. Group PF had a liquid diet but had no alcohol. The alcohol was replaced with a calorically equal substance in the diet of Group PF. To be sure that the quantity of liquid diet was the same in Group E and Group PF, each rat in Group PF was given the same amount of food as a rat chosen from Group E. This is called pair-feeding in this study, but a more general term for it is to say that the control group was *yoked* to the experimental group. A yoke is an old-fashioned wooden device that hitches two farm animals side by side so that they can pull a vehicle. The scientific use of this term means that the behavior of one participant determines what happens to another participant.

CAUSE AND EFFECT

The experiment is a very powerful way of testing hypotheses. However, it is often not possible to do an experiment, and other scientific methods must be used. The advantage of a carefully conducted experiment is that it allows us to draw conclusions about cause and effect. One of the reasons why psychology exists is to find causes for behavior. The experiment is the only way to do this with any confidence. In our everyday lives, we do not generally require an experiment before we conclude that some event has caused a certain behavior. For example, if you are backing your car out of a parking spot and hit a telephone pole, you may become angry. It is quite likely that the event of hitting the pole was the cause of your anger. We do not need to do an experiment in which a large randomly assigned group of people damages cars and another group does not in order to believe that accidents make us feel angry. This is not an important question. However, there are many important questions that psychology can address using the most powerful method yet developed for determining cause and effect: the experiment. Nonexperimental methods may tell us a great deal about behavior, but they should not be used to conclude that an independent variable is the cause of a dependent outcome or effect. As you will see, even true experiments are always limited in their scope, and we believe that conclusions about cause and effect from experiments should be made with appropriate caution.

There are many other scientific approaches discussed in this book, as well as a number of other experiments. As we will stress, these scientific methods are not perfect or flawless, but they are a great deal better than other approaches to knowledge such as hunches, guesses, intuitions, individual experiences, or the uncritical opinions of others.

RIGHTS OF RESEARCH PARTICIPANTS— THE ETHICAL ISSUE

There are committees in research institutions that examine each research proposal to ensure that the rights of the participants are considered. Even in research with rats, it is required that the research not be trivial and that the research design be sufficient to permit robust conclusions to be drawn. For humane reasons, researchers would have to describe what was going to happen to the rats at the conclusion of the research. The rights of research participants have been a major issue since the late 1960s and, as a result, it is now fairly difficult to do psychological research on any organisms. When the participants are people, the ethics of deception is an issue: is it fair to allow humans to participate in an experiment when they are not fully aware of the hypothesis?

Informed consent is now required before people can be research participants. People must be given quite a bit of information about what will happen to them in the study before they finally decide to participate. In some cases, this may mean that it is not possible to conduct an experiment in which the participants are unaware, or blind, to the conditions. It must also be made clear to participants that they are free to leave, without penalty, at any time during the experiment.

REFERENCES

American Psychological Association (1994). *Publication manual of the American Psychological Association* (4th ed.). Washington, DC: Author.

Astley, S. J., Clarren, S. K., Little, R. E., Sampson, P. D., & Daling, J. R. (1992). Analysis of facial shape in children gestationally exposed to marijuana, alcohol, and/or cocaine. *Pediatrics, 89,* 67–77.

Kim, C., Kalynchuk, L., Kornecook, T., Mumby, D., Dadgar, N., Pinel, J., & Weinberg, J. (1997). Object-recognition and spatial learning and memory in rats prenatally exposed to ethanol. *Behavioral Neuroscience, 111,* 985–995.

Rosenthal, R. (1973, September). The Pygmalion effect lives. *Psychology Today, 1,* 56–63.

Streissguth, A. P., Barr, H. M., Sampson, P. D., & Bookstein, F. L. (1994). Prenatal alcohol and offspring development: The first fourteen years. *Drug & Alcohol Dependence, 36,* 89–99.

CHAPTER 2

PSYCHICS AND SCIENTISTS

Do you know what this chapter is about? Then you must be psychic! (Or maybe you read the title.) This illustrates the main point of the chapter: although many people believe in psychic phenomena, there are also perfectly normal explanations for these seemingly paranormal happenings. There is no need to resort to unknown powers of the mind.

Many of us have had the experience of thinking about someone when the phone rings, and the phone call turns out to be from the person of whom we were thinking. Is this really *precognition*, the ability to predict the future through psychic means? It is possible to collect a little data to study this question. Keep a piece of paper near the phone and, each time it rings, guess who it is and write the guess down before answering. Circle the guesses that turn out to be correct. If someone in particular usually calls you at about the same time every day, you are likely to be correct in guessing his or her name because you would recognize the time he or she usually calls. Time of day explains those cases, so set them aside. The real test of your precognitive ability is to be able to correctly identify the unexpected callers. You will be correct once in a while just by chance. These unusual occasions on which you are correct are likely to be remembered clearly. The thousands of times you are not correct are forgotten; they are too ordinary to be memorable. Keeping a record will illustrate this for you, if you need illustration. The failure to remember thousands of disconfirming instances while remembering a few successes probably explains psychic precognitive identification of phone callers. The correct guesses are examples of coincidences.

Coincidence is a technical term that means that two events have occurred together either by accident or by chance. When someone you have not heard from in years phones you while you happen to be thinking of him or her, it is probably a coincidence. In order to think clearly about these things, you need to know that in a large set of events, coincidences are highly probable. They are almost *certain* to happen. Imagine that you have five unbiased coins. If you toss all five at once, the probability that they will all come up heads is 1 in 32, or about 3 percent. If you toss them 100 times, however, the probability of getting 5 heads at least once is 96 percent. It is almost certain to happen. Media reports often speak of "remarkable" coincidences as if they were

Incorporating the research of R. Wiseman, D. West, and R. Stemman, "An Experimental Test of Psychic Detection," 1996, *Journal of the Society for Psychical Research, 61*, pp. 34–45.

unexpected. In a large series of events, coincidences are not unexpected or remarkable. If you receive about five phone calls a day you will have almost 10,000 calls in five years. With that many opportunities, it would not be at all surprising if you were to occasionally guess the correct identity of an unusual caller in advance.

Cable television and the Internet have many advertisements for psychics who claim to be able to use special powers to delve into your life and predict what will happen in the future. We believe that if they could really predict the future, they would be in Las Vegas predicting the future of roulette wheels and raking in the money. Of course, at the four dollars a minute they charge for talking to people on the phone, they are making $240.00 an hour, so they are not doing too badly. One of the best-known psychics in recent times was the late Jeanne Dixon. Some people believe that in 1956 she predicted the assassination of President Kennedy seven years before it happened. What she actually predicted was that the person, unknown to her, who won the 1960 election would "be assassinated or die in office, but not necessarily in the first term." This vague statement was a reasonable surmise given that seven of the twentieth-century presidents either died in office (McKinley, Harding, Roosevelt), were very seriously ill (Wilson and Eisenhower), or experienced assassination attempts (Truman). It is also noteworthy that Jeanne Dixon failed to predict her own death in 1997.

The words *psi* and *parapsychology* are used as blanket terms to refer to unusual human processes of information or energy transfer, such as sensing or moving things, that are currently unexplained in terms of known physical, biological, or psychological mechanisms. This includes a variety of supposed happenings such as:

telepathy—knowing others' thoughts

psychokinesis—moving and otherwise affecting objects in the physical world through thought processes

clairvoyance—receiving information about remote events using pathways other than recognized sense organs

Some people who want to believe in psychic phenomena feel that the scientific community has somehow "ganged up" to suppress evidence of psi because it violates accepted theories or beliefs. This is not the case. There have been hundreds of research studies investigating paranormal phenomena, and nothing of substance has been found (Blackmore, 1996). Psi has not been rejected because it violates accepted scientific notions. It has been rejected as an explanation because there are plenty of ordinary rational explanations for the observed phenomena. The scientific arena is rigorous. Methods and procedures are scrutinized carefully before studies are accepted for publication. Yet, many initially unpopular ideas have passed the test of this scrutiny and have been accepted. Ideas such as continental drift and the circulation of the blood received acceptance in science because the evidence for them was compelling. At this point, there is no convincing evidence for psi. Magician James Randi, who has been a crusader in exposing fake psychics, offered $10,000 to anyone who could demonstrate psi in properly controlled conditions (Randi, 1982). He made this public offer in 1968 and has not yet had to pay the reward money. In a typical case of an attempt to win the prize money, a psychic claimed that he could use psychokinesis to turn the pages of a phone book without touching them. Randi gave him the chance to do so, but being a magician himself, Randi knew that these tricks are usually accomplished with small streams of compressed air emanating from somewhere, such as the psychic's sleeve. In what was to be a television demonstration of psychic page turning, Randi instituted a simple but elegant control. He scattered Styrofoam beads around the phone book, which would move at the slightest puff of air. The psychic walked around the book for 10 minutes sweating and scowling before claiming that bright lights were inhibiting his psychic powers (Gardner, 1989).

Although it may be widely believed that police use psychics in finding solutions to crime, the data available present a different picture. Sweat and Durm (1993) conducted a survey of police departments in the 50 largest cities in the United States. Although 17 percent of the police departments that responded said that they handled information from psychics "differently" than information from the general public, *all* police respondents noted that psychic information was no more helpful than information from the general public.

Psychics have frequently claimed to be able to use their powers to assist law enforcement agencies in the solution of baffling crimes (Nickell, 1994). The difficulty is that the reports are anecdotal. When scientists speak of *anecdotes*, they are referring to stories that people tell of personal experiences or hearsay. The intention is to use the story as evidence for some assertion about behavior. In this case, someone might say, "I heard about a psychic who was able to solve a murder that stumped the police." If you are thinking critically about this assertion, you should begin to question the source and the quality of the information. Psychics may make several vague and sometimes conflicting predictions about a crime. Once the real story of the crime is known, the correct predictions are remembered and the incorrect ones are forgotten (Hoebens, 1985; Rowe, 1993). This situation is very similar to the one we described concerning precognition and telephone calls. The rare instance that seems to confirm psi is remembered, and all the failures to confirm are forgotten.

An additional problem in evaluating the work of psychics in crime detection was identified by Lyons and Truzzi (1991). They pointed out that success in information about crimes should be measured against a baseline expectation. For example, a psychic may have told police that a person who suddenly disappeared is now dead, and this was later found to be accurate. In order to evaluate critically the extent of clairvoyant abilities, it would be necessary to know what percentage of people who suddenly disappear are later found to be dead. If this was a high-frequency outcome, then there may be nothing spectacular or important about the accuracy of the prediction. Anyone could have made it with no knowledge about the crime. If the psychic prediction referred to a highly unusual means of victim disposal, then it might have warranted more attention.

One of the earliest scientific investigations of psychic ability in crime detection involved four psychics who were shown photographs and objects that might have been related to crimes. Some of this material was evidence in criminal cases and some had nothing to do with any crimes. The psychics were asked to describe the crimes that might have involved the pictures and objects. The final report of this demonstration concluded that nothing of interest to police was produced by the psychics (Brink, 1960). Martin Reiser of the Los Angeles police department and his colleagues carried out a similar study with 12 psychics (Reiser, Ludwig, Saxe, & Wagner, 1979). Each psychic was presented with physical evidence from real crimes. The procedure was double blind: neither the psychics nor the experimenters knew anything about the crimes in advance. Psychics made predictions that were sorted into categories such as type of crime, victim, and suspect. These descriptions were compared with actual information about the crimes. The performance of the psychics was poor. On one crime, police had established 21 real facts. The psychics averaged 4 correct. On another, 33 facts were known and the psychics averaged 1.8 correct descriptions. Lyons and Truzzi (1991) have criticized this study and similar ones for methodological flaws. The data coding involved assessing a match or mismatch between each psychic statement and the key facts in the case. Other things that psychics said were simply discarded. For example, one crime involved the murder of a church historian. One of the psychics believed that the crime had something to do with a church, but there was no way in the coding scheme to categorize this small, but accurate, assessment. Another methodological problem was that if psychics produced no information about a particular key fact, it was scored as a wrong response. This meant that, for example, not stating the sex of the victim was scored the same as saying the victim was male, when, in fact, she was female. These methodological issues might seem to put psychics at a disadvantage, thus lowering their scores and ignoring responses that did contain some correct information.

The research, which is the focus of this chapter, is from a study by Richard Wiseman, Donald West, and Roy Stemman (1996). They compared three self-proclaimed psychics against three college students in a test of psychic ability. One of their goals was to overcome shortcomings of earlier studies. The authors were contacted by a television production company that wanted to produce a program about psychic ability for a syndicated television series, *Arthur C. Clarke's Mysterious Universe*. The producers wanted to film a well-controlled test of psychic ability, and they were prepared to allow the psychologists to design the study and to specify the details of methodology to be followed.

PARTICIPANTS

Participants included three well-known psychics residing in Great Britain. One of these people had recently received considerable attention in the British news media because of claims that he had consistently and accurately predicted several crimes, terrorist attacks, and airplane disasters. He claimed that these predictions occurred in dreams. Although he had not been subjected to any formal assessment of accuracy, his local police department issued a statement saying he was "taken seriously," and that the information he provided was "acted upon immediately." The other two psychics in the study both worked as professional psychics. The participants in the other group for the study were three students recruited from the psychology department at the University of Hertfordshire. None of them claimed to have any psychic powers or any particular interest in solving crimes.

PROCEDURE

This study is an example of a research design called a quasi experiment. A difference between a quasi experiment and a true experiment is that the participants are not randomly assigned to groups. They cannot be, because they already belong to the groups to be studied before the research begins. In this case, they were either psychics or nonpsychics (students). Within psychology, opinions differ about whether or not this difference should be called an *independent variable.* There is no disagreement when this term is used to designate an experimental manipulation done to randomly assigned participants. Issues arise when the researcher does not create the input variable; rather it is already a characteristic of the participants before the beginning of the study. In the strictest sense, being a psychic or being a student is not an independent variable because the experimenter has not created it. We will adopt this strict sense. We do this not to be pedantic or picky, but because occasionally precision of thought and of phrasing is warranted. Unless there is an experimenter-created independent variable, no evidence has been produced for cause and effect. Often the main interest in behavior is to attempt to uncover causal components, and we believe that the somewhat common broad use of *independent variable* only clouds critical analysis of results. The only reason why we raise this issue is that published studies sometimes say that preexisting group characteristics, such as *gender* or *intelligence level*, are independent variables. Some statistical analyses also refer to preexisting group differences as independent variables. Although we allow that this is a judgment call, we are going to use the strict definition of an independent variable as something created by an experimenter. Instead, terms such as *predictors, antecedents, correlates,* or *participant variables* may be used to describe the relationship between group membership and outcomes measured in a quasi-experimental design.

The Essex Police Museum supplied three objects, each of which had been involved in a different actual crime. These objects were an old and rotting shoe belonging to a woman who had been murdered and buried, a deformed bullet recovered from the scene of a gunshot murder, and a red scarf that was used in a strangulation. Each of the crimes had been solved, and a great deal of detail was known about each one. Great care was taken to ensure that the people with whom the participants interacted in the lab had no knowledge of the crime. Sergeant Fred Feather, curator of the police museum, brought the objects to the lab, placed them on a table, and labeled them A, B, and C. He left the test area and waited in a distant part of the building while the tests were being conducted. The researcher who interacted with the participants during the tests knew nothing about the crimes or the objects. Participants were brought, one at a time, to the room where the objects were laying on a table. They were encouraged to handle the objects and to speak aloud any ideas, images, or thoughts that might be related to the crimes. They were told they could take as much time as they wished and could say as little or as much as they liked. During the test they were left alone in the room. With their full cooperation and knowledge, everything they said or did was filmed through a one-way mirror.

In advance, Sergeant Feather had supplied information for each of the crimes. This information permitted one of the researchers to construct six statements that were true of that particular crime, but untrue of the other crimes. These statements referred to specific aspects of the particular crime that were not likely to be true of crimes in general. This was done to eliminate correct answers from educated guessing that had nothing to do with psychic powers. For example, one might guess that a stabbing crime in a home occurred in the kitchen, because that is where most knives are kept. The three sets of 6 statements were combined and randomly ordered into a single list of 18 statements. Examples of these were:

> An accomplice involved
> Perpetrator aged in his twenties
> A link with milk
> Victim had only one son, aged four

After each participant was finished handling the objects and talking about them, one copy of the list of 18 crime descriptors was provided for each object. Participants were told that six of the statements were true for the crime associated with each object. Their task was to make check marks beside the six true statements for the particular crime connected with each object. They were allowed to take as much time as they wanted to complete this task. When they finished, they were ushered to a waiting area away from participants who had not yet been tested.

RESULTS

The number of correctly identified statements for each participant, out of six possible, is shown in Figure 2.1.

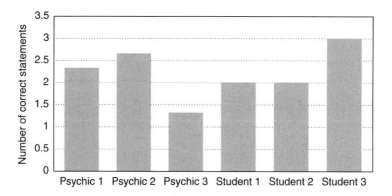

FIGURE 2.1   Participant's Identification of Statements. Average number of correct statements selected by each participant for all three objects combined. The statements about a crime were chosen from a list of 18 statements, 6 of which were correct. Total possible correct was 6.

The data in Figure 2.1 are the average number correct for each participant averaged across all three objects. The mean correct for the psychics as a group was 2.09 and for the student group it was 2.33. None of the means, individual or group, were statistically significantly different from the rest. The psychics did not appear to be better or worse than the students in identifying correct statements about crime objects.

Wiseman et al. (1996) wanted to be sure that the ability of the psychics was not underestimated by the methodology of the study. Choosing statements from a list did not take into account correct statements that the psychics might have made in handling and talking about the objects. To assess this qualitative information, a rater who was not involved in the test transcribed and separated each comment made by any of the participants. A list was made of all comments each participant made relating to a single crime. On this list, the order of these statements about each crime was randomized. These lists were then presented to two additional people, who had read about the crimes, acting as judges. The judges were asked to rate each of the statements about the crimes on a scale from 1 (very inaccurate) to 7 (very accurate). The ratings of the two judges for each participant were averaged and are shown in Figure 2.2.

The psychics made a total of 39 statements, and the students made 20 statements. There was no significant difference between the mean accuracy of the psychics and of the students (psychic mean = 3.83, student mean = 5.63). The reason why the accuracy level of these statements was so high is that many of the comments were obvious from the nature of the object. For example, one of the objects was a scarf and most of the comments correctly predicted that it had been used in a strangulation murder. A deformed bullet elicited comments such as "loud bang heard," "involved a shooting," and "looks like a squashed bullet." These are accurate, but unsurprising. Wiseman and his colleagues noted that no participant produced even one piece of information that would have been helpful to police in the investigation of the crimes.

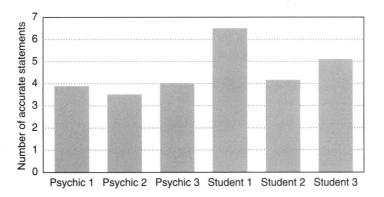

FIGURE 2.2 Comments Judged to Be Accurate. Average number of unrestricted comments and statements made about crimes that were judged as being correct. Total possible correct was seven.

DISCUSSION

The results in this study showed that the psychics were as unsuccessful as students at choosing correct statements about crimes. Neither group performed above the chance level. In addition a more qualitative analysis of free comments also showed the psychics to perform at the same level as the students. After the study, all the participants were told about the findings. When presented with their results, none of the students thought that they had performed very well. However, all three psychics thought they had been "very successful." Throughout the study, the psychics appeared eager and willing to participate under the test conditions. As the psychics happily talked about their performances, they began to rebuild the history of what had happened. They emphasized small, vague, or somewhat correct statements and seemingly forgot they had said things that had been contradictory or wrong.

Following the test, one of the psychics appeared on a nationally televised talk show and said: "I have proved it [my psychic ability] in laboratories. In fact, only three weeks ago I did a test at the Department of Psychology at Hatfield University [The University of Hertfordshire in Hatfield, U.K.], which—I mean—they are just going around thinking 'How does he do this?' I don't know how I do it but it does happen." This was, of course, completely untrue. Nothing amazing or out of the ordinary happened in the test reported by Wiseman and his coauthors. The psychic's assertion was challenged on the program by psychologist Dr. Susan Blackmore and later Wiseman appeared on a different program in the same series to further deny the suggestion that the Hertfordshire test had resulted in anything other than negative findings.

Susan Blackmore (1996) spent years doing research on psi, working very hard to find evidence for psychic phenomena. The conclusion she drew from this work makes a fitting conclusion for this chapter, as well:

> I now know that the very idea of psi has got me nowhere. Parapsychology is often held up as the science of the future, the science that will tackle all those questions about the nature of mind or the farther reaches of human experience, the science that will force a new paradigm to topple the old and serve as a route to spirituality. But it does not deliver.

REFERENCES

Blackmore, S. J. (1996). *In search of the light: Adventures of a parapsychologist.* Buffalo, NY: Prometheus Books.

Brink, F. (1960). Parapsychology and police investigations. *International Criminal Police Review, 134,* 3–9.

Gardner, M. (1989). *How not to test a psychic: Ten years of remarkable experiments with Pavel Stepanek.* Buffalo, NY: Prometheus Books.

Hoebens, P. H. (1985). Reflections on psychic sleuths. In M. Truzzi and P. Kurtz (Eds.), *A skeptic's handbook of parapsychology.* Buffalo, NY: Prometheus Books.

Lyons, A., & Truzzi, M. (1991). *The blue sense.* New York: Warner Books.

Nickell, J. (1994). *Psychic sleuths: ESP and sensational cases.* Buffalo, NY: Prometheus Books.

Randi, J. (1982). *Flim flam: Psychics, ESP, unicorns and other delusions.* Buffalo, NY: Prometheus Books.

Reiser, M., Ludwig, L., Saxe, S., & Wagner, C. (1979). An evaluation of the use of psychics in the investigation of major crimes. *Journal of Police Science and Administration, 7,* 18–25.

Rowe, W. F. (1993). Psychic detectives: A critical examination. *Skeptical Inquirer, 17,* 159–165.

Sweat, J. A., & Durm, M. W. (1993). Psychics! Do police departments really use them? *Skeptical Inquirer, 17,* 148–158.

Wiseman, R., West, D., & Stemman, R. (1996). An experimental test of psychic detection. *Journal of the Society for Psychical Research, 61,* 34–45.

CHAPTER 3

RUN FOR YOUR LIFE

The relationship between physical fitness, life stress, and health is widely discussed in the media. The general assumption is that a state of good fitness will act to strengthen the individual against the aversive stresses of life and furthermore serve to maintain a state of good health. The following synopsis of research shows that good physical fitness has been associated with *medical benefits:*

- Reduced cardiovascular illness and death (Oberman, 1985)
- Lowered blood pressure (Blair, Goodyear, Gibbons, & Cooper, 1984)
- More effective carbohydrate metabolism (Lennon et al., 1983)
- More effective fat metabolism (Rosenthal, Haskell, Solomon, Widstrom, & Reavan, 1983)

Research has also shown the following positive *psychological benefits* are associated with being in good physical shape:

- Improved self-concept (Hughes, 1984)
- Reduced depressive mood states (Folkins & Sime, 1981)
- Improved cognitive functioning (Tomporowski & Ellis, 1986)

The accumulating research suggests that being physically fit is an important component of physical and psychological health. The focus of Jonathan Brown's research described in this chapter is whether physical fitness does indeed have a positive stress-buffering effect, reducing or moderating the negative effects of stress. Some research (Brown & Siegel, 1988; Holmes & Roth, 1985) has found that physically fit individuals, compared to those who are less fit, have less physiological reactivity to induced or naturally occurring stress. A potential problem in much of this previous research was the use of participants' self-reports as the dominant measures. Previous research relied heavily on participants' reports of how much they exercised and how often they became ill. Participants' reports of their own behavior can be a source of error because they are subjective. Subjective reports by participants often rely on memories or opin-

Incorporating the research of J. D. Brown, "Staying Fit and Staying Well: Physical Fitness as a Moderator of Life Stress," 1991, *Journal of Personality and Social Psychology, 60*, pp. 555–561.

TABLE 3.1   **Measurement Examples**

BEHAVIOR	OBJECTIVE MEASURE	SUBJECTIVE MEASURE
Typing	Words per minute	Self-report of typing skill
Driving	Number of accidents or tickets	Self or instructor rating of skill
Intelligence	IQ score	How smart you believe you are
Reading	Pages read per hour	Self-report of books read
TV viewing	Minutes watched per day	Personal estimate of TV viewing

ions. Although a number of self-report assessments are part of the research reported in this chapter, Brown seeks to add objective indicators of exercise, fitness level, and physical health to help eliminate sources of subjectivity. In contrast to subjective reports, objective indicators are typically assessed on numerical scales. The issue of measurement of behavior is a central concern for psychologists. Objectivity in measurement is preferred over the subjective approach because it minimizes error. For example, if you attempted to assess whether your child has fever, a numerical measure of body temperature taken with a thermometer is a better measure than the subjective approach of holding your hand on her head or asking her if she feels warm. Table 3.1 provides some examples of both types of measurements.

CORRELATIONAL RESEARCH

A research design typically used in research about fitness and health is correlational. We will see this same correlational strategy in a number of other chapters including Chapter 13 about Field's research on the relationship between day care for young children and later measures of personality, social skills, and academic development. The correlational approach to research looks at the relationship between variables under investigation. As you will see in reviewing the results of this research, the findings are expressed in terms of a statistic called the correlation coefficient. The correlation coefficient is often symbolized by the lowercase letter r. A correlation coefficient gives two pieces of information about the relationship between variables: the strength and the direction. The strength component of the correlation coefficients occurs on a scale ranging from −1.00 to +1.00. The closer the number is to 1.00 (+ or −), the stronger the magnitude of the relationship between variables. Direction is indicated by the sign (+ or −) of the correlation. Correlations that are negative reflect an inverse relationship between the two variables being measured. An inverse relationship means that as one variable increases, the other variable decreases (or vice versa). A positive correlation means that both variables being assessed either increase or decrease together. As the absolute value of the number in the correlation coefficient increases, either toward −1.00 or +1.00, the strength of the relationship is greater. For example a correlation of −.86 is stronger than a correlation of +.59. The strength of the relationship is solely based on the number and not on the sign. Initially many students make the mistake of assuming a correlation with a positive sign is stronger than a negative one; again, the sign tells you about the direction of the relationship and the number tells you about how powerful it is. This means that as the number increases toward 1.00, in either a positive or negative direction, the strength of the relationship and therefore the predictive "power" is increased. The sign (+ or –) tells you how the variables are related (direct or inverse). Table 3.2 provides an illustration of the correlation range with qualitative descriptions of the strength of the correlations relationship at various points, while Table 3.3 presents some examples of variables that are likely to be correlated positively, negatively, and not much at all. We believe the positive and negative relationships in Table 3.3 would be quite strong.

TABLE 3.2   Examples of Positive, Negative, and No Correlation

STRONG POSITIVE CORRELATIONS
Study hours and grade point average
Calories consumed and body weight
Watching TV violence and engaging in aggressive behavior

STRONG NEGATIVE CORRELATIONS
Altitude and percentage of oxygen in air
Optimism and illness
Shyness and number of friendships

LITTLE OR NO CORRELATION
College ID number and grade point average
IQ in infancy and IQ in adulthood
Blood type and level of depression

TABLE 3.3   The Range of Correlation Coefficients

"APPROXIMATE" CORRELATION STRENGTH	CORRELATION COEFFICIENT
Very strong	*–1.0* to *–.80*
Strong	*–.80* to *–.60*
Moderate	*–.60* to *–.30*
Weak	*–.30* to *–.10*
No correlation	*–.10* to **+.10**
Weak	**+.10** to **+.30**
Moderate	**+.30** to **+.60**
Strong	**+.60** to **+.80**
Very strong	**+.80** to **+1.00**

Italics = inverse relationship or negative correlation

Bold = direct relationship or positive correlation

The predictive power of strong correlations can be seen because if you know the value of one variable, you can make a fairly good prediction about the value of the other. If I were the admissions director of a college and knew there was a strong positive relationship between a college entrance exam and final college grade point average, entrance exams would be a powerful tool for making admissions selection decisions. If I, as admissions director, wanted solely to consider accepting students who would have high grade point averages at graduation, such an examination would be an excellent selection tool because of its predictive power. As correlation coefficients approach zero (either – or +) it is likely that the variables studied have little relationship to one another and little predictive power. The relationship between hair length and IQ is probably near zero, as is the relationship between shoe size and family size.

Be aware that even a strong relationship between the two variables in correlational research does not ensure that those two variables are linked in a causal relationship. Making causal assertions from correlational data is a very common error in everyday life. For example, the number of churches in a city and the amount of criminal activity are positively correlated. We would probably not make the causal assumption that these two measures are positively related because churches are a breeding ground for crime or because criminal activities lead to church construction. This example illustrates how a variable that is not being measured and is not under study can influence the two variables you are studying. In this example, population is a likely "causal" factor that affects both the crime rate and the rate of church construction. Where population is large there are more churches and more crime. Other factors such as income and education levels also contribute. Of course it may be the case that two variables that are correlated do have a causal relationship, however correlational design does not provide information about causality that would permit a researcher to make a causal claim based on correlational design. In many cases it is possible to use an experimental design to explore causality. However, in some cases experimental designs are inappropriate. For example, the presumed link between smoking and cancer in humans is correlational because we cannot place humans in experimental designs that may initiate a disease. If we employed human participants in such an experimental study, our dependent variable, that is, the data we would be collecting, would be symptoms of a disease that we, as researchers, initiated by placing participants in various smoking groups. This is obviously unethical. There is a place for correlational research and through replication (repeating a study to gain more confidence in the findings) and more sophisticated correlational techniques we may be able to gain more confidence in our conclusions. As a general rule we want you to be very cautious about making causal conclusions based solely on simple correlational research designs.

Participants

The participants in this research were introductory psychology students, 37 males and 73 females, who were followed for an academic year. At the start of the research they were given a complete description of the research program and they signed an informed consent agreement.

Measures

Objective measures:

- Number of appointments at the health center for physical illness.
- Resting heart rate measure obtained in a standardized manner consisting of the average of two readings obtained 30 seconds apart.
- Physical fitness assessed on an ergocycle. Each participant's heart rate and workload were measured after a standard workout to obtain an objective index of aerobic physical fitness. The maximal oxygen intake for participants was obtained utilizing the heart rate and workload data obtained on participants during the final two minutes on the ergometer. This procedure has yielded accurate indices of aerobic fitness in previous research (Astrand & Rodahl, 1977).

Subjective measures:

- All participants completed the Physical Activity Questionnaire or PAQ (Brown, 1989) to obtain a self-report of how much time they spend engaging in a wide variety of aerobic activities in a typical week. This questionnaire has been used previously and been shown to be a reliable measure (Brown & Siegel, 1988).
- The Life Experiences Survey or LES (Sarason, Johnson, & Siegel, 1978), a measure of stress associated with events occurring to the participant during the past year. The life stress score was the number of negative life events reported.
- Participants' reported medical conditions and illnesses on a standard checklist indicated which illness they had experienced during the past six months. An illness score was determined by totaling the checked items.
- Psychological distress was measured by combining the scores of the following three self-report scales: Rosenberg Self-Esteem Scale (1965), Center for Epidemiology Studies Depression Scale (CES-D; Radloff, 1997), and an emotional mood measure developed by Watson, Clark, and Tellegen (1988). Statistical analyses of the three measures showed considerable overlap, and Brown decided to merge the three measures to create a unified index of psychological distress.

Participants Who Drop Out

Ninety of the 110 participants completed the research program over the course of the academic year. Incomplete participation was a result of students leaving school, denying researchers permission to examine health records, or administrative errors. Students who did not complete the entire program were compared with those who had complete data sets, and the two groups were not found to be significantly different on any dimensions. It is important for researchers to track down participant "dropouts" to make sure they do not differ from the remaining participants in any important ways. For example, if it were determined that the "dropouts" all had lower or higher levels of physical fitness compared to the non-"dropouts," it would represent an important difference and would mean that the remaining participants would be less representative than the initial participants.

Statistical Significance

In psychology the findings of studies are usually assessed with some sort of statistical analysis to help the reader to decide how much confidence to put in the findings. In order to understand the basics of these statistical analyses, imagine an exercise in which you consult a table of random numbers often found in the back of statistics books. This table consists of a long column of numbers generated by some random process, such as drawing the numbers from a hat. Next, you select ten of these random numbers from one column and ten other random numbers from another column. Calculate an arithmetic mean for each of the two columns. It is likely that the means will be at least slightly different because, after all, the numbers were selected at random. The difference between the means in this case is a direct result of chance factors because all the numbers were random in the first place.

Now imagine that you have conducted a little psychology experiment and you have two columns of scores from the measure that is your dependent variable. You calculate the arithmetic mean for each column and you find that the means are slightly different. You need to know if that difference is the result of your independent variable, or if it is a result of chance factors. In this case *chance factors* could be a number of things that you did not control, such as how much sleep your participants had the night before the study, whether they were hungry or not, how interested they were in the study, and other things like that. If the difference between the means for your dependent variable was only the result of uncontrolled chance variation, your finding is meaningless.

There is no way to be absolutely sure whether an outcome in an experiment is a result of chance factors or the independent variable. However, statistical tests can assess how likely it is that an outcome is the result of chance and that is the way these tests are used in science. The result of a statistical test is a statement indicating the probability that a difference—such as a difference between two means—is the result of chance. Scientists have arbitrarily decided on a probability level at which they are willing to agree that differences measured are not likely to be the result of chance. The arbitrary level selected is a probability of 5 percent. If the statistical test shows that there is only a 5 percent or less probability that the difference is a result of chance factors, scientists are willing to assume that the difference was the result of the research manipulation, not other, uncontrolled, events. The notation that is used to indicate this is $p < .05$, meaning probability is less than 5 percent that differences are the result of chance. Perhaps needless to say, smaller probabilities are also accepted as indications that differences are not a result of chance. Probabilities such as $p < .01$, $p < .001$, and $p < .001$ may be commonly found in research reports. These and any others indicating a 5 percent or smaller likelihood of chance are called *statistically significant* findings. This term is reserved for probabilities of chance at 5 percent or lower. Above 5 percent, such as $p < .06$ or $p < .10$, findings should be considered statistically nonsignificant. Sometimes this is abbreviated in research reports with the notation *NS*, for *not significant.*

Findings

In this research, as well as many correlational studies, a number of measures are correlated to one another to look at relationships. Remember that correlations only examine the relationship between two variables. In order to look at all the relationships between the many measures of fitness, stress, and health, many correlations are reported. In correlational studies with many measures, the outcomes may include relationships between variables that are positive, negative, or have no relationship. Correlations, through statistical analysis, can be designated as statistically significant. Statistically significant correlations are seen to represent genuine relationships between the two variables and not to be a result of chance or luck. Therefore if a correlation is presented as statistically significant, we can place greater confidence that it represents a true relationship between the variables. Usually when a correlation is said to be statistically significant, this means that it is significantly different from a zero correlation; that is, it is significantly different from no relationship at all. Following are the significant positive and negative correlations, as well as the significant sex differences for this study. Correlations not reported did not attain statistical significance.

Positive Correlations

- Participants' self-reports of exercise were related to physical fitness. Participants who reported that they exercised had higher levels of objectively measured physical fitness ($r = +.28$).
- Stressful life events were related to psychological distress. Participants who reported lower levels of psychological distress also reported lower levels of stressful life events ($r = +.23$).
- Stressful life events were related to self-reports of illness. Participants who reported lower levels of illness also reported lower levels of stressful life events ($r = +.37$).
- Stressful life events were related to visits to health center. Participants who had lower numbers of health center visits also reported lower levels of stressful life events ($r = +.23$).
- Psychological distress was related to self-reports of illness. Participants who reported lower levels of psychological distress also reported lower levels of health complaints ($r = +.22$).
- Health center visits were related to resting heart rate. Participants who obtained higher resting heart rates had greater numbers of health center visits ($r = +.28$).
- Health center visits were related to self-reported illness. Participants who had greater numbers of health center visits had higher numbers of self-reported illnesses ($r = +.37$).

Negative Correlations

- Self-reported exercise was related to resting heart rate. Participants who exercised had lower resting heart rates ($r = -.22$).
- Physical fitness was related to resting heart rate. Participants who higher levels of objectively measured physical fitness had lower resting heart rates ($r = -.41$).
- Self-reported physical fitness was related to psychological distress. Participants who were physically fit reported lower levels of psychological distress ($r = -.18$).

Participant Sex Differences

- Male gender was associated with self-reported exercise ($r = +.39$).
- Male gender was associated with physical fitness ($r = +.58$).
- Female gender was associated with self-reported illnesses ($r = +.23$).
- Female gender was associated with health center visits ($r = +.27$).

In reviewing the correlational outcomes, we find some support for the relationships between fitness, stress, and health. The correlations indicate that participants who were physically fit on the objective ergocycle measure or on self-report had lower resting heart rates, had higher rates of self-reported exercise, and had lower levels of psychological distress. It was also demonstrated that lower levels of psychological distress were associated with lower levels of health complaints, as well as lower levels of stressful events in their lives. Participants' sex was interesting, as women had higher usage of health centers and self-reported more illnesses. Males indicated more self-reported exercise and better physical fitness.

In addition to interpreting the various correlations, Brown explored interactions between the stress and fitness variables. Interactions are a bit more complex way of looking at the data. They focus on the effect that one variable may have on another variable with reference to the level of the other variable. In this study it was found that illness reports increased with increased stress for participants who did not engage in frequent exercise. This was not the case for participants who were regular exercisers. Therefore, the interaction observed was that illness reports increased for high-stress participants who were not physically fit. Under high-stress conditions, the physically fit did not have high illness reports. This finding does provide increased confidence that physical fitness can serve to buffer the adverse effect of stresses in life. Despite this important finding, one needs be cautious in interpreting and generalizing the results. Some correlations that one would have expected to support the overall hypothesis showed no significant differences. It would be interesting to explore the reasons behind this lack of relationship. Is this because of subjective self-report data that do not adequately measure what they purport to assess? Subjective measures can be inconsistent or unstable. Brown deserves credit in using some objective fitness and health measures. But even with the objective measure of the number of health visits to the student health center there are potential problems. Participants may visit the health center at the slightest indication of illness whereas others only seek health care if their condition is dire. Finally some students may visit the health center to seek information and not actually be ill.

Future research might consider using a more objective assessment of life stress. The measure used in this research is self-report and therefore open to a good deal of subjectivity both by participants while taking the assessment and by researchers in making sense of the accumulated data. An additional issue in this research concerns the use of college students as participants. Although college students are commonly used in investigations, largely because of their ready availability to researchers, they are not representative of the larger population. College students are younger, healthier, and brighter than the population at large and therefore may not serve as a good model for the experience of middle-aged or older individuals. Middle-aged or older people are likely to suffer from more serious illnesses than college students. Can fitness moderate the effect of stress in these populations? The problem is not unique to this area of study. Nevertheless, this research provides us with data supporting the hypothesis that physical fitness can shield us from the negative effects of life stress. Brown's research, discussed in this chapter, is certainly a step forward in examining the links between fitness, health, and life stress. His use of multiple measures and most importantly objective measures represents an improvement over research, which relies exclusively on subjective self-report data. In this area of research the next steps forward would be to explore these issues using an experimental design and a more representative participant pool.

REFERENCES

Astrand, P., & Rodahl, K. (1977). *Textbook of work physiology: Physiological bases of exercise* (2nd ed.). New York: McGraw-Hill.

Blair, S. N., Goodyear, N. N., Gibbons, L. W., & Cooper, K. H. (1984). Physical fitness and incidence of hypertension in healthy normotensive men and women. *Journal of the American Medical Association, 252*, 487–490.

Brown, J. D. (1989). *Measuring physical fitness by self-report.* Unpublished manuscript, Southern Methodist University.

Brown, J. D. (1991). Staying fit and staying well: Physical fitness as a moderator of life stress. *Journal of Personality and Social Psychology, 60*, 555–561.

Brown, J. D., & Siegel, J. M. (1988). Exercise as a buffer of life stress: A prospective study of adolescent health. *Health Psychology, 7*, 341–353.

Folkins, C. H., & Sime, W. E. (1981). Physical fitness training and mental health. *American Psychologist, 36*, 373–389.

Holmes, D. S., & Roth, D. L. (1985). Association of aerobic fitness with pulse rate and subjective responses to psychological stress. *Psychophysiology, 22*, 525–529.

Hughes, J. R. (1984). Psychological effects of exercise. *Preventive Medicine, 13*, 66–78.

Lennon, D., Stratman, F. W., Shrago, E., Nagle, F. J., Hanson, P. G., Maddon, M., & Spennetta, T. (1983). Total cholesterol and HDL-cholesterol changes during acute, moderate intensity exercise in men and women. *Metabolism, 32*, 244–249.

Oberman, A. (1985). Exercise and the primary prevention of cardiovascular disease. *American Journal of Cardiology, 55*, 10D–20D.

Radloff, L. S. (1977). The CES-D scale: A self-report depression scale for research in the general population. *Applied Psychological Measurement, 1*, 385–401.

Rosenberg, M. (1965). *Society and the adolescent self-image.* Princeton, NJ: Princeton University Press.

Rosenthal, M., Haskell, W. L., Solomon, R., Widstrom, A., & Reavan, G. M. (1983). Demonstration of a relationship between level of physical training and insulin stimulated glucose utilization in normal humans. *Diabetes, 32*, 408–411.

Sarason, I. G., Johnson, J. H., & Siegel, J. M. (1978). Assessing the impact of life changes: Development of the life experiences survey. *Journal of Consulting and Clinical Psychology, 46*, 932–946.

Tomporowski, P. D., & Ellis, N. R. (1986). Effects of exercise on cognitive processes: A review. *Psychological Bulletin, 99*, 338–346.

Watson, D., Clark, L. A., & Tellegen, A. (1988). Development and validation of brief measures of positive and negative affect: The PANAS scales. *Journal of Personality and Social Psychology, 54*, 1063–1070.

CHAPTER 4

HALF AND HALF

It has been known for a long time that some parts of the brain are related to some specific aspects of our behavior. As early as 1861 French surgeon Paul Broca noticed a patient who could not speak but was otherwise fine. When this patient died, an autopsy showed damage to a small area on the left side of the brain, later called *Broca's area*, which seemed to be the center for the production of language. Subsequently, a part of the brain that seemed to control language understanding, called *Wernicke's area*, was also found on the left side of the brain. Sadly, in the last 150 years a string of wars have also contributed quite a bit to our understanding of localized brain functions through the numbers of people who sustain injury to specific parts of the head.

SURGICAL EXPLORATIONS

The notion that individual psychological functions were located in specific parts of the brain also gained substantial support from observations accompanying brain surgery. Beginning in 1928, neurosurgeon Wilder Penfield of McGill University pioneered techniques for locating specific functions on the surface of a patient's brain, a technique called *brain mapping*. Penfield's original purpose was to surgically remove scar tissue on the cortex of the brain. It was believed to be one of the causal components of epilepsy. Before surgery was done, it was important to determine how essential the scarred area was to the functioning of the individual. For example, if the tissue that was to be removed was in the area that is involved with language understanding, the treatment could be worse than the disorder. Given the choice, unless the seizures were continuous and severe, most people would rather suffer epileptic seizures than become unable to understand language.

The method of brain mapping developed by Penfield involved removing a large section of the skull to expose the area of the brain where the scar tissue was located. Often, the scar tissue was the result of an injury to the head, so its general location was known. The patient was awake and alert during surgery. Penfield touched the surface of the brain with a small probe that gave, in his words, "gentle electrical currents" to a section of the brain. The patient was asked what was felt, seen, or experienced. Even though these patients had experienced the sawing open of their skulls and were lying

Incorporating the research of K. Patterson, F. Vargha-Khadem, and C. E. Polkey, "Reading with One Hemisphere," 1989, *Brain, 112*, pp. 39–63.

on an operating table with their brains exposed for all to see, they were able to chat about what was happening to them. Penfield operated on over 400 patients and only found small variations in the location of brain functions. Penfield confirmed the location of language areas on the left side of the brain and managed to pinpoint many other specific brain functions (Hothersall, 1990).

Roger Sperry (1982) contributed additional information about the localization of functions in the brain. He and his research team studied people in whom the right and left halves of the brain had been surgically separated as a treatment for severe epilepsy (Gazzaniga, 1967). Through the work of these and other researchers, much was learned about the differences between the right and the left hemispheres of the brain. In summary, this research indicated that the right hemisphere was largely responsible for thinking about the relationships of objects in space and for the creative parts of our lives. In contrast, the left hemisphere, in addition to being associated with language, was also thought to be more involved in mathematics and logical thought.

Sperry's work soon caught the imagination of popular culture, and some media reports suggested that people could be dominated by one side of the brain or the other. People were thought to be either right-brained or left-brained. For example, lawyers have to be articulate and logical, so they were supposed to be dominated by the left sides of their brains. Conversely, the creativity of an artist was supposed to be the result of a dominant right brain. These kinds of assumptions went well beyond the data (Farah, 1994). Clearly, a lawyer has to be articulate, logical, *and* creative in arguments. An artist needs to be creative, but will have to know about the technical specifications of materials such as paint, ceramics, metal, or ink. The simplistic notion of domination by a section of the brain overlooks the obvious point that we use psychological functions traditionally associated with both hemispheres in order to get through life.

A second complication is that the localization of functions is not as precise as some people are inclined to believe. The brain has two hemispheres, one on the left and one on the right. It has been suspected for a while that people may have some language capability in both hemispheres. For example, people who experience damage to the left hemisphere resulting in language loss still may be able to sing quite clearly, even though they may not speak very well. This implies that the language that is connected to music is not only controlled by the left hemisphere language areas. You do not have to be a brain surgeon to know that the brain is very complex. Individual nerve cells may be able to communicate with as many as 200 other nerve cells. The brain is a massively interconnected network. One of the best ways to describe the relationship between a part of the brain and a psychological function is to say, for example, the left hemisphere *mediates* language. This phrasing allows for a specific brain area to play a role without suggesting that it is the entire control system. As we will see, the notion of *control* being vested in a single brain area is misleading to the point of being false.

THE CASE STUDY

The research method illustrated by the work in this chapter, the case study, typically involves intensive study of one or a few individuals. Often, considerable information about the past history of the individuals is collected, and a great deal of descriptive information about the current state of the individuals is recorded. You will have guessed by now that, as a research method, the case study can have many shortcomings. Historical data may depend upon someone's recollection or upon written records that may be biased or otherwise inaccurate. Researcher bias may easily creep in because much of the data might be qualitative—words, rather than quantitative—numbers. Words are not necessarily more biased than numbers, but a number is less susceptible to various interpretations than a verbal description such as "seems depressed" or "moves slowly." Another problem is that case studies investigate only one or a few individuals, and those individuals are not likely to be representative of the general population. Additionally, a case study may be so rooted in a particular period that its findings cannot be generalized to the future. Many of the clinical case studies of Victorian psychoanalyst Sigmund Freud suffered this fate.

Given these problems, it is important to understand why and when the case study is an appropriate research strategy. Although an experiment is a much more powerful research method, there are some situations in which experiments cannot be done. The removal of a cerebral hemisphere is certainly one of these. We doubt that very many of you would want to be in an experiment where you would be randomly assigned to the group who was going to have the right hemisphere removed or the group that was going to have the left hemisphere removed. In this case, an experiment can be ruled out. One might be able to do some kind of correlational study taking large groups of people who had lost one hemisphere and comparing them to a group who had lost the other. The difficulty, as you have probably guessed, is that there are no large groups of people who have only one hemisphere. Because this condition is rare and could not be created in an experiment, the case study may be the best way to approach it.

The case study is only as important as the problem being studied. Sometimes case study results are reported in areas where correlational studies or experiments could easily have been done. Imagine, for example, the case study of a child who does poorly in school. It might tell us something about this one child. School performance is a question about which correlational data could be collected because, unfortunately, there are lots of kids who do poorly in school. A case study of such a child might be compelling and dramatic, but it would also be trivial. If you look at some of the popular books that are supposed to involve psychology, you are certain to find some of these. They will be compellingly written cases about rather common situations, and we are expected to believe that the details of the case are generalizable to other individuals. One of the benefits of the study of psychology is that you should be able to evaluate the importance of these case studies. Some of them are worthless. There are better and more representative ways than case studies to find out about why kids do poorly in school. As an illustration, there is a good study of school achievement later in this book (Chapter 14). Doing studies with large samples may enable us to help many kids improve school performance. A study of one kid is not likely to help much, no matter how interesting it is to read. This illustrates one of the shortfalls of the case study.

Radical Surgery

A stark illustration of the function of brain hemispheres is presented in a study by Patterson, Vargha-Khadem, and Polkey (1989). They present a case study of two unrelated girls. Owing to severe illness, one girl had her right hemisphere removed and the other girl had her left hemisphere removed. This research presented precisely the kind of material that made a good case study. The problem was important, it was very rare, and careful steps were taken to measure and quantify the aspects of behavior that were studied.

In case studies, individuals are usually identified by initials or by some kind of nickname to preserve their anonymity. In order to help you remember which of the two research participants we are referring to, we will not use their real initials. Instead, we are going to use the initials R. H. for the girl who retained her right hemisphere and L. H. for the girl who retained her left hemisphere.

These girls had developed normally in the early years of their lives. The first serious evidence of problems for each of them was the appearance of epilepsy. For R. H., this took the form of early convulsions and lethargy that developed over several weeks into seizure activity consisting of frequent small attacks lasting 30–40 seconds, but occurring at such a high frequency that they were virtually continuous. L. H. seemed normal until one day she was found passed out and totally unresponsive. Over the following weeks, she also developed seizures that affected part of her body and were as frequent as six episodes per hour. CAT scans of the heads of these girls eventually showed severe atrophy in their brains; for R. H. the problem was in the left hemisphere and for L. H. it was in the right hemisphere. Both were diagnosed with Rasmussen's encephalitis. This is a poorly understood and rare disorder in which the person has seizures affecting one side of the body and progressive degeneration of the brain on the opposite side from the seizures. The causes of this disease are unknown. A summary of case study data on the early history of these girls is found in Table 4.1.

Each of these girls had a brain hemisphere that was disintegrating. The only treatment for this was the removal of the hemisphere. It is important to understand that these decisions were not taken lightly. Sometimes popular media like to depict doctors who do exploratory brain surgery as the "mad scientists" with flashing eyes, disheveled hair, and a manic disregard for the patient as anything other than a research subject. For R. H. and L. H. the surgery would remove debilitating seizures and restore the individual to a more normal life. For R. H., however, there was another issue. Because she was

TABLE 4.1   Background Information on R.H. and L.H.

	R.H.	L.H.
General:		
Hemisphere removed	L	R
Original handedness	R	R
Year of birth	1969	1970
Age at symptom onset (yrs.)	13	10
Age at operation (yrs.)	15	15
Age at testing (yrs.)	17	17

going to lose what remained of her left hemisphere, attempts were made before surgery to discover what effect this might have on her language ability.

One way to do this is to anesthetize the hemispheres of the brain one at a time as a way of simulating the effects of being without a hemisphere. R. H.'s left hemisphere was injected on three successive trials and her right hemisphere was injected once in an attempt to determine the functions of each before the operation. The evidence from these tests was not completely clear, but speech arrest, the seeming inability to talk, was only evident when her *right* hemisphere was paralyzed. This suggested that she was already using her right hemisphere to control much of her language. This may have been a neurological response to the progressive degeneration of the left hemisphere, which is usually associated with language ability. This kind of flexibility, called *plasticity*, is not uncommon. When one part of the brain is damaged, sometimes other parts are able to take over. It has generally been observed that plasticity is greater among younger people.

In order to evaluate the information that follows, it is essential to understand that before becoming ill, both of these girls were doing well in school and performing normally. Following surgery, R. H.'s speech was halting, as can be seen from this fragment of an interview quoted from Patterson et al. (1989):

K. P.:   What do you particularly like to eat?

[R. H.]:   I like . . . er . . . you know . . . the . . . I can't say it now . . . well, I like . . . I don't like chips a lot but . . . I like Bolognaise.

K. P.:   Do you cook?

[R. H.]:   Yes.

K. P.:   What do you cook?

[R. H.]:   Different things. I made . . . er . . . I made . . . these (pointing to the apple she was eating). But not that . . . these. . . .

K. P.:   What did you do with them?

[R. H.]:   Crust over the top.

K. P.:   What's that called?

[R. H.]:   An apple.

K. P.:   Yes that's an apple, but with the crust over the top, what do we call it?

[R. H.]:   I can't remember.

K. P.:   An apple . . .

[R. H.]:   Pie!

Clearly, R. H. possessed language ability but she sometimes could not actually produce the words without considerable prompting. Although her language deficits may seem striking, it is even more striking that her right hemisphere is as skilled as it appears to be in producing language. Earlier research on the brain suggested that language was a left hemisphere function and implied that without the left hemisphere, language would cease.

In order to probe more closely the language skills of the right and the left hemispheres, these two girls were given a group of tests, called a *battery* of tests. These instruments were aimed at making careful assessments of different components of the overall language skill, such as letter naming, word recognition, and various kinds of reading. The cases of these girls were particularly illuminating because any language skills displayed had to be the work of a single hemisphere. Because surgery left the girls with such different skill levels, it was not always possible to test them with the same instruments. R. H. showed some severe debilitation, whereas L. H. was more typically just below normal. It was not a complete surprise that they had some problems when we consider that each of these girls had undergone years of debilitating seizures. Nevertheless, the differences between them were such that some tasks that challenged R. H. would have been pointlessly easy for L. H. In these cases, the tests were only performed on R. H.

Letter Naming (R. H. Only)

Individual uppercase letters were presented in random order and R. H. was asked to name the letter or give the sound it makes in a word. Letter recognition was further tested by showing pairs of letters, short words, and nonwords in which the pair of stimuli were either the same (although different in case) or different (see description below). The correct answer was "yes" when the members of the pair were the same and "no" when they were different. For example:

	LETTER	**WORD**	**NONWORD**
Correct answer YES:	G-g	ROAD–ROAD	FERB–FERB
Correct answer NO:	G-y	ROAD–ROAR	FERB–FERD

R. H. was poor at naming randomly presented letters. The strategy she used to solve these problems was to start with the letter *A* and speak her way through the alphabet, trying to recognize the letter when she came to it. She often got lost and had to start over at the beginning. As Patterson et al. (1989) pointed out, this made the tests very slow to administer. She was only correct—defined by stopping at the correct place in her alphabetic recitation—on 7 out of 17 letters. Her ability to sound letters was even worse: she was only able to sound the letter *S*. In contrast, she was 100 percent correct in matching letters and words and 95 percent correct in matching nonwords. She was also given a test that presented one- to four-digit numbers and asked her to read them aloud. No number higher than 23 was actually tested, however, because she used the same strategy as she had with the alphabet, starting with one and counting up. In contrast, L. H. was fast and accurate at number reading including multidigit numbers and dates. In summary, R. H. could visually match the patterns of letters and words. If she presented the sounds of letters to herself by rattling off the alphabet, she could sometimes recognize the match between what she had said and the letter in front of her. She could not spontaneously produce the sounds of letters in response to their visual image.

Word Recognition (Both R. H. and L. H.)

Recognition of printed words was tested in two ways. The girls were asked to say "yes" if they recognized a letter string as a word and "no" if they did not for a list of 76 familiar three- to five-letter words plus 76 nonwords. The nonwords were made by changing a single letter of each of the words. A second test consisted of a list of words that were chosen to be of high, middle, and low familiarity and encompassed four levels of imageability, from high to low. Imageability refers to the ease with which a word can be pictured. For example, PROOF and CHOOSE are low-imageability words, whereas MONEY and KNIGHT have high imageability. Nonwords were created by changing a single letter. Patterson et al. (1989) gave the example of NERVOUS and NERDOUS.

L. H. performed well on this task, but showed some lack of vocabulary in her inability to recognize some low-familiarity words, such as KNIGHT and VAGUE. R. H. recognized many real words, but she also thought that a number of nonwords were actually words. This shows the value of testing nonwords. Without them, it might have seemed that she was good at word recognition, but that was called into question by her positive responses to nonwords. This asking of nonwords is an example of a *control*. It allowed the researchers to determine if R. H. was really recognizing words, or if she was merely making many positive responses. It was found that, indeed, she was making many positive responses. R. H. had particular difficulty with this task when the words were of low imageability, showing again the dependence of her language on visual images.

Single-Word Reading (Both R. H. and L. H.)

Words were printed on individual cards, and the patient was given a stack of cards and asked to move at her own pace reading them aloud. Self-corrections were accepted as correct responses. L. H. did not have much difficulty with this task. However, R. H. sometimes had to talk herself around the word. For FRUIT she said "juice . . . it's apples and pears and . . . fruit" and for RABBIT, she said "ears and . . . not a hamster . . . rabbit." R. H. had a great deal of trouble with words such as END, PART, and PLACE, which do not refer to a particular concrete thing. Words that were imageable were easier for her to read, although she was not very good at reading any of them. The patterns of R. H.'s responses suggested some comprehension of the printed words, but she seemed to be lacking the usual means to translate the group of letters into the sound for the word. It is important to remember that in talking her way through the single-word reading task, R. H. was demonstrating considerable language skill, even though the task also pointed to a specific language deficit. It seems that the pattern of letters had meaning for her, but that she had difficulty in finding the sound of the word. As described above for single-letter recognition, she had difficulty in linking sounds and visual images.

Comparison of Reading with Naming (R. H. only)

R. H. was asked to name common actions by looking at line drawings of people performing these actions, such as climbing a ladder, combing hair, and for comparison, by

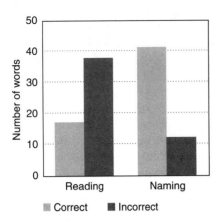

FIGURE 4.1   Comparison of Correct and Incorrect Responses for R. H. in Reading and Naming 54 Common Action Words

reading about these actions. For reading, each of these drawings was converted into a simple sentence with the verb underlined. There were 54 action words and, correspondingly, 54 drawings. Figure 4.1 shows the total correct for reading and for naming out of 54 possible.

R. H. was much better at naming than she was at reading, again illustrating the close link between her language ability and visual images.

Nonword Reading (Both R. H. and L. H.)

Both girls were asked to read aloud thirty simple nonsense words printed on individual cards. These were words such as NEG, LOAT, and FOD. L. H.'s performance was normal for her age and showed no evidence of her brain surgery. In contrast, R. H. could not read any of the nonwords. When asked to repeat the same 30 nonwords immediately after hearing them, she repeated every one perfectly. This task showed similarity to the letter recognition and single-word reading tasks. She had trouble associating sounds with visual images, but her difficulty was not merely a matter of inability to produce the sounds.

Rhyming Tasks (Both R. H. and L. H.)

Two word pairs were spoken to each girl and each was asked if the words rhymed. Thirty pairs did rhyme and 30 pairs did not. Next, they were asked to produce a rhyme for 20 single-syllable spoken words. Each of them made a few errors on the rhyme recognition task, but they were both quite good at it. However, unlike L. H., R. H. totally failed on the other task. When asked to produce a rhyme, she could only repeat what had been said to her. If she was given BAT and CAT as a sample rhyme and then asked for a another word that rhymed with CAT, she would repeat BAT. She was incapable of finding any other word that rhymed with CAT. In light of her performance on other tasks, it is not surprising that she had difficulty with this task that is so dependent upon recognizing, processing, and manipulating the sounds of words.

CONCLUSIONS

It is clear from this work that the right hemisphere may mediate a considerable amount of language ability. In spite of her deficits on specific tasks, R. H. could understand instructions that were given to her and she could talk, although somewhat haltingly.

Patterson and colleagues conducted a number of additional tests with L. H. and R. H., which all pointed to the same general picture of right-hemisphere capabilities. R. H.'s pattern of language performance was not merely a matter of sweeping and generalized impairment. She was successful at recognizing letters, not very good at naming them, and unable to give their sound equivalents. She was fairly good at recognizing common words, but very inaccurate when faced with uncommon words. She could comprehend words that named common concrete objects and had some degree of success in reading concrete familiar words. When words were difficult to picture, that is, when they were not imageable, she had trouble. It was not a coincidence that R. H. could read words aloud that were understandable to her, but not sound out even simple nonsense words such as NEG, LOAT, and FOD. She could not use the pattern of letters to translate a printed word into a spoken sound unless the word had meaning for her. If the word had no meaning, she could not say it.

Patterson rejected the idea that R. H. presented an unusual case of competence in the right hemisphere. Critics might say the primary language areas for R. H. were, for some reason, unusually located in her right hemisphere from birth. However, if this were so, there would be no explanation for the sudden decrement in language following the removal of her left hemisphere. In addition, this is statistically unlikely because in a study of 140 right-handed people who had their left hemispheres anesthetized, 96 percent of them had the primary language areas in the left hemisphere. R. H. could have been otherwise, but it is unlikely. It is not obvious how much of R. H.'s right-hemisphere language skill was the result of the right hemisphere taking over the functions from the ailing left hemisphere as disease progressed. More information will be required to settle this question, but it is interesting that she was much more competent with things she heard than with things she read. In order to explain this, one could assume that as her disease progressed, her right hemisphere took over the most important functions of the ailing left hemisphere. Listening and responding might be considered more important than reading and perhaps they were taken over first. Nevertheless, this case raises the alternative intriguing possibility that R. H. exhibits the normal linguistic capabilities of the right hemisphere in a school-aged girl. These may be poor compared to the language ability associated with the left hemisphere, but they are much better than would be expected if we were to adopt the view that language is totally *controlled* by the left hemisphere. Traditionally, the right hemisphere has been associated with mental images, and it seems clear that the language ability of R. H. is very closely tied to these kinds of visual images.

Following surgery, the seizures were totally arrested for both girls. L. H. attended a local college and could do regular course work. R. H. enrolled in a nonacademic college where she took courses in cooking and handicrafts. Certainly, further research will be required to assess the possibility that the right hemisphere routinely has some sort of language ability. The information available suggests that Sperry (1982) was correct in rejecting a common characterization of the right hemisphere as "the so-called subordinate or minor hemisphere . . . illiterate and mentally retarded and thought by some authorities not even to be conscious."

REFERENCES

Farah, M. (1994). Neuropsychological inference with an interactive brain: A critique of the "locality" assumption. *Behavioral and Brain Sciences, 17*, 43–61.

Gazzaniga, M. (1967). The split brain in man. *Scientific American, 217*, 24–29.

Hothersall, D. (1990). *History of psychology* (2nd ed.). New York: McGraw-Hill.

Patterson, K., Vargha-Khadem, F., & Polkey, C. E. (1989). Reading with one hemisphere. *Brain, 112*, 39–63.

Sperry, R. (1982). Some effects of disconnecting the cerebral hemispheres. *Science, 217*, 1223–1226.

CHAPTER 5

THE WOLF
IN SHEEPDOG'S CLOTHING

The research in this chapter is an illustration of the research method called a *naturalistic observation*. Naturalistic observation qualifies for inclusion as a scientific method because it can be used as a means of hypothesis testing. This method is a sort of a maverick within the study of behavior. Some psychologists consider it to be the weakest possible approach to research, a last resort to be used only when all other methods have been ruled out. Others might celebrate this method because it examines real behavior in real settings. Opinions differ widely about the value of naturalistic observations because this label is used to describe a variety of actual research procedures. The common factor is the observation of behavior within a natural context. This description hinges on something difficult to define: a *natural context*. It is probably not productive to try to create a strict definition for this term, but usually natural contexts are considered to be the places where animals are typically found. For wild animals, it is the wild, but it might also be a zoo. The natural environment of a farm animal is, we suppose, a farm. For humans, it might be homes, workplaces, cars, recreational sites, and shopping areas. With humans, it is easier to say what a naturalistic observation is *not*: it is not a contrived lab setting in which people are randomly assigned to various experimental groups. It is not a survey, it is not an interview, and it is not a psychological test. Could a naturalistic observation of people be done in a lab? Maybe. If people were behaving without any particular instruction from the researcher, we might consider lab observations to be naturalistic. There are several examples like this in the chapters that follow. Even though they take place in labs, we believe they qualify as naturalistic observations. Naturalistic observations are sometimes used as one of the outcome measures in a study that employs other research methods as well.

At one extreme, naturalistic observations can be totally descriptive, producing only narrative text about behavior. Early studies of animal behavior were often like this: the animal was watched and actions were described (Lorenz, 1952). More recently, Dian Fossey's work on mountain gorillas was largely descriptive (Fossey, 1983). However, it is also possible to produce numerical data from naturalistic observations, sometimes including making alterations in the natural environment and watching to see how behavior is affected. Early examples, which still make compelling reading, can be found

Incorporating previously unpublished observations of L. C. Shaffer and N. Tinbergen. Adapted from research presented in L. C. Shaffer, "Man Bites Dog," 1998, *Discovery*. Leeds, UK: Yorkshire Television.

in the work of Tinbergen (1958, 1974), who studied a wide variety of animals in outdoor settings. Although many people associate naturalistic observation with the study of non-human animals, sometimes it can be a very good way of finding things out about people as well. Let us presume you wanted to know whether men or women drivers are more likely to wear seat belts. You could observe cars going underneath a highway overpass, while making recordings of sex of driver and seat belt wearing. We believe these data might be better than those you could collect in an interview or survey, because surveys are susceptible to errors from faulty memories or purposeful attempts to misrepresent behavior. A published example of this method can be found in the work of Hoxie and Rubenstein (1994), who observed that traffic lights did not stay red long enough to allow elderly people to cross a busy street safely. An example from a different area of study can be found in the work of Martin and Ross (1996) who went to people's homes to make observations of parents responding to aggression in children.

A STUDY OF SHEEPDOGS

The researchers for this chapter, Lary Shaffer and Niko Tinbergen, worked in the north of England, near the Scottish border, making science documentaries for British television. In addition to being filmmakers, both of them had degrees in zoology, specializing in animal behavior. Indeed, during the course of the study to be described, Tinbergen was awarded a Nobel Prize for his enduring contributions to the study of animal behavior. While traveling in the rolling green farmland of northern England, they had numerous opportunities to observe border collie sheepdogs at work herding vast flocks of sheep. On distant hillsides the white mass of sheep looked like a single organism, stretching out, bunching up, and forming into strings while being forced through gates in the stone walls. If Shaffer and Tinbergen looked carefully, they could sometimes see the single dog that was responsible for all this activity: a black and white speck, darting this way and that, rounding up errant branches of the flock. Thinking this behavior might be worthy of a research study, they asked a friend, Jimmy Rose, for help. Jimmy lived in the Pennine Hills, where there are many sheep farms, and he said he knew just the place to do a study of dogs. This was a lucky break for Shaffer and Tinbergen. They were fortunate to know someone who could make some introductions.

Two weeks later, Shaffer and Tinbergen, in the company of Jimmy, found themselves on their way to Dufton Village for an introduction to the Dargues, a family who had been farming the hills around Dufton for almost 1,000 years. The farms in that area were mostly family farms, staffed by sprawling extended families of parents, offspring, aunts, uncles, cousins, and grandparents, all living under one roof and all working, in some capacity, at the daily chores of the farm. Jimmy had known the Dargues for years and, following the customs of the area, he drove up to the farmhouse and went right in without knocking. Shaffer and Tinbergen followed shyly behind. The Dargues were having their midday meal, seated around a big oak table covered with steaming mountains of food. After a one-sentence introduction from Jimmy, all three guests were invited to pull up to the table and "have a bit of dinner." No one paid any particular attention to the newly arrived guests, and food was shoveled down while the talk centered on cattle feed prices and the weather. Almost as an aside, Jimmy said, "Oh, by the way, Lary and Niko would like to hang about here in the next year or two, watch you work with your sheepdogs, and make a film about it." The head of the family, old John Dargue, slowly looked up from his plate. Chewing along without missing a beat he gazed first at Shaffer, then at Tinbergen, then at Shaffer again and softly said "Aye" between bites. That was all it took to seal the deal. Permission from "Boss" John Dargue meant that the whole farm would be at Shaffer and Tinbergen's disposal for as long as was necessary to complete the project. Shaffer shot a questioning glance at Tinbergen, who returned a meek little shrug and forked a roast potato into his mouth.

Jimmy Rose was correct in thinking that the Dargue's farm would be a good place to watch sheep and dogs. As with most of the farms in the area, their farm was too small to easily provide both food and pasture space for the number of sheep they owned. This fact necessitated a considerable amount of moving sheep from one place to another. Although the entire Dargue family would pitch in when needed, Edwin did most of the shepherding. At 50 years old, Edwin Dargue was short, stoutish, and strong as an ox. He had a quick wit and enjoyed the company afforded by Shaffer and Tinbergen on his rambles around the hills, shepherding his flock. At first, Shaffer and Tinbergen spent a great deal of time just watching the dogs. Sometimes naturalistic observations have a hypothesis immediately but, in this case, hypotheses grew out of weeks of initial observations. Tinbergen was one of the pioneers in the use of naturalistic observation, and he strongly believed that the way to approach a new research project was to "observe, observe, and observe again." As the researcher became acquainted with the behavior, questions would begin to appear. At first these might be small questions or puzzles, but, over numerous observations, they would gradually form into more specific and important questions. This research method required faith that sufficient observations of behavior in a natural setting could be counted on to lead to testable hypotheses. Naturalistic observations are also used by many scientists to suggest hypotheses that will later be tested by other research methods, such as experiments.

Although there were no specific and testable hypotheses at the start of the investigation, Shaffer and Tinbergen both believed that the spectacular performances of the sheepdogs were not merely a matter of training. Dogs are closely related to wolves, and good scientific studies of wolves were beginning to appear (Mech, 1970). Shaffer and Tinbergen suspected that much of the herding behavior was really thinly disguised pack hunting behavior. In the domestication of the dog, humans had created breeds by selective mating that emphasized different characteristics. In the sheepdog, Shaffer and Tinbergen believed that aspects of ancestral wolflike hunting behavior, which might have been useful in herding flock animals, had been retained through generations of selective breeding.

GETTING STARTED

Their first unsystematic observations seemed to confirm the idea that at times the dogs were behaving as a wolf pack. When groups of dogs worked together, a clear dominance hierarchy could be seen among the dogs. The same kinds of status arrangements are found in wolf packs. The dog who seemed to be in the role of the alpha male, or the head of the pack, was always out in front of the others as they trotted to the fields where they would work. If another dog tried to pass him, he would charge at it, chasing it back with the others. In particular, the lead dog spent a great deal of time rebuffing one particular challenger, who usually seemed to be in second place. The alpha male frequently urinated on rocks and tufts of grass. The number two dog would stop, sniff and urinate in the same places, followed by the other male dogs in a predictable order. Female dogs played no obvious part in this scent marking. One day, the dog who had been running second in the dog pack picked a fight with the lead male, which turned into a ferocious battle of flashing teeth and flying fur. The other dogs gathered around to watch. Shaffer and Tinbergen were surprised that Edwin did nothing to break up this fight, which looked as if it would certainly end in injury for both dogs, and maybe death for one. Edwin said, "If you let them fight, they will sort it out for themselves. If you break it up, they will be trying for a rematch every time they see each other. This way, both dogs may get hurt but when it is over they will know who is boss and will be able to work together without any more fighting." After a few minutes of fierce combat, the number two dog went squealing away from the fight. It was over, and the alpha male was still in charge. Edwin was correct about the reestablishment of order. Shaffer and Tinbergen saw no further fighting between these dogs. These observations further convinced Shaffer and Tinbergen that, at times, the dogs were behaving as a wolf pack.

After initial observations and discussions, Tinbergen returned to his busy professorship at Oxford University, reluctantly leaving much of the daily observation to Shaffer. At regular intervals, Tinbergen returned to Dufton to have some days among the dogs, discuss the work, generate new ideas, and debate interpretations.

Shaffer gradually got used to the routine of farm life. After a few weeks, he ceased to notice the smell of farm animals and hardly noticed when running sheep kicked up a spray of liquid manure, which flew in all directions, landing on his clothes and face. As Tinbergen predicted, he began to notice things about the dogs. For most ordinary work around the farm, Edwin used only one dog, a 5-year-old male named Spot. Most border collies have large patches of black and white on their backs, but Spot was almost all black with a white nose, a white bib, and a white spot just behind his ears.

Shaffer marveled at how Spot seemed to know just what to do, requiring very few commands from Edwin. They worked together like a well-rehearsed ballet when moving large flocks or isolating single sheep for specific purposes. When Shaffer asked Edwin about Spot's training, the response was, "They either have it in them, or they don't—you work them and they soon figure out what to do." As Shaffer observed, he was struck by the sorts of commands that Edwin was giving. There seemed to be many more commands telling Spot to *stop* doing some behavior than there were to tell him to *start* doing a particular behavior. Once Shaffer had this idea, it was easy to do the empirical checking. In his little notebook, Shaffer began to record the circumstances of Edwin's commands. The original intention had been to study the dogs, but Shaffer was coming to the realization that the dog behavior made no sense without some understanding of the shepherd and the sheep. For 3 weeks in ordinary work around the farm, Shaffer noted each of Edwin's commands and scored it as a command either to stop a behavior or start a behavior. Other utterances, such as "Good lad, Spot," were not

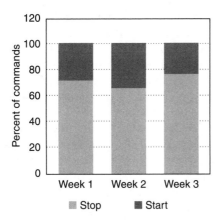

FIGURE 5.1   Frequency of Stop and Start Commands

scored because they did not tell the dog to do anything specific. The overall frequencies of these commands are shown in Figure 5.1.

Although the data here only involve one dog and one shepherd, Shaffer's hunch that most of the commands were *stop* commands was confirmed. Shaffer was excited about this because it was the beginning of systematic observations and the start of an emerging story about sheepdog behavior. Although 3 weeks might seem to be a long time to spend confirming such a small point, at the same time Shaffer was beginning work on a documentary film about sheepdogs that was paying for the project, and the film work limited the amount of time each day that could be spent in unencumbered observation.

Having convinced himself that most commands were *stop* commands, the next question seemed to appear automatically: Stop doing what? Another bout of research was launched with Edwin and Spot. Shaffer tried, over a series of days, to find a way to put Spot's behavior into meaningful categories. Initially, this proved to be a challenge. The behaviors of sheep and dog seemed chaotic at first. There seemed to be so many completely different kinds of situations in which Spot had to be stopped by a stream of shouted invective. Tinbergen gave Shaffer a lot of encouragement to keep watching, waiting, and thinking. Patience is more than a virtue in naturalistic observation; it has to be an obsession. Shaffer persevered and, rather suddenly, the clouds of confusion began to clear. For a few days Edwin and Spot had been moving sheep from one field to another, down a narrow road with high stone walls on both sides.

MISTAKES AND INSIGHTS

Edwin's Uncle Joss was helping with this using his dog, Meg, as was Cousin John with a dog called Moss. Moss was just over a year old and was still a big, shaggy, good-natured pup. He would bound around, dividing his time between getting in trouble and working in useful ways. The high stone walls and gates on each side of the roadway focused the errors that a dog could make by squeezing the sheep from both sides. Unlike an open field, the sheep could only go forward or back. At some point, this constriction from the sides, combined with the large number of errors made by Moss, resulted in a flash of insight for Shaffer about the herding behavior of dogs. Moss, Meg, and Spot really had very little work to do in order to keep the sheep moving. The dogs would dart back and forth behind the last row of sheep. If any sheep from the last row tried to turn around and run away from the flock the dogs would charge at these individuals, causing them to turn around and rejoin the flock. If the sheep did not act quickly enough, it was likely to get a little bite on one of its hind legs, causing it to launch into the air and land among the flock. While the dogs were working at this, it became obvious that Moss was also often moving around the side of the flock, pushing in between the sheep and the stone wall, as if he were going to work his way to the front of the flock and stop them. Each time he did this, John would yell at him to stop and come back where he belonged. Shaffer noticed that this was also a common error for Spot, and even for old Meg. These were more than random errors of an untrained puppy: the older dogs were doing the same thing.

Shaffer had been reading about the hunting of wolves and other pack-hunting carnivores, and the reading suggested a reason for this "error." The breakthrough came when Shaffer realized that the dog was acting as a social hunter, treating the shepherd as the head of the hunting pack. In a carnivore pack hunt, the hunters will try to isolate one or a few animals from a large flock. In the early phases, pack hunters split up and spread around the prey trying to make a grab for an individual.

Shaffer believed that this was the situation in which the dogs found themselves. They had moved in close to a small flock and if they were to use patterns of ancestral hunting behavior, the sensible thing to do first would be to spread out around the sheep. The farmers needed to have the sheep driven down the road. However, for a hunting pack, nothing is gained by endlessly driving prey in one direction with all the pack members close together. In the narrow lane, the dogs appeared to be reverting to an ancestral hunting strategy in the tendency to surround the sheep. In order to understand this, you have to remember that although the dogs had their own dominance hierarchy within the pack, they also treated the shepherd as the ultimate pack member.

Shaffer's head began to whirl as he tried to think about the other mistakes he had seen the dogs make. Had most or all of these "mistakes" really been pack-hunting maneuvers that happened to interfere with the dog's role as a sheepdog? Were the dogs depending upon a pack-hunting ancestry in the mistakes they made as well as in their successes? Shaffer thought so, but needed to confirm this hunch with new observations.

Much of sheepdog work involves handling sheep in close quarters in small fields. On other occasions, however, the dog has to run distances of a mile or more away from the shepherd to bring a distant flock back down to the shepherd. As Shaffer reflected upon this, it occurred to him that there were four basic kinds of interactions involving shepherds, dogs, and sheep. These are shown in Figure 5.2, top and bottom.

Figure 5.2 shows that there are two elements in the observed situations that closely resemble a pack hunt: pack members surrounding the sheep and pack members

being close to the sheep. The plus and minus signs in the top part of Figure 5.2 became
the hypothesis for further observations. The logic of the pack hunt is that it is important for the pack members, in this case shepherd and dogs, to surround the prey,
preparatory to catching one of them. This is found in the upper left cell, and it has a
double plus, because Shaffer thought it was very like a pack-hunting situation and,

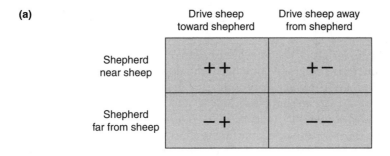

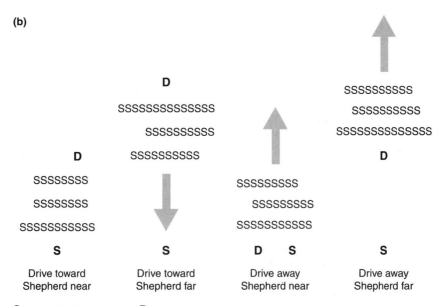

S = shepherd, S = sheep, **D** = dog.
Arrows indicate direction in which shepherd would like sheep to move.

FIGURE 5.2   Categories of Sheepdog Behavior with Sheep and Shepherd.
(a) Shepherd, sheepdog, and sheep maneuvers reduced to basic examples. The plus
signs indicate Shaffer's guess that the situation is something the dog would do readily
based on hunting ancestry: driving toward the shepherd and being near the sheep.
The minus signs suggest that a dog would be expected to have trouble performing
well in the situation, as in driving sheep away and being far from the shepherd. Mixed
signs predict mixed success. (b) Schematic representations of the maneuvers in (a).

therefore something the dogs should do well. Shepherds typically use this arrangement when it is necessary to surround and catch one sheep from a flock so that it can be given some medicine or other treatment

Moving across the top of Figure 5.2, the upper right cell is the situation that the dogs had encountered in the narrow lane. "Pack members" were all near the sheep, but the shepherd wanted the sheep driven away from themselves and the dogs. This has a mixed sign because it is like the hunt in having pack members near the sheep, but it also has the nonhunting element in that the goal is to drive the sheep away from the pack members.

The lower left cell has one hunting element: the pack has the sheep surrounded. The shepherd is a long way away from the dog and the sheep. In hunting terms, the head of the pack is too far away to help with the hunt. This is the situation that can occur when the dog is sent up a hillside to fetch sheep back to the shepherd.

The remaining cell in Figure 5.2 is an unlikely event in which the shepherd is far away from the flock and wants the dog to show itself and chase the sheep further away. Neither element of this, being far from the pack or chasing sheep farther from the pack, would have any obvious role in a pack hunt. As Shaffer worked out this theoretical scheme, he could not remember seeing any actual field situations that would fit in the lower right cell.

The next step was to go to the field and try to do observations that would support the model. The best times for getting observations of a number of different dogs was during the gathering days when sheep were brought down from the high moors where they shared common grazing during the summer. Because the sheep from many farms had been been grazing on hundreds of square miles of open moorland, gathering is a big job, requiring shepherds and dogs from all the farms in the area. Shaffer took this opportunity to observe behavior of several different dogs and to rate the overall success of each individual maneuver. The outcome was judged to be successful if fewer than 10 percent of commands given by the shepherd were attempts to get the dog to stop doing behaviors. This is a fairly high standard for success, and you should know that it was chosen somewhat arbitrarily. There are no established rules for observing and rating behavior. This leaves it up to the researcher to make a decision. Needless to say, Shaffer tried to avoid introducing bias into the data. Several different operational definitions of the successful maneuver did not produce very different patterns of results. The results of these observations are shown in Figure 5.3.

The data offer some confirmation of the initial observation that closely surrounding the sheep, dog on one side of the sheep and shepherd on the other, was something that the dogs did readily and well. In this figure, the last column for each dog is the situation on the right at the bottom of Figure 5.2 that rarely, if ever, occurred: the dog is sent by the shepherd to approach a distant flock and chase them further away. This had no application for a pack hunter and made little sense in sheepherding. Shaffer asked Edwin if he had ever done this and, after some thought, Edwin responded that occasionally he needed a dog to run at distant intruding neighbor sheep and move them out of the way in order to prevent mixing with his own flock. Zeros have been entered as data for this column in Figure 5.3, because Shaffer asked each of the shepherds to try to get their dogs to do it, and the result was a complete failure. The dogs

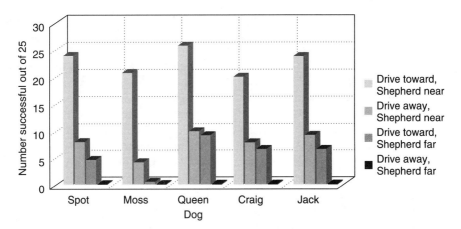

FIGURE 5.3   Success in Maneuvers for Several Dogs. Number of successful maneuvers of four different types by five different dogs. Success was defined as a herding event in which less than 10 percent of commands were telling the dog to *stop* a particular behavior.

refused to do this in spite of a barrage of commands from the red-faced, arm-waving shepherd. The dogs were practically incapable of this behavior.

It is important to make a distinction between these rough working farm dogs and the polished and trained dogs who perform in the spectator events called sheepdog trials. Dog trials are local and national competitions that are held to show off the peak achievements of herding dogs who have been meticulously taught to follow instructions. The training of these dogs is so intense and thorough that they appear to be radio controlled. The dogs trained for exhibition in sheepdog trials demonstrate that it is possible to teach these dogs to do exactly what the shepherd wants. For Shaffer and Tinbergen, however, the rough farm dogs provided a better window into the workings of canine behavior.

The observations described here illustrated an important, but rarely appreciated, aspect of learning. People sometimes think of learning as adding a new behavior to a list of behaviors that can already be performed. For example, as a child, you learned to do arithmetical operations such as multiplication. It might be easy to conclude that this learning only involved adding new responses to a behavior repertoire. What is less obvious is that learning also includes eliminating responses: learning *not* to perform certain behaviors. To perform multiplication, we must learn to put the numbers in straight columns above each other, but this includes learning to avoid having the response of having columns so misaligned that arithmetic becomes impossible. Much of the sheepdog behavior involved learning *not* to do things. Remember that most of the commands given to the dogs were "stop" commands.

Shaffer and Tinbergen were also interested in the development of sheepdog behavior. During their work with Edwin, they had an opportunity to watch him raise a pup, Jill. At first Jill seemed to have no particular interest in sheep. When she was around 8 months old, she rather suddenly started to run along beside Spot, doing what he was doing. It seemed to Shaffer and Tinbergen that Jill was learning as much from Spot as she was from Edwin. By the time she was a year and a half old, she was able to work on her own and be useful in herding the sheep. Years ago, Jill's behavior might have been described as a herding instinct, suggesting that it was caused by her genetic endowment. We now believe that this sort of label is too simple to be of any use. Herding behavior certainly has some genetic components. This becomes clear if, facetiously, we ask why *dogs* are used for herding? Why not cats? *Sheepcats?* Shaffer and Tinbergen believed that the dogs carried a genetic package that predisposed them to perform many of the behaviors needed by the farmer. These behaviors were thinly disguised hunting behaviors, and probably this genetic component had come to the dogs through ancestral lines. The spectacular levels of performance in sheep trial dogs clearly showed that learning was involved. Much of this learning was the elimination of undesirable responses. Immediate situational components such as nutrition, time of day, and the behavior of other dogs also made a difference. One of the recurrent themes of contemporary psychological research is that a behavior does not have a single cause. All behaviors have genetic, biological, experiential, and situational components. As you will see in subsequent chapters, these components, and the interactions among them, are the primary topic for psychological investigations today.

People who know little about contemporary psychology may consider that most human behavior is learned: we use misleading phrases such as "the child learned to walk." Although learning is certainly a component of walking, other factors are also involved. For example, research by Esther Thelen (1992) has shown that the appearance of walking is delayed by the leg muscle strength of babies. The legs of young babies are so heavy that their underdeveloped muscles cannot move the legs in walking motions without assistance. Walking does not simply appear as the result of learning. Much as with the sheepdog behavior described in this article, human walking has many components, not a single cause.

REFERENCES

Fossey, D. (1983). *Gorillas in the mist.* Boston: Houghton Mifflin.

Hoxie, R., & Rubenstein, L. (1994). Are older pedestrians allowed enough time to cross intersections safely? *The Journal of the American Geriatrics Society, 42,* 241–244.

Lorenz, K. (1952). *King Solomon's ring.* London: Crowell.

Martin, J., & Ross, H. (1996). Do mitigating circumstances influence family reactions to physical aggression? *Child Development, 67,* 1455–1466.

Mech, L. D. (1970). *The wolf.* New York: Natural History Press.

Thelen, E. (1992). Development as a dynamic system. *Current Directions in Psychological Science, 1,* 189–193.

Tinbergen, N. (1958). *Curious naturalists.* London: Country Life.

Tinbergen, N. (1974). *Curious naturalists* (rev. ed.). Amherst: University of Massachusetts Press.

CHAPTER 6

ZIPPING UP THE GENES

Where does personality come from? The readings about personality in this book have each, in their own way, tried to provide some answers to this question. As you will come to understand, there is no single source of personality; rather, it is part of a complex interaction among many factors. We wish it was possible to give you simple answers, but, for this question, simple answers are wrong answers. One of the differences that has been found between high school students and upper-level college students is that the college students are better able to deal with multiple answers to a single question (Perry, 1981). High school seems to prepare students to seek THE answer, whereas the college experience seems to help people understand that this is often too simple. The style of thinking exhibited by high school students has been called *dichotomous thinking*. They are likely to see the world in terms of dichotomies; that is, they see the world as being either one thing or another. A national sports figure may be either a god or pond scum, not a realistic mix of attributes of all sorts. In the distant past, the field of psychology thought in the same way as a high school kid: mind *or* body and nature *or* nurture are examples of discarded dichotomies. Psychology now takes a multidetermined approach to areas where dichotomous thinking was once common. As an example of this, genes are now appreciated as a component of behavior acting in concert with many other influences.

THE MEASUREMENT OF VARIABILITY

In trying to find out where personality comes from, we are really asking why some people have different personalities from others; why there are so many differences in personality. Usually, the question is about a particular trait: why are some people so optimistic and some so pessimistic? Differences among people can be measured with a statistic called the *variance*. Variance is a measure of the differences that can be found

Incorporating the research of T. Bouchard and M. McGue, "Genetic and Rearing Environmental Influences on Adult Personality: An Analysis of Adopted Twins Reared Apart," 1990, *Journal of Personality, 58,* pp. 263–292.

within a particular trait among members of some group. If you have taken a course on statistics you may know how to calculate the variance, but the calculation of it is not required for the understanding of this chapter.

If you line up a group of 12-year-olds, you will be able to see considerable variation in the extent of their physical development. A statistical measure of that variability, such as the variance, would yield a high score for physical development within that group. To take a behavioral example, the variance in juvenile delinquency would probably be quite high within most junior high schools. Some kids would commit many delinquent acts, some would commit none, and there would be a group in the middle. There would be quite a bit of variability, so the value of the variance would be high. Variance can only be measured within some specific group. It may be possible to imagine measuring the variance for juvenile delinquency for U.S. kids in all junior high schools, but practically speaking, we could not. To do that would involve assessing the delinquency of each individual kid. Usually, if you are interested in the variance of some population (such as all kids in the United States) you will try to take a *representative* sample of the population and assume that the variance of that sample is similar to the population. If the sample is large, a random sample will probably be representative. With small samples, representativeness is more difficult to achieve, even with random selection.

The same applies to personality traits. The variance must be obtained from studying a particular group. We cannot know what the variance is for optimism within the United States, but we might be able to estimate it with research samples that were representative of the entire country. These samples can be difficult to construct but if they are large and carefully selected, they can yield good estimates of the variation within a large population.

SOURCES OF VARIABILITY

An important comparison can be made here between life sciences, including psychology, and some of the physical sciences. In physical sciences, variability is often largely the result of errors made in the scientific procedures. Imagine a simple demonstration of the physics of falling objects. If you want to know the speed at which objects fall you might drop 10 bricks, one at a time, from a tall building and have a friend measure the falling time of each brick with a stopwatch. Variability might be introduced because you dropped some bricks end first and some side first. Perhaps a few times the bricks hit window ledges on the way down. The human who is timing the fall of the bricks may also introduce some variability because he might not be paying full attention to the task after a number of bricks had fallen. This variability found in brick falling would be the result of errors and imprecision.

In psychology, variability may also be the result of error and imprecision but, much more importantly, the variability may reflect important real differences among people. For example, the driving ability of elderly people has been shown to deteriorate as the people get older, partially because of slowing of reaction time (Hakamies-Blomqvist, Johansson, & Lundberg, 1996). This variability is more than measurement error—some people are better drivers than others. In psychology, the variability is usually more than error—it can be the main focus of the study. Among people, differences are usually more interesting than similarities. If we were to tell you that all of the kids in a particular classroom have IQs that are about average, you might think "So what?" In contrast, if we were to tell you that there was a classroom in which some kids had very low IQs and some kids had high IQs, then you immediately have a question for psychological science: Why are these kids different? This could also be phrased, "What accounts for the variance in IQ in this classroom?" Either way, it is the same question.

The answer to the question, "Where does personality come from?" requires a clear understanding of the nature of variability within a group. The variance is one measure of this variability. We believe you can understand this, no matter how skilled or unskilled you are in statistics. Statistics are an important part of measurement in psychology, but at the introductory level it is probably more important to understand the concepts than it is to understand the math.

Once variability itself is grasped, the next step in finding out where personality comes from is to ask how much of the variability of a trait within a group is the result of the variability in any one specific factor. We might ask, for example, how much of the variance in a personality trait is accounted for by variability in genes, parenting, schooling, nutrition, or socioeconomic status. Note we are *not* asking how *much* of personality is accounted for by each factor. Rather, we are saying that we can measure personality, find a range of variation in a trait, and find out how much of the *variation* in the personality trait is the result of the variation in some other specific factor (see Figure 6.1). The research and statistical methods exist to enable us to answer this question.

You should be able to guess that variability in no one factor such as genes, parenting, or school will ever account for 100 percent of the variance in a psychological trait or a behavior. Nevertheless, some factors have been shown to account for rather large amounts of measured variation. It may come as a surprise to learn that for personality, painstaking research has indicated that a large amount of the variance is the result of variation in genetic factors. With proper research methods, to be discussed below, it is possible to find out how much of the variation is the result of individual nongenetic components and how much is the result of genes. The amount of variance in a trait that is the result of genetic factors is called the *heritability* of that trait.

TWINS

The usual way to approach the measurement of heritability in a human population is to measure the trait in question among individuals of known genetic relatedness—fathers and sons, siblings, half-siblings, cousins, or other relatives. A team of scientists

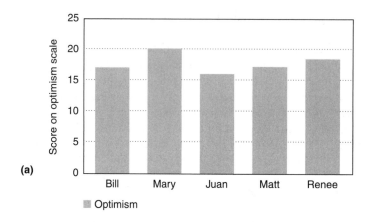

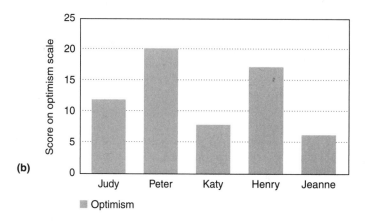

FIGURE 6.1   Illustration of Variance. (a) Optimism for Group A. (b) Optimism for Group B. Imagine that these are data on samples of students who have been selected from two classrooms, Group A from one class and Group B from another. Both have been given a pencil-and-paper optimism scale designed to measure their outlook about life. It is easy to see that there is more variation in Group B than in Group A. It would be interesting to do a larger study to find out why the members of Group A are so similar. The study we would do would ask why Group A has less variability than Group B. It would also ask what is the source of this variance. Perhaps, for example, the scores in Group B also have considerable variance, and the people who are not very optimistic, Judy, Katy and Jeanne, are doing poorly in the class. As you can see, one way to approach this problem would be to calculate correlations between grades and optimism score. That might explain some of the variance. If Group A is a small class where students get a lot of individual attention and Group B is a large class, this might also explain some of the variance. You can, perhaps, think of other factors that might explain some of the variance.

at the University of Minnesota has been working on the heritability question for a number of years. Rather than relying on other family members who may share only small amounts of genetic material, this team has concentrated on twins. There are two kinds of twins, dizygotic and monozygotic. Dizygotic (DZ) twins are the result of two eggs being fertilized at the same time by two different sperm (*di* means two and a *zygote* is a fertilized egg). These individuals are no more closely related genetically than any other siblings. This means that they share, on the average, half their genes. They just happen to have been conceived at the same time. Monozygotic (MZ) twins are the result of one fertilized egg splitting into two individuals (*mono* means one and a *zygote* is a fertilized egg). Because they came from one zygote, their genetic material is the same. These twins are sometimes called "identical twins." They are interesting as research participants because differences between them cannot be caused by genes— their genes are the same. The similarities between MZ twins certainly *may* have a genetic explanation, but they may also have something to do with the shared experiences and environments that are usual for MZ twins. Again, *similarities* between MZ twins do *not* have to result only from their shared genes.

Participants

In order to sort out the effects of genetic influences on personality, Thomas Bouchard and the research team from Minnesota located a group of twins, MZ and DZ, who had been separated early in life and raised apart in different environments. These were called *MZA* and *DZA*, short for *MZ apart* and *DZ apart* (Tellegen et al., 1988).

If personality measures of monozygotic twins raised apart show strong correlations, we might be able to conclude the similarities are the result of genetic influences. The dizygotic twins in this study form a very important control group. The dizygotic twins share no more genes than ordinary brothers or sisters. On the average, this is 50 percent. If the DZAs show about half as much similarity as the MZAs in personality, then we have some additional evidence for the role of genes in personality.

It might seem that it would be difficult to find many separated twins and, once found, some of these twins might not want to be studied. The research team from Minnesota found that, indeed, separated twins are quite rare. However, with hard work, quite a number of pairs were located. Bouchard and his colleagues noted that the twins seemed to enjoy being studied. The Minnesota team worked hard to make the lab visits of all twins interesting and worthwhile so that they would remain in the study (Lykken, 1982).

Twins do not always know if they are MZ or DZ. In everyday life, this decision is usually made based on physical appearance: if the twins look quite similar, they are assumed to be MZ twins. Clearly this is not good enough for genetic research, because some DZ twins may appear to be quite similar, in the same way that nontwin siblings may sometimes look quite a bit alike. Bouchard and McGue verified the MZ and DZ status of all twins in the study by testing blood samples to examine a variety of indicators of genetic relatedness. In addition, they examined fingerprints and other physical indices. Given these measures, the probability that a DZ pair would end up misclassified as an MZ pair in this research was less than 1 in 1,000.

Participants were 45 MZA pairs and 26 DZA pairs. In a study such as this, it is very important to know how much contact the twins had with each other. In a perfect study, the twins would have been separated at birth and would not have been reunited until after personality had been assessed. However, real life does not produce this situation very often. Nevertheless, Bouchard and McGue were able to assure themselves that their twin pairs had been apart for a sufficiently long enough time so that shared environmental conditions were unlikely to account for personality. Extensive interviews were conducted to collect information on the length of time that had passed before the twins were separated and on the amount of time they had spent together after they were reunited. The mean values for separation time are found in Table 6.1. This table also shows the range for each mean. The range is the lowest score in the group and the highest score in the group. It is a fairly crude measure of variability because if there is one individual with an extreme score, that person will distort one end of the range. If you look at the means and at the ranges together, you can get a better picture of the variability than you will get from looking at one or the other alone. For example, one MZA twin pair was together for 48.7 months before they were separated, but that could not be typical of many other MZA pairs, or the mean for the whole group would be higher than 5.1 months.

Total contact months shown in Table 6.1 is the amount of time before separation combined with the amount of contact twins experienced after reunion.

Procedure

When the twins were brought to the Minnesota lab, they engaged in about 50 hours of medical and psychological assessment. The researchers were interested in collecting as much information as possible on them because this may have been the last research of this kind to be done. Adoption agencies are now very reluctant to separate twins. In contrast, this was commonly done when the people in this study were children. Although we are primarily presenting information about personality, quite a bit of

TABLE 6.1 **Means and Ranges for Age and Contact in MZA and DZA Twins**

	AGE	% FEMALES	MONTHS, YEARS PRIOR TO SEPARATION	CONTACT REUNION	TOTAL MONTHS
MZA (N = 45)					
Mean	41.0	65.2	5.1	30.0	26.5
Range	19 to 68		0 to 48.7	.5 to 64.7	.3 to 284.5
DZA* (N = 26)					
Mean	42.0	75.0	12.7	37.3	13.1
Range	25 to 61		.1 to 54.8	17 to 57.9	.2 to 54.2

*There were three opposite sex sets of twins in the DZA sample.

other information has been collected about twins by the Minnesota researchers (Lykken, Bouchard, McGue, & Tellegen, 1993).

The personality measure used by Bouchard and McGue was the California Psychological Inventory, or CPI. The CPI is a widely used personality test, probably selected because it has been shown to be a valid measure of personality. The form of the CPI that was used had 480 items designed to measure "aspects and attributes of interpersonal behavior that are to be found in all cultures and societies, and that possess a direct relationship to . . . social interactions." In addition, Bouchard and McGue asked the twins to assess their rearing environment using the Family Environment Scale, or FES. The FES is a self-report questionnaire made up of a wide range of statements about family environments. The twins' spouses were used as a comparison control group to ensure that the twins were not in some way different in personality simply because they were separated twins. The spouses were useful for this comparison because they were not twins, and they had not been separated from siblings.

Results

The combined CPI scores of all MZA twins look about the same as the scores for all DZA twins combined. The combined scores for a few of the CPI scales are shown in Table 6.2.

These scores are not different than those found for typical adults, nor were they different from those found for the control group of spouses of twins. In terms of personality, as a group, the twins looked about like the rest of us. As a group, MZA and DZA twins were also similar for the Family Environment Scale measures. On FES family variables such as cohesion, expressiveness, conflict, independence, achievement orientation, intellectual-cultural orientation, active-recreational orientation, moral/religious orientation, organization, and control, the two groups of twins were not different. Both MZA and DZA samples were similar to the FES scores of the group of nonadopted spouses, suggesting that any effects seen were not merely the result of having been raised in an adoptive home.

TABLE 6.2   Examples of Mean CPI Scores for MZA-Combined and DZA-Combined Samples

SCALE ON CPI	MEAN MZA	MEAN DZA
Dominance	25.5	24.2
Sociability	22.5	19.5
Self-acceptance	19.4	18.3
Tolerance	20.7	20.0
Responsibility	26.9	26.2
Self-control	30.1	30.0
Flexibility	9.3	8.1

The twins were separated early in life. When comparisons were made within a pair of twins, the data from the FES showed that there was no reason to think that their adoptive environments were particularly similar. Obviously, if both twins of a pair are placed in highly similar adoptive homes, similarity between twins in adulthood could be a result of home characteristics, shared genes, or both. Correlations were calculated for the Family Environment Scale ratings of each twin pair. High correlations would mean that the different adoptive homes were quite similar in family interaction style. Only a few of these correlations were significantly different from zero, suggesting that the adoptive homes were not very similar when one member of a twin pair was compared to the other twin in the pair.

In contrast, the members of a twin pair, particularly the MZA pairs, showed fairly strong correlations for personality when one twin was compared to the other. Table 6.3 shows some examples of correlations for MZA pairs and DZA pairs. A third column shows the heritability for the listed factors. These heritabilities have been calculated from the twin data in this study and represent, as you will remember, the proportion of variability that is the result of genetic factors. Heritability may range from zero—where there is no genetic influence, to a theoretical 1.00—where genes are the only source of observed variation.

The difference between correlations for MZA twins and DZA twins is striking, and the heritabilities range around .5, suggesting that about half of the variation observed in the personalities of these people was a result of genetic factors. A few personality traits not shown in Table 6.3 had lower heritability, such as *communality* (= .104) and *flexibility* (= .051) but these were rare.

TABLE 6.3   Examples of Correlations for MZA and DZA Twins and Heritabilities for California Psychological Inventory Scales

CPI SCALE	CORRELATION FOR MZA	CORRELATION FOR DZA	HERITABILITY*
Dominance	.53	.24	.541
Capacity for status	.60	.39	.652
Self-acceptance	.62	.11	.616
Well-being	.59	.17	.583
Responsibility	.48	.34	.626
Socialization	.53	.39	.577
Self-control	.68	−.28	.612
Tolerance	.55	.22	.602
Good impression	.53	−.19	.464
Achieve via conformance	.44	.02	.414
Achieve via independence	.62	.25	.665

*Note: Be careful not to confuse heritability with the correlation coefficients. Although the arrangement of the digits is superficially similar, they are very different measures. Heritability is the proportion of variance for a particular trait that is the result of genetic factors.

Discussion

This is not an isolated finding. Research with other personality assessments (Tellegen et al., 1988) and with other groups in other countries (Rose, Koskenvuo, Kaprio, Langinvainio, & Sarna, 1988) have found substantially the same thing. Bouchard and McGue note that our intuitive estimates of the effects of environmental factors in personality are often inflated. Although we have not presented the data for MZ twins reared together, you may be quite surprised to learn that MZ twins show about the same levels of personality correlations when reared together as when reared apart. Summing up the literature, Bouchard and McGue say "We are led to what must for some seem a rather remarkable conclusion: The degree of MZ twin resemblance on self-reported personality characteristics does not appear to depend upon whether the twins are reared together or apart, whether they are adolescent or adult, in what industrialized country they reside . . . degree of personality similarity between reared-apart and reared-together twins suggests that common familial environmental factors do not have a substantial influence upon adult personality."

If 50% of the variance in personality is accounted for by genes, what about the rest? As in the introductory example involving falling bricks, some of it will be a result of error in measurement and other unsystematic factors. One twin may have had more rest than the other on the day of testing. The personality test questions may mean slightly different things to different members of a twin pair.

Aside from heritability and error, Bouchard and McGue conclude that most of the rest of the variance is accounted for by idiosyncratic environmental factors. Idiosyncratic factors are those that are different from one person to the next, even from one twin to the next. One way to understand these factors is to think about your own experience compared to that of other people raised in what may be naïvely called "the same environment." If you had siblings, you may be able to use them as examples; if not, think of a group setting such as a schoolroom. Individual homes and schools may seem like the *same* environment for the kids in them, but the current thinking in psychology suggests this is not the case. As Sandra Scarr (1992) pointed out, the actual experience of these contexts varies greatly from one individual to the next because, among other reasons, different people elicit or evoke different responses from the so-called *same* situations. Many of us may remember being hunted down and punished for specific behaviors while siblings and classmates seemed to get away with the same behavior. Perhaps when others told the teacher that the dog had eaten their homework, the teacher expressed concern for them. When you said the same thing, the teacher yelled at you and expressed concern for your dog. On the flip side, many of us will also remember having a special relationship with a teacher, very different from that person's relations with our classmates. Parents may love all their kids, but the kids get treated differently from one another. These are the idiosyncratic factors that can make a superficially similar environment into a very different place for each individual.

So, after all this, where does personality come from? You will now recognize that there is no easy answer to this question. Bouchard and McGue have demonstrated that genetics play a considerable role in personality differences among people. This is likely to be one reason why, as in other personality chapters in this book, personality seems to be quite consistent across situations and over parts of the life span. Does this mean that personality cannot change? No. We will have more complete answers to this question when we understand more about the idiosyncratic environmental factors that also seem to be involved in personality. The first step in that understanding has been a big one. It has involved the acceptance of the idea that personality is not merely the result of learning *or* biology. Whatever the future holds for this line of research, it is already clear that there are important things going on down there in your genes.

REFERENCES

Bouchard, T., & McGue, M. (1990). Genetic and rearing environmental influences on adult personality: An analysis of adopted twins reared apart. *Journal of Personality, 58*, 263–292.

Hakamies-Blomqvist, L., Johansson, K., & Lundberg, C. (1996). Medical screening of older drivers as a traffic safety measure: A comparative Finnish-Swedish Evaluation study. *Journal of the American Geriatrics Society, 44*, 650–653.

Lykken, D. (1982). Research with twins: The concept of emergenesis. *Psychophysiology, 19*, 361–373.

Lykken, D. T., Bouchard, T. J., McGue, M., & Tellegen, A. (1993). Heritability of interests: A Twin Study. *Journal of Applied Psychology, 78*, 649–661.

Perry, W. G. (1981). Cognitive and ethical growth. In A. Chickering (Ed.), *The Modern American College* (pp. 76–116). San Francisco: Jossey-Bass.

Rose, R. J., Koskenvuo, M., Kaprio, J., Langinvainio, H., & Sarna, S. (1988). Shared genes, shared experiences and similarity of personality: Data from 14,288 adult Finnish co-twins. *Journal of Personality and Social Psychology, 54*, 161–171.

Scarr, S. (1992). Developmental theories for the 1990s: Developmental and individual differences. *Child Development, 63*, 1–19.

Tellegen, A., Lykken, D. T., Bouchard, T. J., Jr., Wilcox, K. J., Segal, N. L., & Rich, S. (1988). Personality similarity in twins reared apart and together. *Journal of Personality and Social Psychology, 54*, 1031–1039.

CHAPTER 7

SMALL WAIST + BIG HIPS = ATTRACTIVE LADY

EVOLUTIONARY PSYCHOLOGY: AN INTRODUCTION

Quite recently psychologists have begun to take notice of the explanatory power of evolutionary theory in understanding human behavior. Charles Darwin first proposed the contemporary version of evolutionary theory in 1859. It quickly became the basis for most thinking in biology because it explained many previously unexplained observations, and it unified data from many areas of biology. Although evolution is still called a "theory" and some details of what happened in the past are considered controversial by some, we will adopt the stance of the overwhelming majority of scientists that evolution is a fact. We are not so naive as to think that scientific facts are the *truth*. We understand that scientific facts can be modified by further research and that other factors (e.g., culture, learning, and genetics) are also likely to play significant roles. We believe that evolution happens. Although we hope that you will share this belief, there is no way that we can force you to agree. We do hope that you will work to understand evolutionary ideas whatever you happen to believe. It is possible to understand a position even if one does not believe it is correct, and this is all that is required to understand the research in this area.

Evolutionary theory proposes that among the variation we observe in structure or behavior within populations of organisms, there are some variants that make some individuals more likely to survive than others. If these characteristics are passed from parent to offspring, then the offspring of these individuals are also more likely to survive and to have surviving offspring themselves. In this way, the genes of the surviving and breeding individuals will, over generations, spread through the population and take over. Genes of organisms that do not survive to reproduce will disappear, also known as being *selected out*. Notice two important things about this description. First,

Incorporating the research of D. Singh, "Adaptive Significance of Female Physical Attractiveness: Role of Waist-to-Hip Ratio," 1993, *Journal of Personality and Social Psychology, 65*, pp. 293–307.

some individuals are taking over the population with their genes, so the competition here is *within* the species. This is the rabbits versus the rabbits, not the rabbits versus the foxes. Second, to be successful in this system, the individual must reproduce itself to a greater extent than other individuals—merely surviving or being healthy and strong are evolutionarily useless unless the individuals also outbreeds the competitors. It is in this sense that the old catch phrase, *survival of the fittest*, is misleading. Survival of the fittest was a concept proposed by Herbert Spencer, not Charles Darwin.

The new thinking embodied in evolutionary psychology is that much of human behavior is adaptive; that is, it operates to ensure that individuals will survive and successfully reproduce. That is what we would expect, because the humans who are alive today are the descendents of many generations of evolutionarily successful competitors who managed to outbreed other humans. The result is us. We are not always aware of the evolutionary underpinnings of our behavior. For example, we are reluctant to eat food that smells bad. We would say, "That smells rotten, so I will not eat it." The rotten smell is the *proximal* or *immediate reason*, and it is usually the reason we give. The adaptive or long-term reason, called the *ultimate reason*, is that individuals who eat rotten food are likely to get ill, die, and therefore not reproduce. In the past, individuals who readily ate rotten food were selected out, leaving the rest of us. Evolutionary psychologists stress that we may be often blissfully unaware of ultimate reasons for most of our behavior. Conscious awareness of the ultimate reasons for our behavior does not matter for survival. What matters is that the behavior, in some way, promotes survival and reproductive success.

HUMAN MATING STRATEGY

Evolutionary psychologists note that in mammals, males and females have different goals when it comes to sexual reproduction. Females are always certain that their offspring are their own—they are present at the birth. Males can never be totally certain that they are the parents of a mate's offspring. In addition, females are limited in the number of opportunities to pass on genetic material. That is, females have only a limited number of pregnancy cycles during the fertile portion of their life span. Males, in contrast, are almost unlimited in the numbers of potential offspring. Indeed the number of sperm in one ejaculation could fertilize all the women in the United States if dispensed door to door. This is especially important for humans because males may invest considerable energy and resources for extended periods of time after the child is born. From an evolutionary standpoint, it would be a very costly error for a male to lavish attention, time, money, and other resources on a child who was genetically unrelated to him. Remember, conscious or not, the major goal of evolution is passing on your genes to your children and subsequent descendents. Therefore, it makes no evolutionary sense for a male to contribute to the development of children he did not father. Males must maximize the chances of parenting their own genetic children. Women do not have any doubt that they are related to their children but, nevertheless, are at risk of being alone during the child-rearing years. The evolutionary task of a woman must be to maintain her mate's investment in the relationship with her and their children. If a man has an extramarital affair, his commitment to his marriage is at risk, and this can bring significant threat to the wife's ability to parent effectively. Evolutionary psychology would predict that a male's emotional investment in another woman would pose a major threat to his mate. A strong emotional investment, rather than a purely sexual affair, may lead to the demise of the marriage, resulting in the wife being burdened by the tasks of child rearing with limited or no spousal support. This burden significantly increases the risk of being less successful in passing on gene copies to the next generation.

The focus of Devendra Singh's research is what makes a woman attractive to a man. We often think of attractiveness in terms of facial beauty, hairstyle, clothing, status, and other variables. Women seem to spend a great deal of time and money to improve their appearance through cosmetics, dress, hair styling, and even plastic surgery. Singh's approach to the study of female attractiveness does not focus on these aspects but, instead, focuses on a relatively simple concept of beauty—the ratio between size of waist and hips. You might think this to be a very unusual concept, because we often think of the variables mentioned earlier (hair, dress) as the key dimensions of attractiveness. The waist-to-hip ratio (WHR) is really not a newly discovered dimension of beauty, but has historical roots. In Victorian society, a small waist and large hips were attained by wearing corsets that cinched the waist tightly and bustles, artificial structures attached to the rear of dresses to increase hip size.

The work of Singh grows out of the tradition of evolutionary psychology and specifically focuses on the role of attractiveness as a variable in mate selection. Evolutionary psychology suggests that both sexes desire mates who will enhance their own opportunities to reproduce more effectively. Women should choose high-status males who can provide the necessary resources to help raise children over a sustained period of time. A man should choose a woman who is fertile and capable of nurturing her offspring. It may not be too difficult to assess a man's status, because the resources associated with one's status are obvious. With women, however, status in terms of reproductive health may be less obvious.

Evolutionary psychologists state that because the major signs of female reproductive ability are hidden (e.g., ovulation), a potential mate must use other more indirect data (e.g., physical attractiveness) as a sign of health. Evolutionary psychology includes physical attractiveness as a sign of youth, and youth is a positive index of fertility. The difficulty with assessing attractiveness is that it is culturally specific, and the particular qualities may even vary over time within a culture. If one compares the standards of beauty in Renaissance paintings of women to contemporary standards of beauty as exemplified by fashion models, one can readily see the difference over time and culture. Even during the past 40 years the preferred body shape of the Miss America participants has evolved in favor of a slimmer look. Taking a cross-cultural perspective, the difficulties of finding a uniform standard have proved difficult. Women differ considerably in terms of facial features, skin color, hairstyle, skin adornment, and alteration of body features. These characteristics are predominantly culturally based and are important.

However, if evolutionary theory plays a significant role, a cross-cultural biophysical marker of fertility must exist. It is vitally important that relatively obvious physical signs are available for males and females to use as significant factors in mate selection. Singh's research focuses on distribution of body fat, specifically in terms of a ratio between waist and hip size, as the biophysical measure. It is his thesis that WHR is a cross-cultural biophysical feature that relates to attractiveness because it is an indication of reproductive health. Singh certainly recognizes that culturally based variables play a part in the perception of attractiveness, but suggests that the biophysical factors, such as WHR, are of primary importance.

CALCULATING WHR

The calculation of WHR is made by dividing waist measurement by hip measurement. For example, if your waist measured 26 inches and your hips measured 36 you would have a WHR of .72. This ratio is low and indicative of attractiveness. However, if your waist measured 38 and your hips measured 42 your WHR would be approximately .90, a higher and less-attractive ratio. Remember, as you will see in this chapter, overall weight does also play a role.

WHY WAIST-TO-HIP RATIO?

It has been demonstrated that sex hormones affect the accumulation of fat. Testosterone, the male hormone, increases fat deposits in the abdominal area and decreases fat deposits in the hip-buttock-thigh area. In contrast, estrogen, the female hormone, inhibits fat in the abdominal region and increases fat deposits in the hip-buttock-thigh region. Therefore mature men and women have opposite body features in the waist and hip region due largely to the function of different hormones. WHR is seen to be a stable, easily obtained measure that reflects the underlying biological processes.

The next step that needs to be established is the link between WHR and reproductive health status. There is evidence that girls with lower WHR experience earlier endocrine activity (DeRidder et al., 1990). DeRidder's research established a relationship between WHR and fertility. In this research, females with higher WHR had more difficulty becoming pregnant and experienced their initial childbirth at a later age than females with lower WHR. WHR also serves to indicate a general state of health. For example, research indicates that lower WHR is associated with decreased risk for diabetes, coronary disease, and stroke. Obviously women who are in a more favorable state of health may be better prepared for pregnancy, childbirth, and the demands of childcare and nurturing.

It is important to note that if the WHR is such a good index of general and reproductive health, then it is absolutely essential to this argument that males be able to detect this feature easily and use it to assess the attractiveness of a potential mate. It is important for readers to understand that, in mating from an evolutionary perspective, males are primarily focused in getting their genetic material represented in succeeding generations. In doing so, it makes most sense for them to select as mates the most fertile women. Singh's research studied whether men use WHR as important criteria in assessing the attractiveness of women.

Research has shown that even though the overall weight standard of female attractiveness has changed over the past three decades in favor of a lower overall weight, the hourglass figure as the ideal has remained unchanged. Measurements of Miss America participants from the 1940s through the mid-1980s indicate that WHRs have remained constant, even though body weight and height have changed (Mazur, 1986.) Gardner, Garfinkel, Schwartz, and Thompson (1980), in examining body measurement data for Playboy centerfolds from 1960 to 1978, found a fairly constant WHR that was very close to the Miss America data. In both samples a WHR of approximately .70 was found. The notion of women's bodies changing to a more androgynous, tubular look may find some support in the upper body, the bust. However the WHR, even in models that look similar to Twiggy, a famous twiglike English model, tend to have low WHR. Twiggy is said to have physical measurements of 31–24–33, which yields a WHR of .73. Therefore it appears that weight variations in females, high or low, do not invalidate the concept of WHR. Women who are attractive to men have WHRs in the low .70s.

DO MEN USE WHR IN ASSESSING ATTRACTIVENESS OF WOMEN?

It is interesting to observe that Miss America contestants and Playboy magazine models have consistently conformed to WHRs in the low .70s. However, it is even more important to demonstrate that men use the WHR data as an important factor in determining a woman's attractiveness. Women have many other physical features such as legs, breasts, facial characteristics, and hairstyle that may convey information regarding general and reproductive health. If WHR is to be considered an important criterion, it has to be shown that men's ratings of women's beauty correlate with WHR. The following study does just that—if the researcher manipulates WHR, will men's ratings of a woman's attractiveness change?

In this first study, 106 Caucasian and Hispanic college men volunteered to participate as part of class requirements. This is a common practice in psychological research, even though it raises ethical questions. Are you really a volunteer if you participate as a course requirement? The participants were asked to rank 12 line drawings of average height female figures at four different levels of WHR (.7, .8, .9, and 1.0) and three levels of body weight (underweight—90 lbs., normal weight—120 lbs., and overweight—150 lbs.). The figures were printed on normal letter-size paper in a random order. Participants could review all figures prior to making ratings. The line drawings are presented in Figure 7.1.

The participants were told that they were in a research project concerning "Body Types and Personality." The participant's task was to review all 12 drawings and rank them from most attractive (i.e., 1) to least attractive (i.e., 12). Information about the participants such as age, height, weight, religion, and ethnic background was collected

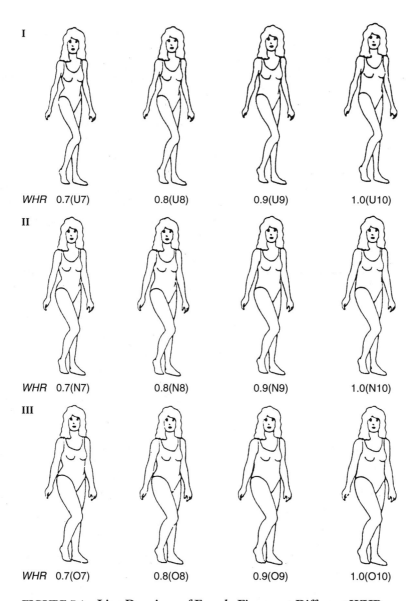

WHR   0.7(U7)   0.8(U8)   0.9(U9)   1.0(U10)

WHR   0.7(N7)   0.8(N8)   0.9(N9)   1.0(N10)

WHR   0.7(O7)   0.8(O8)   0.9(O9)   1.0(O10)

FIGURE 7.1   Line Drawings of Female Figures at Different WHR and Body Weight Levels. Stimulus figures used to represent three body weight categories (underweight, normal weight, and overweight) and four WHR ratings. Participants were given the 12 stimulus figures in random order without any notation of weight or WHR.

From "Adaptive Significance of Female Physical Attractiveness: Role of Waist-to-Hip Ratio," by D. Singh, 1993, *Journal of Personality and Social Psychology, 65,* pp. 293–307. Copyright © 1993 by the American Psychological Association. Reprinted with permission.

before the ranking task. After the ranking was completed participants were debriefed. Debriefing means that the research participants were given all the facts about the research project. In this research it was felt that giving the participants all the facts prior to the ranking would have altered the results. Therefore, participants are often given a "cover story" that will enable them to participate without knowing what the investigators are interested in studying. When this is done, it is mandatory to let participants know about the genuine purposes of the research after they complete their participation.

The attractiveness scores for both Caucasian and Hispanic participants in this study were compared and found to be similar. The participant's own body type, as assessed by a weight/height index, was not found to be a factor that impacted their ranking of attractiveness of the drawings. The attractiveness ranking scores are displayed in Table 7.1. This table depicts the percentage of participants ranking each of the drawings as most attractive (rank 1) and least attractive (rank 12); the choice is a function of body weight status (underweight, normal weight, overweight) and WHR (.7, .8, .9, and 1.0).

Within all three weight categories, the attractiveness rating, as seen in Table 7.1, increased as the WHR moved from 1.0 to .7. The normal weight figure with a WHR

TABLE 7.1   Attractiveness Ranking Scores

	PERCENTAGE RATING MOST ATTRACTIVE	PERCENTAGE RATING LEAST ATTRACTIVE
UNDERWEIGHT FIGURES		
WHR = .7	20	0
WHR = .8	11	0
WHR = .9	0	3
WHR = 1.0	0	8
NORMAL WEIGHT FIGURES		
WHR = .7	48	0
WHR = .8	8	0
WHR = .9	2	0
WHR = 1.0	1	0
OVERWEIGHT FIGURES		
WHR = .7	0	3
WHR = .8	0	3
WHR = .9	0	9
WHR = 1.0	0	11

of .7 was ranked as most attractive, with the underweight WHR of .7 in second place. The figures in the normal weight category were overall most often assigned the highest rank (i.e., 1) and never assigned the lowest rank (i.e., 12) with the exception of the normal figure with the WHR of 1.0. Singh notes that the normal body weight figures accounted for approximately two-thirds of the attractiveness rankings, whereas the underweight figures accounted for approximately one-third of the attractiveness rankings. It is interesting to note that despite the widespread American belief that thinness is a marker of beauty, the data from this study indicate that men prefer normal weight when rating attractiveness. The low attractiveness ratings for overweight females were consistent with previous research (Harris, Walters, & Walshull, 1991), however, the lower attractive scores for underweight women were unexpected. Singh states that there is some evidence to suggest being under- or overweight can negatively impact reproductive health in the following ways: retardation of the onset of menstrual cycle, increasing the length of menstrual cycle, and a higher incidence of infertility due to ovulation problems. Data also indicate that underweight women have offspring who are born at low birth weights, have delays in growth, and may suffer impairments in physical and cognitive development (Supy, Steer, McCusker, Steele, & Jacobs, 1988). Overweight women also experience reproductive health issues.

In order to determine if older men would rank female attractiveness in the same way as the college-age males, a second study using the same methodology was undertaken. The participants in this study were Caucasian males ages 25 to 85. A wide range of socioeconomic and educational status was included in this participant group. The findings in this second study were remarkably similar to the initial investigation. No age group differences were noted. This second study, a replication, provides additional strength for the concept that males utilize WHR as a sign of physical attractiveness. Indeed, these findings imply that the WHR plays a critical role in male decisions regarding attractiveness. Certainly the data indicate that weight is an important factor and the two physical variables (weight and WHR) are both central to male decision making regarding a woman's beauty status. To be considered highly attractive, a woman must have a low WHR and a normal body weight. If a woman's weight deviates from normal or if her WHR increases, she is likely to be judged less attractive by males. These results indicate that males have the ability to detect the WHR signal and utilize the information in formulating judgments regarding beauty.

IS WHR ADAPTIVE?

Men and women have radically different energy requirements when it comes to the process of reproduction. Women need to supply energy for the development of the fetus during a nine-month gestation period. After birth, the need to supply milk for nursing continues to demand significant energy. A woman's success in the reproduction and child rearing process requires a high level of stored fat. The fat deposits women have in the hips, buttocks, and thigh region are used almost exclusively during pregnancy and during the nursing of infants. There is considerable evidence that the reproductive process in a woman cannot begin until a reasonable amount of fat is stored to ensure the viability of the pregnancy, the birth process, and lactation. It is obvious that the investment in fat storage for a man's reproductive success is irrelevant. In fact, for males to store fat in a pattern similar to women would be counterproductive, as they would be less able to protect and defend their mates and offspring. What is required for males is muscularity and strength. Singh notes that another advantage of gluteofemoral fat in women is that it may serve as a signal to males of reproductive ability. It is a good signal because it can be seen well from side, front, or back. Women's breasts, often associated with attractiveness, do not have the same signal potential and do not always mirror reproductive health.

IS WHR THE ONLY THING THAT MATTERS?

Singh does not mean to suggest that men select women only on the basis of WHR. He does make the case that WHR is likely to be involved in the initial process of decision making about a woman's beauty. Singh regards men as using WHR as an initial screening filter to exclude some women who may be poor candidates for reproductive success. If a woman passes this initial screening, based on WHR, other finer, more discreet filters may be applied to serve in decision making regarding attractiveness. At the next level of decision making, the forces of culture come to bear and operate. These may include body stature, facial features, skin decoration, hairstyle, and use of cosmetics, jewelry, and ornamentation. These variables are seen to operate as long as they do not interrupt or interfere with the biological signals (i.e., WHR) that are viewed as taking primary importance. Facial characteristics have been given considerable attention as an important dimension because of the ability of the human face to convey signals. Eibl-Eibesfeldt (1989) found that facial expression of emotion is relatively free of cultural constraints and is used to convey sexual intentions. Singh contends that the third level of decision making regarding female attractiveness (1st = WHR, 2nd = cultural) involves personality factors and other learned societal variables. Some examples of these factors would be religious identification, attitudes, personality traits, and family values. In order to provide further support for Singh's views, especially the hierarchical arrangement that places WHR as a primary filter, it would be necessary to collect cross-cultural data to assess validity. If his thesis is correct, other biological factors such as body stature, breast size, and facial features, as well as cultural factors and personality factors, should be of lower importance than WHR.

In 1995 Singh and Luis published a cross-cultural study that replicated the research procedures described in this chapter with young Indonesian, African American, and Caucasian American participants of both sexes. The findings indicate that neither the sex nor the cultural background of the participants affected their ratings of female attractiveness. Normal weight females with low WHR were rated as most attractive. Note that in this study, female participants also had similar ratings to their male counterparts. These findings are important because they show that evolutionary hypothesis operates in a similar manner in very different cultures.

Singh does not deal directly with the issue of male attractiveness to women in this study. However, one can speculate that a single or cluster of biophysical markers for male attractiveness may not be found to be useful in modern society. It is likely that in primitive human societies a man's strength, endurance, and speed as evidenced by a muscular, athletic physique would provide such a marker. In primitive societies those characteristics, evidenced in body type, would mark a male as a potentially better provider who could sustain a woman through pregnancy, and, more importantly, be a strong, supportive partner during the years of child rearing. In today's society, the characteristics in a male who will demonstrate nurturance, support, and protection for his mate and offspring seem not to be available through a biophysical marker. A person's socioeconomic status is likely be a better indicator of the characteristics that women look for in a potential mate in order to be assured of protection and support. Bill Gates is now the ideal, not Tarzan.

REFERENCES

DeRidder, C. M., Bruning, P. F., Zonderland, M. L., Thijssen, J. H. H., Bonfer, J. M. G., Blankenstein, M. A., Huisveld, I. A., & Erich, W. B. M. (1990). Body mass fat, body fat distribution and plasmahormones in early puberty in females. *Journal of Clinical Endocrinology and Metabolism, 70,* 888–893.

Eibl-Eibesfeldt, I., (1989). *Human ethology.* Chicago: Aldine.

Gardner, D. M., Garfinkel, P. E., Schwartz, D., & Thompson, M. (1980). Cultural expectation of thinness in women. *Psychological Reports, 47,* 183–191.

Harris, M. B., Walters, L. C., & Walshull, S. (1991). Gender and ethnic differences in obesity-related behaviors and attitudes in a college sample. *Journal of Applied Social Psychology, 21,* 1545–1577.

Mazur, A. (1986). U.S. trends in feminine beauty and overadaptation. *Journal of Sex Research, 22,* 281–303.

Singh, D. (1993). Adaptive significance of female physical attractiveness: Role of waist-to-hip ratio. *Journal of Personality and Social Psychology, 65,* 293–307.

Singh, D., & Luis, S. (1995). Ethnic and gender consensus for the effect of wasit-to-hip ratio on judgment of women's attractiveness. *Human Nature, 6,* 51–65.

Supy, Z. M. V. D., Steer, P. J., McCusker, M., Steele, S. J., & Jacobs, H. S. (1988). Outcome of pregnancy in underweight women after spontaneous and induced ovulation. *British Medical Journal, 296,* 962–965.

CHAPTER 8

ATTRACTIVENESS OF BREAST ODORS TO BABIES

After reading the title of this chapter you might conclude that this is an odd area of investigation, maybe even trivial to human behavior. The sense of smell is given a great deal of importance in nonhuman animal interactions, including parent-offspring relationships and mating. Often when we think of odors we think of something unpleasant or something to be avoided. However, the sense of smell may well play a vital role in areas of central concern to the human experience. A body of research has shown, however, that not only do maternal odors play a positive role in relation to their infants, they have been found to be downright appealing to newborns. Maternal odors are likely to be a significant factor in mother-child bonding or attachment (Porter, Balogh, & Makin, 1988). Recent research (Cernoch & Porter, 1985; Macfarlane, 1975; Russell, 1976) suggests that breast-fed newborns prefer their mothers' breast or underarm odors to the same odors from unknown lactating females. This phenomenon has not been observed in bottle-fed babies (Cernoch & Porter, 1985). Researchers Balogh and Porter (1986) suggest that this difference in response to underarm odors may be a result of the two styles of feeding. Breast-feeding requires close contact with the mother's skin, whereas bottle feeding may be done while the mother is clothed and without face-to-skin contact. It may also be that breast-feeding mothers produce special odors that newborns can identify. Leon (1983), from research on other animals, suggests that such odors may serve to bond babies to mothers. The research by Makin and Porter described in this chapter focuses on whether or not the breast and underarm odors from lactating women are attractive to bottle-fed infants.

John Bowlby (1969) and Mary Ainsworth (1979) have proposed that caregiver-infant attachment during the initial year of life may profoundly impact the later development of the infant. Bowlby's view regarding attachment focuses on patterns of infant behavior (e.g., cooing, smiling, and crying) that serve to promote a strong bond with its caregiver. Attachment is also seen to be a reciprocal relationship in which caregiver characteristics, such as emotion and affect, also play an important role (Goldberg, MacKay-Soroka, & Rochester, 1994). Other research by the Harlows (Harlow &

Incorporating the research of J. W. Makin and R. W. Porter, "Attractiveness of Lactating Females' Breast Odors to Neonates," 1989, *Child Development, 60,* pp. 803–810.

Harlow, 1962), using infant rhesus monkeys as participants, suggests that the sense of touch, specifically "contact comfort" between infant and mother, fosters the attachment bond. The process of bonding that occurs between caregiver and infant is likely to be multidetermined like many other significant behaviors. It is therefore important to see how our sense of smell—the ability to detect and recognize odors—may play a vital role in the bond of newborn infants and their mothers. This information provided may have significant practical use in guiding new moms in infant care.

A secondary value of the research in this chapter is to show how inventive and clever researchers can be in setting up methods to assess behaviors. Makin and Porter had to come up with some objective methods of determining how attractive breast odors were to 2-week-old infants. These infants have very limited behavioral repertoires, and they don't complete surveys or preference questionnaires. Part of the fun of research is to devise measures to capture significant human experiences.

METHOD

The participants were healthy bottle-fed infants. In the first experiment both male and female infants were participants. In the three succeeding experiments only female infants were participants. The reason for only using female infants is a result of the findings of the first experiment. Participants in all experiments were approximately equally divided between Caucasian and African American babies and were between the ages of 12 and 17 days of age.

The infants were placed in a hospital-style bassinet for the research testing. A metal device was attached to the bassinet so that its two end pieces could be positioned close to each side of the infants' face. Attached to the ends of the device were gauze pads that contained the stimulus odor. Infant testing sessions were recorded on videotape.

The breast and underarm odors were collected by giving two gauze pads to lactating women and two gauze pads to adult women who have never had children. The women wore the gauze pads either on both breasts covering the nipple area or on one breast and under one arm. The pads were worn for an 8-hour overnight period and then sealed in separate zip-type plastic bags. The women from whom the samples were obtained were asked not to use perfume or deodorants while the odor samples were being collected.

The infants, age 13 to 15 days, were tested with the odor stimuli in their homes. The infants, who were alert at the time of testing, were placed on their backs with the odor stimuli pads hanging close to their cheeks. The infants were also swaddled to immobilize their arms. The gauze pads were situated so that if the infants turned their heads their noses would be approximately 1–2 cm from the hanging pads. The testing procedure began with the researcher moving the infant's head toward each of the gauze pads to give the infant a sample of each odor. The infant's head was then moved to a position centered between the pads and a timer measured the number of seconds the infants turned to each pad. Each infant was given two 1-minute trials separated by a 2-minute break. For each infant the odor stimuli were the same except that they were reversed in position on the second trial. The initial assignments of odors to positions were determined randomly. The trials were videotaped so that two raters could assess the duration of time each infant oriented to each pad at a later time. Inter-rater reliabilities across all experiments achieved correlation coefficients between .98 and 1.00. The raters, in reviewing the videotapes, recorded the duration of time for both trials during which infants turned toward each pad. Turning was operationally defined as a deviation from a centerline position toward one side or the other.

EXPERIMENT 1

The focus of this initial experiment was to understand how responsive exclusively bottle-fed infants are to breast odors of lactating women who are unknown and unrelated to them. Thirteen male and 13 female infants participated in this experiment. Using the bassinet described earlier, the infants were tested with gauze pads containing odors from lactating women's breasts or clean gauze pads. Each of the infants was tested with breast odor pads from different women. The women from whom the breast odors were obtained had given birth to their own infants within nine days of the birth of the infants who served as participants in this experiment.

The group mean duration times for male infants were 40.54 seconds for lactating female breast odor and 47.31 seconds for a clean pad. For female infants the group mean duration times were 84.77 seconds for lactating female breast odor and 18.08 seconds for a clean pad. As the duration times indicated, female infants demonstrated a significant preference for the lactating mother's pad. No significant preference differences were found for male infants. These results are illustrated in Figure 8.1. The findings show that female infants had a clear attraction to the breast odors of lactating

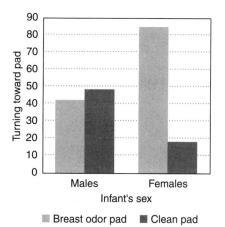

FIGURE 8.1   Experiment 1—Mean Duration of Turning toward Pads

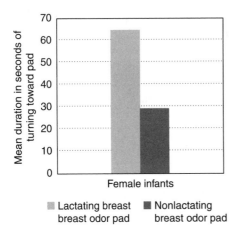

FIGURE 8.2   Experiment 2—Mean Duration of Turning toward Pads

females whom were unknown to them. Male infants showed no preference between a clean pad and a lactating female's breast pad odors.

EXPERIMENT 2

The first experiment demonstrated that breast odors from lactating females were attractive to female infants who were bottle-fed. The researchers, Makin and Porter, asserted that it was possible that the infant girls were responding to the presence of odor over the absence of odor. In order to be certain that the infants were preferentially attending to breast odors, a second experiment was conducted. In this experiment bottle-fed female infants were placed in the same procedural setup as in the first study. This time they were given a choice between the breast odor of an unfamiliar nonlactating female and the breast odor of an unfamiliar lactating female. Because male infants were unresponsive to the differences in the initial study, only female infants were used in this and succeeding experiments. The findings from this experiment are presented in Figure 8.2. The results indicate that the infants spent significantly more time turned in the direction of the lactating female's breast pad. Although these babies had always been bottle fed, they were significantly more attracted to the breast odors of lactating women than the breast odors of nonlactating women.

EXPERIMENT 3

Cernoch and Porter's (1985) research, noted at the beginning of this chapter, found that breast-fed infants preferred their mother's underarm odor to the underarm odors

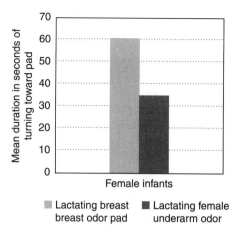

**FIGURE 8.3   Experiment 3—Mean
Duration of Turning toward Pads**

of other women, lactating or not. The third experiment sought to determine whether or not bottle-fed female infants are more attracted to breast or underarm odors of unfamiliar lactating women. Using the same research format as the previous experiments, female infants were given the opportunity to show preferences by turning toward suspended gauze pads containing each of the odors. The findings are presented in Figure 8.3. As can be seen, the female infants spent significantly more time with their heads turned toward the breast odor pad than the pad containing underarm odors. This study suggested that bottle-fed infant females preferred the breast odors of lactating females to the underarm odors of lactating females.

EXPERIMENT 4

This final experiment was designed to test whether or not odor intensity was responsible for infant preferences in the previous experiments. It is possible that the intensity of the breast odors from milk saturated pads, may be the critical variable rather than the breast odor itself. In this fourth experiment, infants were given the opportunity to choose between the underarm pad (high in odor intensity) of an unknown lactating mother and a clean pad (low in odor intensity). The thinking behind this design was that if odor intensity is the important factor guiding infant choices in the three previous investigations, then the infants in this experiment should choose the underarm pad in preference to the clean pad. If there was no preference difference, the infants were not selecting on odor intensity. The experimental method was the same as previous studies. The participants were 16 bottle-fed girls. The results, available in Figure 8.4, show there was no significant difference in infant preferences and therefore no indications that the infants were responding to odor intensity.

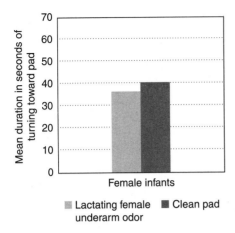

FIGURE 8.4   Experiment 4—Mean Duration of Turning toward Pads

DISCUSSING THE EXPERIMENTS

In the initial experiment it was found that female bottle-fed infants preferred gauze pads with breast odors to clean pads. Infant boys, on the other hand, did not demonstrate this preference. Research by Balogh and Porter (1986) found that infant boys preferred to turn their heads toward the right and as a consequence would not sample odors presented on the left as often. Other researchers (Liederman & Coryell, 1981; Turkewitz, 1977) have also found a right-turning head preference in some experimental conditions. Coryell and Michel (1978) have suggested such head-turning preferences may be associated with handedness. If such were the case, especially with males, the right-turning bias might prevent the male infants from responding to olfactory stimuli. Therefore, the inability of male infants in the initial study to show odor preferences may really not be a lack of ability to discern odors. It is also possible that male infants may have odor detection ability, but at lower levels than female infants. It is interesting to note that olfaction research indicates that females, at ages that range from childhood to old age, have significantly better odor detection ability than males (Doty, 1981; Doty et al., 1984). The next step in looking at gender differences in odor discrimination among young infants would be to utilize a dependent variable that does not require the head-turning response but still taps odor preferences. The search for such a response in a 2-week-old infant is likely to be challenging, because the available repertoire of behaviors is limited.

The findings of the second experiment, infant preferences for breast odors of lactating versus nonlactating women, suggest the possibility that odors from lactating women are attractive to infants. Steiner (1977) found that newborns are sensitive to food odors and can react differentially with various facial expressions denoting approval or rejection. In addition to breast odors being connected with milk as a food source, lactating women produce sebum, a substance found on the skin (Burton, Shuster, Cartlidge, Libman, & Martell, 1973). Researchers (Epple, 1980; Nikolaides, 1974; Shorey, 1976) have discovered that sebum is significant for olfactory communication in animals. Burton et al. (1973) reported that sebum production increases late in pregnancy and is seen in higher rates in lactating females than nonlacting or nonpregnant women. Additional research has shown that breast-fed infants can identify the unique odor pattern of their own mother (Cernoch & Porter, 1985; Russell, 1976). This ability would be adaptive in helping the infant to locate and latch onto the nipple and, as a result, to nurse effectively. The survival of an infant who is attracted to the breast by odor would not only benefit from the nutrition provided by breast feeding, but also would benefit positively from the mother-infant bonding relationship (Bowlby, 1969; Schaffer, 1971).

REFERENCES

Ainsworth, M. D. S. (1979). Infant-mother attachment. *American Psychologist, 34,* 932–937.

Balogh, R. D., & Porter, R. H. (1986). Olfactory preferences resulting from mere exposure in human neonates. *Infant Behavior and Development, 9,* 395–401.

Bowlby, J. (1969). *Attachment and loss: Vol. 1. Attachment.* New York: Basic.

Burton, J. L., Shuster, S., Cartlidge, M., Libman, L. J., & Martell, U. (1973). Lactation, sebum excretion, and melanocyte-stimulating hormone. *Nature, 243,* 349–350.

Cernoch, J. M., & Porter, R. H. (1985) Recognition of maternal axillary odors by infants. *Child Development, 56,* 1593–1598.

Coryell, J. F., & Michel, G. F. (1978). How supine postural preferences of infants can contribute toward the development of handedness. *Infant Behavior and Development, 1,* 245–247.

Doty, R. L. (1981). Olfactory communication in humans. *Chemical Senses, 6,* 351–376.

Doty, R. L., Shaman, P., Applebaum, S. L., Giberson, R., Sikorski, L., & Rosenberg, L. (1984). Smell identification ability: Changes with age. *Science, 226,* 141–143.

Epple, G. (1980). Relationships between aggression, scent marking, and gonadal state in a primate, the tamarin *Saguinus fuscicollis.* In D. Muller-Schwarze & R. M. Silverstein (Eds.), *Chemical signals, vertebrates and aquatic invertebrates* (pp. 87–105). New York: Plenum.

Goldberg, S., MacKay-Soroka, S., & Rochester, M. (1994). Affect, attachment and maternal responsiveness. *Infant Behavior and Development, 17,* 335–339.

Harlow, H. F., & Harlow, M. K. (1962). The effect of rearing conditions on behavior. *Bulletin of Menninger Clinic, 26,* 213–224.

Leon, M. (1983). Chemical communication in mother-young interactions. In J. G. Vandenberg (Ed.), *Pheromones and reproduction in mammals* (pp. 39–77). New York: Academic Press.

Liederman, J., & Coryell, J. (1981). Right-hand preference facilitated by rightward turning during infancy. *Developmental Psychobiology, 14*(5), 439–450.

MacFarlane, A. (1975). Olfaction in the development of social preferences in the human neonate. In *Parent-infant interactions.* Ciba Foundation Symposium No. 33 (pp. 103–117). New York: Elsevier.

Makin, J. W., & Porter, R. W. (1989). Attractiveness of lactating females' breast odors to neonates. *Child Development, 60,* 803–810.

Nicolaides, N. (1974). Skin lipids: Their biochemical uniqueness. *Science, 186,* 19–26.

Porter, R. H., Balogh, R. D., & Makin, J. W. (1988). Olfactory influences on mother-infant interactions. In C. Rovee-Collier & L. Lipsitt (Eds.), *Advances in infancy research* (Vol. 5, pp. 39–68). Norwood, NJ: Ablex.

Russell, M. J. (1976). Human olfactory communication. *Nature, 260,* 520–522.

Schaffer, H. R. (1971). *The growth of sociability.* Harmondsworth, Middlesex: Penguin.

Shorey, H. H. (1976). *Animal communication by pheromones.* New York: Academic Press.

Steiner, J. E. (1977). Facial expressions of the neonate infant indicating the hedonics of food-related chemical stimuli. In J. M. Weifenbach (Ed.), *Taste and development: The genesis of sweet preference* (pp. 173–188) (DHEW Publication No. [NIH] 77-1068). Bethesda, MD: DHEW.

Turkewitz, G. (1977). The development of lateral differentiation in the human infant. *Annals of the New York Academy of Sciences, 299,* 309–318.

CHAPTER 9

BEING SICK OF THE HOSPITAL

Usually, people go to the hospital when they are ill. This chapter considers the reverse: the learning process through which the hospital, and the treatment associated with it, can make people sick. When you first consider a hospital making people sick, you may be tempted to focus on the food, which is stereotypically considered to be bad. In defense of the food, it is not like Mommy makes, but it is exactly what Mommy *would* make if she had to feed 1,000 or more people, many of whom are on highly specialized diets.

Because we are not talking about the food, what is it about a hospital that can make people sick? First, we need to be clear about what we mean by "sick." We mean *sick*, physically sick; sick in a way that can be measured using the kinds of assessments available to contemporary medicine. It is important to be precise about this; we are talking about the kind of illness that is technically called *somatoform* illness. Sometimes the older label for this disorder, *psychosomatic illness*, is used in popular media to mean an imaginary illness, one that has no physical basis. That is not correct. In a somatoform illness, a person really has observable symptoms but, unlike other illnesses, the cause is not some obvious disease organism, such as a virus or a bacterium. This is not to suggest the causes of somatoform illness are mystical or unknowable. The causes of somatoform disorders are just as concrete as viruses and bacteria. In the case to be discussed here, no one would argue about the concreteness of the causes: the hospital was made of concrete. We are doing more than playing with words. The research to be discussed has shown that a hospital, in all its concrete and glass glory, can make people sick.

In order to understand how this can happen, we have to follow a path that connects the hospital to the illness through a process of learning. The special kind of learning that was implicated in this example is called classical conditioning, or Pavlovian conditioning, after its discoverer, Ivan Pavlov (1849–1936). We will briefly consider Pavlov's work before returning to the illustration of somatoform illness. There are at least two reasons for this detour. First, you should know a few things about Pavlov. Although we try to focus on contemporary psychology in this book, there are a few examples of psychological phenomena that are so well known that they are familiar to

Incorporating the research of D. H. Bovbjerg, W. H. Redd, L. A. Maier, J. C. Holland, L. M. Lesko, D. Niedzwiecki, S. C. Rubin, and T. B. Hakes, "Anticipatory Immune Suppression and Nausea in Women Receiving Cyclic Chemotherapy for Ovarian Cancer," 1990, *Journal of Consulting and Clinical Psychology, 58*, pp. 153–157.

any educated person. Pavlov's work is one of these. It is an important model, or way of thinking, about certain types of events in psychology. These models are sometimes called paradigms (pronounced *pair-ah-dimes*). A second and perhaps more compelling reason is that the hospital illustration, and many other examples from life, cannot be understood without a clear understanding of the Pavlovian paradigm.

GOING TO THE DOGS

Initially Pavlov did not seek to find out about somatoform illness, or even about learning. Pavlov lived and worked in Russia and was educated as a physiologist. He studied at the University of St. Petersburg, a center of intellectual life in a largely agrarian country, which otherwise had high levels of illiteracy. In this setting, Pavlov was aware of the privilege afforded by a university education. As a young man he was very much influenced by the study of reflexes. Reflexes were considered to be automatic responses to stimuli, responses that did not require any conscious thought or planning. With some slight refinement, this basic definition is still used today. The physiologists of Pavlov's student days considered reflexes to be the basic building blocks of behavior. Complex behaviors were presumed to be made of reflexes, in the same way that a brick wall is made of bricks. In particular, Pavlov was greatly impressed by the work of Sechenov, the professor of physiology at St. Petersburg. Sechenov believed that all physical acts were reflexes and that the study of reflexes would move psychology away from philosophy and "the deceitful voice of consciousness [to] positive facts or points of departure that can be verified at any time by experiment" (quoted from Frolov, 1938, p. 6). Clearly, the scientific establishment of the time felt some uncertainty about the emerging field of psychology and wished its approach and content to be more like that of other sciences. So do we.

Pavlov worked for many years studying digestive physiology. He approached digestion by observing it in animals who were alive and who were functioning as normally as possible. He developed masterful surgical techniques for collecting and studying saliva and gastric juices from the stomach. Pavlov even augmented his meager research budget by selling gastric juice from dogs to the general public as a supposed aid for stomach problems (Babkin, 1940). This stuff did not turn out to be a miracle cure and probably tasted just as you might imagine it would. If anything, its sales bring credit to Pavlov's ability to sell his ideas to others.

In 1904 Pavlov was awarded the Nobel Prize for his research on digestion. Pavlov's formal speech on the occasion of the award spoke little about digestion but, rather, presented some other observations he had made while doing the digestion research. The observations he recounted took him to the forefront of psychology. He retains this position today, almost 100 years later.

In his work on the digestive processes of dogs, Pavlov had perfected a little operation in which a cut was made in the dog's cheek, allowing a tube to be introduced through the cheek and into the salivary duct. A glass vial at the end of this tube collected and measured the saliva produced in response to various stimuli (see Figure 9.1).

FIGURE 9.1   Classical Conditioning Apparatus Similar to That Used by Pavlov

AN UNEXPECTED OBSERVATION

Pavlov was interested in studying the amount and timing of saliva production in response to various foods. Salivation was clearly a reflex because it did not have to be consciously turned on or off; it was an automatic response to food being placed in the dog's mouth. However, in the course of this work, Pavlov noticed dogs often salivated before the food was in the mouth. The dogs salivated when they saw food, when they saw a food bowl, or even when they heard the footsteps of laboratory personnel at feeding time. At first these responses were considered no more than nuisances that interfered with the study of digestion (Anokhin, 1971). Over time, Pavlov and his coworkers came to realize they had observed something very important. Because the stimulus for these salivary responses was not the usual stimulus, food in the mouth, something unusual was happening. Pavlov came to understand that he had observed a basic kind of learning.

Pavlov developed some terminology for describing this situation and, with slight modification, his descriptions continue to be used today. In the situation Pavlov described, the food is called the *unconditioned stimulus* (UCS) and the salivation is the *unconditioned response* (UCR). The word *conditioned* merely means learned, so when you are attempting to decode a situation using Pavlovian terms, you may find it helpful to substitute the word *learned* whenever you read the word *conditioned*. If you do this, it becomes a straightforward task to put a situation into Pavlovian terms. An *unconditioned* stimulus should always result in a particular *unconditioned* response without any learning, as that is the definition of *unconditioned*. Think of these responses to stimuli as reflexes. They are unlearned and automatic, requiring no thought or planning. If food is put in your mouth, you salivate. You do not have to plan or think about the response. You do not need to learn how to do this. If we were to pop a balloon right behind you, you would make a startle response—this is another example of an unconditioned stimulus and an unconditioned response. Yet another one: if you touch a hot iron you will pull your hand away quickly. In each of these examples, the stimulus is called the UCS (unconditioned stimulus) and the response is called the UCR (unconditioned response).

Pavlov's dogs experienced a repeated pairing of some other stimuli with the unconditioned stimulus (food). For example, each time a dog was given food—the UCS—this food was paired with the footsteps of a laboratory worker bringing it. After a number of pairings, the dogs learned that footsteps signaled the approach of food. Once this was learned, the saliva would begin to flow in response to the sound of the footsteps. In this new pairing of stimulus and response, the footsteps and the saliva were called, respectively, the *conditioned stimulus* and the *conditioned response*, or the CS and the CR. They were called the *conditioned stimulus* and the *conditioned response* because they were learned: the dog learned to make this response to a new stimulus. One way to diagrammatically represent this can be found in Figure 9.2.

When you are trying to analyze a Pavlovian or classical conditioning situation into its elements, you can use four guidelines to check your analysis:

1. The UCR and the CR will be responses—something that the organism does. The UCS and the CS will be stimuli, usually something in the environment, such as food or footsteps.
2. The UCR will be the organism's reflexive response, one that requires no learning. If the response has to be learned, it is not a UCR. By this logic, you should expect the same UCR to follow a particular UCS in all the members of a particular species.
3. The stimulus that will become the CS should not lead to the response being studied until it has been paired with the UCS. Footsteps only resulted in salivation

FIGURE 9.2 Pavlovian Analysis of Salivation

when repeatedly paired with the UCS, the food. Sometimes many pairings are required for classical conditioning; sometimes few are sufficient.

4. The UCR and the CR will appear to be the same behavior. The difference between them is that in one instance the response is not learned and in the other case the response is learned. The difference between the UCR and the CR is how behavior came to be produced by a stimulus: not learned or learned.

If you survey a number of sources that discuss classical conditioning, you may be surprised at how many give examples that contain errors because they do not pass these little tests. Probably the fourth guideline, similarity of UCR and CR, is the most often violated.

As a footnote to Pavlov's work, popular culture usually remembers the CS as a bell, not footsteps. Pavlov's early work on conditioning used a variety of stimuli for the CS including footsteps, a metronome, a variety of tones, and some visual stimuli.

Not all learning involves Pavlovian conditioning. In spite of the importance of the Pavlovian paradigm, it is quite restricted because it requires an unlearned association as the basis for subsequent learning. Although subsequent studies identified so-called higher-order conditioning in which an additional stimulus is paired with an already established CS, classical conditioning has to start with an unlearned association. Once you understand the components of the Pavlovian paradigm, you should quickly be able to determine if classical conditioning is at work in behavior you observe. Learning to play basketball, for example, has little if anything to do with classical conditioning. It is much better explained by the imitation of behavior and the resulting rewards, such as the ball going through the hoop or the cheers of others.

Probably the only way for you to thoroughly understand classical conditioning is for you to use the terms we have described and to try to apply them to new examples. When you can do this for novel examples, you own this concept. To give you a start, try to do a Pavlovian analysis, identifying the UCS, UCR, CS, and CR, in the following situation:

Imagine that you live in an old building with problematic plumbing. If you are in the shower and someone in the bathroom next door flushes the toilet, the cold water disappears from your shower. You feel the water temperature go from pleasantly warm to scalding, and you jump out of the shower. After a few experiences with this situation, you jump out when you hear the next-door toilet flush. Once you have assigned classical conditioning terms, you can check your Pavlovian analysis against Figure 9.3.

So much for dogs and toilets. You should, by now have a sufficient grasp of the concepts of classical conditioning to allow us to discuss the work of Dana Bovbjerg and colleagues about hospitals making people sick (Bovbjerg et al., 1990). It has been known since the 1980s that cancer patients who receive chemotherapy often experience two side effects of the treatment: nausea and suppression of the immune system (DeVita, Hellman, & Rosenberg, 1985). These outcomes were first noticed shortly after the treatment. However, some patients showed more puzzling symptoms of nausea or vomiting *before* each treatment. This was called Anticipatory Nausea and Vomiting, or ANV. Between one-quarter and three-quarters of patients were troubled by ANV. ANV seemed to be triggered by things as diverse as the sight of the clinic, the sound of a nurse's voice, or even the mere thought of treatment.

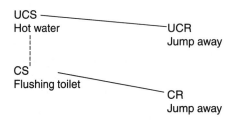

**FIGURE 9.3   Pavlovian Analysis of
Jumping Away from Hot Water**

A number of clinical studies investigated ANV and the conclusions pointed to classical conditioning (Redd, 1989). If you want to test your ability to analyze this example in Pavlovian terms, stop here, look away, and do so before we give you the answer. The toxic drugs that are used in chemotherapy (UCS) make people feel nauseated (UCR). The hospital (CS) is constantly paired with the drug treatment (UCS) until the hospital (CS) itself makes people feel nauseated (CR). This is diagrammed in Figure 9.4.

The effects of this classical conditioning are so powerful that hospitals can still nauseate some former patients years after chemotherapy has ended (Cella, Pratt, & Holland, 1986). This fits with other research, which has shown that for many animals classical conditioning has long-lasting effects when feeling ill was the CR (see, for example, Gustafson, Garcia, Hawkins, & Rusinak, 1974).

The study by Bovbjerg et al. (1990) further investigated ANV and, in addition, sought evidence that anticipatory immune suppression (AIS) was also taking place in cancer patients. Immune suppression is the name given to a number of physiological responses that result in depressed functioning of the immune system. The immune system is the body's way of recognizing and dealing with disease organisms. When the immune system function decreases before some event, in this case chemotherapy, it is called Anticipatory Immune Suppression or AIS. AIS has been the subject of a number of other research studies because of its importance to clinical medicine (see, for example, Kiecolt-Glaser & Glaser, 1988).

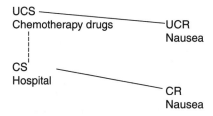

**FIGURE 9.4   Pavlovian Analysis of
ANV**

PARTICIPANTS

Thirty-six patients were identified who had all undergone surgical treatment for ovarian cancer. These women also met other criteria for being participants, including: they had not been treated with chemotherapy for any prior illness, their treatment plan called for chemotherapy, they had already received at least three treatments, and they lived within a 2-hour driving time of the hospital where the chemotherapy was being given. Twenty-seven of the original 36 eligible women agreed to be in the study. Of these 27, 7 had to be dropped for a variety of reasons including eventual change of their chemotherapy treatment and difficulty in drawing blood from their veins.

PROCEDURES

During the course of the study, an appointment was made for a home visit at least 3 days before chemotherapy treatments. Blood was drawn for later analysis in order to assess immune system functioning. During the home visits, an experienced research technician administered some rating instruments called *scales*. On the scale, patients were asked to rate their current level of nausea. They rated this by choosing a number from a visual scale in which numbers were arranged as if they were numbers on a thermometer. This is called a visual analog scale, or VAS. The VAS is a useful tool for the quantification of feelings. Turning subjective states into numbers makes it possible to deal with the data quantitatively by computing averages and drawing graphs. The amount of anxiety being experienced was recorded on a questionnaire, the Spielberger State-Trait Anxiety Inventory, or STAI, as well as by asking for a single assessment on another visual analog scale. These two anxiety measures were used so that one could be a reliability check for the other. Measures of anxiety can be imprecise, and having more than one was a way of boosting confidence in the results of the study.

Later, when participants arrived at the hospital, the anxiety measures were repeated. Participants were asked to recall and rate past feelings of nausea at three times before chemotherapy: the previous evening, on awakening the morning of chemotherapy, and immediately before chemotherapy was administered. Another sample of blood was drawn just before chemotherapy. The independent variable in this part of the study was the setting: home or hospital. The dependent measures were the ratings of anxiety, nausea, and analysis of immune functioning. This part of the study is a so-called *within-subjects* design. It is an experiment, but unlike some other experiments, the participants are their own control group. We saw this research design in the previous chapter. The same participants are exposed to two different situations, in this case, home and hospital.

RESULTS

Biochemical analyses of blood samples taken at home and at the hospital showed that there was not much suppression of the immune system at home. However, by the time the participants had arrived at the hospital, their blood samples showed biochemical indicators of immune function that were statistically significantly lower than in the home blood samples ($p < .001$). Lower immune function indicated that the immune response was worse. Sixteen of the 20 patients elected to receive some sedative drugs upon arrival at the hospital, prior to blood drawing. To ensure that these sedatives were not responsible for immune suppression, a separate statistical analysis was performed on the patients who did not wish to have any sedatives. The patients who had no sedatives also showed immune suppression, suggesting that sedatives were not suppressing the immune system. Although the researchers might have preferred to have no sedatives given to any of the participants in the study, it is important to understand that these "participants" were also people. In older studies the participants were usually referred to as *subjects*. This terminology is still used in phrases such as *within subjects design*, where no reference is made to specific people. The American Psychological Association now suggests that authors avoid the impersonal term *subjects* in the preparation of research reports (American Psychological Association, 1994). The word *subjects* is sterile, and one might forget that these participants were women, each recovering from surgical treatment of a frightening disease. It speaks very well of them that they were willing to participate in research and to tolerate additional procedures in the home and hospital in order to help advance scientific understanding.

The measures of anxiety, the Spielberger State-Trait Anxiety Inventory and the visual scale (VAS), both indicated higher levels of anxiety in the hospital than at home ($p = .036$; $p < .001$). In addition, the visual scale for nausea indicated that anticipatory nausea was a greater problem in the hospital than at home ($p = .008$) (see Figure 9.5).

In summary, levels of all three symptoms were statistically significantly lower at home than in the hospital.

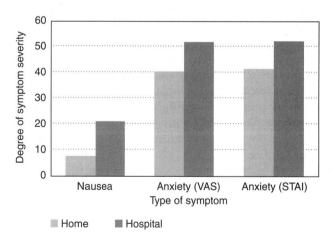

FIGURE 9.5   Degree of Symptoms Reported by Chemotherapy Patients at Home and in the Hospital

Although, as a group, the women showed immune suppression in the hospital, five individuals within the group did not. An additional data analysis was performed in which these five women were considered as one group and the other women were placed in another group. In this quasi-experimental analysis, immune suppression was the variable that was being investigated by comparing the groups; one group had it and one group did not. Nausea and anxiety continued to be outcome measures. The finding was that there were no significant differences between the anxiety measures when the AIS group was compared to the non-AIS group. Both groups were anxious in the hospital. This can be interpreted as meaning that the subjective feelings of anxiety were not always linked to immune suppression. This was important because it indicated that anxiety was not always associated with immune suppression. It follows that finding ways to lower the anxiety felt by these women would not be expected to also help them with immune suppression. Anxiety and immune suppression are separate responses to the situation.

In contrast, in this analysis, the patients who had immune suppression also reported higher levels of nausea in the hospital than those who had no immune suppression (p = .04). In this case it seems possible that, because these symptoms are linked, dealing with one of them might help to treat the other. The discovery of a link of some sort can point the way to future research that may find causal links.

DISCUSSION

Bovbjerg et al. (1990) acknowledge their debt to studies of laboratory animals that pointed the way to this research. Lab animals can be used in studies that would not be ethically acceptable for human participants. It might be interesting to know what types of stimuli, other than hospitals, can serve as conditioned stimuli for immune suppression but ethics rightly limit research manipulations that can be performed on humans.

The sample in the Bovbjerg et al. (1990) study is small and the validity of the conclusions could be enhanced by replications on other groups of people. All science is tentative, particularly when studies report findings that have not been observed before. Nevertheless, this study was carefully conducted, and its findings make some important suggestions about anticipatory nausea and vomiting (ANV) and anticipatory immune suppression (AIS). In particular, it appears that increased anxiety is not, by itself, responsible for AIS. It is known that people undergoing stressful life events may show immune suppression (Kiecolt-Glaser & Glaser, 1988). In this study, however, small-group analysis suggested that anxiety did not always accompany immune suppression. If this finding were to be confirmed by other studies, it might lead to the practical suggestion that counseling to relieve anxiety would not be expected to help chemotherapy patients avoid AIS.

Both ANV and AIS were seen in this study in response to the hospital environment. Probably the best explanation for this was that they were simultaneously classical conditioned. Chemotherapy, the UCS, caused both nausea and immune suppression, the UCRs. As the chemotherapy was repeatedly paired with the hospital, the hospital itself became the CS for the CRs of ANV and AIS. This seems like alphabet soup, but when you can read this through and understand it, you are getting a grasp of classical conditioning.

The importance of the research can be illustrated by one case. Among the group of women studied by Bovbjerg et al. (1990), one person showed a dramatic 50 percent decrease in one of the measures of immune function. A person who is immuno-compromised to this extent, even before the chemotherapy has been administered, is at considerable risk for contracting other diseases. In spite of sanitation procedures, hospitals are, after all, full of diseases waiting for people to come by. For people with AIS, the hospital might not merely make them nauseated, it might play a role in making them severely ill owing to poor immune function.

Understanding is the first step toward finding a remedy. Other classically conditioned responses, such as unreasonable fears—called *phobias*—have been successfully treated by programs designed to gradually expose the participant to the fear-producing object. It is not clear that this process of systematic desensitization would help the chemotherapy patients, but it is an illustration that understanding classical conditioning can lead to treatment. Perhaps further work in this area will assure that, in the future, there is no need for the hospital to make people any sicker than they already are.

REFERENCES

American Psychological Association (1994). *Publication manual of the American Psychological Association* (4th ed.). Washington DC: Author.

Anokhin, P. K. (1971, March). Three giants of Soviet psychology. *Psychology Today*, 43–78.

Babkin, B. P. (1940). *Pavlov: A biography.* Chicago: University of Chicago Press.

Bovbjerg, D. H., Redd, W. H., Maier, L. A., Holland, J. C., Lesko, L. M., Niedzwiecki, D., Rubin, S. C., & Hakes, T. B. (1990). Anticipatory immune suppression and nausea in women receiving cyclic chemotherapy for ovarian cancer. *Journal of Consulting and Clinical Psychology, 58,* 153–157.

Cella, D. F., Pratt, A., & Holland, J. C. (1986). Persistent anticipatory nausea, vomiting and anxiety in cured Hodgkin's disease patients after completion of chemotherapy. *American Journal of Psychiatry, 143,* 641–643.

DeVita, V. T., Hellman, S., & Rosenberg, S. A. (1985). *Cancer: Principles and practice of oncology.* Philadelphia, PA: Lippincott.

Frolov, Y. P. (1938). *Pavlov and his school.* London: Kegan, Paul, Tench, Trubner.

Gustafson, C. R., Garcia, J., Hawkins, W., & Rusinak, K. (1974). Coyote predation control by aversive conditioning. *Science, 184,* 581–583.

Kiecolt-Glaser, J. K., & Glaser, R. (1988). Psychological influences on immunity: Implications for AIDS. *American Psychologist, 43,* 892–898,

Redd, W. H. (1989). Anticipatory nausea and vomiting and their management. In J. Holland & J. Rowland (Eds.), *Psychooncology* (pp. 423–433). New York: Oxford University Press.

CHAPTER 10

YOKING SMOKING

B. F. Skinner (1904–1990) started his academic life wanting to be a writer with an academic major in English. By the time his career was over, he was the best-known empirical psychologist of his time. He was a confirmed behaviorist and had little use for things inside the body, including mental events. He believed that mental characteristics were unobservable and, therefore, beyond the reach of science. For Skinner, proper scientific psychology should center its attention on the manipulation and measurement of the frequency of behavior. A great deal of Skinnerian psychology, also known as *operant conditioning*, can be summarized by the statement, *behavior is maintained by its consequences*. Skinner believed that the events that followed a behavior played a significant role in the subsequent frequency of the behavior. If pleasant stimuli followed a behavior, the behavior would increase in frequency. On the other hand, if unpleasant events followed the behavior, its frequency would decrease. If the behavior actually produced the consequences, Skinner would say that the consequences were *contingent* on the behavior.

PULLING HABITS OUT OF A RAT

Skinner believed that control over consequences would mean control over behavior. Many of his studies were carried out in an apparatus that he called an *operant chamber*, but almost everyone else calls it a *Skinner box*. The steps in the development of this device were amusingly described by Skinner (1956) in a well-known article entitled "A Case History in Scientific Method."

The Skinner box was a chamber tailored to the size of the organism under study. For example, a typical Skinner box for a rat might have dimensions of a little less than 1 foot on a side. The walls and lid were usually made of clear plastic to facilitate observation of the animal. The floor was a series of closely spaced metal bars. Usually one wall of the box was a control panel with a device variously called a *bar* or *lever* protruding from it. This smooth metal object was the correct height so that a rat could push it down. The wall with the control panel also typically included an automatic food or

Incorporating the research of J. M. Roll, S. T. Higgins, and G. J. Badger, "An Experimental Comparison of Three Different Schedules of Reinforcement of Drug Abstinence Using Cigarette Smoking as an Exemplar," 1996, *Journal of Applied Behavior Analysis, 29*, pp. 495–505.

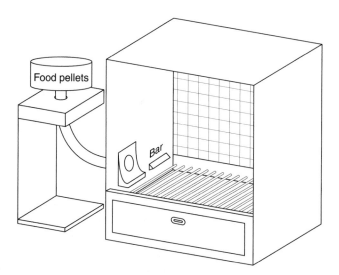

FIGURE 10.1   Skinner Box. An example of the sort of
Skinner box that might be used in studies of learning with rats.

water dispenser, which could be programmed to deliver water or food rewards to the
animal in a manner controlled by the researcher (see Figure 10.1).

The researcher was able to program the Skinner box creating a contingency, or
causal link, between a behavior (pressing the bar down) and a pleasant event (receiving
food or water). Skinner devised operant chambers for many different types of organisms. Although design of the device might be different, the point would be the same: to
alter the frequency of behavior by changing consequences. A Skinner box for pigeons
might have a little window that the pigeon could peck and a feeder that delivered bird-
seed, but the idea, and the resulting behavior, were not much different from a rat in a
Skinner box.

In a typical Skinnerian training situation the researcher would watch a hungry rat
and, using a handheld switch, reward it for small movements, thereby coercing it
nearer to the bar. At first the researcher might reward the rat for turning toward the
bar. Each time the rat turned that way, it would be rewarded. The effect of this contingent consequence was that the rat would begin to turn toward the bar more frequently.
Next, the experimenter would reward only steps in the direction of the bar. The rat
would move successively nearer the bar. Following this, the criteria would be
restricted, and only a lift of the paw in the direction of the bar would be rewarded. Next
the rat would have to touch the bar for a reward, and finally it would have to push the
bar down to get food. This procedure of training a rat to press the bar by rewarding
successive approximations to the desired behavior is called *shaping*. In the space of two
or three shaping sessions in a Skinner box, a hungry rat can learn to press the bar and
feed itself. Skinner was not merely interested in teaching rats to feed themselves. He
wanted to predict and control behavior. He found that changing the consequences of
behavior rapidly changed the behavior itself.

REINFORCEMENTS AND PUNISHMENTS

Skinner believed that for humans, the world was like a big Skinner box. We usually experience consequences following behavior, and he expected that the nature of those consequences would determine the frequency of our behavior. Consequences that increased the frequency of behavior were called *reinforcements*, and those that decreased behavior frequency were called *punishments*. An additional complication is introduced by saying that both reward and punishment can be administered in one of two ways: a stimulus can be added to the situation or it can be taken away. When the consequences following a behavior involve adding a stimulus, we say that the reinforcement or punishment is *positive*. When the consequences involve removing a stimulus, we speak of negative reinforcement or negative punishment being applied to the behavior. Notice that the words *positive* and *negative* do not mean good or bad; they are only technical labels telling us that a stimulus has been added or removed.

This is best understood with a little patience and a few examples. In *positive reinforcement* there are two components: *positive* means that a stimulus is being added, *reinforcement* means that the frequency of the behavior is going to increase. If you mow someone's lawn and they give you 20 dollars, you have been positively reinforced. The consequences of the behavior were that a stimulus was added ($20) and the behavior frequency was likely to increase (you will do this again if you can). Here's another one: you are watching television and a particularly annoying commercial comes on with loud music of a sort you hate. You press the mute button on the remote control and find the silence to be a relief. You find that you do this more often when this commercial comes on. You have been negatively reinforced. A stimulus has been removed (annoying music), and the frequency of the behavior (pushing mute button) increases. It is very likely that the stimulus that is removed in negative reinforcement is something aversive or irritating. The removal of this unpleasant event is likely to increase the frequency of the behavior. People sometimes use the term *negative reinforcement* when they are really referring to *punishment*. This is a common error, and you should learn to discriminate between these two operant situations. Imagine that you catch your finger in the car door as you slam it. It hurts. It hurts a lot. You do not do that again. This is positive punishment. A stimulus (pain) has been added following the door-slamming behavior. The frequency of the behavior decreases. Negative punishment may be a bit difficult to picture, although there are a few common examples of it (Cautela & Kearney, 1986). Probably one of the best is the application of so called "time-out" to reduce various undesirable behaviors in children. It may help you to see this as negative punishment if we tell you that the original name of this procedure was *time-out from reinforcement*. A child does not get its way and throws a tantrum. The child is taken to some quiet place and told that he or she can return to the family when the crying stops. This is punishment because the goal is to decrease the frequency of the behavior (tantrum). It is negative punishment because a stimulus has been removed (interaction with family and toys). This will be easier to see if you understand that the child is being placed into a neutral environment that has few, if any, sources of reward or reinforcement. Schools sometimes have a room designed to be a time-out environment. It is quiet and ordinary, perhaps carpeted with a chair or two but it has no other source of entertainment or reinforcement. Because most kids prefer to be around other people, toys, and things to do, removing these things decreases the frequency of the behavior. This is negative punishment. In recent years negative punishment has largely replaced positive punishment in the management of child behavior. Positive punishment required adding a stimulus, generally a painful one. Spankings and other physical forms of positive punishment have been associated with undesirable outcomes, such as increased aggressive behavior toward others (Strassberg, Dodge, Pettit, & Bates, 1994). The four operant learning situations described above are diagrammed in Figure 10.2.

In trying to analyze behavior in Skinnerian or operant terms it is important to remember that the consequences must follow the behavior and must be seen to have a contingency with the behavior in order for reinforcement or punishment to be effective in behavior change.

In order to do an operant analysis of behavior, you must answer two questions: Is behavior going to increase or decrease following consequences (reinforcement or punishment)? Is a stimulus being added or taken away as a consequence of behavior (positive or negative)? Operant analysis of behavior into these four categories can be challenging and calls for precision. The target behavior and target organism must be clearly specified before this analysis can take place. For example, a child in a grocery store checkout line starts screaming because he or she wants some candy that is displayed next to the cash register. The parent eventually gives in and buys some candy. To do an operant analysis of this situation we first have to decide who is the target: parent or child. If it is the parent, then the situation is negative reinforcement. Immediately following candy buying, a stimulus (screaming) is removed. The parent is more likely to make this response in the future because it works. If the target organism is the child, then the situation is positive reinforcement. The response (screaming) is rewarded with candy. The screaming behavior is more likely to happen in the future. In this case, both individuals in the setting are receiving reinforcement, so it is easy to imagine more screaming and candy buying in their future.

	Behavior frequency increases	Behavior frequency decreases
Add stimulus	Positive reinforcement	Positive punishment
Take stimulus away	Negative reinforcement	Negative punishment

FIGURE 10.2   Positive and Negative Types of Reinforcement and Punishment

SCHEDULES OF REINFORCEMENT

Skinner discovered quite early in his career that it was not necessary to reinforce every single response in order to maintain a high level of responding. There are a variety of ways to manipulate the frequency of rewarded responses. Collectively, these methods are called *intermittent* or *partial reinforcement*. Procedures of partial reinforcement can be seen to belong to one of four basic categories. In thinking about these, it is important to remember that reinforcement is an event that follows a response: the response must come first in operant conditioning. It is possible to issue reinforcements in some ratio to the number of responses. For example, every third response might be reinforced. This is what would happen if a rat in a Skinner box was given a food reward following three bar presses. This is partial reinforcement, because not every response is reinforced. The first two presses would not be followed by reinforcement, but the third would be. Correspondingly, the next two presses would not be rewarded but the third would, and so on. This kind of schedule is called a *fixed ratio* schedule, because every third response is rewarded. The ratio between responses and rewards does not change. Contrast this with a long operant session in which, *on the average*, one response in three is rewarded. Sometimes reinforcements occur close together, sometimes they do not, but, over time, the ratio *averages* to one in three. This is a type of partial reinforcement called a *variable ratio* schedule. The rat must make responses in order to receive reinforcements, but it is impossible for the rat to predict which particular response will be followed by food reward. A shorthand used for this situation is VR 3, or variable ratio three.

Instead for reinforcing on a ratio schedule, it is, alternatively, possible to reinforce responses after a particular *time* interval has passed. Partial reinforcement schedules that work this way are called *interval schedules*. If we continue to use a Skinner box example, the important thing to remember is that the rat in the Skinner box must still make a response. In an interval schedule the time interval since the last reward is what matters, not the number of responses the rat makes. In a *fixed interval* schedule, the first response after some period of time, for example 2 minutes, will be rewarded. The rat can do anything it likes during the interval, but only the first bar press after every 2-minute interval will be reinforced. The rat must make a response. Simply sitting and waiting will not be reinforced. However, only one response is required, and that has to occur at least 2 minutes after the previous reinforcement. This would be called an FI 2 schedule, meaning that there is a fixed interval of 2 minutes before another reinforcement can be obtained. After some experience of FI 2 schedules, rats will respond with few bar presses until the 2-minute interval approaches. There will be a burst of responses around the end of the interval until the reinforcement is delivered. Responding is then likely to decrease until the end of the interval again draws near. The last of the basic schedules is the variable interval schedule. In this schedule, over a long session the rat is rewarded after an *average* time interval, for example, 2 minutes. The Skinner box would be programmed to pay off after a series of time periods that, over the course of a long session would average to 2 minutes. In this situation the rat cannot figure out the length of the interval. Merely sitting and waiting will not be reinforced, the rat must continue to respond and, when one of the programmed variable intervals passes, the next response will be rewarded. As you will have guessed, this schedule

Payoff

		Predictable or regular	Unpredictable or irregular
	Time	Fixed interval	Variable interval
Reinforcement only after:			
	Responses	Fixed ratio	Variable ratio

FIGURE 10.3   Four Schedules of Reinforcement

would be called a VI 2, indicating a variable interval averaging overall to 2 minutes. These schedules are diagrammed in Figure 10.3.

We have chosen three responses and 2 minutes for use in describing the ratio and interval schedules. Be aware that these were arbitrary choices for the purposes of example, and either schedule might have any reasonable number attached to it.

THE HUMAN SIDE OF REINFORCEMENT SCHEDULES

Skinner firmly believed that these schedules of reinforcement were part of everyday life. We have used Skinner box situations as examples, but we would not want you to think that these phenomena are restricted to rats in operant chambers. For example, imagine that a class you are in meets on Mondays, Wednesdays, and Fridays and has a quiz every Friday. You do well on the quizzes, and this reinforces your studying and hard work. You are on a fixed interval schedule. This is an interval schedule, because the reinforcement is issued only after a period of time (1 week) goes by. It is not dependent on your responses. In contrast, another Monday, Wednesday, Friday class has pop quizzes that can happen any time, during any day of class. The instructor has decided that the average frequency will be two each week, but you do not know when they will happen. There may be four of them the first week and none the second week. You are on a variable interval schedule. If you are like many students, these two schedules would influence your study patterns. The fixed interval schedule tends to make you put off studying until it is almost time for class on Friday. The variable interval schedule tends to result in more continual study patterns. These frequency differences in your behavior are similar to those that would be seen in a rat responding in a Skinner box. Skinner believed that the schedule would determine the behavior frequency, and the species of organism did not matter very much. If you were to work in a car salesroom where you were given a bonus for every five cars you sold, you would be operating on a fixed ratio schedule. You get the bonus after five sales. Time does not matter. If you sell five cars in a morning you get the same bonus you would get by selling five cars in two weeks. A variable ratio schedule is illustrated by a slot machine. It is programmed to pay off at some average low frequency but only after a varying number of responses. Time does not matter to a slot machine. It is not operating on an interval schedule, so waiting around does not make it more likely to pay off.

CHANGING THE FREQUENCY OF BEHAVIOR

The rather simple notions of reinforcement and punishment and the schedules of reinforcement have been shown to be powerful means of changing behavior. For many psychologists, Skinner's radical behaviorism has been tempered by cognitive approaches, yet it continues to provide a useful technology for implementing behavior change. John Roll, Stephen Higgins, and Gary Badger (1996) investigated the use of schedules of reinforcement to promote and sustain abstinence from cigarette smoking. Their study was not intended to be a treatment for people who wanted to quit smoking. Instead, they studied people who did not want to quit smoking in order to demonstrate the power of reinforcers to increase abstinence. Because none of the participants wanted to quit or was trying to quit, any cessation of smoking among the participants was probably a result of reinforcements, not other factors. Roll and his colleagues pointed out that use of addictive drugs is a kind of operant behavior. It is maintained by the reinforcing consequences of the drug effects. The researchers believed that alternate nondrug reinforcers should be able to increase drug abstinence if they were sufficiently attractive to the participants and if the reinforcers were delivered on an optimum schedule. The schedules of reinforcement used in this study were more complex than the basic examples we have described, but they are not difficult to understand once you have mastered the basics.

Participants

The participants were 60 adult smokers who responded to descriptions of the study in newspaper advertisements or flyers posted on bulletin boards. Twenty-one of them were females and 39 were males. The mean age was 30 years, and the mean number of years they had smoked was 13. On the average they smoked 26 cigarettes per day, with a range from 10 to 50. The extent of their addiction was measured with a scale called the Fagerstrom Tolerance Questionnaire (Fagerstrom & Schneider, 1989). The Fagerstrom Tolerance Questionnaire is scored from 0 to 11, with higher numbers representing more nicotine dependence. The participants had a mean Fagerstrom score of 6.5, with a range of 4 to 9. In order to be eligible for the study, participants had to be over 18 years of age and appear for the initial meeting with an initial exhaled carbon monoxide (CO) reading of at least 18 parts per million (ppm). This was assessed with a carbon monoxide meter that measured exhaled CO. Smokers have high levels of CO in their lungs, so this was one way of assessing whether or not a person was a smoker. To be included, participants also had to answer "no" to the question, "Are you currently trying to, or do you want to, quit smoking?" Lastly, people were allowed to participate only if they showed no signs of physical or psychiatric problems. Questionnaires were administered that collected information on drug use, as well as medical and psychiatric history. Following this initial interview, the study took 5 days to complete.

Procedure

All participants agreed to either visit the laboratory or to be visited by the researchers at a prearranged place three times a day for the duration of the study. These visits occurred between 9:00 and 11:00 A.M., 3:00 and 5:00 P.M., and 8:00 and 11:00 P.M. The first visit of the study took place on a Monday morning. Participants were told that they should stop smoking by the previous Friday night. On each of the visits a CO level was taken to assess whether or not the participant had remained abstinent from smoking. Abstinence was defined as having a CO level equal to, or less than, 11 ppm. Participants were given immediate feedback about their CO level at each visit. They were also offered a supply of their own brand of cigarettes at each visit. Presumably, this was to ensure that abstinence was a result of the reinforcement schedule, not merely lack of access to cigarettes.

Participants were randomly assigned to one of three reinforcement schedules:

Progressive reinforcement group: The first time the CO level indicated abstinence, the participant received $3.00. On each subsequent consecutive measurement indicating abstinence, the amount of money was increased by $.50. In addition, every third consecutive abstinent visit was rewarded with an extra $10.00 bonus. A participant in this group who remained abstinent for four visits would earn for those four visits respectively, $3.00, $3.50, $14.00 ($4.00 + $10.00 bonus), and $4.50. If a participant was over the 11 ppm level, indicating that smoking had taken place, payment was withheld for that visit. On the next visit in which abstinence was demonstrated, the reinforcement was reset to the initial $3.00 level. If the participant had three abstinent visits following a reset, the reinforcement level was restored to the high value that had been received before the reset occurred. It was felt that this would support efforts to achieve abstinence again following a reset because the early gains made in level of reinforcement would be given back to the participant after three abstinent visits.

Fixed reinforcement group: Participants were paid $9.80 each time they made an abstinent visit to the researchers. There was no bonus money and there were no resets. The reason why the amount $9.80 was chosen was that this made it possible for a completely abstinent individual in this group to earn the same amount of money overall as a completely abstinent participant in the progressive reinforcement group.

Control group: Payments to control participants were yoked to the average of payments to the first 10 participants to be assigned to the progressive reinforcement group. Yoking was described in the earlier chapter (Chapter 1, "Oh Rats!") where a control group was fed the same quantity of food as an experimental group ate. In the smoking study the concept was the same: the control group received the same payment as another group; however, the payment was not contingent upon the control group's behavior. The control group was paid no matter what CO level they had at any given visit. They were told to try to achieve a CO level at or below 11 ppm, but there were no reward contingencies attached to this request.

Each participant received a detailed oral and written explanation of his or her reinforcement schedule. It was made clear to them exactly what they would have to do in order to receive payment. Money was paid in cash immediately following each CO assessment. In addition, participants were given an additional $50.00 on completion of the study. This encouraged them to finish the study, even if they were having problems achieving abstinence.

Results

Reinforcement contingencies were found to make a difference in abstinence as measured by the mean percentage of visits with CO readings at or below 11 ppm. These data are shown in Figure 10.4.

Mean abstinence levels in the progressive and fixed group differed significantly from the control group ($p < .05$), but not from each other. This measure showed that contingent reinforcement could lead to abstinence from smoking. The control group showed that even noncontingent reinforcement had some effect, but less than with other groups. Using other measures, we can see a difference between the progressive and the fixed schedules. An immediate difference could be seen between the groups in their ability to achieve an initial period of abstinence indicated by three consecutive visits with CO levels under 11ppm. These data are shown in Figure 10.5.

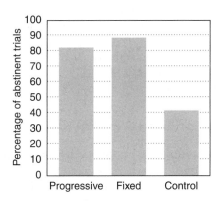

FIGURE 10.4   Abstinence by Group.
Mean percentage of CO readings at 15 trials at which participants were abstinent during the course of the 5-day study.

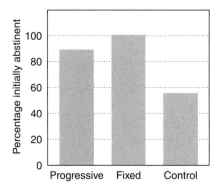

FIGURE 10.5   Achievement of Initial Abstinence. Percentage of participants from each group who achieved initial abstinence as defined by having the first three visits show levels of CO at or below 11 ppm.

The control group is significantly lower on this measure than the other two groups ($p < .01$). The fixed group appears to be a little higher in abstinence on this measure, although not statistically significantly so. The percentage of participants from each group who resumed smoking during any part of the study following an initial period of three abstinent visits is shown in Figure 10.6.

The progressive group had significantly fewer individuals resuming smoking than in the fixed or control groups ($p < .02$ and $p < .01$, respectively). Although they appear to be different in Figure 10.6, the fixed and control groups were not statistically significantly different on this measure. A last interesting measure was the percentage of individuals who remained abstinent through the entire course of the study. These data are shown in Figure 10.7.

The first thing to notice here is that the scale on the y-axis has changed. In order to think critically about data, it is important to look at the scales on graphs. Whereas on the previous figures, a bar reaching almost to the top would indicate 100 percent, on this graph it only indicates 60 percent. This does not diminish the importance of the findings shown in Figure 10.7, but it illustrates the importance of paying attention to the scaling. The progressive and fixed groups were each statistically significantly different from the control group ($p < .01$ and $p < .04$, respectively), but not from each other. Another question you might ask at this point is "How many people are we talking about?" Percentages do not, by themselves, tell you how many individuals are presented in each bar of the graph. Remembering that there were 20 participants in each group, you can figure out that the numbers abstaining throughout the entire study were: 10 progressive group members, 6 fixed group members, and 1 control group member. These numbers are quite small for making sweeping generalizations about large populations, nevertheless, the differences between them are interesting.

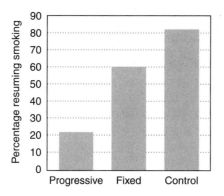

FIGURE 10.6   Resumption of Smoking. Percentage of participants in each group who, following an initial period of abstinence, resumed smoking.

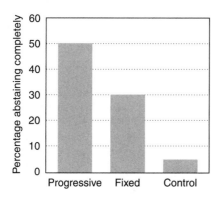

FIGURE 10.7   Abstaining throughout Study. Percentage of participants in each group who were abstinent on all 15 visits during the course of the 5-day study.

DISCUSSION

This study was not intended to be a treatment program, but it provided information that might be useful in treatments for nicotine addiction. Often the most difficult part of quitting smoking is the first week or two. This study suggested that monetary rewards were effective in increasing abstinence during this period of time, at least with a progressive reinforcement schedule. Even small amounts of tobacco use during attempts to quit have been found to be a significant predictor of long-term failure to remain abstinent (Chornock, Stitzer, Gross, & Leischow, 1992; Hughes, Gulliver,

Fenwick, Valliere, & Flynn, 1986). Progressive reinforcement might help people to remain abstinent, improving their chances of long-term abstinence. You might argue that this was an expensive program, costing about $150 per participant in reward money for only 5 days. This has to be put in the context that a two-pack-a-day smoker may be spending up to $2,000 a year on cigarettes. In this context, the money required to get through initial weeks of quitting is small. Although the study did not address this issue, it is also possible that people who want to quit would be more amenable to abstinence than the participants in this study and might find it easier to achieve and maintain. Further study will be required if the hopeful outcomes reported here are to become part of attempts to treat drug addictions.

REFERENCES

Cautela, J. R., & Kearney, J. A. (1986). *The covert conditioning handbook.* New York: Springer.

Chornock, W. M., Stitzer, M. L., Gross, J., & Leischow, S. (1992). Experimental model of smoking reexposure: Effects on relapse. *Psychopharmacology, 108,* 495–500.

Fagerstrom, K. O., & Schneider, N. G. (1989). Measuring nicotine dependence: A review of the Fagerstrom tolerance questionnaire. *Journal of Behavioral Medicine, 12,* 159–182.

Hughes, J. R., Gulliver, S. B., Fenwick, J. W., Valliere, L. J., & Flynn, B. S. (1986). Smoking cessation among self-quitters. *Health Psychology, 11,* 331–334.

Roll, J. M., Higgins, S. T., & Badger, G. J. (1996). An experimental comparison of three different schedules of reinforcement of drug abstinence using cigarette smoking as an exemplar. *Journal of Applied Behavior Analysis, 29,* 495–505.

Skinner, B. F. (1956). A case history in scientific method. *American Psychologist, 11,* 221–233.

Strassberg, Z., Dodge, K. A., Pettit, G. S., & Bates, J. E. (1994). Spanking in the home and children's subsequent aggression toward kindergarten peers. *Development and Psychopathology, 6,* 445–461.

CHAPTER 11

I DO!

Previous chapters have described two kinds of learning: *classical* (Pavlovian) conditioning and *operant* (Skinnerian) conditioning. A third broad category of learning, *social learning*, or *imitation*, will be described in this chapter. Although many behaviors owe their existence to classical conditioning or to operant conditioning, it is apparent that these two types of learning do not account for everything we do. Imagine trying to teach someone to hit a baseball with a bat using these techniques. It is difficult to imagine any significant role for classical conditioning: batting is not a reflex and classical conditioning must begin with a reflexive response. Operant conditioning could certainly play a role: the consequences of a successful hit, or a strikeout, probably have the effect of increasing the frequency of hits and decreasing strikeouts. Even though operant conditioning plays a role, it is not the only process involved in learning to bat. It would take a very long time to teach someone to hit a baseball if we had to depend entirely on operant processes. We would have to wait for the person to emit behaviors and then reinforce or punish them to alter the behavior frequency. If a person had never seen baseball being played, it could take a long time before any of the appropriate behaviors were emitted spontaneously.

SOCIAL LEARNING

We can learn a great deal by watching others. If a person had a chance to watch other people playing baseball for a while, that person would probably be able to make a credible start at playing the game. Many of the behaviors could be learned, at least in rudimentary form, by watching others. Of course, additional practice and operant consequences would further shape the behavior, but the basics could be learned by imitating others. This process is called *social learning*, and it is responsible for much of our behavior.

The most widely known early studies of social learning were conducted by psychologist Albert Bandura and his colleagues (Bandura, Ross, & Ross, 1961). Since

Incorporating the research of P. W. Dowrick and J. M. Raeburn, "Self-Modeling: Rapid Skill Training for Children with Physical Disabilities," 1995, *Journal of Developmental and Physical Disabilities*, 7, pp. 25–37.

Bandura's early research, hundreds of studies have been done showing the wide applicability of the principles of social learning (Bandura, 1986). The classic research demonstration of social learning by Bandura, Ross, and Ross (1961) is sometimes known as the Bobo Doll Study because some of the best-known findings involved one of these dolls. The Bobo doll was a child-sized inflatable plastic doll, painted to resemble a clown. It had a rounded weighted base so that it would fall over and stand back up when it was punched in the face. Punching it in the face was the most common response to this toy. In this study and subsequent literature, people demonstrating behavior to be imitated are called *models*. In this classic investigation, children were given the opportunity to observe adults performing unusual acts of aggression directed at the Bobo doll. The adult models pushed the Bobo on its side and punched it in the face while holding it down. The models also struck the Bobo with a mallet that was lying around. These behaviors were not typically observed in children playing with a Bobo until after the children had observed others doing these unusual acts of aggression. Bandura, Ross, and Ross found that children readily learned novel acts of aggression by watching adult models.

In the research that followed this study, a body of thought developed that is called social learning theory (Bandura, 1977, 1986). Its findings helped to delineate the characteristics that increased the probability of social learning. Models were shown to be readily imitated if they were *attractive* (Loken & Howard-Pitney, 1988), *powerful* (Bandura, Ross, & Ross, 1963), *personally warm* (LaVoie & Adams, 1978), *celebrities* (McCracken, 1989), or *enviable* (Hosford & Krumboltz, 1969). Another of the principles established empirically by social learning research was that when there were greater similarities between model and observer, the power of the model to elicit behavior change through imitation was enhanced (Kazdin, 1974).

THE SELF AS A MODEL

If similarity of model to observer is important, then it follows that one of the best models for any of us would be ourselves. The appearance of home videotape technology enabled researchers to study the effects of individuals being their own models. In 1983, Peter Dowrick defined self-modeling as "the behavioral change which results from observation of oneself in videotapes that only show desired behaviors." For example, Bray and Kehle (1996) made videotapes of children who stuttered. All episodes of stuttering were edited out, so that the children could see and hear themselves speaking fluently. This study showed that using these tapes, children could be powerful models for themselves. This medium showed children images of themselves functioning at a superior level of performance, a level that they had not yet attained. They saw what they would look like at a point in the future when they might have mastered the behavior. Dowrick (1983) called this *feedforward*, making an analogy with a technique called *feedback* in which children merely watched videotapes of unedited current performance to show them how well they had done in the past. In feedforward, children are shown how they would be able to perform in the future, once the behavior has been learned.

In the time since this formulation, video self-modeling, or *VSM*, has become a powerful tool for treatment of some kinds of behavior disorders. For example, Woltersdorf (1992) used VSM to treat some problem classroom behaviors associated with children who had Attention-Deficit Hyperactivity Disorder. These kids tended to play with pencils and pens instead of working, they talked and made noises when they were supposed to be quiet, and they were easily distracted. Children were taped, problem behaviors were edited out, and children were shown the tapes. In this instance, VSM was successful as a treatment for behaviors that interfered with classroom learning.

The standard treatment for childhood physical disability is training from physical and occupational therapists using verbal instruction, adult demonstration, and guided practice in which problems with behavior patterns are singled out for additional work. The outcomes of this standard form of treatment have been only modestly successful when evaluated empirically (see, for example, Batshaw & Perret, 1992). Peter Dowrick and John Raeburn (1995) used VSM to treat children with disabilities. They argued that particularly with these children, self-modeling might be more effective than other social learning approaches. One social learning approach might be to get other, able-bodied children to serve as models for behavior. However, Dowrick and Raeburn felt that using nondisabled children as models might be less effective because it is difficult for disabled children to see able-bodied children as similar to themselves.

Participants

The participants were recruited by occupational therapists and physical therapists from facilities attended by children with disabilities, such as day programs, inpatient services at a pediatric hospital, and special classrooms for disabled children. The eighteen children chosen for participation had to be available during the times required by the study. A summary description of the participants can be found in Table 11.1.

As you can see from Table 11.1, the children had a number of different disabilities. They were also diverse in terms of their cognitive capability, with IQs ranging from 45 to 95. At the lower end of the IQ range found in this study, cognitive impairment was sufficient to cause considerable problems in understanding and learning.

Procedure

A therapist who had been working with each child for at least 2 months selected two target skills. These skills were of approximately equal importance in daily life and in difficulty. Each of the skills was a behavior that normally would be fully developed in a child of the participant's age. The disabilities of the participants had slowed their behavior development, but the therapists and the researchers believed each target behavior was something the participant could learn to do. One of the two target behaviors was randomly assigned to be treated through self-modeling, the other target behavior was treated as a control. This random assignment was done to ensure that VSM was the only systematic difference between the group of target behaviors and the group of control behaviors. The target behaviors are shown in Table 11.2.

TABLE 11.1   Summary of Sex, Age, IQ, and Disability for Participants

NUMBER OF PARTICIPANTS	SEX	MEAN AGE	MEAN IQ	DISABILITY
7	3F, 4M	7.7	74.8	Spina bifida[a]
6	4F, 2M	8.3	75.5	Cerebral palsy[b]
2	2M	8.5	75.5	Muscular dystrophy[c]
1	1F	7	90	Hemiplegia (acquired)[d]
1	1F	8	89	Brain stem tumor[e]
1	1M	10	76	Multiple congenital abnormalities[f]

Notes:

[a]Spina bifida: developmental disability in which newborn has part of spinal cord exposed through a gap in the backbone. Outcomes may include paralysis of legs and mental retardation.

[b]Cerebral palsy: developmental abnormality of the brain caused by factors such as injury or lack of oxygen during birth and viral infections before birth. Outcomes may include weakness and lack of coordination in limbs.

[c]Muscular dystrophy: any one of a group of muscle diseases in which there is a pattern of genetic inheritance marked by a weakness or wasting of muscle tissue with associated problems in movement.

[d]Hemiplegia: disease of one hemisphere of the brain. Affects movements on the (opposite) side of the body, which are mediated by the diseased hemisphere.

[e]Brain stem tumor: tumor in the brain stem, the effects of which can include disability in fine motor coordination.

[f]Multiple congenital abnormalities: combinations of types of disabilities listed above, perhaps including others.

One way to set up experimental groups would be to assign some children to a self-modeling treatment and other children to a control group that did not experience self-modeling. In this study, each child served as its own control. For each child, amount of change in a behavior treated with VSM was compared to amount of change in another of that child's behaviors, one that was not being treated with VSM. As noted in Chapter 9, "Being Sick of the Hospital," this kind of research design is called a *within-subjects design* because one behavior is compared with another within a single group of participants. If the experimental and control conditions consisted of different people, the research design would be called a *between-subjects design*.

Both target behaviors for each child were videotaped. During the taping, the children were encouraged to do their best. They were also helped to perform difficult maneuvers. For example, a girl who had difficulty stepping over a small obstacle was helped by having a therapist hold her hand. At this time the camera was aimed at her feet, so that the therapist's assistance would not show in the final version that was used for self-modeling. About 15 minutes of tape was recorded for each participant doing each task, and this was edited down to about 2 minutes for the self-modeling version. In this editing, any parts of the tape where the children performed poorly, or where assistance was evident, were edited out. The final version showed each child performing the task in a smooth and error-free manner. As noted earlier, one of the behaviors

TABLE 11.2   **Target Behaviors for Each Participant**

PARTICIPANT	SELF-MODELING	VIDEO TAKEN BUT NOT SHOWN
1	Exercises on floor	Manipulation of blocks
2	Ball skills, wheelchair	Attention to reading
3	Exercises on floor	Dressing outer clothes
4	Walking unaided	Dressing upper garments
5	Clapping to instruction	Drawing between dots
6	Clearing away	Playing concentration
7	Dressing outer clothes	Walking, prosthetics
8	Putting on shoes	Walking up steps
9	Walking unaided	Dressing upper garments
10	Walking with posture	Ball skills, standing
11	Ball skills, standing	Balance on one foot
12	Attending to writing	Dressing self
13	Maintaining posture	Feeding self with spoon
14	Dressing self	Writing from copy
15	Ball skills, wheelchair	Dismounting wheelchair
16	Ball skills, standing	Dressing upper garments
17	Trampoline skills	Exercises for feet
18	Trampoline skills	Ball skills, standing

was randomly chosen for treatment by self-modeling. The other behavior was taped, but the tape was never shown to the children. It was necessary to tape both behaviors because in an experiment an attempt is made to make the experiences of experimental condition, or group, as similar as possible to the control condition in every way except for the independent variable. Doing this helps ensure that differences in outcomes between the groups are the result of the independent variable, not unintended factors. In this study, if only one of the behaviors had been taped it would have been difficult to know whether behavior changes were the result of taping, VSM, or both. Although it may seem unlikely that a behavior will change because it is taped, it is possible that the close attention given to behavior performance during taping would result in changes in the behavior. This may sound far-fetched, but it is known that people will sometimes change their behavior merely because psychologists are paying attention to it.

The classic example of this was a series of studies conducted at the Hawthorne, Illinois, plant of Western Electric Company. Psychologists studying worker productivity found that increased illumination in the factory was associated with higher work output. However, they also found that lower illumination boosted productivity. They gradually came to realize that it did not matter what they did. As long as they were studying the workers, productivity increased (Roethlisberger & Dickson, 1939). The *Hawthorne effect* is the name given to the phenomenon that behavior can change merely because participants know they are being studied. It is important to avoid

Hawthorne effects in designing experimental studies, and one way to do this is to treat different groups or conditions of participants equally in all ways except for the independent variable.

The VSM treatment for the target behavior chosen consisted of participants watching the edited videotape of themselves, without any discussion, for 2 minutes on six occasions over a 2-week period. Children received no discussion of the tape because Dowrick and Raeburn wanted to demonstrate the effects of self-modeling alone, without other factors being included. If discussion had been included with the tape, it would have been difficult to know which was responsible for behavior change: discussion or VSM. Although this could be the topic of another study, Dowrick and Raeburn chose to investigate only VSM as a variable. Previous observations of VSM suggested that six presentations over 2 weeks might be sufficient to result in behavior change, and so this was adopted as the treatment protocol in this study.

Data Collection

The observations that formed the basis for the data in this study were made by the therapists, mentioned above, who worked with the children. Following the selection of two target behaviors, the therapists carefully observed each behavior and made detailed records of the child's performance. The therapists used standardized checklists that are common behavior assessments in occupational and physical therapy. The initial behavior assessment, before any intervention, was called a *baseline*. It was a measure of what the child could do before any treatment was undertaken. Next, each skilled therapist was asked to use his or her experience to make a prediction about the amount of progress expected for each behavior during the next 3 weeks. These estimates were based on the therapist's knowledge of the child and experience with the treatment of the particular disability. It is critical to understand that while the therapists had helped with the taping of the two target behaviors, they were not made aware of which of the two had been chosen for treatment by VSM. During the 2 weeks of self-modeling treatment, the therapists continued to work with the children, doing the usual occupational or physical therapy for a wide range of behavior problems, including both target behaviors. Therapist's predictions of change over the VSM period were based on their expectations from the usual occupational and physical therapy. They did not know which behavior received additional treatment from VSM, so their predictions could not include the effects of VSM.

During the next 2 weeks, one target behavior was treated with self-modeling. Following this, the therapists again made careful assessments of both target behaviors. These new assessments were compared with the baseline assessments made at the start of the study as a means of measuring improvements in either target behavior. If the improvement observed was at the level the therapists would have predicted after a 3-week course of standard occupational or physical therapy, the behavior was rated 100 percent. If progress was different from the prediction, it was assigned a percentage based on how advanced or behind the current skill level was when compared to the initial prediction made by the therapist. For example, if the progress actually seen at 3 weeks was at the level that would usually be expected after 6 weeks, it was given a score of 200 percent. If progress observed at 3 weeks was similar to the progress normally predicted for a week and a half, the behavior would be scored 50 percent. The therapists gave a rating of "equal" to small amounts of change in a behavior that, although noticeable, represented a minimal change and, for practical or clinical purposes, an unimportant amount of change.

The reliability of the observations by therapists was checked by having other observers review videotapes of target behaviors made before and after the self-modeling intervention. The other observers were psychologists who did not know the children. They were shown the videotapes and, based on a number of specific evaluations, ultimately asked to make a choice of which of the two target skills for each child showed the greatest amount of improvement. There was 100 percent agreement between the ratings of "more progress," "less progress," and "equal" when these other psychologists' opinions were compared to the ratings of the therapists. Checking the accuracy of observations using multiple observers is a standard procedure in psychological research. It is a way of detecting bias or inaccuracy in the observations of a single observer.

Results

The overall results suggested that VSM had been a successful treatment. Fourteen of the eighteen participants showed more progress in the behavior that was self-modeled than in the behavior that was taped but never shown. For three children the differences were too slight to be considered important, or clinically significant. This is particularly striking when we remember that the VSM treatment only consisted of six viewings of a 2-minute tape over a period of 2 weeks. The amount of improvement seen in VSM target behaviors and in control target behaviors, based on the ratings of the therapists, can be seen in Figure 11.1.

As you look at Figure 11.1, it is important to remember that a 100 percent improvement means that the behavior progressed exactly as expected using standard occupational and physical therapy. Behavior change that was higher than 100 percent exceeded the expectations of the therapists, below 100 percent behavior change was less than expected. Figure 11.1 shows that the VSM behaviors more frequently exceeded the expectations of the therapists than did the behaviors assigned to the control conditions. One-third of the VSM behaviors fall in the highest category, 181 to 200 percent improvement, meaning that they showed progress almost twice as fast as would be expected in standard therapy, alone. In contrast, half of the control behaviors were near the expected level for standard therapy, in the category of 81 to 100 percent. The average for the controls was 106 percent, near enough to 100 percent to suggest that the therapists' estimates of progress with standard treatment were accurate.

Because the progress of some participants had been so great, the charts for 15 of the children were examined 1 year after the VSM treatment to see if these rather

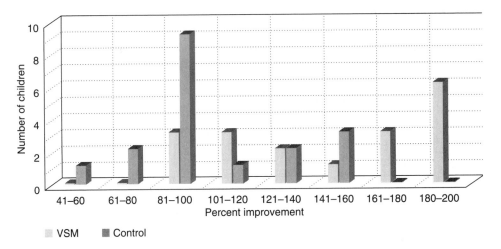

FIGURE 11.1 Improvement in Behavior. Percentage of improvement seen in VSM target behaviors compared to control target behaviors as rated by the therapists. One way to interpret this graph is to ask yourself which behaviors, the VSM or the control, appear to be more frequent above 120 percent? Which appear more frequent below 120 percent?

sudden behavior gains had been maintained. In all cases except a boy with the degenerative disease muscular dystrophy, the developmental gains were retained and, beyond that, the participants had continued to progress.

DISCUSSION

VSM treatment was shown to be successful for a variety of specific disabilities. The IQ of each child appeared to be unrelated to the success of VSM treatment. For example, the children with the lowest and the highest IQ scores were two of the four children who did not respond to VSM treatment. However, the children with the second-highest and second-lowest IQs did respond to VSM.

Only one child improved his nonmodeled behavior more than the one that was self-modeled. It was not known why this child showed behavior improvement in the nonmodeled skill but, certainly, the weight of evidence suggests that self-modeling is a useful therapy for problem behaviors of disabled children. Because people are so diverse and so many variables may influence behavior, the results of scientific psychology are probabilistic. Rarely, if ever, do all participants react in the same way to research manipulations. As in the results of this study, it is important to look carefully at the outcomes and to make your own decision about the confidence you think you should have about the findings. Although you might be more confident of the value of self-modeling if all the children had shown benefits from this procedure, nevertheless, the success rate of the group as a whole was quite high. We believe that even the most cautious professionals would agree that a treatment that did not cost much money or take a long time, yet which helped almost 80 percent of the children, was worthwhile. There are no absolute guidelines for deciding when a therapeutic approach is effective. This has to be a decision for you to make, based on factors such as the expense, the success rate and the confidence that you place in the research demonstrating success. When you make this decision and have some reasons why, you are thinking critically about psychology. As we have said in earlier sections, this is our primary goal for you: to be able to evaluate assertions about behavior. We want you to be able to assess your confidence in assertions about behavior and to have reasons that you can use to convince others. This is a practical skill that will be very useful to you. Would we still feel that self-modeling was a worthwhile approach if 50 percent of the children had improved? Maybe. What if only one child had improved? Probably not, although it would be worth further investigation to try to discover why that child was helped and others were not.

Dowrick and Raeburn noted that their tapes were crudely edited using the quality of videotape recorders manufactured for household use. Nevertheless, their results suggest that relatively little exposure to these somewhat roughly edited tapes can dramatically improve the behavior of many disabled children. This certainly seems to be a useful and cost-effective approach to some behavior problems.

REFERENCES

Bandura, A. (1977). *Social learning theory.* Upper Saddle River, NJ: Prentice Hall.

Bandura, A. (1986). *Social foundations of thought and action: A social cognitive theory.* Upper Saddle River, NJ: Prentice Hall.

Bandura, A., Ross, D., & Ross, S. A. (1961). Transmission of aggression through imitation of aggressive models. *Journal of Abnormal and Social Psychology, 63,* 575–582.

Bandura, A., Ross, D., & Ross, S. A. (1963). Vicarious reinforcement and imitative learning. *Journal of Abnormal and Social Psychology, 67,* 601–607.

Batshaw, M. L., & Perret, Y. M. (1992). *Children with disabilities: A medical primer* (3rd ed.). Baltimore: Paul H. Brookes.

Bray, M. A., & Kehle, T. J. (1996). Self-modeling as an intervention for stuttering. *School Psychology Review, 25,* 358–369.

Dowrick. P. W. (1983). Video training of alternatives to cross-gender behaviors in a 4-year-old boy. *Child & Family Behavior Therapy, 5,* 59–65.

Dowrick, P. W., & Raeburn, J. M. (1995). Self-modeling: Rapid skill training for children with physical disabilities. *Journal of Developmental and Physical Disabilities, 7,* 25–37.

Hosford, R., & Krumboltz, J. (1969). Behavioral counseling: A contemporary overview. *The Counseling Psychologist, 1,* 1–33.

Kazdin, A. (1974). Covert modeling, model similarity, and reduction of avoidance behavior. *Behavior Therapy, 5,* 325–340.

LaVoie, J. C., & Adams, G. R. (1978). Physical and interpersonal attractiveness of the model and imitation in adults. *Journal of Social Psychology, 106,* 191–202.

Loken, B., & Howard-Pitney, B. (1988). Effectiveness of cigarette advertisements on women: An experimental study. *Journal of Applied Psychology, 73,* 378–382.

McCracken, G. (1989). Who is the celebrity endorser? Cultural foundations of the endorsement process. *Journal of Consumer Research, 16,* 310–321.

Roethlisberger, F. J., & Dickson, W. J. (1939). *Management and the worker: An account of a research program conducted by the Western Electric Company, Chicago.* Cambridge, MA: Harvard University Press.

Woltersdorf, M. A. (1992). Videotape self-modeling in the treatment of attention-deficit hyperactivity disorder. *Child & Family Behavior Therapy, 14,* 53–73.

CHAPTER 12

NOW YOU SEE IT, NOW YOU DON'T

Jean Piaget (1896–1980) was one of the founding fathers of modern developmental psychology. Most of his life work involved studying the cognitive processes of children. Probably his most important discovery was that children think differently from adults. Piaget first noticed this while he was giving individually administered intelligence tests to children. Because this task involved having to ask the same questions over and over, he began to notice that different children independently and repeatedly came up with the same wrong answers to questions on the test. For example, children would repeatedly fail to understand the abstract point that objects can belong to two classes at once: a marble may be both red and round. Over time, Piaget came to see that these answers were only "wrong" from the adult perspective. Children think differently than adults do and, from the perspective of the children, their answers were right.

Later, Piaget did a number of classic demonstrations of childhood thought processes using his own children as participants (Piaget, 1954). He recounted his interpretations of these demonstrations in his early and important books about cognitive development in children. Piaget's books were very influential because his work was a new approach to understanding the development of mental processes. Many researchers were soon working hard to find solid empirical confirmation for the charming observations he reported.

Piaget turned his observations into a stage theory of cognitive development in which a child progresses through a number of stages as childhood thinking comes to resemble adult thinking. In summary, this cognitive development consists of two major components: (1) the child being able to understand the viewpoints of others and (2) the child coming to deal with abstract ideas. One way to think about these abstract ideas is to contrast them with concrete ideas. *House* is a concrete word, *beauty* is an abstract word. Small children have difficulty grasping the meaning of ideas that are not tied to observable objects and events. The central idea of a stage theory is that the transition between stages is quite rapid compared to the longer time spent within the stage. Much

Incorporating the research of R. Baillargeon & J. DeVos, "Object Permanence in Young Infants: Further Evidence," 1991, *Child Development*, 62, pp. 1227–1246.

of the research on this topic attempted to evaluate the timetables Piaget proposed for the stages of development.

It may seem a bit strange, but part of the fun of science consists of taking on the established notions or theories of others and finding problems with them. This is an adult version of the giggle that a child might get when a feared authority figure gets a pie in the face. Although many textbooks correctly stress the value of science, few of them point out the fun. The most stolid scientists might not want to admit this, but it can be great fun, even for adults, to throw a pie at the establishment. The scientific way to do this is to conduct carefully designed research that contradicts long-held and widely believed notions. Often this involves redoing parts of earlier research, a process called *replication.* You can see one reason why science is self-correcting: a flawed theory is likely to be attacked from a number of directions. If these attacks find problems for the theory, then the theory is likely to be modified. In extreme cases, a theory may be found to be so badly flawed that it is discarded completely.

CONSERVATION

Piaget's entire theory is not exactly spinning around the drain, but it has been successfully attacked by a number of contemporary researchers. These attacks have occurred on a number of Piagetian fronts. For example Samuel and Bryant (1984) studied a well-known Piagetian task called *conservation.* The classic conservation task is designed to show that young children are unable to mentally manipulate ideas about concrete events. In the classic demonstration of conservation, a child is presented with two balls of clay that are identical in size and shape and asked if they are the same. The child responds that they are. Next, while the child watches, one of the balls is rolled into some obviously different shape, such as a pizza or a hot dog. Then the child is asked again whether the two objects still have the same amount of clay. Piaget found that children younger than about 5 years old tended to answer "no" to this question, indicating that one lump of clay or the other now contained more clay. He believed that the child could not grasp the transformation that the clay had undergone and was misled by the obvious visual difference between the two portions of clay.

Samuel and Bryant wondered if, perhaps, the children were also responding to being asked the same question twice in a row. Children learn that when they are asked a question twice, often it is because they are expected to change their answer. For example, if a child is being interrogated about some misdeed and the adult does not get an admission of guilt, the child is asked the same question again and is expected to change the answer. "Now I want you to tell me the truth, *did you scratch your initials in the side of the piano?"* Standard Piagetian conservation testing asked the same question twice and the "correct" outcome was to change the answer. Samuel and Bryant examined this by asking the question only once. The children were shown two objects that were equivalent and, without any questions being asked of them, watched while one was changed. Only then were they asked the question about equivalence. The children in this situation made fewer errors than children who were asked the question twice, in the usual Piagetian manner. This suggested that being asked the question twice played a role in the changed answer.

Winer, Craig, and Weinbaum (1992) studied the classic conservation task with college students as participants and found that the wording of the question also played a role in correct responses. Remember: Piaget expected children to be fully conservational by about age 6. He also expected that once people were fully conservational, they would stay that way. This is an important issue because the conservation task was considered by Piaget to be a hallmark achievement defining the boundary between two major stages of cognitive development. A stage theory suggests a one-way progression of development, and Piaget did not expect cognitive achievement to come and go depending upon factors such as the number and nature of the questions being asked.

One of the more successful of the scientists leading commando raids into Piagetian territory has been Renée Baillargeon (pronounced *bay-r-jon*). One of the focuses of her research has been the timing of another important cognitive achievement, *object permanence*.

OBJECT PERMANENCE

Object permanence is the name given to the ability of children to understand that objects continue to exist, or are permanent, even when they are out of sight. Piaget believed that children younger than about 9 months did not yet have object permanence. His conclusions were based on observations of his young son and daughter. Piaget took an attractive toy away from his kids and hid it under a piece of cloth while they watched. At ages younger than 9 months, they would make no effort to recover it. Piaget concluded that his kids did not try to recover the toy because they thought that it ceased to exist when it was out of sight (Piaget, 1954).

It is easy to jump to wrong conclusions based on simple observations where the researcher is emotionally involved with the observation. If you have ever tried to change a baby's diaper and had the infant use the instant of nakedness to urinate, you could probably convince yourself that the infant had planned this as a way to frustrate you. Your conclusion would have some of the same problems that Piaget's research had—you only made one observation, and you were a part of the event you were trying to observe. You might come to different conclusions if you were to observe a large number of caregivers diapering infants. As we discussed in Chapter 4, "Half and Half," case studies should be confined to unusual situations in which the study of larger groups is not possible.

Sometimes students wonder why object permanence is given such prominence in the research literature. Much research energy has been devoted to object permanence because it is an early, clear, and important indication that a child is beginning to think the way an adult does. It is not possible to think rationally about the world if you believe that anything you cannot see no longer exists and that when things reappear to you, they have suddenly started to exist again.

HABITUATION

It is always a problem to know what an infant has heard or seen. Inability to use language is a defining characteristic of infancy. One of the most common research methods for getting babies to show us what they know is a strategy called *habituation*. In habituation, a baby is exposed to the same stimulus—for example, a visual event—over and over until it shows significant decreases in responding to the stimulus. Although we do not know what the baby is actually thinking, if you were to watch a baby becoming habituated, it would be easy to conclude that the baby has just become bored with the repetitious event. Then the visual event is changed. Typically when the baby first sees the change, strong responding will reappear. The return of responding indicates that the baby can tell something new has happened. Several different infant responses have been used by researchers to indicate that a baby is reacting to a new event. These have included staring at the new visual stimulus, as well as more subtle measures such as pupil dilation or heart rate changes. As long as the baby does something different when the event is changed, we know that the baby has noticed the change.

In 1991, Renée Baillargeon and Julie DeVos published an article that questioned Piaget's notions about the age at which object permanence first appeared. Baillargeon and DeVos used much more sophisticated methodology than Piaget and, unlike Piaget, they went to great lengths to ensure that their own beliefs and other uncontrolled factors were unlikely to bias their results. Baillargeon and DeVos believed that Piaget's observations may have misled him because in his demonstration the child was required to do at least two things at once. Piaget's children had to understand (1) that objects continued to exist when hidden *and* (2) to be able to plan and execute a search for the object. Planning a search involves knowing what to do first, what to do next, and so on. It is a fairly complex task that we, as adults, take for granted. A young child might know that an object continues to exist but may be unable to plan an orderly search for it— these are different tasks. Piaget's situation was even more complex because his kids had to plan the search as well as have the cognitive and motor skills to carry it out.

In order to disentangle object permanence from other cognitive and motor skills, a number of researchers have simplified the tasks children must perform to demonstrate early object permanence. For example, infants have been given tests requiring only visual responses, which can be much easier for an infant than the crawling and reaching required by Piaget's tasks.

Baillargeon and DeVos studied object permanence with a habituation situation called, in the developmental psychology literature, the *possible event* and the *impossible event*. Special effects in the movies have trained us to think that no visual event is impossible. However, for a baby, disappearing and reappearing objects should be surprising any time after object permanence develops. For example, imagine a simple visual test of object permanence in which a child watches while a toy car is rolled down a ramp. At one point the car rolls behind a piece of cardboard that momentarily blocks the child's view of the car. On some trials, while the car is behind the cardboard screen, the researcher, unseen, grabs it off the ramp and hides it. Unaware of this, the infant continues to turn its eyes as if tracking the car behind the screen and then, perhaps, shows some surprise that the car has not reappeared at the downhill side of the cardboard screen. The little car failing to appear on the other side of the cardboard screen is called the *impossible event*. It is "impossible" because the car disappears into thin air. You should be able to figure out why showing surprise at this would be an indication of object permanence. The infants with object permanence show surprise because they are wondering, as we might, where the car has gone. In contrast, if these children did not have object permanence, if they thought objects ceased to exist when not visible, there would be no reason for them to show any particular surprise when a car vanished behind a screen and did not reappear: the car has ceased to exist.

You might make the argument that a disappearing and reappearing car is a surprising event in itself and that even children without object permanence would show surprise as cars come and go. This is why it is important to compare impossible event responses to those of a child watching the *possible event:* a car rolls down a ramp, behind a screen, and out the other side. If a child did not have object permanence, the reaction to these events should be the same—cars here and there, coming and going. However, if the child has object permanence, then the reaction to the possible and impossible events should be different. The impossible event should be a surprise. The possible event, which does not contradict object permanence, should be less interesting and maybe even boring. Because you have object permanence yourself (or you are going to have trouble in life), you can imagine the surprise of the impossible event compared to the ordinary nature of the possible event.

Baillargeon and DeVos (1991) presented a well-controlled series of experiments that used visual tasks such as this in an attempt to find the youngest age at which children could demonstrate the achievement of object permanence in visual tasks. Several related studies are presented in the main article. This kind of presentation can be interesting because we can see the evolution of the researcher's ideas. Usually later studies are done to fix methodological oversights or to extend findings from earlier studies. We will present one of their studies in some detail and refer to the findings of two others.

OBJECT PERMANENCE EXPERIMENT

The method used in the research to be discussed here is the *experiment*. Remember, although that word is often used very loosely in everyday parlance, within psychology it refers to a specific set of operations that can lead to confident conclusions about cause and effect. In the most basic kind of experiment, there is an experimental group that gets some particular kind of experience or treatment. There is also a control group, which does not get the special experience. By comparing the outcomes of the two groups, one can see the effect of the special treatment. The experiment described here involved a within-subjects comparison similar to those described in earlier chapters. The participants were their own control group.

Participants

The participants were 32 healthy, full-term infants ranging in age from 3 months, 23 days to 4 months, 13 days old (mean = 3 months, 24 days). The names of the infants were found in the birth announcements in a newspaper. Parents were contacted and offered some money for travel expenses, but they were not otherwise paid. This may be important because it suggests that all the parents had some interest in the study itself. They were not merely doing it for the money.

Procedure

Baillargeon and DeVos described the apparatus and procedures in great detail. This was done so that other researchers could replicate the study. Think of this apparatus as being like a small stage upon which infants could observe events. The infants were held on the parent's lap in front of the apparatus during the trials. The parent was asked to close his or her eyes and not to interact with the child during the experimental procedures. In this way the parent could not transmit his or her own reactions to the infant. The infants were watched by two observers looking through peepholes in cloth-covered frames on each side of the apparatus. The observers could not see each other nor, presumably, hear each other in any way. Additionally, they could not see the events on the little stage from where they were and they did not know the order in which the events were presented. These arrangements prevented them from unknowingly biasing the data in some way. Each observer had a button that was wired to a computer. The observer's job was to watch the baby and to push the button when the baby showed interest or surprise by attending to the events presented. The computer could record whether the two observers agreed on the direction of the infant's gaze. Agreement averaged 91 percent or more, suggesting that they were both observing quite accurately. There is no minimum level of observer agreement, which is universally accepted in psychology. However, it is not possible to place much confidence in results unless the agreement between observers is quite high. In practice, studies are published with agreements ranging upward from about 80 percent. If the event being observed is relatively unimportant to the main point of the study, one might accept slightly lower levels. If the event is central to the study, higher levels might be sought.

The habituation event in this study consisted of the infants seeing a little ramp that had a track on it with additional track extending from the base of the ramp along the floor. A screen blocked the view of part of the track. The screen was lifted for a short period of time so that the infants could see the whole track set up. The screen was lowered, and a little car rolled down the track, passed behind the screen, and reappeared rolling along the track on the other side of the screen (see Figure 12.1).

The impossible test event in this study was like the habituation event, except that before the car was rolled down the ramp, the screen was raised to reveal a large plastic mouse sitting directly on the tracks. The screen was then lowered and, unseen to the infants, the mouse was removed from behind. The car was then rolled down the ramp and appeared rolling at the far side of the screen. The mouse was then quickly replaced and so that when the screen was raised, the mouse appeared to the infant to have been sitting on the track all along.

The possible test event was like the impossible one, except that the mouse was placed 10 cm behind the track. Although the mouse was behind the track and it would not have impeded the rolling of the car, it was removed during the time when the

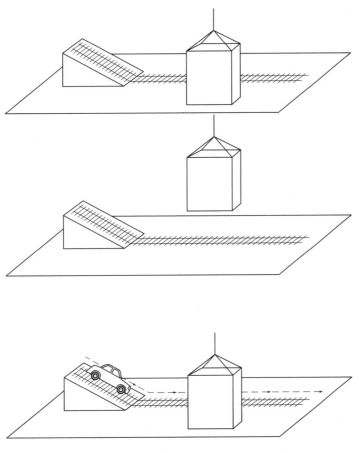

FIGURE 12.1   The Habituation Event. Infants are shown the ramp and track, the cardboard screen is lowered, and the little car rolls down the track, behind the screen, and out the other side.

screen was down so that any small noises associated with mouse removal would be the same for both the possible and the impossible event (see Figure 12.2).

Before they were presented with the habituation events, each infant was given a chance to see the mouse on the tracks and off the tracks in order to become familiar with the two positions. Half of the infants saw mouse-on-the-tracks first and half saw mouse-off-the-tracks first. Following these familiarization trials, the infants were habituated to the event shown in Figure 12.1 in which the car merely rolled down the track. Habituation was operationally defined as a 50 percent decrease in time attending the event or nine full trials. Once one of these criteria had been reached, infants were presented with the impossible and possible mouse events in alternating trials.

During these tests, some infants became fussy and one started to fall asleep. Their data were included—as far as they went—even if they did not finish the experiment. It

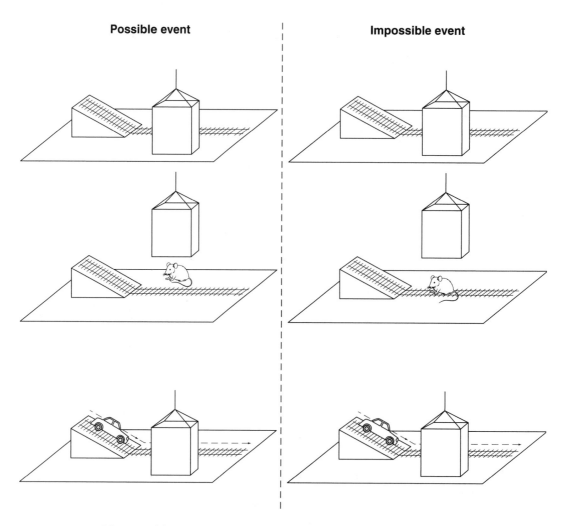

FIGURE 12.2   The Possible and Impossible Test Events. In the possible event, the mouse is shown behind the track. In the impossible event it is on the track. In both cases, the cardboard screen is lowered before the car rolls behind the block and out the other side.

is possible to bias data by leaving subjects in or by dropping them out. In this case, there is no reason to think that including data from these individuals had any adverse effect on the outcome of the study.

Results

As shown in Figure 12.3, both male and female infants showed decreases in looking at the event, which defined habituation.

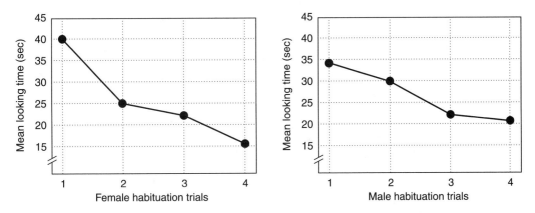

FIGURE 12.3   **Female and Male Habituation Trials.** Mean age = 3 months, 29 days.

Following habituation, infants were presented with the possible and impossible events. When all infants were considered together, the statistical analysis of the data for the test trials indicated that infants did not look longer at the impossible event (mean = 27.4 sec) than at the possible event (mean = 25.8 sec). However, when the group was divided by sex, female infants looked longer ($p < .05$) at the impossible event (mean = 31.1 sec) than at the possible event (mean = 23.7 sec), but males did not seem to notice the difference (possible mean = 27.6 sec, impossible mean = 24.1 sec, $p > .05$). The data for male and female test trials are presented in Figure 12.4.

It is easy to see the female differences in this figure. The males seemed to look longer at the possible event early in the trials, but ended up looking about equally at possible and impossible events. There were no significant differences in looking times on the familiarization or habituation trials, only on the test trials. Studies by other researchers have shown that male infants lag several weeks behind females in some visual skills such as depth perception (Gwiazda, Bauer, & Held, 1989), and this may be the reason why the males seemed to be developmentally behind in the mouse studies of object permanence. The visual displays used by Baillargeon and DeVos require depth perception as well as object permanence.

Baillargeon and DeVos ran this study again with other infants. The only change was that the possible event had the mouse placed in front of the tracks, not behind the tracks. This was done to eliminate the possibility that the females who responded most strongly were merely more interested in the mouse when it was nearer to them. This rival explanation of the data was not supported. The results showed the same finding as in the first study: female infants looked longer than male infants at the impossible event. When the study was done one more time with younger females (3 months, 6 days to 3 months, 22 days, mean = 3 months, 16 days) the effect disappeared, as can be seen in Figure 12.5.

Probably these infants were too cognitively immature to figure this out or too visually immature to see the differences in the mouse positions. Through repeated

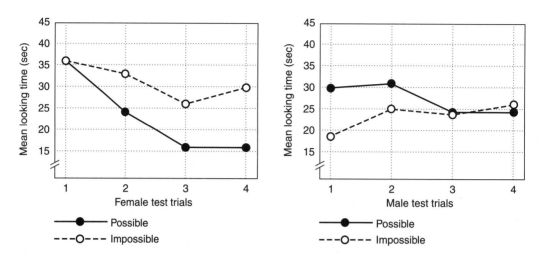

FIGURE 12.4   Female and Male Test Trial Data. Mean age = 3 months, 29 days.

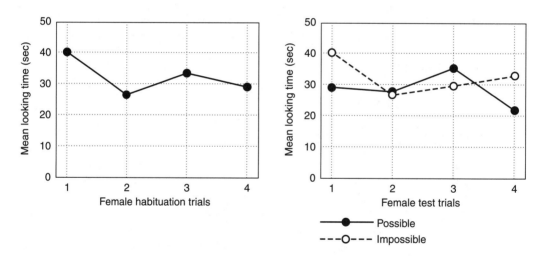

FIGURE 12.5   Female Habituation and Test Trials in Younger Females. Mean age = 3 months, 16 days.

testing, Baillargeon and DeVos pushed the envelope of this study design as far as it would go and demonstrated the age boundary for object permanence, at least when tested in this situation. It is worth a reminder that Piaget did not find object permanence in his children until they were 8 or 9 months old.

The carefully planned and conducted experiments of Baillargeon and DeVos demonstrate striking abilities in children as young as 3.5 months old. We doubt that many parents, even those having considerable experience with infants, would have predicted this level of reasoning in such young children. All but the last of the mouse studies gives evidence that at least young females knew the mouse existed even when it was out of sight. They could figure out the trajectory of the car, understanding that, at times, the mouse was in the way of the car. These children knew that objects continued to exist when they were out of sight. They understood that objects retained their solidity and other physical properties when they were hidden. They also knew that the interactions between physical objects did not change merely because they were out of sight. It seems likely that Piaget did not notice these things in young children because his methods were lacking in adequate experimental procedures and controls. Even though Baillargeon and DeVos have revised Piaget's view of cognition in childhood, it must be remembered that Piaget's crude observations pointed the way to more sophisticated analyses of behavior. As a scientist, Piaget would probably have been well pleased with this outcome.

REFERENCES

Baillargeon, R., & DeVos, J. (1991). Object permanence in young infants: Further evidence. *Child Development, 62,* 1227–1246.

Gwiazda, J., Bauer, J., & Held, R. (1989). Binocular function in human infants: Correlation of stereoscopic and fusion-rivalry discriminations. *Journal of Pediatric Ophthalmology and Strabismus, 26,* 128–132.

Piaget, J. (1954). *The construction of reality in the child.* New York: Basic Books.

Samuel, J., & Bryant, P. (1984). Asking only one question in the conservation experiment. *Journal of Child Psychology and Psychiatry, 25,* 315–318.

Winer, G., Craig, R., & Weinbaum, E. (1992). Adults' failure on misleading weight-conservation tests: A developmental analysis. *Developmental Psychology, 28,* 109–120.

CHAPTER 13

TO DAY CARE OR NOT TO DAY CARE: THAT IS THE QUESTION

One of the most difficult decisions facing parents is the issue of providing child care prior to entering grade school. Parents wonder what is best for their children, and high-profile media reports of abuse and neglect in child-care environments have only served to heighten stress. The development of the child-care center is relatively recent, and standards of care and training of workers may vary considerably. What constitutes acceptable or quality child care is unclear. During the past 20 years placing young children in child care has grown significantly as a common practice for preschool children. The advent of two-parent families, both of whom work outside the home, and the rise of the single-parent family have likely contributed to the need for day care as an institution to nurture infants and preschool children. The definition of day care can vary from a baby-sitter who comes to the family residence and provides one-on-one care to large centers where children are given more institutionalized services. Quality variables such as worker-to-child ratio, physical size of areas used, sleep, eating, worker training, and quality and type of play materials can certainly play a very important role in contributing toward the quality of the child's experience. In 1990 less than 10 percent of infants and children were placed in institutional child-care centers, and the trend toward increasing enrollments is growing rapidly (Kisker, Hoffereth, Phillips, & Farquhar, 1991). However, the quality of care in center-based child care is often inadequate (Cost, Quality, & Outcomes Study Team, 1995), and there is little evidence about how specifics of the child-care environment impact on infant and child growth and development.

HIGH-QUALITY DAY CARE AS PRIMARY PREVENTION

Inadequate child care is important because infants who receive poor-quality care may not receive the stimulation and interactions necessary to develop the social, personal,

Incorporating the research of T. Field, "Quality Infant Day-Care and Grade School Behavior and Performance," 1991, *Child Development, 62*, pp. 863–870.

emotional, and cognitive skills that are needed to succeed. Furthermore, the impact of poor infant and child care may be costly to us as a society by producing children and later adults who are greatly lacking in the attributes to function adaptively. High-quality child care may in fact be a cheap, primary prevention strategy to ensure fully functioning healthy youngsters and productive citizens. Primary prevention refers to impeding the onset of some negative consequences by taking early action. In medicine, the use of vaccines to inoculate children for all sorts of diseases prevents the disease process (certainly a negative consequence) from ever happening. It is likely that the success of vaccine development has done more for the prestige and power of medicine than almost any other medical development, not to mention the many children and adults spared from the symptoms of measles, mumps, or polio. In terms of child care, it may be that we can identify factors in high-quality centers that serve, like an inoculation, to prevent later problematic patterns such as dropping out of school, underemployment, criminal behavior, alcohol and substance abuse, and dysfunctional patterns of adult and family life. The research by Tiffany Field presented in this report targets specific factors in excellent quality infant and child-care centers and looks at how they relate to a number of very significant personal, social, and cognitive variables as children mature.

TIFFANY FIELD'S RESEARCH

Tiffany Field reports that many investigators have contradictory findings with respect to the effect of day-care experience on personal and social behaviors such as sociability and aggression. It is Field's thinking that many studies do not evaluate the quality of the day-care center and that quality of care may be an important factor in whether children are likely to become more or less sociable as a result of day care. Clearly, Field's reasoning that high-quality day-care centers promote and foster positive development will be evident as the child matures, whereas many studies of day-care centers of questionable quality may yield very different findings. As you will see, Field does a good job of describing clearly what is meant by "high-quality" day care.

In an earlier study (Field, Masi, Goldstein, Perry, & Parl, 1988) we can see the emergence of Tiffany Field's thinking and ideas. She and her colleagues studied infants and children who began day care prior to 6 months of age and those who began as infants, but after 6 months of age. Both of these groups attended a high-quality day-care center on a full-time basis. Another group of infants, who attended a different, high-quality day-care center on a part-time basis, was also studied. The results of this investigation indicated that in early entry, before 6 months, and later entry, after 6 months, infants and children did not differ in attachment behavior with their parents; that is, their parental reunion behavior patterns (when parents were reunited with their child at the end of the day) were similar. All children who had more months of day-care involvement were seen to be more engaged socially with their contemporaries. Early starters and full-timers showed less watching behavior, less solitary play, less comfort-seeking from teachers, more cooperative play, and more positive emotional expression than part-timers. Early-starter full-timers also spent more time interacting with peers and had more frequent positive verbal exchanges. The data from this study and others suggested positive findings, but provided no data about how these early patterns of behavior would evolve as the child progressed into grade school. This is the genesis of the present Tiffany Field research discussed here—*How do these same children fare as they venture forward into elementary school?*

The investigation actually consists of two studies. In Study 1 the children in the Field et al. study of 1988 are followed as they progress in grade school, and in Study 2 we look at the relationship of a variety of high-quality day-care centers on children as they enter their preteen years. It is Field's hypothesis that the more time children spend in a high-quality day-care facility, the more likely they are to be better socialized (assertive, nonaggressive) as they grow older. This view is proposed because the day-care experience involves considerable contact with adults and peers and is monitored so children learn more prosocial behaviors while antisocial behaviors are discouraged. Because day care is a group experience, children learn to be assertive and active. It is hypothesized that social experience derived from the day-care experience may positively impact self-esteem and academic performance in school.

Study 1

The same children who participated in full-time infant/child care in the Field et al. 1988 study were the participants in this study. It is important to describe what Field uses as her definition of the high-quality day-care center described in this study. The following description of the day-care center is a good example of an operational definition. An operational definition is often used in psychological research and eliminates subjectivity and error. As described in the first chapter, an operational definition takes a concept, environment, or abstract idea and defines it in specific, concrete terms. For example the abstract notion of "intellectual ability" can be operationally defined as a score on a specific assessment measure (e.g., IQ). Field deliberately and in very precise terms describes her definition of "high-quality child-care environment" so there is no mistake as to what is meant.

The high-quality day-care center was divided into an infant nursery and a toddler nursery. The infant nursery had 16 babies in a room with a door that could partition sleep from activity areas. The room was enriched with many stimulating environmental features including a multilevel structure, sunken waterbed, slopes, stairs, and tunnels. The toddler room was equally enriched with many, many stimulating structures and materials. In addition, a separate outdoor area, which had many play structures and materials was accessible outside each room. The teacher: infant ratio was 1:4 in the infant room, while the toddler room had a 1:5 ratio. The teachers in both rooms were experienced and had training in early childhood education. The head teachers had master's degrees, and all teachers were stable employees. The day-care atmosphere and teacher attitudes were noted to be very positive.

Method

The 28 youngsters in this study averaged 7 years of age (range = 5–8 years). Typically the children were in the second grade (range = K–4th grade). The children all began day care prior to age 2, and the average age of initiating day care was 6.7 months (range = 1–22 months). The children typically spent the remaining preschool years in day care (average = 3.1 years) until they entered kindergarten. The parents of the children were judged to be of middle socioeconomic status (SES) and were employed as medical professionals and staff members. The average number of years of maternal and paternal education was 17 and 20 respectively. The parents were typically stable, two-parent, dual-career family units.

Mothers of the day-care center "graduates" (number = 40) were sent a questionnaire packet in order to gather data on parental perceptions. Because the mothers were well educated, the researchers expected them to be reliable reporters. Because of family relocations only 28 of the participants could be located. The researchers compared the 28 remaining participants to the 12 participants that could not be located to explore for any differences on previously collected measures. Because no differences were noted, the 28 remaining participants were considered to be representative of the original sample. It is common in longitudinal research to "lose" participants as the study proceeds. It is vitally important, as Fields has done, to make sure that the participants who "drop out" don't differ in some important way from the participants who remain. Also it is important to realize that questionnaire and rating measures in psychological research are subject to bias and may therefore be prone to error. This is a general word of caution and is not meant to suggest that the assessment in these studies was flawed.

The questionnaire packet included the following for the mother to complete:

- *Demographic questionnaire.* This questionnaire requested information on the child's age, number of years in school, school awards, and participation in gifted programs, extracurricular activities, and friendship patterns.
- *Internalizer/Externalizer Scale* (Buck, 1977). This scale measures introversion/ extroversion and was included to see if this dimension in the mother correlated with her child's ratings or performance.
- *Behavior Rating Scale* (Santrock & Warshak, 1979). This scale measures peer relations, work/study habits, emotional well-being, and adult/child relations.
- *Parental Ratings of Child.* The children were rated on a five-point scale for the following sociability factors: attractiveness, assertiveness, aggressivity, popularity, and leadership.

The children were assessed on the following measures:

- *Piers-Harris Children's Self-Concept Scale* (Piers & Harris, 1969). This scale includes 85 "yes-no" questions, such as "I have good ideas" and "I am a happy person."
- *Child Self-Portraits.* The children were requested to provide self-drawings using various colored felt markers. These drawings were scored for use of dull colors, single-color usage, absent body parts, displaced or distorted body parts, size of drawing, and facial expression. The scoring focus was to measure depression.
- *Internalizer/Externalizer Scale* (Buck, 1977). The children's version of this scale was administered to measure introversion/extroversion.

What Was Found

The results of this study were based on correlations between measures of the amount of time spent in stable, high-quality day-care and later personal, emotional, and social behaviors. Correlational methods as well as interpreting correlation coefficients were presented in Chapter 3, "Run For Your Life." The major findings from this study are presented in Table 13.1. Correlations significant at $p < .05$ are reported, while insignificant correlations are omitted. Remember, this probability notation ($p < .05$) indicates that the results found in this study would likely happen by luck or chance in no more than 5 opportunities in 100. Thus, we can be assured that the findings were not the outcome of luck at a 95 percent confidence level. Therefore, as readers, we can trust the outcomes observed in the children were associated with the day-care experience.

TABLE 13.1   Study 1—Correlations between Months of Day Care and Background, Personal, Social, and Academic Measures

	CORRELATION(r)
BACKGROUND VARIABLES	
Age	*
Years in day care	*
Current school grade	*
Children in gifted program (number)	*
Honors (number)	*
Extracurricular activities (number)	.40
Friends (number)	.48
CHILD VARIABLES	
Self-drawing	−.80
Piers-Harris Self-Concept	*
Internalizer/externalizer	*
PARENT RATINGS	
Internalizer/externalizer	*
CHILD BEHAVIORS	
Peer relations	*
Study habits	*
Emotional well-being	.38
Adult/child relations	*
Attractiveness	.39
Assertiveness	.39
Aggressivity	−.57
Popularity	.47
Leadership	.40

The reported correlation coefficients are significant at $p < .05$.

*These unreported correlations were nonsignificant.

The outcomes of this study included the following; more than half the group were in gifted grade school programs, the children averaged 1.5 academic honors, children participated in 2.2 extracurricular activities ($r = .40$), and had four friends ($r = .48$). Significant correlations were also found in the following areas: parent ratings of emotional well-being ($r = .31$), leadership ($r = .40$), popularity ($r = .47$), attractiveness ($r = .34$), assertiveness ($r = .34$), and aggressivity ($r = -.57$). Finally, the children's drawings, scored for depressive ideation, were negatively correlated ($r = -.80$). These drawings suggest that the more time spent in quality day care, the less "depression" was evident in the drawings of the children. It is also important for the reader to note that there were many areas of the children's functioning where length of time in day care was not significantly correlated. In Table 13.1 the areas of functioning with no correlation coefficient listed indicate the lack of a significant relationship. The "nonsignificant" areas include most background variables, two of three child variables, the parent ratings, and three of nine child behavior measures.

From parental ratings and children's responses, the data indicate that children coming from a background of high-quality day care function better socially and emotionally in the elementary school period of their lives. Their self-drawings indicated high levels of self-esteem and low levels of depressive content. Parental reports indicated that the children had more friends, engaged in more extracurricular activities, were more popular among their peers, and were seen as more attractive. The results also indicate that the children were better leaders and were more assertive. These findings were expected by Field and were attributed to the extensive experience with other children and adults in the preschool years at the day-care center. There were no undesirable outcomes seen in the data for the children. However, it is hard to explain why there was a significant correlation found for many of the measures assessed. For example, self-esteem, peer relationships, and adult/child relationships would seem to be linked to the intensity of quality day care, yet no significant findings were obtained. Field views the high-quality day-care experience as the simplest and most direct explanation for the findings. However, as in almost all studies, unassessed variables are likely to exist and to play important roles. In this study the "parenting variable" is likely to be important, but is not assessed by Field. Looking at the very high education level of the parents makes one think that such highly educated parents may be responsible, in part, for the favorable outcomes in their children. It is possible that these children might have shown favorable outcomes even if they didn't attend high-quality day care. This is an interesting question; however, the design of this study doesn't allow for this comparison to be made.

Study 2

This study is important because it extends and amplifies upon the findings of Study 1. Any time you replicate a study and obtain similar findings, your confidence in those results is strengthened. The children in this study attended a variety of quality day-care centers starting at different ages in infancy and childhood. These children were also followed into their preteens years when a number of significant assessments were made. The 56 children in this study were from diverse ethnic backgrounds (Caucasian,

African American, Hispanic). At the time of follow-up the children were in two sixth-grade classes in a university laboratory elementary school. The children were on average 11.5 years of age and lived in middle-SES families. Both parents were highly educated, and each family relied on two incomes. The children all began day care before the age of two and remained in the same day-care program until they began kindergarten. The six different day-care centers they came from had similar characteristics to the center described in Study 1.

The following assessments were made on the children:

- *Videotaped Interactions:* The children were placed in best friend's dyads and videotaped having a conversation about anything they desired. These videotapes were coded for affect, vocalizations, activity level, physical affect, and playfulness. Coding is a procedure that is important to know about because it is often used in psychological investigations. Coding typically involves the translation of observational or interview data (images and words) into numbers. However, one has to be sure the translation is reliable—one can check this by having two individuals code and check their agreement. Thus, the numbers that emerge represent the behavior observed or recorded. The advantage of having numbers as an outcome is that they eliminate subjectivity and can be manipulated arithmetically.
- *Piers-Harris Children's Self-Concept Scale* (Piers & Harris, 1969): This scale was used in Study 1 and has been described earlier.
- Teachers were given the *Behavior Rating Scale* (Santrock & Warshak, 1979). This scale was used in Study 1 and has been described earlier.
- *Academic records* of the children including performance measures used in gifted program assessment, language arts and math SAT scores, and language arts and math grades at the end of the sixth grade.

What Was Found

As in Study 1, a correlational strategy was used to answer the primary question: How is the duration of infant day care related to later school outcome measures? Table 13.2 presents the correlational findings.

As the findings in the Table 13.2 indicate, neither of the self-ratings was significant. Three of the teacher ratings, emotional well-being, attractiveness, and assertiveness were significant findings. In the peer interaction category only physical affection was found to be significant. Finally, in terms of academic performance, gifted program assignment and math grade was significant.

In Study 1 the longitudinal follow-up ratings were completed by mothers of the children studied, while in Study 2 teachers, who were unaware of which children in their classes participated in the study, completed the follow-up ratings. It is likely that teachers rated all students in their classes so they would not be aware of which of their students came from the high-quality day-care backgrounds. In both studies the children who had experienced more quality day care received significantly higher ratings on emotional well-being, attractiveness, and assertiveness. Field explains the outcome of children being rated significantly higher in physical affection as not surprising. Field

TABLE 13.2   Study 2—Correlations between Duration of Infant Day Care and Outcome Measures at the End of Grade School

	CORRELATION (r)
SELF-RATINGS	
Self-esteem	*
Extraversion	*
TEACHER RATINGS	
Peer relations	*
Study habits	*
Emotional well-being	.32
Adult/child relations	*
Attractiveness	.39
Assertiveness	.29
Aggressivity	*
Popularity	*
Leadership	*
PEER INTERACTION BEHAVIORS	
Affect	*
Vocalizations	*
Activity level	*
Physical affection	.49
Playfulness	*
ACADEMIC PERFORMANCE	
Gifted program	.29
Language arts grade	*
Math grade	.38

The reported correlation coefficients are significant at $p < .05$.

*These unreported correlations were nonsignificant.

believed it was a result of these children having more experience with their peers, which likely included physical affection and touching. Field states that the most unexpected finding concerned academics. The data indicates that the experience in quality day care was significantly correlated with gaining admission to gifted programs and obtaining higher final grades in math. A similar finding was reported in the National Longitudinal Study of Youth data, where children who were placed in day care during their first 2 years received higher math and reading achievement test scores and obtained higher scores on the Peabody Picture Vocabulary Test, a verbal measure of IQ (Vandell & Corasaniti, 1990). Such a finding should not be totally unexpected because the preschool experience resembles the school experience and is likely to prepare a child better for successful learning.

The data reviewed in this research program are interesting and exciting especially in providing clues to the outcomes of the experience of quality day care. However, as Field notes, the data "do not indicate whether the positive effects are the result of infant day-care or the result of longer attendance in high-quality programs." The findings of the study indicate that students who attend quality day care not only are advantaged in grade school, but also benefit in social skills as well. These findings also appear to generalize into emotional and academic areas. This study did not investigate good, average, or poor-quality day care to see what long-term outcomes were obtained for their graduates. Field does note that her findings are consistent with the conclusions of Phillips, McCartney, & Scarr (1987), where high-quality day-care children were also seen to be more socially competent. As you can see from this chapter, research can help answer questions, but often new questions needing further study arise. This is a healthy process in which psychological research gradually reveals the "answers" over time.

REFERENCES

Buck, R. (1977). Nonverbal communication of affect in preschool children: Relationships with personality and skin conductance. *Journal of Personality and Social Psychology, 35*, 235–236.

Cost, Quality, and Outcomes Study Team. (1995). *Cost, quality, and child outcomes in child care centers: Executive summary.* Denver: University of Colorado.

Field, T. (1991). Quality infant day-care and grade school behavior and performance. *Child Development, 62*, 863–870.

Field, T., Masi, W., Goldstein, D., Perry, S., & Parl, S. (1998). Infant day-care facilitates preschool behavior. *Early Childhood Research Quarterly, 3*, 341–359.

Kisker, E. E., Hoffereth, S. L., Phillips, D. A., & Farquar, E. (1991). *A profile of child care settings: Early education and care in 1990* (Vol. 1) Princeton, NJ: Mathematica Policy Research.

Phillips, D. A., McCartney, K., & Scarr, S. (1987). Child care quality and children's social development. *Developmental Psychology, 23*, 537–543.

Piers, E. V., & Harris, D. B. (1969). *The Piers-Harris Children's Self-Concept Scale.* Nashville, TN: Counselors Recordings and Tests.

Santrock, J., & Warshak, R., (1979). Father custody and social development in boys and girls. *Journal of Social Issues, 35*, 112–125.

Vandell, D. L., & Corasaniti, M. A. (1990). Variations in early child care: Do they predict subsequent social, emotional and cognitive differences? *Early Childhood Research Quarterly, 5*, 55–72.

CHAPTER 14

. . . AND ALL OF THE CHILDREN ARE ABOVE AVERAGE

As you are coming to see, studies in psychology can take many forms. No study is perfect and beyond all criticism. Some are better than others because the methodology is more tightly woven. Ideally, the structure of a study would be so tight as to thoroughly exclude all explanations of behavior except those manipulated by the researcher. As you read these studies, critical questions will probably form on the tip of your tongue. You may find yourself thinking something like, "Oh yeah? Well what would have happened if those same people had been studied again, 5 years later?" Often, the best of the studies will have an answer for you, sometimes in the next paragraph. As you read other studies, you may be impressed by how much sheer effort has gone into the creation of the study. Some researchers could hardly have time for any other life because their research projects are so gigantic. We find ourselves asking, "Do these people have time to eat lunch? To blow their noses?"

Although it may seem to be a bit of a surprise, the judgments of quality we make about hard-as-nails scientific studies are not completely based on science. Quality judgments also have an aesthetic side based on the cleverness of the research design. If you were to hang out in places where scientists meet and talk, you would hear the lilting language of aesthetics being used in the discussion of scientific studies. Studies will be described with words such as *beautiful*, *gorgeous*, or *elegant*. As with any beauty contest, there are a number of specific characteristics that make a winner. The more of them a study has, the more beautiful it is. For example, a beautiful study in psychology will have a claim to *validity*. Validity involves a judgment about correctness or accuracy. Validity is often divided into two categories, *internal* and *external*. A study has internal validity if it thoroughly and rigorously tests the correctness of its hypothesis. Appropriateness of group assignment, control conditions, and operational definitions are examples of issues to consider in judging internal validity. To some extent, validity is a matter of opinion; however, validity judgments are not merely some wild and crazy guess. In order to evaluate the validity of a study, one must carefully consider all aspects of the methodology using the kinds of critical thinking skills that are discussed in this

Incorporating the research of H. W. Stevenson and S. Y. Lee, "Contexts of Achievements: A Study of American, Chinese, and Japanese Children," 1990, *Monographs of the Society for Research in Child Development*, 55 (Serial No. 221, Nos. 1–2).

book. It is rarely the case that a study is either valid or not. More often, strengths and weaknesses have to be considered, and we make a judgment about how much confidence to place in the findings.

The term *external validity* is used to indicate that the findings of the study can be generalized to the real world and do not merely apply to a contrived laboratory environment. Size and quality of the sample of participants can be important for external validity. Studies cannot investigate the behavior of all the people on the earth, so a sample of people, called the participants, is chosen for the investigation. To be able to make judgments about validity and to have a basis for making them is to have a precious skill that few people possess.

The concept of *validity* may also be applied to measures within studies and, in this context, it also refers to accuracy. For example, if a psychological test or scale that is supposed to measure depression accurately indicates the amount of depression people are experiencing, it would be considered a valid measure of depression. *Reliability* is a related concept. In earlier chapters we mentioned inter-rater reliability. Reliability means that a finding, or outcome, is repeatable. If two observers watch the same behavior and score it the same way, we say their observations are reliable. If a person takes a test, such as an IQ test, over again and the results are the same, we say that the test is reliable. It is important to understand that reliability and validity are not the same thing. If the fuel gauge on your car is stuck and always reads one-quarter of a tank, it is reliable but not valid, except in the coincidental case in which there really happens to be a quarter of a tank of fuel. This is an unusual example, but it illustrates the difference between reliability and validity. In psychology, reliability is often taken to be an indication of validity. If two observers code a behavior in the same category we know they are reliable and we usually use this as evidence that they are making valid observations. It is, of course, possible that the observations are not valid because both observers may be observing inaccurately in the same way, but this would not be a typical case.

There is enormous variability in the quality of the information about behavior available to you, whether you are among some library bookcases swatting back the cobwebs or dealing with another kind of web, the worldwide one. How much of it are you going to believe? This vast quantity of information is almost valueless to you unless you can evaluate the methodology and make a decision about the validity of the studies that underpin the information.

A reason why these issues have been discussed here is that this study, like most of the studies in this book, has a tightly woven research design that gives considerable justification to claims of external validity, within the confines of the practical restrictions to the study sample.

A CROSS-CULTURAL STUDY
OF SCHOOL ACHIEVEMENT

Harold Stevenson, Shin-Ying Lee, and their many coworkers (1990) provided us with a gorgeous study about school achievement of elementary school children in America, Taiwan, and Japan. Their study was designed to discover correlates of achievement in the context of school, but also in the home lives of children. We would like to be able to talk about *causes* of school achievement, but this is not an experiment, so cause-and-effect terms are inappropriate. In using the weaker word *correlates*, we understand that some of the correlates may well be causes, but this cannot be demonstrated without an experiment. Because of the magnitude of this investigation, the findings were spread over a number of individual journal articles. Needless to say, all the findings will not be discussed here, and much more can be discovered by reading the splendid original articles as well as reports of Stevenson's newer work (Stevenson, Chen, & Lee, 1993). For our discussion, we have selected findings that we thought might be of most interest to an American readership.

Previous to Stevenson and Lee's work, there had been descriptions of education in China and Japan, but these descriptions relied on unsystematic observations in schools and verbal reports from parents or school officials. These approaches can give some general information, but detailed comparisons of schools are impossible without numerical data. Stevenson and Lee collected vast amounts of data from students and parents in the Asian cultures and made comparisons with similarly collected data from America.

A city from each country was selected to be the site of the study: Minneapolis, Minnesota; Taipei, Taiwan; and Sendai, Japan. These cities were similar in population. Even considering national and cultural differences, they were similar in other ways. They were modern industrial cities supporting a broad range of manufacturing and commercial activities. Ten schools were chosen from each of the three cities. With the advice of local officials, these schools were chosen to be representative of the population of the city. Two first-grade classrooms as well as two fifth-grade classrooms were randomly selected from within each school. Permission had to be obtained before data collection could begin. It is interesting that in the Asian schools, permission to study the children was obtained in one-stop shopping from highly placed administrators. In America this was much more complicated because of national standards protecting the rights of human participants: school officials and each parent had to give permission. In order to ensure an adequate target sample, 863 parents in Minneapolis were contacted for permission. Only 38 refused.

The Participants

As mentioned in the first chapter, in order to do psychological research, particularly on humans, permission must also be obtained from a committee that has been set up to protect the rights of the humans who will be participants. Usually, in universities, these committees are made up of staff members from a variety of disciplines. The committee examines the details of research procedures, and if it appears that people might be harmed in any way, including psychologically, permission will not be given for the research to be conducted.

The total sample of kids in the first and fifth grades in three countries was 4,260. Some data were collected on all of them. Because of the practical difficulties of collecting detailed data from this number of participants, much of the data to be reported here comes from a smaller target sample of 240 kids in each city, as well as the mothers and teachers of these kids. This target sample consisted of 12 students from each classroom in the study. These children were two boys and two girls randomly selected from each of three groups: the upper, middle and lower third of scorers on a reading test given to all kids.

In Minneapolis, all but four children in the target sample were born in the United States, and approximately 1 percent of the sample was from minority families. Because they were all from Minneapolis, they were all urban kids. In summary, they were predominantly white, English-speaking, native-born city kids. This should immediately put your antennae up into the problem-detector mode. The most common initial response to this kind of sample is often something like "What is this? In spite of some random selection, this target sample is clearly unrepresentative of the diversity of people who live in America. Nothing important can be learned about America by only looking at these kids." Although this might be a common response, it is somewhat naïve and may not be the best way to look at the situation. It is important to remember that this study is trying to *compare* behavior in Taiwan, Japan, and America. The participants in Taiwan and Japan were Taiwanese and Japanese, respectively. They were ethnically uniform native-born speakers of their languages, and they were city kids. If Stevenson and Lee had gone to some American city where the population was more diverse—and this would have been easy to do—the comparison would not have been fair. If the American sample had included, for example, children who had not grown up speaking standard English, it would be difficult to argue that the test of reading that was given to first graders would have been a comparable assessment. Stevenson and Lee also make the point that because the American kids in the sample were native-born speakers of English, any unfavorable outcomes in American scores could not be the result of background differences within the American sample. This is particularly important because, sadly, it is still common in America that large proportions of kids who speak English as a second language also come from economically disadvantaged homes and may have cultural backgrounds that diverge from school curricula. The kids in Minneapolis are about as advantaged as one can get with a random sample in a large city. If they do not do as well as their Asian counterparts, it is very likely that the situation elsewhere in America is even worse. Cross-cultural evidence from within America has confirmed this (Steinberg, Dornbusch, & Brown, 1992).

"OK," one might say, "but why only city kids?" It seems likely that the constraint was a practical one. If Stevenson and Lee had tried to include kids from isolated farms, villages, and small and large cities, the study might well have become so arduous in the necessity to run from place to place that it could not be done at all. In order to be carried through to completion, studies have to fall within some practical and economic boundaries. For example, we could facetiously suggest that this study would have had better external validity if it had studied every single elementary school kid on the surface of the earth.

Data Collection

Researchers went to homes to interview mothers about attitudes concerning education. The questions were carefully constructed to avoid the problem that direct translation of words does not always exactly translate meaning. You will know this if you have ever tried to follow instructions literally translated from another language: "Please to undertake the front bottom side plate and hold it up in the air. . . ." Some of the questions in the interviews were open ended and some had predefined answers from which mothers could choose. The interviews contained about 200 items. Interview data were tabulated by native speakers of the language in question.

The same care was used in putting together a questionnaire for the teachers of the kids who were in the study. About 70 questions were formulated that asked about teaching style, classroom management, and daily schedules.

In additional interviews, the kids were asked to make a series of ratings to indicate their attitudes about homework, arithmetic, reading, and school attendance. They registered their agreement or disagreement by pointing to one of five faces, ranging from a smile to a frown. This method has frequently been used to quantify ratings from small children. It is particularly helpful in this study because it does not require a verbal response from the child. The kids were also given mathematics achievement tests and reading achievement tests.

Results

The scores on the mathematics achievement tests are presented in Figure 14.1.

These tests were fairly challenging, particularly for the first-grade students: the highest score was only 52 percent correct. By grade five, the high score was 88. The Taiwanese kids had the highest mean scores on the mathematics achievement test in first grade. You can see some evidence of this in the data by locating the peak, or mode, of the distribution and comparing it to the modes of the other countries. The Japanese were second, and the Americans were third. By fifth grade, the Japanese were first, the Taiwanese were second, and the Americans were third. Looking at the data it is easy to see that there is quite a bit of overlap of scores. The average scores, or means, are different, but quite a number of kids in each group scored well and quite a few scored poorly. Comparing the data of the first graders to the fifth graders, one can see that the three national groups seem to be separating by grade five, with the Japanese farther out in front and the Americans further behind.

The differences in the reading scores (not shown) were less pronounced. One reason may be that it is quite difficult to make a culture-fair test of reading when comparing beginning readers in Western and Asian cultures. American kids have to learn an alphabet of 26 characters. In contrast, Taiwanese kids have to learn approximately 3,000 characters, each of which is more complex than any letter in the alphabet. In order to read Japanese with reasonable literacy, kids also have to learn a large set of complex symbols. Although this symbol learning may make language learning more difficult initially, later progress may be facilitated for the Asians. In contrast, the American kids may learn the alphabet easily by singing the little alphabet song. However, when few letters represent many sounds, each letter must represent many different sounds. This can make subsequent learning difficult.

The mean scores for math and verbal skills do not give a particularly clear picture of what is happening. When there is so much variability among scores, it can be quite

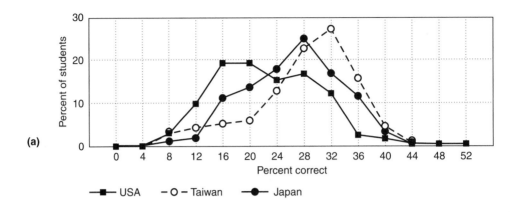

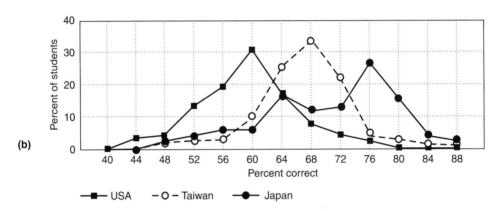

FIGURE 14.1   **(a) Grade 1 Summary Scores**   **(b) Grade 5 Summary Scores.**
Frequency distributions of summary scores obtained for mathematics by first and fifth
graders in each city.

difficult to extract the big picture by considering only the average scores. In this sort of
situation, the mean is an inadequate one-number summary. In order to get a clearer
picture of these data, Stevenson and Lee examined the nationalities of the 100 top
scorers and the 100 bottom-scoring kids on the vocabulary and reading test, as well as
the mathematics test. These data are shown in Figure 14.2.

An examination of Figure 14.2 shows the Americans being in the majority among
bottom scorers in reading. However, among the top scorers in reading, the picture
does not look as bad; Americans show up as a considerable proportion of the total bar.
In mathematics, however, there are many Americans in the bottom scorers and very
few in the top, particularly in fifth grade, where only one American student scored
among the top 100 students. The bar representing only one student is so thin that it
does not show at all on this graph.

These data are particularly interesting in the light of other data collected in the
study. Class sizes were larger in Japan and Taiwan than in the United States. In the

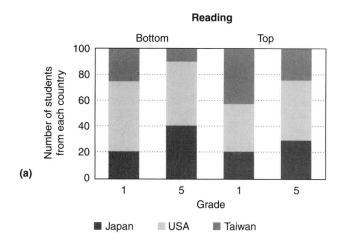

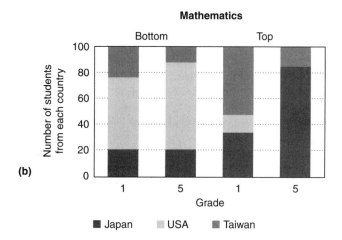

FIGURE 14.2   Number of Children Representing Each Nationality within the Top 100 and Bottom 100 Scorers in Reading and Mathematics Tests. The order in which the three countries occur in each bar makes no difference: the thing to examine is the *proportion* of each bar that is occupied by a given country. If there were no national differences, each country would have an equal share of each bar; we would expect to find about 33 kids from each country in the top 100 and the same in the bottom 100 for each test.

Asian countries first and fifth grades ranged in average size from 39 to 48 students, whereas in Minneapolis the average was between 21 and 23 students per class. This seems to contradict an idea that is almost common sense that smaller classes are associated with better learning. In contrast, more time in school is associated with better performance. When day and year length were combined, first graders in all three countries spent from 1,044 to 1,162 hours in school. However, fifth graders in Japan spent 1,466 hours per year, in Taiwan it was 1,655 hours per year, but in the United States fifth graders only spent 1,044 hours. It seems likely that this extra time spent in school played a role in some of the achievement test differences.

In Japan and Taiwan, all students have a curriculum established by the state. In the United States it is much more likely that school boards, principals, and teachers will create their own curriculum. In the Asian countries, all of the students pass to the next grade each year, and there is no special provision for slow learners. The philosophy seems to be that the faster ones will pull along the slow learners. It is also believed that the faster ones will benefit from hearing material repeated while waiting for the slower learners to catch up. In the United States slow learners tend to be isolated in remedial groups designed to help them along.

The research team also made over 1,000 observations of about 40 minutes each in the classrooms of the kids who were in the study. These observations were made according to a randomly generated schedule covering the school day to ensure that classes were not repeatedly observed at the same time each day. From these observations, estimates could be made of the number of hours spent each week on language-related learning and on math. These are presented in Table 14.1.

In the data for first grade, the U.S. sample looks quite similar to the Asian samples in language arts, but not in math. By the fifth grade students in Taiwan are spending a bit more time on the language arts, but the time spent on math in the U.S. classrooms has fallen even further behind both Asian countries. The poor performance of the Americans on the math achievement test is probably related to the lack of time on task. Not only did American kids spend less fifth-grade time on math and fewer hours in school each year, but they also spent less of their school time in academic activities as can be seen in Table 14.2.

The American percentages are lower than the Asian countries, but Stevenson and Lee also note that the U.S. fifth graders are spending even less time on academics than the U.S. first graders.

TABLE 14.1   Estimates of the Number of Hours Spent Each Week in Language Arts (Reading) and Mathematics

	UNITED STATES	TAIWAN	JAPAN
Grade 1			
Language Arts	10.5	10.4	8.7
Mathematics	2.7	4.0	5.8
Grade 5			
Language Arts	7.9	11.1	8.0
Mathematics	3.4	11.7	7.8

TABLE 14.2   Percentage of Time Spent on Academic Activities in School

	FIRST GRADERS	FIFTH GRADERS
United States	70%	64%
Taiwan	85%	92%
Japan	79%	87%

School and Home Environments

The interviews with the teachers showed that the teachers in the Asian countries had much less formal education than the American teachers, which implies that the kinds of differences seen in students were not a reflection of teacher education. In Minneapolis, all 40 of the teachers had college degrees, and 11 of them had graduate degrees. In Taiwan, most of the teachers had one extra year beyond high school, and only one had a bachelor's degree. About three-quarters of the Japanese teachers had bachelor's degrees, but only one had a graduate degree.

In seeking other factors that may have had an influence, Stevenson and Lee examined the data from the interviews with mothers and found that maternal employment was not related to child achievement in either grade in any of the three countries. At least in these samples, there is no support for the commonsense belief that working mothers put their kids at an academic disadvantage. The number of years of education that the parents had completed was not found to be useful in explanation of the cultural differences in child achievement. Low level of maternal education has often been singled out as a risk factor for the academic success in children within American culture, but considerable evidence suggests that this may be because low educational level has a strong positive correlation with another factor: poverty. When these influences are separated statistically, poverty has been found to be a larger problem than maternal educational level (Brooks-Gunn, Klebanov, & Duncan, 1996).

The home lives of the children were examined through interviews. Between the first and the fifth grades, time devoted to play declined sharply in the Asian countries and less sharply in Minneapolis. The Japanese kids watched the most television, followed by the Americans and the Taiwanese. The children themselves did not describe TV watching as something that they especially liked to do. Stevenson and Lee conclude that kids turn to TV because it is available, more than because they really enjoy it. Thirty-four percent of the American kids had chores to do around the house, whereas only 6 percent of the Taiwanese kids and 9 percent of the Japanese kids had chores. According to the Asian mothers, chores were purposely not assigned so that their kids would have more time for homework.

The Asian kids had more homework to do. The Japanese fifth-grade teachers estimated that the kids had an average of 37 minutes of homework per night; in Taiwan, the kids had 78 minutes per night; and the Minneapolis kids only had 20 minutes per night. Only 63 percent of the American fifth graders had their own desk and a nice quiet place to work, whereas 95 percent of the Taiwanese and 98 percent of the Japanese had their own workplace.

Attitudes toward school were assessed in several ways, but one of the most telling findings was that 50 percent of the Minneapolis mothers reported that their children had, at one time or another, simply refused to go to school on a particular day. This kind of refusal was reported by 11 percent of the mothers in Taiwan and 26 percent of the Japanese mothers.

The fifth-grade children were asked to rate themselves on how smart they were and on how good they were at school subjects. The results showed that the American kids were more likely than kids in the Asian countries to think that they were intelligent. They were also more likely to think that they were good at schoolwork in general and at math in particular. This is in marked contrast to the actual achievement scores of the Americans. An analysis of the math textbooks in the three countries suggested that the American math curriculum was easier, and this may be one reason why kids who are doing poorly in math can think that they are good at it. Specific math concepts are introduced later in American curricula than in the state-mandated Japanese curriculum.

Stevenson and Lee noted that perceptions of intelligence and other signs of high confidence among the American kids might be a factor in preventing them from working hard. American kids may think they do not have to work hard because they believe they are smart. There was no evidence, as is popularly believed, that the Taiwanese and Japanese children were particularly stressed about academics. They worked harder on academics in and out of school, and the results of this work was shown by their high placement on achievement tests. Crystal et al. (1994) showed that even among the highest-achieving high school students, Japanese and Taiwanese were less stressed than Americans. American students found stress in the high expectation to excel in athletic, social, and academic domains all at the same time.

Effort versus Innate Ability

The culture that surrounds the Asian students supports their work habits. Stevenson and Lee noted major differences between American and Asian students in the pervasive cultural beliefs about the causes of academic achievement. In psychology these beliefs are often called *attributions*, because behavior is attributed to, or thought to be a result of, a certain factor or factors.

The recognition that human beings can make changes in their own behavior has long been part of Taiwanese culture and is a basic tenet of the writings of Confucius. In this belief system, achievement is seen to be the result of hard work and persistence. An individual can change achievement levels by increasing effort. Japanese culture shares this belief system. Inborn individual differences are not considered to be important but, in contrast, individual effort is paramount. This is well summarized by the Japanese saying *Yareba dekiru*, which means, "If you try hard, you can do it." In Japan, lack of achievement is likely to be interpreted as failure to work hard enough, rather than as the lack of inborn ability or other insurmountable obstacles.

The picture can be quite different in America. American culture is very diverse, but for the last 100 years at least, there has been a strong undercurrent of belief in the importance of inborn individual differences. The American view of achievement is likely to give considerable weight to factors such as genetics and childhood environment and to place little emphasis on sheer effort. The data collected by Stevenson and Lee reflect these cultural differences.

Mothers in all three cultures were asked to rate the extent of their agreement with interview items that stated that all kids have the same amount of reading and math ability. They also rated statements about the amount of overall inborn ability that kids have. American mothers were least likely to think that all kids had the same natural abilities and most likely to think that children were born with certain amounts of reading and math ability. When mothers were asked to rate other factors that were involved in school success, American mothers gave lower ratings to effort than to other things, such as having good teachers, study habits, curriculum, and home environment. The Asian mothers put good teaching ahead of effort, but after that, effort was the most important consideration.

Humorist Garrison Keillor talks of his mythical home town of Lake Wobegone, Minnesota, by saying that "all of the children are above average, each and every one of them." The statistical joke that *all* of the kids cannot be above average is obvious. Stevenson and Lee found very much the same sort of thinking among mothers. In mean ratings from all three cultural groups, mothers placed their kids at or above average on cognitive abilities such as memory, learning, verbal ability, and intelligence. Isn't that just like Mom? However, the American mothers' ratings were farther above average than either of the Asian groups. American mothers also rated their children more positively on personality characteristics such as being self-confident, sociable, curious, creative, persistent, and obedient.

When the children were asked about the importance of effort, American kids were more likely than Asian kids to consider inborn ability to be more important than effort. Stevenson and Lee believed that this typically American pattern of attributing academic success to inborn ability might result in a confident child who is successful in many situations. However, this is a double-edged sword. An American child who has poor academic achievement may cease trying, and find excuses for failure such as inadequate academic environment or low inborn academic ability. The Asian child, in contrast, might be much more likely to respond to poor academic achievements with an increase in effort, as dictated by the culture. Increased effort is likely to be met with increased success and can lead to an upward achievement spiral.

Mothers were asked to rate their satisfaction with the performance of their children in school and with the job that the school was doing in providing education. In strong contrast to the Asian mothers, American mothers were satisfied with the performance of the kids and with the job that the school was doing in providing education. It is important to remember that these same American children did less well on achievement tests, particularly in the area of math.

CONCLUSIONS

Although our discussion has only brushed the surface of this intensive and extensive study, a story does emerge. It is the story of a part of American culture where unchangeable inborn factors are believed to play a major role in academic achievement. Effort is seen to be less important. In American culture parents and kids are satisfied with lower levels of achievement. Kids spend less time on task, both in and out of school, and end up with lower comparative levels of academic achievement.

We might speculate that the American belief systems and educational practices have managed to survive in the past because there was so little competition from Asian countries and other rapidly developing parts of the world. If so, we can expect dramatic changes in the very near future as the kids who were in this study become adults and begin to compete in a world economy.

REFERENCES

Brooks-Gunn, J., Klebanov, P., & Duncan, G. (1996). Ethnic differences in children's intelligence test scores: Role of economic deprivation, home environment, and maternal characteristics. *Child Development, 67,* 396–408.

Crystal, D., Chen, C., Fuligni, A., Stevenson, H., Hsu, C., Ko, J., Kitamura, S., & Kimura, S. (1994). Psychological maladjustment and academic achievement: A cross-cultural study of Japanese, Taiwanese and American high school students. *Child Development, 65,* 738–753.

Steinberg, L., Dornbusch, S., & Brown, B. (1992). Ethnic differences in adolescent achievement: An ecological perspective. *American Psychologist, 47,* 723–729.

Stevenson, H. W., Chen, C., & Lee, S. Y. (1993). Mathematics achievement of Chinese, Japanese and American children: Ten years later. *Science, 259,* 53–58.

Stevenson, H. W., & Lee, S. Y. (1990). Contexts of achievements: A study of American, Chinese, and Japanese children. *Monographs of the Society for Research in Child Development, 55* (Serial No. 221, Nos. 1–2).

CHAPTER 15

GOLDEN OLDIES: WHAT IT'S LIKE TO BE IN YOUR SEVENTIES

This interesting and engaging study has its origins in one of the oldest and most successful longitudinal studies in psychology. Terman's (1925) study of gifted individuals began in the early 1920s and has continued to follow the same talented men and women throughout their life span. The investigation by Edwin Shneidman described in this chapter takes a sample of the "termites," an affectionate name for the participants in Terman's research, and looks at how they're doing in their seventies. Shneidman states that since the mid-nineteenth century, the definition of what is "old" has been extended in years. Being in your fifties or sixties is no longer seen as old, and being in your seventies could be seen as a "pleasant plateau, even a time of considerable growth, and certainly a time of reasonable and sustained happiness" (Shneidman, 1989). As we enter the twenty-first century, the U.S. population is graying or aging; that is, the average age of an American is becoming older. This is certainly a result of many factors including improvements in health care, lifestyle, and education. In addition the number of children in a typical family is less than it was earlier in the century. We have fewer kids, but adults are living longer. This is a prescription for a longer life and a great deal of time for individuals in the postretirement epoch of life.

Shneidman asserts that there are those who see life in the seventies in quite negative terms, marked by pessimism, health problems, death of loved ones, isolation and loneliness, and depression. A much more optimistic view states that this decade of life can afford people the chance for growth, freedom, and increased opportunities in a number of domains. This is the question that was explored in this investigation—*What is the quality of life as people move through their seventies?* Instead of just speculating or drawing conclusions from isolated cases, Shneidman initiated a program to identify a sample of people in their seventies and explore their lives in some detail. The study described in this chapter is a preliminary study, and as such has limitations. However it serves to show how an investigation can use innovative methods and focus on an age range that has received marginal attention. Obviously, more research needs to be done,

Incorporating the research of E. S. Shneidman, "The Indian Summer of Life: A Preliminary Study of Septuagenarians," 1989, *American Psychologist, 44,* pp. 684–694.

but this inquiry by Shneidman provides us with interesting data and ideas for the future. Because the sample of seventy-year-olds are Termites, we will first describe the Terman study.

THE TERMAN STUDY

The Terman Study began in the early 1920s. This was a study to find out as much as possible about gifted children and to follow them regularly throughout their lives. The Terman sample (1,528 males and females) were students who were recommended by their teachers and who obtained IQs over 140 on the Stanford-Binet Intelligence Test. This IQ score is above the 99th percentile and represents very superior intellectual or cognitive functioning. Percentile ranks are commonly used to translate raw scores into scores that can be easily understood. A percentile rank indicates the percentage of scores that lie below a given score. A person who obtains a percentile rank score on the SAT of 85 has achieved a score that is higher than 85 percent of people who take the SAT. Terman was interested in assessing what the children were like on a number of dimensions and in following them at regular intervals throughout their lives. Data were obtained on their physical, emotional, and psychological development, home and family background, social and educational history, personality profiles, parental ratings, vocational interests, academic achievement scores, and other demographic, social, personal, and educational information. These participants were contacted at regular intervals so that aspects of their lives could be evaluated. Reports of the Termites are available in articles by Terman (1925, 1940), Oden (1968), and Sears (1977). Shneidman reports that in 1980, 1,200 of the 1,528 participants were alive, and the Terman Study was still actively involved with 900 participants. It is amazing for a study that began some 60 years ago to have maintained contact with approximately 75 percent of the living participants.

When this study began in the 1920s it was commonly assumed that mental ability was associated with physical weakness. The prevalent view of the 1920s was that there was an intellectual nerd type of person who was likely to be physically frail, prone to "mental" problems, a poor athlete, and marginally successful in the world. A "just the facts" analysis of the overall Terman findings is that the termites have generally grown up to be cognitively, emotionally, and physically healthy and very successful in many domains of life experience.

SHNEIDMAN'S TERMITES

The group of Termites in this study was males residing in and around Los Angeles. Shneidman chose not to study women because women Termites were the focus of several other studies, and given limited resources he thought it was best to focus on males instead of dealing with smaller numbers of both sexes. This is not an unusual decision, especially when researchers are beginning to focus on an untapped area of study and are not in the first instance interested in sex differences. The male participants were 45 Caucasian college graduates with business or professional backgrounds. Not all 45 participants were available to engage in all phases of the study. This longitudinal study contacted the participants at five intervals during the decade of their seventies (1981, 1983, 1985, 1986, and 1987). During each of the five contacts information was gathered on various aspects of their lives. You should recognize this is a limited sample. They were very bright males, all successful, all living around Los Angeles. However, one can still derive important information from this sample, and these data can be helpful in designing other, more representative, studies. Even though this is a limited sample, one can still learn a great deal that may be applicable to other segments of the population. It is likely that Shneidman's Termites will show the best outcomes that could be expected, and replication with other participant groups is certainly a necessary next step.

Personality Assessment

Twenty-three of the participants were given the Minnesota Multiphasic Personality Inventory (MMPI). This instrument is the dominant self-report clinical assessment of psychopathology measure in use today. It is an empirically keyed inventory that was developed to avoid many of the difficulties found with previous content-keyed measures. There are important differences between these two types of keying in self-report questionnaire development.

The earliest measures were content-keyed, which means that the test items reflect the composition of what is being assessed. For example, "I enjoy reading "(T-F) is a content-keyed questionnaire item that measures whether you like to read (responding T) or whether you prefer not to read (responding F). A problem with this type of item is that testees can figure out what the item is measuring by just reading it. This is not a problem if you assume the testee will be truthful. However, individuals may complete personality/clinical questionnaires in evaluative situations where certain responses are seen to be desirable. For example, in assessing the mental health status of recruits for the military in World War I, the Woodworth Personal Data Sheet, a very early content-keyed personality/clinical questionnaire, was used. At the time there was a great deal of patriotism, and many young men wanted to enlist in the military and go to war. The content-keyed Woodworth had very transparent items clearly reflecting the content of what they were measuring (e.g., "I have the habit of wetting my bed at night"). Obviously the military would not select you for service if you responded "true" to this and other related items. The recruits could easily see what each questionnaire item was measuring, and if they wanted to go "over there" to fight the Germans it would be very easy to alter their responses to portray a problem-free soldier. In the war in Vietnam the military had just the opposite problem. Significant number of draftees did not want to go to war because they disagreed with American policy in Southeast Asia. However, the mental health screening questionnaire in use was now the MMPI, an empirically keyed questionnaire that made it difficult for individuals to falsify their personal adjustment.

The MMPI and other modern personality and clinical assessment questionnaires are composed of a number of scales that measure dimensions of personality. For example, the MMPI has 10 clinical scales that assess depression, schizophrenia, mania, and other clinical features of personality. On the MMPI testees could not easily appear to be mentally ill (i.e., "fake bad") or appear to have excellent mental health status (i.e., "fake good") because there is a lack of relevant content material in the questionnaire items. Empirical keying means that questionnaire items are selected on the basis of whether they discriminate on the criteria they are measuring, not on their specific content. For example, if you are attempting to measure depression in an empirical manner, you might select a group of individuals who have the diagnosis (a medical label) of depression and a group of "normals" that never had a psychiatric diagnosis. Next you would give each group hundreds of potential questionnaire items. As an empirical test builder you are looking for the items that clearly discriminate between the depression and normal groups, that is, items to which most normals respond "true" and many in the depressed group respond "false" and vice versa. Those items that meet this criterion of discriminating between groups would be good items for an empirically keyed questionnaire. Notice that the content of the items has nothing to do with selecting it. An item might say "I like to go to the zoo" or "I have a good appetite"—if the depressed group generally says "false" and the normal group says "true," you've got some good items to use on your Depression Scale. A bunch of these together becomes your Depression Scale. A major advantage for empirically keyed questionnaires is that the item doesn't give away what it is measuring, items on such scales are said to be "subtle." If testees can't figure out what is being assessed, it is much more difficult for them to manage the impression they make, that is "fake good" or "fake bad." In contrast, content-keyed questionnaires, in which items are obvious, should be used with caution. This is especially important when individual questionnaire takers are in evaluative situations where it is advantageous for them to present a favorable image of themselves (e.g., they are applying for a job that they want) or to present an unfavorable image of themselves (e.g., they do not want to be selected for service in the military). In addition to being empirically keyed, the MMPI has very favorable outcomes in terms of validity (it is accurately measuring the personality and clinical dimensions on its scales) and reliability (it is a stable measure that can be counted on to yield consistent outcomes over time).

In Shneidman's sample 23 men, aged 70 to 83, completed the MMPI, which was computer scored. The MMPI profile that emerged was a pattern indicative of depression as a primary symptom. The depression was not of major magnitude, but within the mild to moderate levels. In addition, the profiles suggested concerns over health and somatic issues. The MMPI profiles were not seen to be indicative of psychopathology. Shneidman split the 23 MMPI participants into four age groups (age 70–73, age 74–76, age 77–79, and age 80–83). The typical scores for the three groups in their seventies are quite similar, but the group in their early eighties shows a significantly higher score for depression on the MMPI. Reviewing the specific items for this group of eighty-year-olds suggests they have physical complaints and general distress, along with themes of generalized depression. The data indicate that, in this group, turning eighty is an important milestone for the emergence of some significant psychological issues.

Interviews and Concordances

The interview sessions conducted in Shneidman's project took place over a 7-year period and had 11 lawyers as participants. Shneidman used a very interesting strategy to make sense of the interview data. The approach was to compare words used by participants in the interview to a concordance, which is a list of all words in the interviews, in alphabetical order. This approach is used by scholars in the humanities in the analysis of literature to gain information about the thinking of the author. The actual mechanics of how this was accomplished was as follows; interviews were tape recorded and transcribed into a word processing program. Next a special computer program was used to calculate word frequency totals and to develop concordances. Shneidman believed we could learn about a great deal about participants through an analysis of their language during interviews that took place during their seventies. As a perspective in looking at this form of analysis, you should know that there are approximately 300,000 words in the Random House Dictionary. Herman Melville used 17,560 different words to write *Moby Dick*. Shneidman's participants used 11,659 different words in their interview sessions. This approach to the analysis of qualitative, subjective interview data (i.e., words) has great value because the participant's language is translated into data that are objective and quantified. In a real sense this procedure translates fluid, subjective data of language into a quantifiably numerical measure. The overall data across the decade of the seventies are depicted in Figure 15.1, adapted from Shneidman (1989).

As the figure illustrates there was a decline in number of total words spoken by participants in their late seventies from the period of their early seventies. The data for

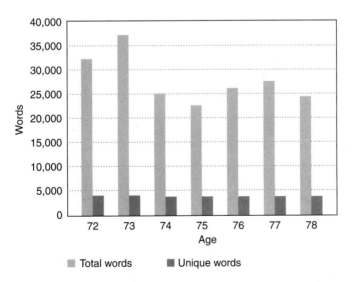

FIGURE 15.1   Number of Total and Unique Words Used in Interviews

unique words also show a decline from around 4,000 words for participants in their early seventies to a bit over 3,000 words for those in their late seventies. Reviewing the concordance, it is possible to determine what an individual's language tells us about lifestyle. In order to do this Shniedman uses Robert Sears (1977) categorization of six major areas of life experience: occupation, family life, friendship, cultural life, service to society, and joy in living. In addition to the Sears' categories, Shneidman adds "health concerns" to the list. Shneidman employed the concordance method to objectively categorize the words of his participants into the seven relevant groups. The words obtained from the interviews were coded into the seven categories. These data, showing the percentage of total words and the percentage of unique words, are displayed in Figure 15.2, adapted from Shneidman (1989).

As the figure shows, the participants spoke largely about their jobs, families, and health status. Their language was not much concerned with friends, service to others, or joy in living. The health category was interesting because it had a large number of unique words, especially medical terms. The data clearly showed that work and family were important, but health emerged as a growing topic of conversation and concern. This can be seen more clearly by examining changes that occurred over time during the eighth decade in the interviews of these men. In Table 15.1, adapted from Shneidman (1989), one sees the specific changes in language focus across the seventies.

Examining this table leads one to conclude that as "health talk" goes up, "family talk" goes down, and "job talk" drops significantly. Leisure pursuits, travel, and cultural concerns remain fairly constant. The remaining three categories—friends, community

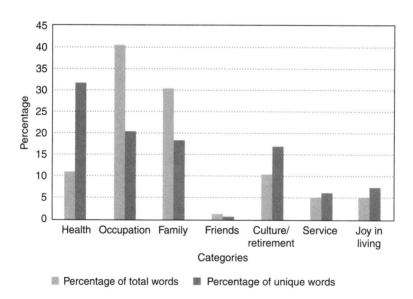

FIGURE 15.2   Percentage of Total and Unique Words in Life Experience Categories

TABLE 15.1   Total Words in Areas of Life Experience

AGE	HEALTH	JOB	FAMILY	FRIENDS	CULTURE & RETIREMENT	SERVICE	JOY IN LIVING
72	95	607	431	26	116	80	74
73	139	682	336	16	177	63	47
74	82	413	285	18	103	34	39
75	89	292	303	28	132	39	40
76	313	353	294	15	96	41	44
77	177	442	350	19	139	33	49
78	130	287	271	22	94	30	29

From Shneidman, 1989.

service, and joy in living comprised a very small amount of interview data and tended to remain constant across the period. In looking at these data, in light of the MMPI findings, showing that turning eighty represented a major negative shift, Shneidman (1989) stated:

> . . . the 70s seem almost like a hiatus, a time before total retirement because of poor health or lowered energy or before catastrophic loss of spouse—like an Indian Summer, a last stretch of rather pleasant weather before the onset of an irreversible winter's frosting. (p. 692)

Shneidman is fully aware that the data in this study were preliminary and that any interpretations should be made with caution. This sample was not broadly representative of humankind; it was a bright, educated, successful group. It is only composed of men. One wonders how the female Termites would have fared. This is characteristic of the research venture: information is discovered and opportunities for follow-up, replication, and extension are made clear. For these participants, the eighth decade of life is seen to be a benign period with no marked diminishment in intellect or vocabulary. One can certainly observe a slowing down, but being in the seventies doesn't represent the stereotypic portrait of problem aging. An interesting observation among these participants was that none of the individuals was completely retired, and they all preferred to continue working. It may be that continued involvement and use of cognitive, social, and personal skills serve us well in maintaining a healthy adaptation. Shneidman suggests that the notion of self-fulfilling prophecy may help explain what is going on. Our ability to keep doing something tells us that we can, in fact, do it, and performing it further tells us that we remain capable. This style of behavior and thinking may serve as prevention for the aging process and its stereotypes. As a reality check Shneidman (1989) notes:

> Indian Summer is not real summer. During the Indian Summer of life there are many premonitions of the imminent winter in which one is embedded, and there is a painful

awareness of one's inescapable death-bound plight. . . . For this reason, a pleasant stretch of weather in the late Fall is doubly welcome, and we enjoy the rays of sun while they last, suppressing our certain knowledge of the threat of what lies beyond the turn. (p. 693)

Our society has touted the importance of love to sustain us in life, but may have missed the equally important value of work and achievement. One of Shneidman' participants who was approaching the end of his seventies noted "If I can't get out to do the weeding and the heavy pruning and climb up in my trees and get the high fruit, then I'll feel I'm side tracked and out of the stream of life." In many ways the data from this investigation give credence to Freud's assertion of the importance of "love and work" in living a long, productive, and meaningful life.

REFERENCES

Oden, M. H. (1968). The fulfillment of promise: 40-year follow-up of the Terman Gifted Group. *Genetic Psychology Monographs*, 3–93.

Sears, R. S. (1977). Sources of life satisfaction of the Terman gifted men. *American Psychologist, 32*, 119–128.

Shneidman, E. S. (1984). Personality and "success" among a selected group of lawyers. *Journal of Personality Assessment, 48*, 609–616.

Shneidman, E. S. (1989). The Indian summer of life: A preliminary study of septuagenarians. *American Psychologist, 44*, 684–694.

Terman, L. M. (1925). *Genetic studies of genius: I. Mental and physical traits of 1000 gifted children*. Stanford, CA: Stanford University Press.

Terman, L. M. (1940). Psychological approaches to the biography of genius. *Science, 92*, 293–301.

CHAPTER 16

KIDS SAY THE DARNDEST THINGS

Memory was a topic of research within psychology before the beginning of scientific psychology over 100 years ago. One of the most surprising findings of recent decades is the extent to which memories can be modified by events that happen subsequently. You will have some hint of this if you have ever heard a friend relating a past incident that included you as a participant. As you listen to your friend's account, you find yourself thinking, "That isn't what happened, that's not the way I remember it."

RECALLING AN ACCIDENT

One of the most formative classic pieces of research about the manipulation of memory was done by Loftus and Palmer (1974). This study demonstrated that memory was unlike a video recorder; it was not a faithful or objective record of what happened. Instead, they found that memory was reconstructive: some aspects of our memory were shown to be accurate, but later events were merged with some existing memories, changing their content.

In an experiment, Loftus and Palmer showed adults a film of a car accident. Following this, participants wrote a description of what they had seen and answered some questions about it. One key question was: "About how fast were the cars going when they *contacted* each other?" Different groups of participants were given different versions of this question. Although some were asked the question with *contacted* as the verb, for other participants this word was replaced with one of the following: *hit*, *bumped*, *collided*, or *smashed*. The speed estimates given by the participants as answers to the question were a dependent variable. These estimates varied depending on the word that had been used in the question. Participants who were asked about the speed as the cars *contacted* each other gave an average speed estimate of 32 miles per hour. Other

Incorporating the research of M. D. Leichtman and S. J. Ceci, "The Effects of Stereotypes and Suggestions on Preschoolers' Reports," 1995, *Developmental Psychology, 31*, pp. 568–578.

words resulted in successively faster estimates, culminating in *smashed*, which resulted in a 41 mph average estimate.

A week later, participants were asked to recall the film and to answer another group of questions. Memory was operationally defined as the responses that participants made to questions about past events. One of the questions asked was, "Did you see any broken glass?" There was no broken glass in the film, but most participants who had heard the word *smashed* in the initial phase of the study also remembered broken glass that was not really there. This nicely illustrates what is meant by reconstructive memory. When we refer back to memories of past events, what we retrieve is a patchwork composed of things that really happened, things that have been changed a bit, and things that were added later. Memory is not like a photograph, unchanged in storage across time. Rather, it is a project constantly under reconstruction.

PRESUPPOSITIONS

In a subsequent study, Loftus (1975) further investigated memory reconstruction as a function of additional information tucked into questions. This extra information was called a presupposition. For example, in the sentence "Did it hurt when the vicious dog bit you?" the question is *"Did it hurt?"* but there is also a presupposition that the dog was vicious. You are not being *asked* if the dog was vicious, you are being *told* this. You are asked about being hurt. Loftus (1975) showed participants a film involving a car hitting a baby carriage. Some participants were asked if they had seen a barn, although there was no barn in the film. Other participants were asked if there was a station wagon parked in front of the barn. In this latter case, the question asked directly about a station wagon and the barn was a presupposition: these participants were not asked about the barn—they were told about it.

When asked a week later, 29.2 percent of the participants who were given false presuppositions, such as the barn, claimed that they actually remembered the nonexistent object. In comparison, surprisingly, only 15.6 percent of people who had false objects introduced as direct questions—for example, "Did you see a barn?"—remembered false objects. Lastly, only 8.7 percent of a control group, which had not been given any false information, remembered false objects. The wider implications of these findings ought to be of great interest to a society that depends on testimony from memory.

These are among many clear research demonstrations of the reconstructive nature of memory. We observe events, but the memory we have of them includes more than perfectly stored observations. Even completely false information can be included merely because it happened to be available around the time of the event. We all feel that there are some things we *know*; things that we remember so clearly that we have no doubt about the objectivity or truthfulness of our memory. The studies of Loftus and others indicate that we should not be so sure of ourselves. What does this say about objectivity? If we accept these research findings as having external validity, it becomes nonsense to instruct someone to "be objective" about past events, as if objectivity were something that could be turned on or off at will. The studies of memory suggest quite different conclusions: the memories in which we put so much stock are mosaics of real and false information.

These observations ought to undermine some of our confidence in the truth of our memories. Usually this does not matter very much. Who cares if we remember that there was potato salad at the family picnic last summer and, in fact, it was a fruit salad? Aunt Mildred may care when you rave about the potato salad she never made. The worst-case scenario might have you remembering a salad as good when it was not and, as a result, Aunt Mildred makes it "especially for you" every time there is a family gathering.

Setting the salads aside, there are cases where memory and confidence in memory can be a matter of life or death. When we take account of research findings, this becomes a scary proposition. Courts of law often consider that eyewitness testimony is a truthful account of events, particularly if it holds up under grueling cross-examination. In the time since the memory studies of the 1970s, psychologists have increasingly questioned this assumption. In the studies discussed above, the participants were adults. However, in the past decade there have been a number of high-profile cases in which the recollections of children have played a pivotal role. If adult memory is questionable, what about the memories of children? The research literature in this area shows, unsurprisingly, that memories of younger kids are even more vulnerable to false information than those of older kids (see Ceci & Bruck, 1993, for a review of the literature).

Michelle Leichtman and Stephen Ceci (1995) identified two classes of reasons for false memories in children: cognitive factors and social factors. Children have difficulty in distinguishing the sources of their stored memories. Younger children are particularly likely to remember performing an act when, in reality, they only repeatedly imagined performing it. This is called *source misattribution*, and it is an example of a cognitive factor. Social factors include bribes, threats, or feeling pressured to respond in ways that will please certain adults. When children are required to testify in court, both cognitive and social influences may be present, setting the stage for false memories. Cognitive factors will operate in court, where it is routine that children are questioned in detail and at great length. It is easy to imagine that some of the questions will contain presuppositions or will be leading questions. Repeated leading questions can make particular scenarios so familiar to children that they become incorporated into the child's memory. In one case involving child sexual abuse, a mother indicated that her daughter had been interviewed between 30 and 50 times by county officials (Humphrey, 1985). It is also easy to imagine a role for social factors: a child might figure out which responses please the adults. The child may give those responses at higher frequencies. A key child witness in a Texas murder case changed her testimony saying, "Originally I think I told police just what I saw. But the more questions I was asked, the more confused I became. I answered questions I wasn't certain about because I wanted to help the adults" (quoted in Leichtman & Ceci, 1995).

Leichtman and Ceci (1995) conducted an experiment in which they studied the recollections of children about a prearranged event. This has become known as the *Sam Stone Study*, because an enactment was staged for the children in which a man called Sam Stone visited their day-care center.

Participants

The participants were 176 preschool children who were enrolled in private day-care centers. The children represented a wide range of socioeconomic status and ethnic groups. The children belonged to one of two age groups: early preschoolers (3- and 4-year-olds) and later preschoolers (5- and 6-year-olds). They spent their days in classrooms consisting of eight children each. Whole classrooms, not individual children, were randomly assigned to an experimental condition. This was done to prevent children within a single class from talking with each other and discovering that different things were going on for different children.

Procedures

There were eight different groups of kids in the study. There was a control group and three experimental groups for the young preschoolers and the same four groups for the older preschoolers. The procedure for the actual visit of Sam Stone was repeated in each of the eight classrooms. A confederate acted the role of Sam. *Confederate*, in this context, means someone who works for the researcher as an actor, pretending to be someone else. You will see this again in later chapters where, for example, confederates pretend to be additional participants in studies. These confederates are sometimes making behavior observations of the real participants. By pretending to be participants themselves, they are able to do so without the awareness of the real participants. In this study the confederate, Sam, was not collecting data, but was playing the role of a classroom visitor. Sam entered the classroom during a story reading session and said hello to the adult in charge. He was introduced to the children. He commented upon the story being read by saying, "I know that story; it's one of my favorites!" He walked around the perimeter of the room, waved to the children, and left. His visit lasted about 2 minutes.

Neither the young nor the older control group had prior knowledge of Sam Stone's visit. Following the visit they were interviewed once a week for 4 weeks. In these interviews they were asked questions about what Sam had done during the visit to their school, but they were given no suggestions or additional information about Sam or his visit.

The *stereotype* experimental groups, one younger and one older, were told about Sam Stone before his visit in a manner designed to create a stereotype of Sam's personality. A research assistant went to these groups once a week for a month before the visit and, while playing with the children, told three different scripted stories about Sam. Over the course of the four visits, these children heard 12 stories that presented a consistent stereotype of Sam. In each story Sam was shown to be a kind person, but somewhat accident prone. In one of these stories, for example, the children were told that Sam Stone had visited the research assistant the previous night and asked to borrow a Barbie doll. On the way down the stairs he tripped and broke the doll, but he was having it fixed. In other versions of the story Sam did other things. They were told he lost a borrowed pen and replaced it; spilled soda on the research assistant but cleaned it up, and accidentally took some board game pieces home but brought them back. After 4 weeks of stereotype building, this group had an identical 2-minute visit from Sam Stone in which he behaved as he did in all groups. Following Sam Stone's visit, this group was treated like the control group in being asked neutral, suggestion-free questions at 1-week intervals for 4 weeks.

For the *suggestion* experimental groups, no attempt was made to create a stereotype of Sam Stone in the month before his visit. Instead, following the visit, at 1-week intervals, the children were asked questions that contained two false suggestions about Sam Stone's visit: that he had ripped a book and that he had gotten dirt on a teddy bear. Children were asked, for example, "When Sam got the bear dirty, did he do it on purpose or was it an accident?" and "Was Sam Stone happy or sad that he got the bear dirty?"

The children in the remaining experimental condition received both the stereotyping information about Sam's clumsiness before his visit and the leading questions once a week after the event. They were called the *stereotype-plus-suggestion* groups. These children were exposed to a stereotypical expectation about Sam for the month before the visit as well as misinformation planted in the month following the visit.

At the completion of the experimental conditions described above, all children were exposed to a final interview conducted by a new person who was not present during Sam's visit or the experimental procedures. The quality of their memory for events was operationally defined as the accuracy of their responses to interview questions. In this interview, the same questions were asked of all children. In this test of memory, the children were first asked to describe, in their own words, the happenings on the day of Sam's visit to their class. Once this free narrative was done, children were asked specific probing questions about whether they had "heard something" about the book or the teddy bear or had seen Sam dealing with either of these objects. If children indicated that they had seen Sam do something, which, in fact, he had not done, other questions were asked to test the strength of belief in the memory, such as "You didn't really see him do this, did you?"

Results

The final interviews were videotaped, and data were produced by having the children's responses coded. The coders were people who did not know which condition the children had been in. Twenty percent of the tapes were randomly selected and recoded by another rater to check for rater reliability. Agreement between raters was found to be 90 percent, certainly high enough to indicate that raters were sufficiently reliable. The coders were looking to see if individual children made false statements either during free narrative or pointed questioning.

As can be seen from Figure 16.1, there were striking differences in the extent to which children made false allegations in their unguided recall about what happened during Sam Stone's visit.

No children from the control group or from the stereotype group made any false statements about the visit in free recall. However, the group that had been given after-the-fact suggestions about tearing the book and soiling the teddy bear did include these events in their free narrative. It is important to remember that these suggestions were presuppositions inserted in questions that were, ostensibly, asking about something else. A stereotype was established for two groups in which Sam was clumsy, likely to spill and break things. It is interesting that the stereotype alone was not enough to result in false

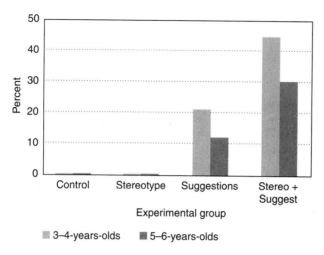

FIGURE 16.1 **Percentage of Children Making False Allegations.** Statements were made during the free recall narrative at the beginning of the fifth interview.

events being reported in free recall. Yet, Figure 16.1 shows that in the *stereotype-plus-suggestion* group, it had an additive effect: levels of false allegations were higher than in the *suggestion-only* group. The stereotype procedure did not have an effect on its own but it made a difference when combined with subsequent suggestions. In these latter two groups there was also a difference between the younger and the older children, with the younger ones being more likely to include false stories in their narratives.

Figure 16.2 shows the control group outcomes for the procedures that followed free narratives in the final interview. These were responses to probing questions about (1) whether the child believed that the book or the teddy bear incidents had occurred, (2) whether they had seen either of them, and (3) whether they would insist on the reality of the events. Because the control group had been given no formal exposure to any of the false events, the expectation was that they would not make false assertions, even when pointed questions were asked. As expected, only a few such responses were seen in this group. Although these children had not been previously exposed to false information about the book and the teddy bear, a few of them were prepared to say they remembered these false events. They had first heard about the book and the bear minutes before, in final interview questions.

Even though the stereotype group did not mention false events during free recall, Figure 16.3 shows that they became likely to assert the reality of false events under pointed questioning. As in all these data, there is an age trend favoring better memory for the older children.

In the suggestion group the levels were even higher as shown in Figure 16.4. Over half of the 3- and 4-year-olds reported one or two false memories under pointed

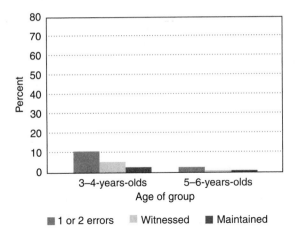

FIGURE 16.2   Erroneous Answers Given by Control Group (No Stereotype; No Suggestions). *1 or 2 errors* indicates that the child asserted that a false event really happened. *Witnessed* indicates that the child claimed to have observed the false event. *Maintained* indicates that the child insisted on having observed the event, despite the attempt at dissuading: "You didn't really see him do this, did you?"

questioning, and there was a noticeable increase in the percentage of younger children who claimed to have witnessed a false event.

Lastly, Figure 16.5 shows the effects of having some training in a stereotype about Sam's personality and then, over time, having a number of embedded suggestions made that are congruent with the stereotype. As in the other groups, there is an age trend when the two age groups are compared. Particularly in the younger children, there are strikingly high levels of reporting false beliefs, claiming to have witnessed the event, and maintaining this stance under gentle, but adverse, questioning.

These are important findings. We know, from earlier studies, that even adult memory can be influenced by presuppositions, but this study presents clear evidence that the memory of a child, particularly a young child, can be greatly influenced especially when previously held stereotypes are supported by subsequent suggestions. The design of the study is very clever in being able to create stereotypes about a person previously unknown to the children and in being able to follow this up with congruent suggestions. These findings are not only important for what they tell us about reconstructive memory; they also bear directly on the issue of children testifying in courtrooms. Children quickly pick up stereotypes. Imagine a child who witnesses a crime committed by a person of an ethnic group different from the child itself. Further imagine that the child has grown up in a home where there is substantial prejudice against

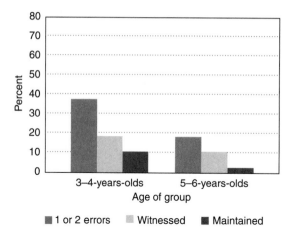

FIGURE 16.3 Erroneous Answers Given by Stereotype Group (Stereotype; No Suggestions). *1 or 2 errors* indicates that the child asserted that a false event really happened. *Witnessed* indicates that the child claimed to have observed the false event. *Maintained* indicates that the child insisted on having observed the event, despite the attempt at dissuading: "You didn't really see him do this, did you?"

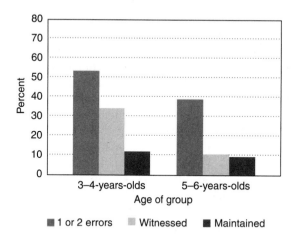

FIGURE 16.4 Erroneous Answers Given by Suggestion Group (No Stereotype; Suggestions). *1 or 2 errors* indicates that the child asserted that a false event really happened. *Witnessed* indicates that the child claimed to have observed the false event. *Maintained* indicates that the child insisted on having observed the event, despite the attempt at dissuading: "You didn't really see him do this, did you?"

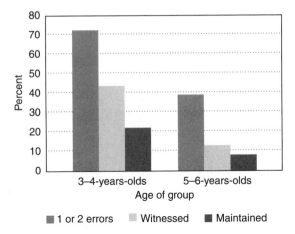

**FIGURE 16.5   Erroneous Answers Given by
Stereotype Plus Suggestion Group (Stereotype;
Suggestions).** *1 or 2 errors* indicates that the child
asserted that a false event really happened. *Witnessed*
indicates that the child claimed to have observed the
false event. *Maintained* indicates that the child insisted
on having observed the event, despite the attempt at
dissuading: "You didn't really see him do this, did you?"

other ethnic groups. In addition, imagine that, following the crime, the child is repeatedly questioned by all sorts of people: parents, police, and prosecuting attorneys.
Unless these interrogators are extraordinarily careful in the wording of questions, it
would be easy for them to unknowingly make presuppositions or suggestions such
as, "Did the long-haired man with the knife yell at the store clerk?" In this question
there are presuppositions about the man having long hair and a knife, yet the child
has not been asked about either of these. It takes little imagination to apply the findings of the Leichtman and Ceci (1995) research to the real world. It creates a chilling
picture.

    This research suggests what should be avoided with child witnesses, but it also
suggests what should be done to maximize the value of their recollections. As can be
seen in Figure 16.1, the free narratives of children in the stereotype group are factually
accurate, in spite of experience with stereotypical information. Although the stereotype in this study may be weaker than real-life stereotypes embedded by repeated
expression in a child's daily environment, the data here indicated that stereotypes play
no role in false allegations during free narrative. The problems begin to occur when
suggestions are made. A conclusion that might be drawn by police and prosecutors is
that evidence from the free narrative might be more accurate than evidence under
pointed questioning. Free narratives of child witnesses should be solicited and carefully
recorded at the earliest possible time following a crime. At the least, any additional

questions should be carefully structured, and court officials should caution parents and others against questioning the child further, possibly inadvertently adding suggestions that become part of memory.

CAN ADULTS DETECT INACCURATE REPORTS FROM CHILDREN?

Leichtman and Ceci (1995) were interested in applications of their research to real-world settings. They believed that adults who had no knowledge of the history of Sam Stone's visit would be unable to determine the extent to which children were giving accurate accounts. In contrast to their beliefs, they cited Goodman (1990) as having stated that adults can easily detect false reports in the narratives of young children.

As noted above, the final interview responses of the children experiencing free recall, probing questions, and challenging questions had been videotaped. Leichtman and Ceci (1995) showed some of these tapes to adults, asking them to try to detect false statements. The videos chosen were of a 3-year-old, a 4-year-old, and a 5-year-old. Each of these children was selected from the *stereotype-plus-suggestion* group. The particular children were chosen because they were coherent and seemed engaged by the interviewer. On the tape, the 3-year-old spontaneously asserted that Sam had done the false acts. The 4-year-old was a soft-spoken child who made no false allegations in her narrative or in subsequent prompting. The 5-year-old included no false acts in his narrative, but assented to false memories under prompted questioning.

At a conference, these tapes were shown to 119 researchers and clinicians who worked in the area of children's testimony. This audience was only told that each child had witnessed the same visit by Sam Stone. Based on the three videotapes, the audience was asked to rate their confidence about which events really happened. They were also asked to rate their confidence in the overall account given by each child. These ratings were made on a seven-point scale, where seven represented the most confidence and one represented least confidence. The data are presented in Figures 16.6 and 16.7. Figure 16.6 shows that although the adults tended not to believe that Sam soiled the bear, they had considerable confidence that he ripped the book. This showed that even skilled professionals who are interested in children's testimony could come to have confidence in some false memories reported by children.

Interestingly, Figure 16.7 shows that the adults had the least confidence in the reports of the four-year-old, even though she was the only child giving accurate reports. One of the reasons for this may have been that the three-year-old child provided the most detail in her story. A story rich in detail may seem more credible. If this is so, it may be useful for school children to give more detail with the old excuse about how the dog ate their homework. What kind of dog was it? How long did it take him to eat it? Did he spit out the staple? Although details may not have formed the entire basis for audience judgment of credibility, it was probably part of it. Whatever the reason, the data suggested that adults, even interested and motivated adults, are not very good at determining the accuracy of reports by children.

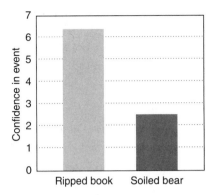

FIGURE 16.6   Mean Confidence Levels That Events Occurred. Confidence ratings of professional adults that events occurred, based on videotapes of children (1 = sure it didn't, 7 = sure it did).

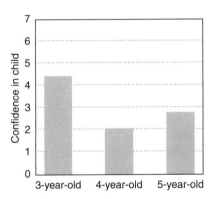

FIGURE 16.7   Mean Confidence Levels in Accounts Given. Confidence ratings of professional adults in the accounts given by three children.

We hope that you will bear the findings of this study in mind as you watch media accounts of children in courtrooms. It would be nice to think that results of carefully conducted research, such as that presented by Leichtman and Ceci (1995), will find their way into the daily practice of people who are professionally involved with children's testimony. Media depictions suggest to us that the scientific studies concerning eyewitness testimony have not yet resulted in standardized procedures for dealing with eyewitness accounts. Maybe the general public, even members of the educated general public such as police, judges, and lawyers, do not understand research about behavior. *Psychology* means many things to different people, but few people associate it with a cautious, empirical approach to understanding behavior. In reading these articles, you are coming to see that no research study is perfect. Those who are ignorant about psychological research may use this fact to conclude that psychology is useless and meaningless. It is our contention that a person with adequate skills in understanding psychological research can assess and evaluate studies, making decisions about when and how results can be applied to daily life. We believe that this is the point of learning about psychology. We hope that you agree.

REFERENCES

Ceci, S. J., & Bruck, M. (1993). Suggestibility of the child witness: A historical review and synthesis. *Psychological Bulletin, 113*, 403–439.

Goodman, G. S. (1990). Media effects and children's testimony. In D. Singer (Chair), *The impact of the media on the judicial system.* Symposium conducted at the 98th Annual Convention of the American Psychological Association, Boston.

Humphrey, H. H., III (1985). *Report on Scott County Investigations.* Minneapolis, MN: Attorney General's Office.

Leichtman, M. D., & Ceci, S. J. (1995). The effects of stereotypes and suggestions on preschoolers' reports. *Developmental Psychology, 31*, 568–578.

Loftus, E. F. (1975). Leading questions and the eyewitness report. *Cognitive Psychology, 7*, 560–572.

Loftus, E. F., & Palmer, J. C. (1974). Reconstruction of automobile destruction: An example of the interaction between language and memory. *Journal of Verbal Learning and Verbal Behavior, 13*, 585–589.

CHAPTER 17

FLASH IN THE PAN

Quite a bit of day-to-day life depends on things we remember. Our interactions with other people often depend on memories we share with them. We recall the first time we met someone else, happy times we had together, and countless small, ordinary occurrences. For the mundane operation of our lives, our memories seem to be adequate. Although we sometimes notice that our recollections of specific events are slightly different from the recollections of others, usually this is not much of a problem. We do not forget where we live, the names of friends and relatives, what time of day our classes are, or the thousands of big and little things that are required for daily functioning.

Nevertheless, psychological studies have found memories to be unreliable. Neisser and Harsch (1992) noted that psychologists have found it difficult to reconcile the fallibility of memories for some events with the dependability of others. Many studies have shown that memories created in laboratory situations are reconstructive: available information, which is unrelated to the lab event, finds its way into memory. Memory seems to be a patchwork of things that really happened and things that did not (Loftus, 1979).

Neisser and Harsch (1992) studied a particular kind of memory called *flashbulb memory*. This term has been used to describe the recall of very specific images about a rare, striking, or significant event, personal or public. The word *flashbulb* was used because these memories were supposed to capture the action the way a camera flash did, creating a memory that was permanent and rich in vivid detail. Weddings, graduations, and births as well as personal tragedies were the kinds of personal events that were supposed to be captured by flashbulb memories. Significant national events that had a big emotional impact were also supposed to be remembered in this way. The emotional content of these kinds of memories has been discussed within psychology for a long time. For example, researchers have suggested that the emotion that accompanies these memories may strengthen them (Brown & Kulik, 1977). We are sure you have experienced events about which you have said, "I will *never* forget that. I remember everything so clearly." Among an earlier generation of Americans, many people

Incorporating the research of U. Neisser and N. Harsch, "Phantom Flashbulbs: False Recollections of Hearing the News about *Challenger*," 1992. In E. Winograd and U. Neisser (Eds.), *Affect and Accuracy in Recall: Studies of "Flashbulb" Memories*, (pp. 9–31). New York: Cambridge University Press.

believed they could remember exactly what they were doing at the moment they heard that President Kennedy had been assassinated in 1963. People in younger age groups may remember details of what they were doing when they heard about the bombings of two U.S. embassies in Africa in 1998 or the death of Princess Diana of Britain in 1997.

Many Americans older than age 25 have seemingly clear memories about what they were doing when they first heard that the *Challenger* space shuttle had exploded shortly following its takeoff from Cape Canaveral a little after 11:00 EST on January 28, 1986. The entire seven-person crew was killed in this disaster, including a civilian schoolteacher from New Hampshire, Christa McAuliffe. Before the flight, Ms. McAuliffe had been profiled in a number of national news stories detailing her excitement about being chosen to go on the *Challenger*. Partially because of this, there was more public awareness of the *Challenger* mission than for typical space shuttle flights. The live television images of the takeoff reached a large audience and were replayed many times in the days and weeks that followed.

Neisser and Harsch were able to report particularly interesting findings concerning flashbulb memories because the participants in their study were among a large group of students in a psychology class at Emory University who were asked by the researchers to fill out a questionnaire about the *Challenger* disaster the morning after it happened. Years later the students were tracked down and questioned again about their vivid memories of this event. The existence of the earlier questionnaires allowed Neisser and Harsch to assess the accuracy of the flashbulb memories for this event.

PARTICIPANTS AND INITIAL PROCEDURE

The initial participants were 106 students in a large psychology class who were asked to fill out a questionnaire on the morning following the *Challenger* disaster. The questionnaire collected information about the circumstances in which they first heard of the tragedy. First, the students were asked to write a free description of how they had heard about the disaster. On the next page they answered questions about the disaster such as: "What time was it; how did you hear about it; where were you; what were you doing; who told you; who else was there; how did you feel about it; what did you do afterward?"

1988 PROCEDURE

Two and one half years later, in the autumn of 1988, the freshmen who had been in this class were starting their senior year at Emory University. The student directory was searched for the names of the original 106 students in the class. Almost all of the students remaining on campus agreed to participate in what was described as a "brief" research project. There were 30 women and 14 men willing to participate. This is quite a large attrition rate. Although no detailed information is available about the participants who did not continue in this study, it is usual that authors will present evidence about the similarity of participants who drop out to those who do not. In this study, for example, if many dropouts had been people who were no longer at college because they forgot to do homework or forgot to register for classes, the representativeness of the sample and resulting external validity might be compromised.

If participants asked why they had been selected for the study, they were told their names had come from a list of students enrolled in introductory psychology several years ago. The *Challenger* disaster was not mentioned. They were offered $3 to help pay for their participation time.

They came to the lab individually or in groups and were then told that the study involved their recollections about the *Challenger* disaster. They filled out a questionnaire that was similar to the one they had filled out years earlier: they wrote a description and answered some specific questions. This time, however, each question was accompanied by a five-point scale that was used by participants to rate their confidence in each of their answers. On this scale, 1 = *just guessing* and 5 = *absolutely certain*. A final item asked if they had ever filled out a questionnaire on the *Challenger* disaster before.

1989 PROCEDURE

A preliminary analysis of the data from the 1988 questionnaires suggested that more thorough interviews might be illuminating, and the participants were invited to return to the lab in the spring of 1989. In March and April of 1989, 40 of the original 44 agreed to return to the lab again for further research. This time they were offered $5 for their help. They were not told what the research was about, but, of course, they may have guessed that it was some kind of follow-up to the 1988 data collection. On this last return to the lab, researcher Nicole Harsch interviewed them individually for about 45 minutes each. During the interviews she was "masked" with respect to memory accuracy because, with two exceptions, she did not know if the person had been accurate in recalling the event or not. This is important because it ensured that she could not unintentionally influence the direction or tone of the interview by subtly communicating feedback to the participants about the accuracy of their memories.

The participants were asked to recount, again, how they had heard the news of the disaster. They rated the quality of their memory and its vividness. They were given a procedure called a *cognitive interview*, which has been used in other contexts to elicit additional information from eyewitnesses soon after an event (Geiselman, Fisher, MacKinnon, & Holland, 1985). In the cognitive interview, the participants were asked to try to recreate in their minds the specifics of the situation in which they first heard about the disaster. They were told to:

1. Reinstate mentally the original location
2. Reinstate mentally the *emotional* context
3. Recall the event in backward order
4. Recall the event from a different perspective

It was possible that the cognitive interview strategy only called up the situation as the individual already remembered it. Because of this, a further attempt was made to restore accurate memories. They were asked to:

1. Recall the events of the entire day
2. Describe another way they might have heard the news
3. Describe how a friend might have heard it
4. Recall whatever possible from January, 1986

After each response they were asked if they now remembered more about their first experience with the shuttle disaster. They were encouraged to relate anything that came to mind, no matter how unimportant it seemed. Up to this point, the interview had consisted of generalized small nudges designed to shake loose memories and to help participants recall accurately. Following these approaches, more drastic tactics were unleashed. First, they were shown the questionnaires they had filled out the previous semester. Differences between that account and the one they had just given were pointed out. These differences were usually slight. In a stronger attempt to stir the correct story out of memory, participants were asked a preprepared question designed from their own original 1986 one-day-later account of events. This question was designed individually for each participant. It suggested what really happened to them. For example, a person who falsely remembered seeing the event on TV was asked: "Is it possible that you already knew about the explosion before seeing it on TV?"

As the final attempt to dredge up the original memory, participants were shown their original 1986 report of events in their own handwriting. If the old and new accounts of their story were different, they were asked why they had "said one thing now and something different a couple of years ago." They were also asked which version of the story they liked better and believed more.

CODING THE DATA

Neisser and Harsch pointed out that "Accuracy is not all-or-none: Many subjects [participants] had memories that were partly right and partly wrong." It was necessary to find a way to rate the accuracy of each story numerically in order to be able to express the general trends in the data quantitatively. There is no particular standard way to operationally define story accuracy. Researchers involved in cutting-edge investigations often have to design an approach to the coding process that seems to most accurately translate qualitative descriptions into numbers. In so doing, researchers work to avoid the introduction of incidental bias into the data. Additionally, their methods are described as completely as possible in the research report. This is done so that subsequent researchers working on similar questions can replicate the earlier work using the same operational definitions. Replications are one way of increasing confidence in the validity of research findings.

After trying several coding schemes, Neisser and Harsch adopted one in which raters considered five attributes of the story: *location, activity, informant, time,* and *others present*. Each of these were scored on a three-point scale in which a score of "2" was given to essentially correct responses, "0" was given to versions that were obviously wrong, and "1" was the score for intermediate cases. This provided numbers for statistical analysis. In the final scoring, *location*, *activity*, and *informant* were considered to be the more important than *time of day* and *others present*. The scores on the first three attributes were weighted so that they counted more than the other two attributes in the determination of an individual's overall accuracy score.

RESULTS

In the first return to the lab in 1988, there was a finding that served as an exemplar for the rest of the findings in this study: only 11 participants (25 percent) remembered filling out the 1986 questionnaire about the *Challenger* disaster. Although this may not seem too important, it was the first indication of the extent to which memories for the events of past years were gone.

One of the aims of this research was to investigate the accuracy of details in memory. Accuracy scores were, of course, always the result of a comparison between the participant's original story recorded in 1986 and the subsequent recollections. For the purposes of this study it was assumed that the 1986 story was essentially accurate because it had been written a day after the event. Figure 17.1 presents the weighted accuracy scores for all participants on the first follow-up recall questionnaire given in 1988. Because of the way the data were coded and weighted, accuracy scores ranged from 0 to 7, with higher numbers reflecting greater accuracy.

Although three participants remembered the events of 1986 and were essentially accurate when asked in 1988, not every participant was correct in recollection. Eleven

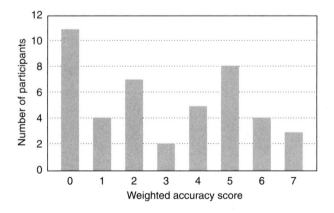

FIGURE 17.1 Accuracy of 1988 Recollections. Number of participants attaining each accuracy rating from 0 (very inaccurate) to 7 (completely, or almost completely, accurate).

participants, or 25 percent of them, were wrong about everything. The mean accuracy score for the entire group was 2.95 out of a possible 7. This does not fit with the picture of detailed accuracy that is commonly accorded to flashbulb memories. This finding was rendered even more striking by the high degree of confidence participants had in their stories that, in some cases, were completely inaccurate. The confidence ratings of the participants on the major story attributes of *location, activity,* and *informant* ranged as high as 5, where higher numbers indicated more confidence. The accuracy for all participants at a particular level of confidence is shown in Figure 17.2.

At the low end of the confidence scale shown in Figure 17.2, people appropriately have no confidence in their scores. Their stories are not accurate, and they seemed to know it. However, excepting the first two bars, which only represented two people, as confidence in the story increased, accuracy did not particularly increase. The data were somewhat saw-toothed, which suggested that there was not a very strong relationship between confidence and accuracy. The correlation between accuracy and confidence for the entire group of 44 participants was .29 and it was statistically non-significant. Thirteen participants contributed to the mean at the highest level of confidence, and yet their mean accuracy on a 7-point scale was only 3.07.

When participants returned to the lab in the spring of 1989, accuracy was about as bad as it had been in the autumn of 1988. Figure 17.3 presents the mean accuracy scores for the 40 participants who returned for the final interview.

The mean accuracy slipped a little between the autumn of 1988 and spring of 1989, but otherwise, the distributions are very similar. In spite of poor accuracy in this last interview, participants remained confident that their memories were correct. Participants again rated their confidence on a 7-point scale, and the mean confidence for the whole group was high (mean = 5.28). As in 1988, confidence and accuracy were

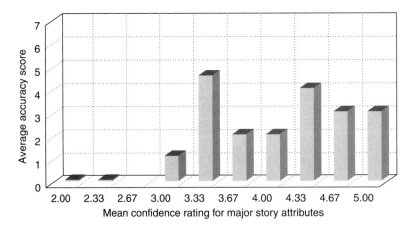

FIGURE 17.2 Accuracy Scores at Each Confidence Level. Mean accuracy scores for participants at each level of confidence about memory accuracy from 1 (little or no confidence) to 5 (very confident of memory accuracy).

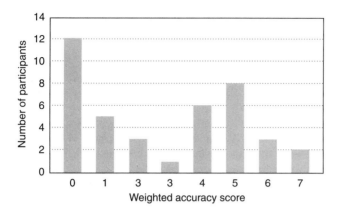

FIGURE 17.3   Accuracy of 1989 Recollections. Number of participants attaining each accuracy rating from 1 (very inaccurate) to 7 (completely, or almost completely, accurate).

unrelated to each other ($r = .30$, nonsignificant). Confidence in memory was somewhat stable from one year to the next. The individuals who were confident of the accuracy of their memories in 1988, tended to remain confident when they were seen again in 1989 ($r = .56$, $p < .001$).

Neisser and Harsch had originally intended to develop two accuracy scores for the final interview—one that would rate the story the participant told at the beginning of the interview and one rating the story the participant told at the end—after all the prompting that was part of that interview. As Neisser and Harsch said, "This proved to be entirely unnecessary. Our attempts to enhance retrieval—asking subjects [participants] to reinstate the context, having them imagine how a friend might have heard the news, and the like—made no difference at all. No subjects changed their minds on any specific point after any of the eight cognitively designed retrieval cues. No one said, 'Oh, now I remember how it really was!' "

Neisser and Harsch acknowledged that cognitive interview techniques might help to refresh memory soon after an event. However, their study indicated that this strategy did not work when years had passed since the event.

STRENGTH OF EMOTION AND RECALL

In order to test the possibility that emotion, or affect, strengthens recall, Neisser and Harsch coded emotions in answers their participants gave to the question "How did you feel about it?" on the first questionnaire in 1986. The logic of this inquiry was that if people had experienced strong emotion when first exposed to the disaster, they might remember it more accurately than those who did not. As in the coding for accuracy described above, a coding scheme had to be developed to turn narrative sentences into numerical data. It would have been possible to have participants rate the strength of their emotions on a numerical scale, eliminating the need for coding. The interpretation would have been made easier, but the richness of the emotional accounts would have been unavailable for subsequent analysis. As we have noted before, there are a number of ways to transform data, and it is the task of the researcher to do this in what seems the best possible way within practical constraints, trying not to introduce bias.

Neisser and Harsch tried several schemes for coding emotional content and finally settled on one that they called SH, for *Shocked and Horrified*. SH scores were defined using criteria including:

> Score 3—Participants used at least two strong negative terms in describing their own reactions: (i.e., shocked, stunned, sickened).
>
> Score 2—Participants used only one such term in describing their reactions.
>
> Score 1—Participants said only things such as "I didn't believe it" or participants qualified stronger statements by saying "However, it's a risk people take."

In spite of the effort made in coding the data for emotion, the ratings of emotion had no predictive value for later recall. The correlation between the emotion score and the accuracy score for recollection in 1988 was –.17, a very weak relationship. There was a slight trend for the emotion score to be associated with confidence, even if it did not lead to accuracy, but this trend was not statistically significant. The correlation between emotion score and confidence in the 1988 recollection was .25, indicating only a moderate relationship with fairly little predictive value. The participants did not remember events very well, and they did not remember their emotions either. There was no significant correlation between the emotions reported in 1986 and those recalled in 1988 ($r = .21$).

THE TELEVISION PRIORITY ERROR

What kind of error was the most common? Neisser and Harsch noticed that many of the erroneous accounts given in 1988 and 1989 mentioned television, whereas fewer of the original 1986 reports cited TV as being the way people learned of the *Challenger* disaster. They went back to the reports and coded instances where TV was involved in mistaken recollections. Figure 17.4 presents these data.

As can be seen from Figure 17.4, between 1986 and 1988, there was a 24 percent increase in the number of participants who recalled TV as the first source of the news about the *Challenger* disaster. Over the 2½-year period, 14 participants changed their recollections about television, but only 2 of them were people who forgot that they saw it first on TV. The rest of them erroneously added TV to their recollections. The shift in recollection depicted in Figure 17.4 was significant at $p < .01$.

Perhaps the capstone finding of this fascinating study is the result obtained at the end of the 1989 interview when participants were shown their own original accounts, in their own handwriting, from the day following the *Challenger* disaster. The partici-

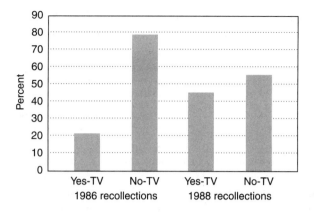

FIGURE 17.4   Percentage Reporting TV as a Source of *Challenger* News. Percentage of participants reporting and not reporting television as the first source of information about the *Challenger* disaster in 1986 and again in 1988.

pants showed complete surprise. No participant did the classic slap on the forehead while saying anything like, "Oh yeah! *Now* I remember! *That's* the way it all happened!" Instead, they found it hard to believe that their current memories were so wrong. They sounded a little confused and said things such as "I still think of it as the other way around."

DISCUSSION AND CONCLUSIONS

When confronted with an unpleasant turn of events, the late Jimmy Durante used to shake his nose (and the rest of his head), stare straight at the camera and say, "What a revoltin' development dis is!" That is somewhat the way we feel about these results. It is not a comforting thought that our memories of important events may be wrong. It is further disconcerting that, oblivious to our erroneous recollections, we can be very confident that we remember events accurately. Television priority was identified as the most frequent error in this study. Related research in memory suggested that one of the problems seen here might have been what was called *wrong time slices* (Brewer, 1988). This term was used to describe what happened when a person remembered a real event but mistook the particular time at which the event happened. In the case of this study, participants may have remembered accurately watching the television account of the *Challenger* explosion but failed to remember that this happened later in the day, after they had already heard about the event. Because the TV images were so vivid, people were confident of their memories—they could clearly remember the explosion and resulting fireball in the sky. The detail that was forgotten was the *time* at which they saw the TV pictures. Memories do not have a time stamp on them. As time goes by and details fade, mislocations of otherwise accurate memories become increasingly likely.

Not all the errors made by participants in this study fit the wrong time slice paradigm. One participant who actually heard the news in the cafeteria where she originally said that it made her so sick she could not finish eating, later remembered first hearing it in her dorm room. By her account, another resident was running down the hall screaming and she recalled wanting to run after her to question her, deciding, instead, to turn on the television to see what was going on. This did not seem to be a time dislocation. It contained elements that are simply wrong, not merely misplaced in time. Another participant who actually heard about the disaster at Emory University like all of the participants, later recalled first hearing about the disaster at home, with her parents. At least one of these accounts is wrong. Did this participant imagine what it would have been like to hear it with parents and then insert that imagined scenario into her memory of the event? As Neisser and Harsch said, "We can only speculate and we may already have speculated quite enough."

Speculation aside, this is an interesting and compelling study. The study has a good claim to external validity because the problem investigated was not an artificial laboratory creation. It should be remembered—even though we do not always remember accurately—that this study explored only one type of memory: the flashbulb memory. Caution should be exercised in generalizing these findings to other kinds of memories. However, the conclusions of this study do support findings of a number of other studies in suggesting that our memories are not as accurate as we may believe them to be.

REFERENCES

Brewer, W. F. (1988). Memory for randomly sampled autobiographical events. In E. Winograd & U. Neisser (Eds.), *Affect and accuracy in recall: Studies of "flashbulb" memories* (pp. 274–305). New York: Cambridge University Press.

Brown, R., & Kulik, J. (1977). Flashbulb memories. *Cognition, 5,* 73–99.

Geiselman, R. E., Fisher, R. P., MacKinnon, D. P., & Holland, H. L. (1985). Eyewitness memory enhancement in the police interview: Cognitive retrieval mnemonics versus hypnosis. *Journal of Applied Psychology, 70,* 401–412.

Loftus, E. F. (1979). *Eyewitness testimony.* Cambridge, MA: Harvard University Press.

Neisser, U., & Harsch, N. (1992). Phantom flashbulbs: False recollections of hearing the news about *Challenger.* In E. Winograd & U. Neisser (Eds.), *Affect and accuracy in recall: Studies of "flashbulb" memories* (pp. 9–31). New York: Cambridge University Press.

CHAPTER 18

STEREOTYPES: A GOOD THING IN THE COGNITIVE TOOLKIT

The term *stereotype* likely will evoke negative thoughts and feelings, perhaps even thoughts of prejudice or discrimination. In psychology however, stereotypes serve a different function. They are a group of characteristics believed to be shared by all individuals who belong to a group. A group might consist of a racial or ethnic group, an occupation, the neighborhood you live in, your gender, or formal membership in a club or organization. When we form opinions or beliefs about individuals based on a stereotype, we tend to ignore their individual qualities and conclude things about them based on the particular stereotype we are using. Furthermore, stereotypes can been seen as cognitive mechanisms that we use to save mental resources and assist in information processing (Allport, 1954; Andersen, Klatzky, & Murray, 1990; Fiske & Neuberg, 1990). Gilbert and Hixon (1991) describe stereotypes as cognitive tools that "jump out" of the mental toolkit "when there is a job to be done." Instead of having to make constant cognitive judgments, stereotypes allow us to rely on simple rules of categorization that can save cognitive energy (Hamilton, 1979; Hamilton, Sherman, & Ruvolo, 1990; Hamilton & Trolier, 1986). Stereotypes help us further by simplifying our perception of the world. In a very real sense, having stereotypes available for ready usage saves us from the difficulty of having to constantly make decisions in a changing, difficult environment (Lippman, 1922).

A number of research studies have shown that we tend to use stereotypes in situations that are difficult and energy draining (Bodenhausen, 1990, 1993; Pratto & Bargh, 1991; Stangor & Duan, 1991). The thinking emphasized in this research is that people under pressure to make a decision will rely on stereotypic thinking to facilitate the task and therefore save energy. It is also possible that stereotypic thinking may be used when people are too lazy or unmotivated to cognitively delve into the task in a critical manner. In summing up this research Macrae, Milne, and Bodenhausen (1994) state, "When the processing environment reaches a sufficient level of difficulty, and perceivers' resources are correspondingly depleted, stereotypes are likely to be activated, and applied in judgmental tasks." The research in this chapter describes more

Incorporating the research of C. N. Macrae, A. B. Milne, and G. V. Bodenhausen, "Stereotypes as Energy Saving Devices: A Peek Inside the Cognitive Toolbox," 1994, *Journal of Personality and Social Psychology, 66,* pp. 37–47.

about the first kind of usage, stereotypes as energy misers (i.e., the use of stereotypes saves cognitive energy and resources that can be available for other assignments). The research in this chapter helps to explain how stereotypes act to save cognitive resources and therefore can be energy misers.

PROCEDURE

Macrae and his colleagues used a *dual-task experimental paradigm* in this investigation. In this procedure participants are placed in a situation in which they are required to handle two tasks at the same time. In a study by Wickens (1976) participants were required to observe the movement of an object on a computer monitor, while simultaneously responding to auditory stimuli. In this situation it is possible to manipulate the difficulty of each of the tasks so that researchers can estimate the amount of cognitive energy used on the primary and secondary tasks. Because the researcher can determine and manipulate characteristics of the primary task, the participant's performance on the secondary task can give you an indication of the amount of excess mental processing capacity not used in carrying out the primary assignment. This is useful because if stereotypes serve to enhance and improve the efficiency of cognitive processing on a primary task, it should be observed in how well a participant performs on a secondary task. If stereotyped information enhances cognitive processing on the primary task, the task should be less difficult to accomplish and, therefore, save mental energy for better cognitive performance on the secondary task. The research in this chapter deals specifically with this issue—Do stereotypes produce energy efficiency in our cognitive toolkit?

METHOD

The participants were 24 female college students from Cardiff, Wales, who were compensated with £2 for taking part in the study. The participants performed two tasks simultaneously. Task 1 required them to form impressions of four males based on trait descriptors provided. While they were engaged in Task 1 they were also required to listen to auditory information about an unfamiliar topic (Task 2). Participants were randomly assigned to stereotype present or stereotype absent group. The independent variable (IV) was whether or not the participants had access to a stereotype during Task 1, which presented them with impressions of four males. Participants were told that they would be assessed later on the trait impression they had formed (Task 1) as well as the information acquired in Task 2. The dependent variables were therefore the recall of the trait data (stereotyped and neutral traits) on Task 1 and scores on a multiple-choice exam regarding the auditory information provided in Task 2.

Participants were each seated in front of a computer monitor and told they would be asked to form impressions of a male individual whose name appeared on the monitor's screen. In order to form impressions, 10 trait descriptors were displayed one at a time beneath the name. A single trait appeared on the monitor at a time for approximately 3 seconds. Five of the 10 traits presented were previously determined to be consistent with a specific stereotype. This stereotype was the job description of the male name being presented on the monitor. In the stereotype-present group, the specific stereotype was given along with the male person's name; in the stereotype-absent group the stereotype label was absent. Both groups were asked to perform the same task, with the difference being the presence or absence of the stereotype label. The rationale was that the presence of the stereotype would simplify the task by giving them a focal point to guide their impressions. Table 18.1 provides the name, stereotype label, and traits used in Task 1. As you can see in Table 18.1, the stereotypes for doctor, artist, skinhead, and estate agent (real estate agent in U.S.) were different from one another. The italicized items beneath each stereotype are trait descriptors congruent with the stereotype. Although this research was done in Wales, the stereotypes are consistent with American stereotypes. In this research the selection of the stereotypes was based on a pilot study to insure the stereotypic traits were accurate and the neutral traits were indeed neutral with respect to all four stereotypes.

While the participants were engaged in Task 1, an audiotape describing the economy and geography of Indonesia was played. Participants were told they would be tested on the information contained in the tape. They also knew that they would be assessed on the traits presented by video monitor. The participants were in a situation that required them to pay attention to two completely different streams of information presented simultaneously. The audiotape (i.e., Task 2) and the video presentation of traits (i.e., Task 1) were synchronized so that both presentations occurred simultaneously and took exactly 2 minutes.

Dependent Variables

The ability of participants to recall traits characteristic of the male person was the dependent measure of Task 1. The participants were given a sheet of paper with each

TABLE 18.1   The Impression Management Task: Names, Stereotypes, and Traits

NAME STEREOTYPE	NIGEL DOCTOR	JULIAN ARTIST	JOHN SKINHEAD	GRAHAM ESTATE AGENT
	caring	*creative*	*rebellious*	*pushy*
	honest	*temperamental*	*aggressive*	*talkative*
	reliable	*unconventional*	*dishonest*	*arrogant*
	upstanding	*sensitive*	*untrustworthy*	*confidant*
	responsible	*individualistic*	*dangerous*	*unscrupulous*
	unlucky	fearless	lucky	musical
	forgetful	active	observant	pessimistic
	passive	cordial	modest	humorless
	clumsy	progressive	optimistic	alert
	enthusiastic	generous	curious	spirited

Italic Text: stereotyped

Plain text: nonstereotyped

male person's name at the top and they were asked to list as many of each person's traits as possible. The dependent variable for Task 2 was a multiple-choice exam to measure the participant's knowledge about topics presented in the audiotape on Indonesia. For example, participants were asked about the official religion of Indonesia and where the capital of Jakarta was located. After both dependent measures were obtained, the participants were debriefed and compensated.

Findings

The experimenters expected that participants who had a stereotype label available would recall more traits than the group of participants who had no access to the stereotypic label. The data are shown in Table 18.2.

As can be seen in Table 18.2, the participants who had the stereotype available were able to recall more than twice as many traits than the participants without access to the stereotypic label. For Task 2, the multiple-choice data is also presented in Table 18.2. Remember that if stereotypes are useful to the participant in making the cognitive processing of information more efficient, then participants who had access to the stereotypic label would have more cognitive resources to handle the audio monitoring task about Indonesia. It would be expected therefore that the group of participants who had access to the stereotype would learn more about Indonesia and obtain higher multiple-choice test scores. The data in Table 18.2 provide confirmation of this hypothesis with the stereotype label group answering significantly more multiple-choice test items ($p < .04$).

The findings of this experiment provided confirmation that stereotypes can facilitate cognitive processing by conserving and economizing cognitive resources. Additional studies by the same researchers (Macrae, Milne, & Bodenhausen, 1994) indicate that the process of using stereotypes operates in an unintentional manner without the perceiver's awareness. Because the use of stereotypes operates in an automatic manner, it lends support for the viewpoint that stereotypic thinking contributes to cognitive efficiency. In a way our cognitive toolkit is set up, by default, to use stereotypes because they are efficient. We are cognitive misers and the verdict is clear—like King Midas, we are misers attempting to preserve cognitive resources. The presence of stereotypes

TABLE 18.2   Participants' Mean Scores on Tasks 1 and 2

TASK 1	STEREOTYPE PRESENT	STEREOTYPE ABSENT
Recalling stereotype consistent traits	4.42	2.08
Recalling neutral traits	1.83	.33
TASK 2		
Correct multiple-choice responses	8.75	6.66

does not mean that the person gives up all conscious, voluntary, and reasoned control of cognition. A person may choose to give up the advantages and savings associated with stereotypes to engage in an active, more complicated mode to cognitive processes in certain circumstances. There is no doubt that stereotypic thinking can lead to negative, prejudicial, and discriminatory beliefs, especially because of the automatic, default nature of its operation. However, one should recognize that the stereotypes are a major part of the cognitive toolkit and have benefits for cognitive functioning. Nevertheless, as we all are aware, the operation of stereotypic thinking can foster prejudices and lead to discrimination. To learn more about the implications of this "negative" aspect of stereotypic thinking, the work of Patricia Devine (1989) is an excellent source. Devine's research also points to solutions to reduce prejudice. The very automatic manner in which stereotypes operate imposes problems for the immediate elimination of prejudiced responses. Devine (1995) states, "People are not always aware of when the stereotype affects their judgments. It (the stereotype) is so easily activated that one has to be extremely vigilant in detecting instances when judgments of others may be clouded by the stereotype." Devine's research supports the findings in this chapter that stereotypes get activated by default. Given this scenario, Devine states that it will take considerable attention, energy, and vigilance to initiate our personal beliefs and values and to inhibit prejudicial stereotypic thinking. You will also learn more about the roots of prejudice in Chapter 32, "I'm OK, You're Not."

REFERENCES

Allport, G. W. (1954). *The nature of prejudice.* Reading, MA: Addison-Wesley.

Andersen, S. M., Klatzky, R. L., & Murray, J. (1990). Traits and social stereotypes: Efficiency differences in social information processing. *Journal of Personality and Social Psychology, 59*, 192–201.

Bodenhausen, G. V. (1990). Stereotypes as judgmental heuristics: Evidence of circadian variations in discrimination. *Psychological Science, 1*, 319–322.

Bodenhausen, G. V. (1993). Emotion, arousal, and stereotypic judgments: A heuristic model of affect and stereotyping. In D. Mackie & D. Hamilton (Eds.), *Affect, cognition, and stereotyping: Interactive processes in group perception* (pp. 13–37). San Diego, CA: Academic Press.

Devine, P. G. (1989). Stereotypes and prejudice: Their automatic and controlled components. *Journal of Personality and Social Psychology, 56*, 5–18.

Devine, P. G. (1995). Getting hooked on research in social psychology: Examples from eyewitness identification and prejudice. In G. C. Brannigan & M. R. Merrens (Eds.), *The social psychologist: Research adventures* (pp. 160–184). New York: McGraw-Hill.

Fiske, S. T., & Neuberg, S. L. (1990). A continuum model of impression formation from category-based to individuating processes: Influences of information and motivation on attention and interpretation. In M. P. Zanna (Ed.), *Advances in experimental social psychology* (Vol. 3, pp. 1–74). San Diego, CA: Academic Press.

Gilbert, D. T., & Hixon, J. G. (1991). The trouble of thinking: Activation and application of stereotypic beliefs. *Journal of Personality and Social Psychology, 60*, 509–517.

Hamilton, D. L. (1979). A cognitive-attributional analysis of stereotyping. In L. Berkowitz (Ed.), *Advances in experimental social psychology* (Vol. 12, pp. 53–84). San Diego, CA: Academic Press.

Hamilton, D. L., Sherman, S. J., & Ruvolo, C. M. (1990). Stereotype-based expectancies: Effects on information processing and social behavior. *Journal of Social Issues, 46*, 35–60.

Hamilton, D. L., & Trolier, T. K. (1986). Stereotypes and stereotyping: An overview of the cognitive approach. In J. Dovidio & S. Gaerther (Eds.), *Prejudice, discrimination, and racism* (pp. 127–163). San Diego, CA: Academic Press.

Lippman, W. (1922). *Public opinion.* New York: Harcourt & Brace.

Macrae, C. N., Milne, A. B., & Bodenhausen, G. V. (1994). Stereotypes as energy saving devices: A peek inside the cognitive toolbox. *Journal of Personality and Social Psychology, 66,* 37–47.

Pratto F., & Bargh, J. A. (1991). Stereotyping based upon apparently individuating information: Trait and global components of sex stereotypes under attention overload. *Journal of Experimental Social Psychology, 27,* 26–47.

Stangor, C., & Duan, C. (1991). Effects of multiple task demands upon memory for information about social groups. *Journal of Experimental Social Psychology, 27,* 357–378.

Wickens, C. D. (1976). The effects of divided attention in information processing in tracking. *Journal of Experimental Psychology: Human Perception and Performance, 2,* 1–13.

CHAPTER 19

MAD ABOUT YOU

The research of David Buss and his colleagues described in this chapter (Buss, Larsen, Westen, & Semmelroth, 1992) attempts to answer another important question derived from evolutionary thinking—do men and women experience jealousy in a relationship in different ways? Evolutionary psychology recognizes that men and women have different interests in a mating relationship. In a sense, they are in competition with one another. Therefore, it would be reasonable to assume that males and females would experience threats to a relationship (i.e., another woman or man) in different ways.

Jealousy is a psychological and physiological feeling that develops when there is a threat to a significant relationship. If the jealousy is centered on a sexual relationship, then it is termed *sexual jealousy*. Likewise, if the focus is an emotional relationship, it is labeled *emotional jealousy*. Evolutionary psychological theory would predict that men and women would respond differently to sexual or emotional threats to their relationship. Specifically, for men sexual threats would arouse more jealousy, whereas for women emotional threats would be the greater threat.

RESEARCH TESTING THE EVOLUTIONARY VIEWPOINT

The first investigation was to determine the very question raised earlier—Is there a differential response between men and women to sexual and emotional infidelity? In this study approximately 200 undergraduates were given the following two scenarios to consider:

Scenario 1

Please think of a serious committed romantic relationship that you have had in the past, that you currently have, or that you would like to have. Imagine that you discover that

Incorporating the research of D. M. Buss, R. J. Larsen, D. Westen, and J. Semmelroth, "Sex Differences in Jealousy: Evolution, Physiology, and Psychology," 1992, *Psychological Science, 3*, pp. 251–255.

the person with whom you've been seriously involved became interested in someone else. What would distress or upset you more?

A—Imagining your partner forming a deep emotional attachment to that person.

or

B—Imagining your partner enjoying passionate sexual intercourse with that other person.

Scenario 2

Please think of a serious committed romantic relationship that you have had in the past, that you currently have, or that you would like to have. Imagine that you discover that the person with whom you've been seriously involved became interested in someone else. What would distress or upset you more?

A—Imagining your partner trying different sexual positions with that other person.

or

B—Imagining your partner falling in love with that other person.

(Both scenarios from Buss et al., 1992)

Between Scenarios 1 and 2 participants were given other questions to consider, but they were not part of the data collection in the study. It was likely that the investigators were providing some distracting material between the two scored scenarios so that participants would not focus solely on the two scenarios. This procedure of using material that will not be scored is a common practice. It is used so that participants were not immediately aware of what the experimenters are studying. In this study the two scenarios that formed the basis for further study were the same with slightly different forced-choice options. Although Buss does not specify his reasoning for this method, it is likely that each participant would have two opportunities to respond and that scores should be in the same direction for each scenario. In a sense it is an internal reliability check. If Buss and his collaborators obtained very different responses to each question within the male or within the female participant group, the reliability of this questionnaire measure would be in doubt. The results from this study are graphically displayed in Figure 19.1

In response to the first scenario, which asks participants to choose whether they would be more upset by sexual infidelity or strong emotional infidelity, 60 percent of the men were found to be upset by sexual infidelity whereas only 17 percent of women felt that way. In contrast, 83 percent of women found it more upsetting for their partner to form a deep emotional relationship. The different response patterns for men and women were found to be statistically significant ($p < .001$). In looking at the data from the second scenario, which asked participants to select between sexual infidelity and love infidelity, we see the same significant sexual differences ($p < .001$). Approximately 45 percent of males experienced more distress over sexual infidelity, whereas this was only found in approximately 13 percent of females. Women view emotional fidelity, in this case, "falling in love," as more distressing than purely sexual involvement.

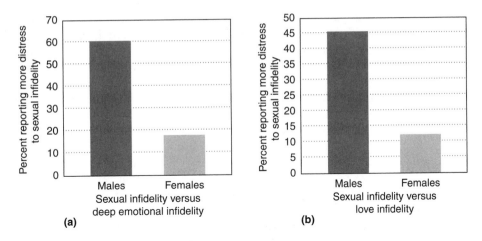

FIGURE 19.1 Distress Responses to Infidelity Jealousy Scenarios. Percentage of participants indicating more distress to sexual rather than emotional (a) and love (b) infidelity jealousy scenarios.

In the first study, participant's behavior was limited to a forced-choice questionnaire response. In the second investigation, the researchers used a number of physiological measures assessing autonomic arousal to determine if the same emotional response (i.e., jealousy) found in the first study, could be measured in a person's physiological response. Autonomic arousal measures involuntary physiological actions that are not under conscious, voluntary control. Therefore, assessment of autonomic responses serves as an additional and quite different source of information regarding jealousy than the forced-choice questionnaire responses. When possible, it is always desirable to have measures from a number of sources.

The following three different physiological arousal measures were used in the second study:

Electrodermal Activity (EDA): Electrodes on the fingers of the right hand measured changes in amplitude of electrodermal activity. This is a measure of changes in electrical activity in the skin. Although it may seem to be an odd measure, increases in it are indicative of increased arousal.

Pulse Rate (PR): Pulse rate in beats per minute was recorded from a device attached to participant's right thumb.

Electromyographic Activity (EMG): The amplitude of electrical activity in a muscle in the brow area of the face associated displays of negative emotion.

The participants in this study were 55 male and female undergraduate students. The procedure involved "hooking up" the participants to the three physiological measures and asking them to relax in a comfortable reclining chair. They were told to relax for 5 minutes before the formal part of the research began. Participants were in a room by themselves and were given instructions over an intercom. In addition, specific instructions for the upcoming imagery tasks were given to the participants in a written format. The participants were asked to imagine three different situations. The first image was used to obtain physiological recordings produced by a neutral situation. This was essentially an opportunity to get a baseline measure of participants' arousal levels and to get them comfortable in the laboratory. In the neutral scene, participants were asked to imagine themselves walking to class while they were feeling neither good nor bad. Participants were told to signal the experimenter by pressing a button when they had the scenario clearly in mind. When participants pressed the button physiological recordings on all measures were made for the next 20 seconds. The second and third images used the same recording procedures, but required the participants to imagine scenarios of sexual infidelity and emotional infidelity. Half of the participants were presented with the sexual infidelity scenario first and half had the emotional infidelity scenario first. This procedure, called counterbalancing, reduces the probability that the order of the presentation may influence the results. You can imagine that always giving the imagination scenario involving sexual jealousy first and emotional jealously second might well create some problems in interpreting the data. As a researcher you want to make every attempt to insure that your data is not a result of some incidental procedural practice. To create the image of sexual infidelity participants were instructed to:

> Please think of a serious romantic relationship that you have had in the past, that you currently have, or that you would like to have. Now imagine that the person with whom you're seriously involved becomes interested in someone else. *Imagine you find that your partner is having sexual intercourse with this person.* Try to feel the feelings you would have if this happened to you." (Buss et al., 1992)

The instructions were exactly the same for the emotional jealousy except the instruction in italics was changed to: *"Imagine that your partner is falling in love and forming an emotional attachment to that person."* The dependent outcomes of this second study were the three sources of physiological data recording following the participant's pressing of the button. Between the three imagination sessions, participants were told to relax for 30 seconds.

MAKING SENSE OF THE DATA

It is not uncommon for psychologists to transform raw data into scores that not only reflect the processes being measured, but also are more readily available to objective analysis. In order to make sense of three sets of physiological data over a 20-second interval the following procedures were used:

> *Electrodermal Activity (EDA):* The score used was the largest EDA amplitude found during the 20-second recording interval.
>
> *Pulse Rate (PR):* The score used was the average number of beats per minute during the 20-second interval.

Electromyographic Activity (EMG): The average amplitude during the 20-second interval.

The next step in processing the data was to obtain a difference score between (1) the two jealousy imagination sessions and (2) the neutral or baseline imagination session for each of the three measures. These difference scores were used in further data analysis.

The results of this second study are summarized in Table 19.1. As you can see, males showed more significant increases in EDA in response to sexual imagery than emotional imagery. For women the results were also significant, but in the opposite direction, that is, they experienced significantly more EDA to emotional imagery than to sexual imagery. For the males the PR findings were similar to the EDA results, or significantly greater arousal to sexual than to emotional imagery. For women elevated scores for emotional versus sexual imagery was seen on PR, but the differences were not significant. The results for both men and women on the EMG measure were similar to the pattern of EDA and PR; males showed greater arousal for sexual scenarios and females showed greater arousal for emotional scenarios, but the findings for both sexes were not significant. Even though some differences were not significant, all of the differences were in the predicted direction—males were more sexually jealous than females.

TABLE 19.1   Mean Difference Scores across Three Physiological Arousal Measures

AROUSAL MEASURE	IMAGERY SCENARIO	MEAN DIFFERENCE	SIGNIFICANT AT $p < .05$
		MALES	
EDA	Sexual	1.30	YES
EDA	Emotional	−.11	
PR	Sexual	4.76	YES
PR	Emotional	3.00	
EMG	Sexual	6.75	NO
EMG	Emotional	1.16	
		FEMALES	
EDA	Sexual	−.07	YES
EDA	Emotional	.21	
PR	Sexual	2.25	NO
PR	Emotional	2.57	
EMG	Sexual	3.03	NO
EMG	Emotional	8.12	

A third study was undertaken to evaluate whether or not having experienced a committed relationship would impact the results. The investigators hypothesized that females who had been in committed relationships would experience greater emotional jealousy than females who had not *and* that males who had been in a committed relationship would experience more sexual jealousy than males who had not. The researchers felt that the experience of being in a committed relationship would be a factor in initiating emotional jealousy for women and sexual jealousy for males.

The participants were more than 300 male and female undergraduate students who were given the following scenario to imagine:

> Please think of a serious or committed romantic relationship that you have had in the past, that you currently have, or that you would like to have. Imagine that you discover the person with whom you've been seriously involved became interested in someone else. What would distress or upset you more?
>
> **A**—Imagining your partner falling in love and forming a deep emotional attachment to that person.
>
> **B**—Imagining your partner having sexual intercourse with that other person.
>
> (From Buss et al., 1992)

The two alternatives were counterbalanced in presentation to the participants. After selecting one of the above options, the participants answered "yes" or "no" to two questions asking if they were ever in a serious or committed relationship. If they were, the participants were asked if it was a sexual relationship. The findings from this larger sample match closely with the results from the initial study. The results of this study are presented in Figure 19.2.

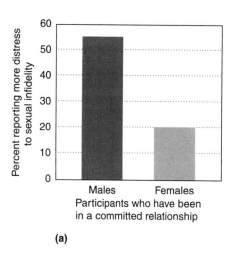
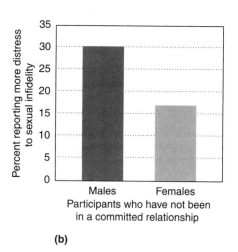

(a)   **(b)**

FIGURE 19.2   Distress Responses of Participants with (a) and without (b) Committed Relationship Experience. Percentage of participants indicating more distress to sexual rather than emotional jealousy.

It was found that a significantly larger percentage of men than women would be more upset if their partner were sexually involved with another person than if their partner was emotionally involved with another person. In looking at whether being in a committed, sexual relationship had an impact, the data are different for men and women. The results for men who experienced a committed sexual relationship was significantly different ($p < .001$) from those who never had. Fifty-five percent of the men with experience in committed, sexual relationships reported they would be more upset by sexual rather than emotional infidelity. In the group of men who never had experienced a committed sexual relationship only 29 percent felt this way. For women the data do not indicate any significant difference between those who had experienced a committed, sexual relationship and those who did not. Both groups of women were upset more by emotional infidelity than sexual infidelity, but for women being in a committed, sexual relationship did not play a significant role as it did with men.

WHAT'S IT ALL ABOUT?

These three studies were conducted to test the evolutionary hypothesis that men and women experience jealousy in different ways. In the initial study, significant differences were seen in male and female responses to stories of sexual infidelity versus emotional infidelity. The second investigation showed that physiological recordings assessing autonomic arousal were able to measure responses to both sexual and emotional jealousy. The Electrodermal and Pulse Rate records were especially sensitive in revealing how jealousy in this study differs between the sexes. The data from the physiological recordings provided an important source of support to the findings from the initial study. In addition, the correspondence in the data between questionnaire and physiological recordings suggests this is a pervasive effect that can be observed in various aspects of behavior. In the final investigation, there is good evidence replicating the findings from the initial study in addition to finding that men who have been in committed sexual relationships are particularly upset by sexual infidelity in their partners. The three studies taken as a group provide support that the jealousy experienced by men and women emerges from different sources; for men, sexual, and for women, emotional. Critics of the evolutionary approach may raise the criticism that the results obtained in these investigations could be a result of cultural conditioning, and not the outcome of biological-evolutionary processes. For the evolutionary viewpoint to respond to its critics who say the findings could be explained by cultural factors, it is important to replicate this study in a variety of different cultures. This is exactly what was done by Buunk, Angleitner, Oubaid, and Buss (1996) in comparing Dutch, German, and American participants and in a recent study by Buss, Shackelford, Kirkpatrick, Choe, Lim, Hasegawa, Hasegawa, and Bennett (1999), which compared Japanese, Korean, and American participants. In both of these research replications across diverse cultures, involving thousands of participants, the evolutionary approach is supported (i.e., males were sexually jealous, while females were emotionally jealous). This is usually seen as strong evidence against the "cultural conditioning" perspective because such conditioning is unlikely to be consistent across very different cultures. The findings in this series of investigations are consistent with evolutionary predictions and represent a good example of the process of empirically testing hypotheses derived from theory. The evolutionary psychology perspective, as new paradigm, often takes a strident stance against existing models in order to make its case. The evidence from this study and related research is certainly supportive of the evolutionary position. However, these findings do not preclude the influence of many other factors (including cultural, physiological, sociological) from playing important roles in determining our behavior.

REFERENCES

Buunk, B. P., Angleitner, A., Oubaid, V., & Buss, D. M. (1996). Sex differences in jealousy in evolutionary and cultural perspective: Tests from the Netherlands, Germany and the United States. *Psychological Science, 7,* 359–363.

Buss, D. M., Larsen, R. J., Westen, D., & Semmelroth, J. (1992). Sex differences in jealousy: Evolution, physiology, and psychology. *Psychological Science, 3,* 251–255.

Buss, D. M., Shackelford, T. K., Kirkpatrick, L. A, Choe, J. C., Lim, H. K., Hasegawa, M., Hasegawa, T., & Bennett, K. (1999). Jealousy and the nature of beliefs about infidelity: Tests of competing hypotheses about sex differences in the United States, Korea, and Japan. *Personal Relationships, 6,* 125–150.

CHAPTER 20

PANTS ON FIRE

Lives can depend on the ability to detect lies. Police and customs officers use this ability on a day-to-day basis. In most other occupations the detection of falsehoods may not be a life or death matter but, in one way or another, all of us hope that we are successful as lie detectors, particularly when it really matters. For example, we hope that we can tell that real estate agents, car dealers, and significant others are telling the truth.

As you might expect, this topic has drawn the attention of a number of psychological researchers. Most of the research in psychology has suggested that lie detection ability is not a stable trait. When we are in different situations or trying to detect lies from different people, our accuracy in lie detection may vary from good to poor (Kraut, 1978, 1980).

If a liar is under emotional strain, facial expressions of emotion might betray the lie. Paul Ekman and his coworkers have long been interested in the relationship between facial expression and emotions (Ekman & Friesen, 1971, 1975). In their 1971 study, they demonstrated that emotions could be recognized across cultures. In this study, pictures of facial emotions from Western societies were shown to people living in an isolated area of New Guinea. These people were asked to identify the emotion depicted. It was found that the research participants were usually more than 80 percent accurate in making these judgments, even though they had not had any extensive contact with Western people.

Ekman (1985) reasoned that so-called high-stake lies, where detection of the lie can result in major negative consequences for the liar, would be accompanied by facial expressions of emotion recognizable to many people. High-stake lies might, for example, be told by criminals attempting to avoid incarceration. If a jury believes the lie, a guilty person escapes penalties. The liar has a high stake in being believed, and Ekman expected the lie to be accompanied by facial expressions of emotion. Individuals who could detect these emotions through observation of facial expressions ought to be accurate high-stake lie detectors. Ekman further argued that people who are accurate high-stake lie detectors should be able to reliably detect lies across different situations, or different liars. This was expected because if an individual was good at detecting

Incorporating the research of M. G. Frank and P. Ekman, "The Ability to Detect Deceit Generalizes across Different Types of High-Stake Lies," 1997, *Journal of Personality and Social Psychology*, 72, pp. 1429–1439.

details of facial expressions, the emotions behind expressions should be noticeable whenever there were high-stake lies. Much of the previous research in psychology investigated the detection of trivial lies that made little or no real difference to the person who was lying. The liar was a confederate of the experimenter who had been told to lie about some small matter so that research participants could be presented with lies to detect. Ekman believed that these low-stake lies were less likely to be accompanied by strong emotion and, as a result, would be more difficult to detect. If this were correct, it would offer an explanation why past psychology studies had not found that lie detection generalized across situations. These trivial lies might be more likely to be detected through verbal behavior than facial expression of strong emotions. Ekman suspected that it is easier to lie with words than with genuine, strong emotions.

STIMULUS MATERIALS

Frank and Ekman (1997) did a carefully designed piece of research to investigate these issues. The first step in this investigation was the construction of videotapes depicting some people telling high-stake lies and some people telling the truth. Much of the first part of this chapter involves the method for constructing the stimulus tapes. Usually the term *participant* is used to refer to the people whose behaviors provide the outcome data for the research. In this study there were two sorts of participants: those involved in creating the stimulus materials and those whose responses were recorded as the data in the study. To avoid confusion, we will adopt the language of Frank and Ekman in calling the people who helped in the creation of stimulus materials *participants*. The people who viewed the stimulus tapes and made the ratings that became the outcome data, will be called *observers*. As will become obvious, the work in this study was divided into two parts: creation of stimulus videotapes and subsequent data collection using these tapes. Because Ekman believed that the facial expressions of emotion accompanying high-stake lies were difficult to fake, the creation of stimulus materials for the experiment required putting people in situations where they really wanted their lies to be believed. This required considerable human engineering.

Creation of the Stimulus Tapes

Twenty male participants age 18 to 28 were involved in the creation of stimulus videotapes. They were recruited from the San Francisco area and were told that they would be paid $10 an hour for participation, but that they might be able to make more. A first engineered situation, called the *crime scenario*, involved a mock theft of money. The "crime" in which they might participate involved taking $50 dollars from an envelope in a briefcase while they were alone in a lab room. They knew that it was not a real crime. They understood that the researchers planned to lose the money. They knew that the researchers expected some other participant to take the money if they did not. This "other participant" was a fictitious person only introduced because pilot testing had suggested that participants became very suspicious about the purpose of the entire procedure if they thought they were the only "suspect." Although the actual instructions to these participants were fairly complex (see Frank & Ekman, 1997), for our purposes it is only important to know that there was a role-play theft in which some of the participants took the money and some did not. Participants believed that the researchers could not be sure if the "thief" was them or the "other participant."

All participants were instructed to deny they had taken the money. Participants were told that if they chose to take the money and were able to convince an interrogator that they had *not* done so, they could keep the $50. If a participant took the money and the interrogator detected the lie, the participant was told he would lose not only the "stolen" $50, but also the $10 per hour that he was being paid for participating in the research. This created the high-stake situation—a successful lie could result in finishing participation with a tidy sum of money. Some participants chose not to take the $50. These participants were, of course, telling the truth when they were interrogated and denied taking the missing money. They were told that if their truthful denials were believed, they would get a $10 bonus in addition to the $10 per hour that they had been promised for being in the research. This was not as much money as the successful liars would get, but it was thought to be an easier task. However, if the interrogator did not believe their truthful denials, they were told they would not get the bonus and would lose their $10 hourly payment as well.

The same participants were also given a second situation in which they could lie or tell the truth. This one was called the *opinion scenario*. Participants were given a questionnaire that asked their opinion about various social issues and allowed them to rate their strength of feeling on the issue from 1 (strongly agree) to 7 (definitely disagree). The issues were things such as the death penalty and the banning of smoking in public places. The opinion that the participant felt most strongly about was selected as the one to be lied about or to be described truthfully. Participants could choose whether they would lie or tell the truth, and the reward structure was the same as in the crime scenario described above. Truth tellers who were believed received a $10 dollar bonus; liars who were believed received a $50 bonus. Liars or truth tellers who were disbelieved lost all money. All participants were instructed to claim that they were being honest in describing their beliefs.

All participants took part in the crime scenario first. They were told that the interrogator knew the money had been taken, but did not know who had taken it. After having the opportunity to take the money or not, they were taken to a small interrogation room. There were two chairs in that room: an uncomfortable metal one that was anchored to the floor and a comfortable padded chair. The participant was led to the metal chair and introduced to the interrogator, who had been described as an expert in deception. The interrogator really did not know if the participant had taken the money. The participant was interrogated for 5 to 7 minutes on a series of 20 questions from a printed list.

At this point, the interrogator left and the researcher reentered and described the opinion scenario. The participant was told that he should choose whether he wanted to lie or tell the truth about his opinion. He was then told that he would have about 2 minutes to think about what he was going to say. After 2 minutes, the interrogator returned and asked another 20 scripted questions, similar to those asked in the crime interrogation. When this was complete, the participant was given a questionnaire that asked about his suspicions concerning the research, how good he felt he had been at convincing the interrogator, and the extent to which he feared the consequences of being judged as a liar.

After this, the participants were told that their part in the research was over. They were informed of the interrogator's judgment concerning whether they had been lying about each scenario. Any bonus money that had been promised was paid. Those accurately judged as having lied were reminded they would not receive any bonus money but, in contrast to expectations, all participants were paid the $10 per hour that they had been promised at the time they volunteered for the research. This was probably part of an effort to restore positive feelings about the research: the promise made during recruitment was kept. They were debriefed about the details of the research and dismissed.

Two videotapes were created, one containing men being interrogated about the crime scenario and one featuring men being interrogated about the opinion scenario. The tapes were assembled using the first six questions a participant answered. For the crime scenario, these were questions such as, "Describe exactly what happened, what you saw and did when you were in that room." "Did you take the money from the envelope?" and "Are you lying to me now?" For the opinion scenario, questions included, "What is your position on this current event issue?" "Is this your true opinion?" and "You didn't just make up this opinion a few minutes ago?" These tapes were edited down so that, in the end, each tape contained five men telling the truth and five men lying. No participant appeared more than once on each tape. For the opinion video, a few specific social issues were selected for inclusion and equal numbers of men were lying and telling the truth about these issues.

Stakes Confirmation

Frank and Ekman believed that the threatened loss of $50 and the $10 hourly fee would be enough to induce strong emotions in the liars. In order to establish that this high-stakes situation was associated with emotion, they had a person trained in scoring emotions look at both of the final edited videotapes. This rater scored the tapes using the Facial Action Coding System (FACS), (Ekman & Friesen, 1978). This is a standardized system that records all visible facial muscle movements, not only those presumed to be involved with emotion. Past research had established that each basic emotion was associated with particular patterns of muscle movements (Ekman, 1985). Based on these findings, it was predicted that the high-stake liars on these videos should show specific facial muscle movements associated with the emotions *fear* (of getting caught) and *disgust* (at oneself for lying). When scores of both videos were combined, the scorer found that 90 percent of the participants could be correctly identified as liars based on facial muscle movements associated with fear and disgust. Seventy percent of the truth tellers could be correctly identified by the absence of facial indicators of fear and disgust. A second FACS trained rater rescored 20 percent of the videos as a reliability check and the agreement between them was 76 percent.

The presence or absence of facial expressions of emotion in the men confirmed two important things. First, it indicated that the liars were, indeed, in a high-stake situation because they displayed empirical evidence of strong emotions. Second, this finding indicated that there was an observable difference when the facial expressions of high-stake liars were compared to those of people telling the truth. The difference had been captured in the participants on the two videotapes. This enabled Frank and Ekman to proceed to their primary research question: How reliable are ordinary people—presumably responding to these differences—at detecting high-stake lies? Their hypothesis was that some people would be consistently better at high-stake lie detection than others. Frank and Ekman were also interested in the overall level of accuracy of lie detection, but made no particular prediction about this before the data were collected.

STUDY 1

The most important outcome measure was the observer's accuracy for each videotape. It might seem that whether the person was lying or not should be considered the independent variable. In a strict technical sense this is not an independent variable because the experimenter did not create it: people chose for themselves whether they were going to lie or tell the truth. Nevertheless it was an important variable and was associated with the most interesting findings in the study. As you know by now, the only reason why this is an issue is that one should be cautious about asserting a cause-and-effect relationship unless dealing with a real, randomly assigned, independent variable. To help you understand this, imagine that all the people who chose to tell the truth were also personally more confident and secure than those who chose to lie. Observers watching the tapes might have responded to the display of confidence, not to the lie. Because this is possible, it is not correct to call lying or being truthful an independent variable in this study. The usual way to solve this in research design is to randomly assign some people to lie and some people to be truthful. Probably Frank and Ekman thought they would get higher quality performances if participants could choose to lie or be truthful. In designing the study the way they did, our confidence about cause-and-effect relationships was undermined. It is our judgment that this study should be considered a quasi-experiment because of the lack of a real independent variable.

Compromise is common in the design of scientific studies. In this case it was necessitated because the participant's performance was the real priority. It may seem that we are worrying too much about a small matter, but we want you to be able to think critically and clearly about study outcomes. Researchers will sometimes consider, for example, gender to be an independent variable. Gender is not a characteristic that is randomly assigned by an experimenter and as a critical thinker you should exercise caution in drawing cause-and-effect conclusions when it is a variable in a study. Some statistical techniques routinely call one variable an *independent variable*, even though it is not really *independent*. For the purposes of this book, we have tried to be consistent, using this term only when the study is a true experiment. We are aware that this degree of caution is unusual, but we think it is important. We want you to be able to think clearly about research findings regardless of the terms that are used by a particular author.

The Judgment Procedure

Forty-nine observers were recruited, and they viewed the videotapes in an attempt to detect lies. They were 32 females and 17 males who were students at San Francisco State University. They received course credit for being observers. They watched the tapes with groups of seven to ten other observers. They were told that they would be seeing 10 men who were being interrogated about a crime and 10 men who were being interrogated about their opinion on a current event topic. One observer did not follow instructions and was dropped from the study. Observers were given a form that permitted them to circle the word *truthful* or *lying* after viewing each participant's segment of the tape. Ability to detect lies was operationally defined as success on this task. The observers were told that between one fourth and three fourths of the men they would see were lying. This was done to prevent observers from merely assuming that all the participants were either lying or truthful. Before and after the videotapes were viewed, observers were asked to rate their own ability to detect lying in other people. These ratings were done on a five point scale where 1 = *very poor* and 5 = *very good*.

Results of Study 1

Accuracy scores of observers were calculated by counting the number of correct judgments, out of 10 possible, for each video. In order to make the results easier to understand, data are presented as percentages. Each video had been constructed to contain five men who were lying and five who were telling the truth. Because there were two choices, lying or truth, an observer who only guessed would average 50 percent correct. Frank and Ekman divided the observers into two groups: high accuracy: those getting 60 percent or more correct and low accuracy, those getting 50 percent or fewer correct. The number of high and low scorers for each scenario is shown in Table 20.1.

As this table shows, people who scored high on the crime scenario were also likely to score high on the opinion scenario. Although less pronounced, the same trend can be seen for low scorers. You can see this by looking at the diagonally positioned cells on the table: the high/high cell in the upper left and the low/low cell in the lower

TABLE 20.1   Number of Observers Scoring High and Low on Each of the Scenarios in Study 1

		OPINION SCENARIO SCORE	
		High	*Low*
CRIME SCENARIO SCORE	*High*	21	6
	Low	9	12

right. In contrast, looking at the diagonal cells in the other direction—the high/low and low/high—there were not too many observers who scored high on one scenario and low on the other. Although it may take a bit of study to understand this table, it is worth your time to do so, because this is a standard method for presenting data assessing two levels of behavior in two situations.

There were also some interesting correlational findings among the results. There was a significant positive correlation ($r = .48$, $p < .001$) between the performance of an observer on the crime scenario and on the opinion scenario. This indicates that those who performed well on one performed well on the other. Those who achieved about the chance level on one did about the same on the other, and those who were poor at lie detection on one videotape were also poor lie detectors when watching the other tape. These accuracy scores for individual observers ranged from 10 percent to 90 percent for the opinion video and from 10 percent to 80 percent for the crime video. These data can be used to illustrate the difference between the detection of ordinary and high-stake lies. In other psychology research, where lies were not high stake, it was unusual for any measured accuracy to surpass 60 percent (DePaulo, Zuckerman, & Rosenthal 1980). Neither the gender of the observer nor the order of videotape presentation had any effect on the results.

No relationship was found between observer's pretest or posttest ratings of *confidence* in their detection ability and their *actual* detection ability. People do not know how good or bad they have been, or are going to be, when it comes to actually detecting lies. Even though these assessments had no relationship to actual detection they did have a relationship to each other: observers who thought they were good lie detectors before seeing the tapes continued to think they were good lie detectors after the tape, even though confidence was, in fact, unrelated to accuracy. This is a good example of a situation in which reliability is not evidence of validity.

STUDY 2

Study 2 was similar to Study 1, but it was also an attempt to directly demonstrate that observers who were good at recognizing facial expressions of emotions would also be good at detecting high-stake lies. In addition, Study 2 provided a replication of Study 1.

The observers in Study 2 were 13 male and 17 female undergraduates from San Jose State University who received course credit for taking part in the research. These observers saw the two deception videotapes developed for Study 1. As in Study 1, they were asked to rate pretest and posttest confidence in their ability to detect lying. Study 2 differed because after judging the videotapes, participants were all given a test of accuracy in judging facial expressions of emotion, called the *microexpression test*.

The 40-item microexpression test consisted of slides of facial expressions of emotions. The emotions depicted were anger, contempt, disgust, fear, happiness, sadness, and surprise. These slides were presented using an apparatus called a tachistoscope, which is essentially a slide projector with a shutterlike device that controls duration of presentation of the slide. In this case, the pictures of facial emotions were on the screen for $\frac{1}{25}$ of a second. Although this may not seem very long, it is easily long enough to see the facial expression. This slide show was videotaped for presentation to the observers. After each picture of an emotion was briefly flashed on the screen, the observer was given the opportunity to identify the emotion by circling the answer from a list of the seven emotions. Presenting the emotions for such a short period of time made the task more challenging and presumably helped to separate those who were good at identifying emotions from those who were not.

As in Study 1, a hypothesis in this study was that observers who were good at finding liars in the crime tape would also be good at finding liars in the opinion tape. Frank and Ekman further predicted that there would be a positive correlation between performance on the microexpression test and the successful detection of lies in the crime and opinion scenarios. As in Study 1, they also expected to find no relationship between confidence in lie detection ability and accuracy at lie detection.

Results of Study 2

As had been found in Study 1, neither the gender of the observer nor the order of videotape presentation had any effect on the results. As in Study 1, observers who were 60 percent accurate or higher were classified as high scorers and those 50 percent and below were considered to be low scorers. Table 20.2 shows the number of observers who were high and low scorers for each tape in Study 2.

A statistically significant positive correlation ($r = .31$, $p < .05$) was found between the detection of lies in the opinion video and the detection of lies in the crime video. There was a significant positive correlation ($r = .34$, $p < .04$) between the successful identification of emotions on the microexpression test and the successful detection of lies in the crime video. The relation between microexpression accuracy and opinion video accuracy was a positive correlation, but it was not statistically significant ($r = .20$, $p = .15$). It is not obvious why this happened, but unanticipated variation from one version of a study to another is not highly unusual. As in Study 1, observer's ratings of pretest and posttest confidence indicated, in Frank and Ekman's words, that "observers seem to have fairly reliable beliefs about their abilities to detect deception, independent of their actual ability" (p. 1436).

TABLE 20.2   Number of Observers Scoring High and Low on Each of the Scenarios in Study 2

		OPINION SCENARIO SCORE	
		High	*Low*
CRIME SCENARIO SCORE	*High*	15	4
	Low	4	7

DISCUSSION AND CONCLUSIONS

The results of these two studies suggest that the ability to detect high-stake lies may not vary much from one lie to the next, but may, instead, be a more general trait that some people possess and some people do not. The ability to accurately read emotions from facial expressions seems to be related to this ability and may well be an important component of it. This kind of cautious language is required here because the data were correlational, so although a relationship was established, there was no evidence for a cause-and-effect relationship between emotion recognition and lie detection. There may, of course, *be* a cause-and-effect relationship here, but a correlation is not sufficient evidence to confirm it.

Given the findings of these studies, it is possible to imagine a true experiment that might help to determine if recognition of emotions is a cause of lie detection. An approach might be to identify a group of people who were not good at emotion recognition, randomly assign them to two groups and train one group to recognize emotions. This presumes that it is possible to train this skill, which, by itself, is another interesting question. Once this skill had been developed, both groups could be given an appropriate lie detection task to see if the group that was taught the emotion detection skill would do better at lie detection. This design could be strengthened if these groups were given a lie detection assessment before training to assure that the groups were not different in lie detection before one group received training. It is easy to *imagine* further research, but we would not want the ease of this interesting activity to distract you from an appreciation of the vast amount of work involved in actually conducting such a study. Aside from the hard work involved in creating the stimulus videotapes, the study that we imagine would also involve a long-term commitment from observers through the training program.

Frank and Ekman showed appropriate caution in the interpretation of their results. Although they believed that the identification of emotions was a component of the detection of deceit, they also stated that lie detection probably involves a number of skills and abilities, some closely related to each other and some not. Because there is no one characteristic that is always present in people who are lying, there can be no one strategy that will always result in successful lie detection. It is highly probable that some people can tell lies, even high-stake lies, while exhibiting no outward evidence of emotional responses. It was clear from this study, however, that many liars do give themselves away, at least to the skilled observer. The significant correlations in this study are of moderate strength, being in the range of .30 to the middle .40s. Although they have some predictive power, it is clear that other, unknown, factors also play a role in lie detection.

Frank and Ekman noted that there are two rather different approaches that might be used in the application of these findings to professional high-stake lie detection in agencies. One approach would be to attempt training using facial emotion recognition. The other would be to identify those people within the organization who are already reliably good at lie detection and have these individuals take responsibility for this task, saving the investment that would be required for training programs. Either way, the future practical application of this important area of research is obvious.

R E F E R E N C E S

DePaulo, B. M., Zuckerman, M., & Rosenthal, R. (1980). Humans as lie detectors. *Journal of Communication, 30,* 129–139.

Ekman, P. (1985). *Telling lies: Clues to deceit in the marketplace, politics and marriage.* New York: Norton.

Ekman, P., & Friesen, W. V. (1971). Constants across cultures in the face and emotion. *Journal of Personality and Social Psychology, 17,* 124–129.

Ekman, P., & Friesen, W. V. (1975). *Unmasking the face: A guide to recognizing emotions from facial cues.* Upper Saddle River, NJ: Prentice Hall.

Ekman, P., & Friesen, W. V. (1978). *The facial action coding system.* Palo Alto, CA: Consulting Psychologists Press.

Frank, M. G., & Ekman, P. (1997). The ability to detect deceit generalizes across different types of high-stake lies. *Journal of Personality and Social Psychology, 72,* 1429–1439.

Kraut. R. E. (1978). Verbal and nonverbal cues in the perception of lying. *Journal of Personality and Social Psychology, 36,* 380–391.

Kraut, R. E. (1980). Humans as lie detectors: Some second thoughts. *Journal of Communication, 30,* 209–216.

CHAPTER 21

AGGRESSION BREEDS AGGRESSION

Popular culture, self-help books, and pop psychology foster the belief that externalizing anger, hostility, or aggression is therapeutic. This process of catharsis or venting feelings, often on inanimate objects, is proposed as a healthy way to reduce the impact of negative emotions. Striking a pillow or hitting a punching bag are advocated as cathartic release techniques. Lee (1993), in a mass market self-help book, advocates that "If you are angry at a particular person, imagine his or her face on the pillow or punching bag, and vent your rage physically and verbally . . . you are not hitting a person. You are hitting the ghost of that person—a ghost from the past, . . . that must be exorcised in a concrete, physical way" (p. 96). The catharsis hypothesis is endorsed widely and has led people to believe that venting anger is a positive, healthy strategy that will make you feel better. The research presented in this chapter focuses on the following questions: (1) Can media endorsement of catharsis lead people to engage in cathartic activities such as venting anger? and (2) If people believe in the benefits of catharsis, will acting in an aggressive manner lead to reduced feelings of aggression?

WHAT IS CATHARSIS
AND DOES IT HAVE SUPPORT?

Catharsis has a long history and has a great deal of contemporary mass media support. Aristotle advocated viewing tragic plays as a means of catharsis to cleanse personal emotional issues. Freud's views, which certainly dominated early-twentieth-century thinking, suggest that the internal build-up of pent-up emotions are responsible for conversion and anxiety disorders. Freud's thinking is often referred to as the *plumbing or hydraulic model*; as negative emotions build up internally the "hydraulic" pressure inside the person increases, like water behind a dam.

Because this pressure represents an uncomfortable state, an external release is proposed as being adaptive for the person (Geen & Quantry, 1977). The self-help book

Incorporating the research of B. J. Bushman, R. F. Baumeister, and A. Stack, "Catharsis, Aggression, and Persuasive Influence: Self-Fulfilling or Self-Defeating Prophecies?" 1999, *Journal of Personality and Social Psychology*, 76, pp. 367–376.

by Lee (1993) mentioned above cites a number of ways to focus your hostilities on inanimate objects including breaking glass, twisting a towel, and using a plastic baseball bat to strike a couch. Exploring the catharsis data from empirical studies, Tavris (1988) determined that there has been almost no research support for the value of catharsis in getting rid of negative feelings. On the other hand, it is very possible that venting anger through a cathartic process can lead to higher levels of feelings of aggression (Berkowitz, 1984; Tice & Baumeister, 1993). In spite of this, however, catharsis continues to be seen in our culture, as a remedy for anger and hostility, and the belief remains resistant to modification.

THE CURRENT SITUATION

Popular Media: Endorses the catharsis hypothesis as truth and produces books, tapes, and articles in support. Because popular media are pervasive, the general public believes this view is fact.

Scientific Psychology: No validation for catharsis but support for just the opposite—acting in a violent manner leads to more violence.

SELF-FULFILLING AND SELF-DEFEATING PROPHECIES

In the first experiment, participants were evaluated to see if pro- or anti-catharsis messages influenced their decision to select a method to cope with anger. The researchers hypothesized that participants exposed to pro-catharsis messages would elect to vent their anger by engaging in aggressive acts against inanimate objects. A second experiment explored the after effects of a participant's choice. Participants were exposed to one of three catharsis messages: pro-catharsis, anti-catharsis, or a control message that said nothing about catharsis. After being encouraged to engage in aggression by striking a punching bag, they were given the chance to engage in aggressive behavior toward a person who has angered them. Would the prepunching message they received be a factor in determining later aggressive behavior? Bushman et al. (1999) suggest that a *self-fulfilling prophecy* viewpoint (a person's beliefs lead to outcomes consistent with expectations) would lead to low aggression after the participants engaged in the physical aggression of hitting the punching bag. On the other hand, a *self-defeating prophecy* (a person's beliefs lead to outcomes opposite to expectations) would lead to higher levels of aggression after engaging in slugging the punching bag. This is not a socially desirable outcome.

First Experiment

The participants in this experiment were 180 male and 180 female introductory psychology students who volunteered and also received additional class credit. They were given a cover story that the investigators were studying people's perceptions in a variety of situations. Participants were assigned randomly to one of three message conditions: pro-catharsis, anti-catharsis, and a control condition. The participants in all conditions were asked to write a brief essay on the topic of abortion, taking either a pro-choice or pro-life position. Half of the participant's essays were assigned to receive very negative evaluations regardless of the quality of the essay, and the other half were assigned to receive very positive evaluations. This was accomplished by comments such as "This is one of the worst essays I have read" in the negative condition or "No suggestions, great essay" in the positive condition. Previous research by Bushman and Baumeister (1998) supported the view that the above manipulation does, in fact, create significantly more anger in the group receiving the negative evaluation than in the group receiving positive evaluations. Next the participants were given 10 activities to place in rank order based on their desire to engage in these activities later in the experiment. Activities in the rank ordering included reading, playing cards, playing computer games, and hitting a punching bag.

This research is an experiment with two independent variables, *media message* (pro-catharsis, anti-catharsis, control), and *anger level* (angered or not angered by feedback). The dependent variable was the participants' preference ranking of "hitting a punching bag" among nine other activities.

Results of Experiment 1

The major results of this experiment are presented in Figure 21.1. Participants who were angry as a result of their essay evaluations and who received the pro-catharsis message ranked hitting the punching bag significantly higher than angry participants who received the anti-catharsis message or those participants who were in the control condition. In the groups of participants that were not angered by the essay grading, the anti-catharsis and pro-catharsis messages played no role in their rank of interest in hitting a punching bag. Overall, participants who received the anti-catharsis message were significantly less likely to want to hit the punching bag than participants who received the pro-catharsis message ($p < .05$). Lastly, sex of participants played a role in wanting to hit the punching bag, with males participants having significantly higher rankings than females ($p < .05$). This experiment shows that messages from such popular media as self-help books, segments on the evening television news, and talk shows can impact an individual's choice to behave in an aggressive manner or not when provoked to anger. The researchers, Bushman, Baumeister, and Strack, thought it was conceivable that demand characteristics found in the experiment may have been responsible for the findings. *Demand characteristics* are environmental or situational stimuli that guide our behavior. Small, seemingly insignificant messages and stimuli can play a major role in determining our behavior. For example, if you are led to believe (even in the mildest way) that a course exam in college will be very difficult, it may affect your test-taking style and performance. This is true even if the exam is quite easy. Similarly, the sanctuary for a religious service contains demand characteristics for being quiet, reverent, and serious. An important interview in your senior year in college for a great job contains demand characteristic for formal dress and formal manners.

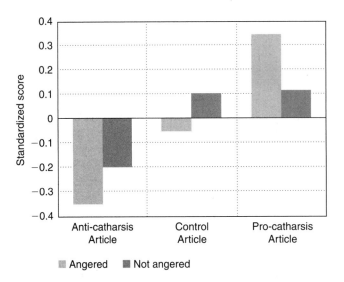

FIGURE 21.1   Bag Punching Preferences as a Function of Anger and Media Message. Preferences are displayed as standardized scores with positive scores indicating greater aggressive preferences, and negative scores indicating lower preferences for aggressive action.

In their initial experiment Bushman et al. (1999) thought it might be feasible that the participants' ranking of "bag punching" might have been affected by the specific mention of "bag punching" in the pro-catharsis message. Were the participants just giving the researchers what they thought researchers wanted? In other words, did "bag punching" in the pro-catharsis message serve as a demand characteristic that affected their later ranking? Remember that only the pro-catharsis group had "bag puching" in their message. The researchers could not simply eliminate this possibility and so designed a second experiment to clarify what was happening.

Second Experiment

In this experiment participants were given the chance to actually express anger toward an individual who had angered them. In the initial experiment, the outcome measure was a self-reported ranking; in this experiment the outcome measure was behavioral. In addition, the researchers were able to determine how cathartic aggressive behavior might impact a person's anger level. Would such actions lower one's anger as the catharsis hypothesis suggests, or not?

The participants were similar to the first experiment with 350 males and 357 females. Participants were evaluated individually and were told that the research project involved the accuracy of perceptions of people in various interactions. Participants were randomly assigned to one of three conditions; pro-catharsis, anti-catharsis, or control condition with no relevancy to catharsis. The next step was similar to the first experiment, with participants writing a brief pro-life or pro-choice essay on abortion. Participants were led to believe that another participant would evaluate the essays. In fact, the essays were *all* given very poor assessments with comments describing poor organization, style, clarity, persuasiveness, and overall quality. As in the initial experiment there was a written comment stating that "This is one of the worst essays I have read." The same ranking procedure used in the initial experiment was used, with one of the 10 possible activities, "hitting a punching bag."

The next step was new to the procedure and involved participants actually hitting a punching bag. Participants were placed in a room with the punching bag, given boxing gloves, and encouraged to hit the bag for 2 minutes. After completing the punching bag exercise participants were asked to indicate their level of enjoyment in slugging the bag. The next step involved having participants engage in what they believed would be a competitive reaction time task. Participants were given instructions to press a button as quickly as they could in response to a signal because they were in competition with another participant. Some of the participants were told that their competitor was the person who evaluated their essay (remember all participants received very negative evaluations designed to induce anger), while other participants were informed that their competitor was unknown to them. The information about their competitor was transmitted to the participants before the bag punching exercise. This was done so that participants could "use" the bag punching exercise as a chance to "vent" their anger *or* to hold on to the anger and direct it against the person who made them angry by insulting them with a negative essay evaluation. The slowest of the pair in the competitive reaction time task would be subjected to a noise blast administered by the winner. The intensity of the noise could be set at one of 10 levels ranging from 60 decibels to 105 decibels. Participants could also select a no-noise condition. A second variable of the noise choice was the duration of the noise to the loser by the winner. The winner administered the noise by holding down a button. The longer the button was depressed the longer the noise was administered. Participants could therefore effectively "punish" other participants by selecting the level and duration of the aversive sound. In summary, the trial winner had control of a "noise gun" that could zap the other competitor. The competitive reaction time task had an initial trial followed by 24 succeeding trials. On the initial trial the "real participant" always won, and on the succeeding 24 trials the "real participant" won half the time. Because the experimental procedure is somewhat complex, the following procedural summary is provided.

- Participants randomly assigned to one of three conditions (Pro-catharsis, anti-catharsis, control)
- Participants write pro-life or pro-choice essays
- All essays given very negative written feedback to induce anger
- Ranking list of activities, which included punching a bag
- Some participants informed they would engage in competitive reaction task later with grader of their essay

- Participants engage in 2-minute punching bag session with enjoyment level measured by self-rating
- Participants engage in competitive reaction task (competitor is believed to be essay grader or non-essay grader)
- Participants could inflict various levels of noise "pain" for various time duration

Results of Experiment 2

Sex of Participants.   Male participants showed a trend toward higher levels of aggressive behavior across all measures.

Angry Pro-Catharsis Participants.   Participant rankings for the 10 activities were quite similar to Experiment 1, with participants who were made angry and exposed to the pro-catharsis message showing significantly more desire to hit the bag than participants made angry who were exposed to the anti-catharsis message ($p < .05$). In addition, participants showed a trend to hit the punching bag more (but not significantly so) when they were aware they would be interacting later with the person who made them angry by evaluating their essay unfavorably ($p < .10$).

Zapping Your Competitor.   An additional component of Experiment 2 was to observe whether or not participants from various conditions, if given the opportunity, would show more hostility in punishing the person who made them angry. The dependent measures to determine this were level of noise intensity chosen and duration of exposure chosen. Both were seen as measures of anger toward the source or the aggression. Since these measures correlated significantly with each other a single *composite intensity + duration measure* was used to assess aggressive interpersonal behavior. The researchers thought that the initial trial (out of 25) represented the best test of aggressive behavior. They reasoned that on the next 24 trials the participant's aggressiveness response would be affected by how aggressive their competitor had been toward them. The results of aggressivity on trial 1 showed a trend for participants who received the pro-catharsis message to be more aggressive than both the anti-catharsis and control message groups ($p < .10$). On the remaining trials the pro-catharsis message group behaved in a significantly more aggressive manner than did the anti-catharsis message group participants do ($p < .05$).

People Like to Punch.   Seventy-two percent of participants liked to hit the punching bag with no differences observed between message conditions. Male participants enjoyed slugging the bag more than females.

Does Hitting the Bag Lead to Catharsis?   Further analyses of pro-catharsis participants who hit the punching bag show higher aggressive levels in the *composite intensity*

+ *duration measure* than participants who did not hit the bag. These findings are contrary to the catharsis hypothesis.

These findings from Experiment 2 supported the results of the initial experiment. Hitting a punching bag does not appear to yield a cathartic effect. On the contrary, it increases aggressive behavior. Experiment 2 also provided a replication of the finding that desire to hit a punching bag ranked higher among the pro-catharsis participants than other groups.

This research shows that messages from the media can impact behavior. Most importantly we discovered that interpersonal aggression is heightened by a pro-catharsis message even after participants have been given a chance to supposedly let off steam by hitting a punching bag. Pro-catharsis participants seem to increase in aggressive behavior rather than show a lessening of anger. The findings support the viewpoint that a belief in catharsis appears to initiate a self-defeating prophecy.

CONCLUSIONS

The researchers in this experiment could not see any beneficial cathartic effect even when participants were given positive messages about its benefits. Catharsis leads to aggressivity rather than dampens it. Why then does the catharsis model retain its current popularity, prestige, and power? Bushman et al. (1999) suggests that the pop media endlessly promotes the catharsis as therapeutic, and people may believe it is a natural, normal process to lower one's anger level. In addition, because it has a long history, people may have come to believe it must be correct.

It is frequently the case that old ideas take a long time to die out, especially in psychology. The Rorschach inkblot technique for personality assessment and clinical diagnosis has consistently been found to have low validity and reliability when scored by traditional methods. However it is still in wide usage among clinicians. This data from this research suggests that pro-catharsis actions are not effective in reducing aggressive behavior. In fact, catharsis promotes aggressive behavior and, therefore, is a hazard to personal, social, and community life. Alternatives to the catharsis hypothesis such as self-control and nonaggressive behavior should be promoted widely.

REFERENCES

Berkowitz, L. (1984). Some effects of thoughts on anti-social and pro-social influences of media effects: A cognitive-neoassociation analysis. *Psychological Bulletin, 95*, 410–427.
Bushman, B. J., & Baumeister, R. F. (1998). Threatened egotism, narcissism, self-esteem, and direct and displaced aggression: Does self-love or self-hate lead to violence? *Journal of Personality and Social Psychology, 75*, 219–229.
Bushman, B. J., Baumeister, R. F., & Stack, A. (1999). Catharsis, aggression, and persuasive influence: Self-fulfilling or self-defeating prophecies? *Journal of Personality and Social Psychology, 76*, 367–376.

Geen, R. G., & Quantry, M. B. (1977). The catharsis of aggression: An evaluation of a hypothesis. In L. Berkowitz (Ed.), *Advances in experimental social psychology* (Vol. 10, pp. 1–37). New York: Academic Press.

Lee, J. (1993). *Facing the fire: Experiencing and expressing anger appropriately.* New York: Bantam.

Tavris, C. (1988). Beyond cartoon killings: Comments on two overlooked effects of television. In S. Oskamp (Ed.), *Television as a social issue* (pp. 189–197). Newbury Park, CA: Sage.

Tice, D. M., & Baumeister, R. F. (1993). Controlling anger: Self-induced emotion change. In D. M. Wegner & J. W. Pennebaker (Eds.), *Handbook of mental control* (pp. 393–409). Upper Saddle River, NJ: Prentice Hall.

CHAPTER 22

PERSONALITY: TRAITS OR SITUATIONS?

Is our personality composed of a number of traits that are consistent across a variety of situations? This trait view of personality would mean that if we possessed the trait of honesty then we would be honest at work, with our friends, with family, and even with strangers. The trait view likens our personality traits to physical traits that are also consistent across situations. For example, a woman with blue eyes is always going to have blue eyes no matter what circumstance she is in. If she wins the state lottery, loses a close friend, obtains a great job, or finds she has a serious illness, her eye color will remain blue. In this same manner, trait theorists in psychology view our personality as composed of a number of relatively enduring characteristics, or traits, that remain constant across a wide variety of situations. Some examples of traits that have been proposed in a number of theories are extraversion/introversion, emotional expressiveness, assertiveness, and self-esteem. In contrast, the situational view of personality proposes that we behave in ways that are a function of the situations we are in. For example, at a funeral, participants usually demonstrate patterns of behavior that may include being reverent, quiet, solemn, and dressing in a particular mode. The same may be true for weddings, job interviews, or being a student in a large lecture hall. The situation of being in a large classroom often elicits behaviors such as sitting passively, having blank expressions, holding pens, and sitting as far back in the classroom as possible. It is likely that highly controlled environments, such as large lecture rooms, tend to produce uniform patterns of behaviors. Such environments are referred to as strongly scripted situations because like actors in a play, we all are given roles and scripts by our culture and we behave or "act out" our "parts." The research investigations of David Funder and C. Randall Colvin reported in this chapter explore this very question: How consistent is our behavior across situations?

In order to understand the competing views of the origin of personality, a mini-digression into trait theory and situational specificity is warranted. Gordon Allport (1937), the "grandfather" of trait theory, presented in clear, concise language the

Incorporating the research of D. C. Funder and C. R. Colvin, "Explorations in Behavioral Consistency: Properties of Persons, Situations, and Behaviors," 1991, *Journal of Personality and Social Psychology*, *60*, pp. 773–794.

fundamental view of traits as basic building blocks of personality. The following presents Allport's assertions regarding traits.

1. Traits are part of the person. They do not just have stated existence. Traits are real.
2. Traits are not just habits. Traits are more generalized. Washing your hands and bathing may be habits, while personal cleanliness may be a trait.
3. Traits are not just frozen structural entities. They are active and determine our behavior.
4. Traits can be assessed by measurement techniques.
5. Traits are relatively independent of other traits.
6. Moral and social judgments are not traits.
7. Traits may be seen in terms of individual personality (the idiographic approach) or in light of their distribution in a population (the nomethetic approach.) Therefore, you can study the trait structure within a person or across a population.
8. A behavior exhibited by a person that is not consistent with a trait within that person is *not* proof that the trait is absent. In a given circumstance a person may choose not to display a particular trait.

The eighth point in the above summary is interesting because it is an escape clause that allowed Allport to maintain a trait theory even though there were obvious exceptions to the theory. This is inconsistent with the general principles of scientific inquiry in which findings that do not conform to a theory force modifications or abandonment of the theory. It is interesting that several major theories of personality, including Sigmund Freud's psychoanalysis and Carl Rogers's client-centered views also have similar escape clauses.

The traditional study of personality developed theories to account for how individuals behave, think, feel, and experience life. The theories that emerged were largely trait models. A by-product of this approach has been the development of personality assessment as a discipline. The assessment techniques that emerged were geared toward assessing significant personality traits, which were assumed to be a good measure of people in a wide variety of human environments. Today, many organizations use personality assessment as part of the hiring and employment process. These organizations use the assessment findings as predictive measures of how prospective employees will function at a later time and in a wide variety of situations. If the human resources department believed that the assessment findings were only situationally specific and therefore limited to the time of the assessment, they would likely find very little utility in the assessment. The organization is not really interested in how a future employee may respond at 9 A.M. on a Tuesday in November, but rather how this person is going to behave in the work environment during a career with the company. In Chapter 15, "Golden Oldies" we discussed the Minnesota Multiphasic Personality Inventory (MMPI), a trait-based questionnaire used to measure aspects of mental illness. In Chapter 6, "Zipping Up the Genes," we discussed the California Psychological Inventory (CPI), a trait-based measure of normal personality features. Both of the above self-report personality inventories are used widely for mental health, personnel, forensic, and research purposes and are based on a trait view of personality.

In sharp contrast to the trait theory of personality, the situational view of personality began to grow in importance with the "power of the situation" social psychology research of the 1960s and 1970s. The approach stresses the importance of the social environment in determining behavior. The research studies of Stanley Milgram (1973), aimed at gaining understanding of obedience to malevolent authority, and the work of Bibb Latané and John Darley (1970), in exploring the apathy of bystanders, found that situational variables played a powerful role in determining significant personal behaviors. As you will see in Chapter 23, Milgram discovered that in response to authority, people could be made to inflict harsh levels of pain on other individuals even if these other people were screaming with pain and said they had heart disease. Milgram found that personality questionnaires, which assessed traits, were not predictive of which participants would obediently inflict pain on others. Milgram's conclusion was that the situation, not personality traits, was the determining factor in understanding how individuals behave. Similarly, Latané and Darley found that altruism, or helping behavior, could not be predicted by trait measures of personality. They found that bystanders witnessing a "medical emergency" acted to help as a direct function of the number of witnesses in the social environment in which the emergency occurred. A person experiencing a medical emergency with a large group of witnesses was less likely to be offered help than if the victim had the emergency with a small group of bystanders. They believed that being part of a large group makes you feel less responsible for taking action to help. They called this finding *diffusion of responsibility*. It is another example of how situations were seen to explain personality. It is important to be aware that Milgram's research on obedience and Latané and Darley's research on bystander apathy placed the participants in strongly scripted situations that were infrequent or extraordinary circumstances. Participants may not be likely to ever encounter such powerful situations; therefore, using these findings to draw sweeping conclusions about how they might act in everyday life is questionable.

The two competing views of personality, personality traits versus situationally determined behavior, form the end points of a continuum as to how we view the origin of behavior. It is likely that somewhere along the continuum between these two extreme views is to be found a more realistic explanation for personality that takes into account both traits and situational views. As we have seen throughout this book, the origin of behavior is likely to be multidetermined and not the result of a single factor. For example, in this chapter the role of genetics has not been discussed. Nevertheless, as we have seen in other chapters, one's genetic makeup is certainly likely to play an important role in personality.

FUNDER AND COLVIN'S RESEARCH

The overall focus of this research project was to compare the behavior of participants in three different situations. The participants were 70 male and 70 female volunteer college students who were paid for their involvement. The three situations created by the researchers were designed to: (1) be low in researcher control and not overtly scripted to allow the expression of personal patterns of behavior, (2) be simple and inexpensive to stage, (3) not involve the deception of participants, and (4) have each situation be different from the other while still having interesting and meaningful content.

The research design involved both observational and correlational methods. The research plan does not involve any deception, cover stories, or confederates. Often in research, as you have seen, researchers may tell participants untruths about what they will be doing in order to conceal the true nature of what is being measured. As you know, participants who know what is being measured may alter their behavior and therefore the data collected may not be valid. As a consequence many researchers have by necessity used deception. Deception is a double-edged sword—it accomplishes the task of gaining a participant who doesn't know what is being assessed, but it certainly can raise ethical problems. Are these participants really given *informed consent* when they are told misinformation? The research in this chapter does not employ any sort of cover stories or deception. The participants are told the truth and the focus of the study is to obtain measures of personality in more natural, less-structured contexts. Two different measures of participant's behaviors, one by friends and acquaintances and the second by raters coding videotaped laboratory sessions, were used in the research. As we shall see, a detailed system of observation was devised to quantify each participant's behavior in all laboratory sessions. In addition, observations outside of the laboratory were obtained from individuals who knew the participants well. These "real-world" data from friends and acquaintances could be compared to laboratory findings. The correlational aspect of this research involved making comparisons between each laboratory session and "out-of-lab" ratings. The research plan, for the lab assessment, was to place participants in three different environments and to videotape their behavior. The initial two sessions were similar and very low in scripting (i.e. participants were given no information on what to do or how to behave). Participants could engage in any behavior. The third session was scripted and consisted of participating in a brief debate. Because each person participated in all three sessions it was possible to examine how consistent people were across the three situations. Did the specific situations yield different behaviors or was there a consistent pattern of personality that was the same in each session? Try to imagine yourself in this study and how you might handle each situation.

Session 1

Participants were randomly assigned to male-female pairs and placed in a small room containing an unconcealed video camera, a VCR, and a couch. The male researcher told the participants to get acquainted with one another. He also told them that he would use the video camera to record their interaction. They were instructed to do whatever they liked and were told that he would return in 5 minutes. The researcher turned on the video camera and he left the room. After 5 minutes, he came back and turned off the camera.

Session 2

Approximately 1 month after the initial session, participants returned to the laboratory and participated in exactly the same situation as Session 1, except each participant had a different partner of the opposite sex.

Session 3

This session took place a few minutes after the conclusion of Session 2, and consisted of a debate between the two participants who were in Session 2. The researcher told the participants they would have a debate about capital punishment. Their position in the debate, pro or con, was determined by a coin toss. The participants were given a writing pad and a minute to organize their thinking before the debate began. At the start of the debate, the researcher started videotaping and left the room. He returned after 5 minutes and turned off the camera.

WHAT WAS MEASURED

Trait Ratings from outside the Laboratory

In order to obtain another personality assessment of the participants, each participant was asked to solicit two people who knew them well and would be willing to come to the research lab to participate in a personality rating of the participant. The researchers were interested in obtaining a measure from outside the laboratory in order to compare it to the data from raters of laboratory sessions. This is an excellent example of procuring external validity for laboratory results. It is much easier to just assume the lab findings are accurate estimates of how participants behave. However, going outside the research lab to get measures of the same characteristics explored in the lab for purposes of comparison makes the findings much more meaningful. This procedure of obtaining external validity certainly strengthens the relevance of the findings.

Of the 140 participants, personality ratings were obtained on 128 of the participants. The raters were friends, roommates, or boy/girlfriends. The raters were compensated and they were informed that their ratings would be kept confidential. The personality assessment completed by the raters consisted of a modified Q-Sort of 100 descriptive personality statements. The Q-Sort task involves a rater sorting a 100-item deck of cards with printed personality statements (e.g., *Is cheerful; Verbally fluent; Basically anxious; Generally fearful*) characterizing the person being evaluated. The rater must sort the 100 Q-Sort cards into 9 separate piles ranging from "not characteristic" in pile 1 to "highly characteristic" in pile 9. In this study and other Q-Sort investigations, different sortings have been compared through correlation coefficients, a statistic that compares the degree of relationship between variables.

Coding the Lab Data

The problem facing Funder and Colvin was how to translate the videotaped sequences of behaviors into objective, numerical data. This process is called coding the data. There are many different approaches to coding, ranging from counting small behaviors such as motor acts or word frequency to making more global, impressionistic judgments. The researchers wanted very much to have their coding system capture the behavior of the participants. In doing this, however, they did not want the raters to be subjective or for the raters to use inferences. In addition, they wanted a system that would be reliable, in which different raters would come up with similar scores. In order to achieve their rating objectives Funder and Colvin again turned to a modified Q-Sort technique. The Q-Sort offered them a way to capture significant behavior in an objective, quantifiable manner. To achieve this, the researchers developed their own behavioral Q-Sort deck based on the Q-Sort (CQ) described earlier. The behavioral Q-Sort (BQ) items were developed by selecting 62 items from the CQ and translating them into behavioral terms. For example, the CQ item "is cheerful" becomes the BQ item "behaves in a cheerful manner." In addition, some items not on the original CQ were developed to evaluate the videotaped behaviors in the three sessions. As you might imagine, when left in a room with a video camera, some participants fooled around and made funny faces while looking at the camera. This sort of behavior was not available in the CQ and therefore a BQ item had to be specifically written so that all behaviors could be evaluated. The raters who coded the three videotaped sessions were individuals who did not know the participants. The following method was used by the raters to code the video sequences: Each rater reviewed the videotape of the 5-minute session they were to code as many times as necessary, and then coded one of the two people in the video session by using the BQ cards. In doing this they had to arrange the cards in typical Q-Sort fashion into 9 piles ranging from "not at all characteristic of the person" to "highly characteristic of the person." Each participant's behavior was coded by approximately six raters. No coders rated more than one session for each participant, and videotaped participants were always rated by different coders. Here is a summary of the types of data collected:

CQ data from Q-Sorts by two acquaintances of each participant

BQ data from Session 1 from raters viewing videotaped lab sessions

BQ data from Session 2 from raters viewing videotaped lab sessions

BQ data from Session 3 from raters viewing videotaped lab sessions

WHAT WAS FOUND

The data indicated a high degree of consistency in participants between Sessions 1 and 2, Sessions 2 and 3, and Sessions 1 and 3. Comparing Sessions 1 and 2, 37 of 62 BQ items attained significant correlations ($p < .001$). For Sessions 2 and 3, 26 of 62 reached this level of consistency. The number reaching this level for comparisons between Sessions 1 and 3 was 18 of 62. The most and least consistent BQ items, averaged across all three sessions are presented in Table 22.1.

Funder and Colvin noted that the correlations were much greater than the highest correlations usually found in personality research literature. Mischel (1968) and Nisbett (1980) suggested the upper limit for personality correlations, or consistency of behavior over different situations, may be in the .30 to .40 range. The findings from this investigation provide convincing evidence that it is no longer reasonable to cling to the idea that a correlation of .30 or .40 is the upper index for consistency of behavior across situations. In their comparisons between Session 1 and 2, 25 items achieved correlations above .40 and some ranged as high as .70 The other cross-session correlations brought to light many behaviors with consistency higher than .40.

TABLE 22.1   Fifteen Most and Least Consistent BQ Items across All Three Sessions

MOST CONSISTENT BQ ITEMS

BQ Item	Average Correlation
Speaks in loud voice	.65
Behaves in fearful or timid manner	.57
Is expressive in face, voice, or gestures	.56
Speaks quickly	.56
Constant eye contact with partner	.54
High enthusiasm and high energy level	.53
Is reserved and unexpressive	.52
Unusual or unconventional appearance	.51
Behaves in a masculine or feminine style	.48
Regards self as physically attractive	.47
Laughs frequently	.46
Behaves in a cheerful manner	.44
Smiles frequently	.44
Awkward interpersonal style	.44
Insecurity or sensitivity	.42

LEAST CONSISTENT BQ ITEMS

BQ Item	Average Correlation
Interest in fantasy & daydreams	−.01
"Interviews" partner	.01
Interested in partner as member of opposite sex	.04
Views interaction as sexual encounter	.05
Tries to obstruct research	.06
Expresses warmth	.06
Interested in topics of power	.08
Brags	.08
Interest in philosophical issues	.08
Discusses very large number of topics	.09
Offers little about self	.10
Expresses guilt	.10
Displays ambition	.11
Seeks advice from partner	.11
Interrupts partner	.12

The comparison between the BQ and the CQ data was extremely important because it makes the case for external validity. Remember the BQ data comes from the raters who did not know the participants reviewing the three lab sessions on videotape, and the CQ data comes from friends and acquaintances of the participants. Is there a relationship between the BQ obtained from laboratory ratings and the CQ that comes from out of lab "real-world" sources? It is very encouraging that the same behavioral items that achieved high correlations in the lab also obtained high correlations between real life and lab. A summary of the 15 highest and lowest BQ-CQ correlations is presented in Table 22.2.

This is a fascinating and very important finding and serves to strengthen the trait notion. However, it should be noted that correlations between lab and real-world situ-

TABLE 22.2   Relationship between BQ and CQ Ratings: The 15 Highest and Lowest Correlations

15 HIGHEST CORRELATIONS

Views self as physically attractive	.41
Interested in intellectual matters	.40
High intelligence	.34
Ambitious	.33
Emotionally reserved	.32
Sex-typed behavior	.32
Socially skilled	.31
Cheerful	.31
Talkative	.30
Dominant interpersonally	.29
Shows self-pity	.28
Rapid speech	.28
Keeps people at distance	.26
Physically expressive	.25
Verbal fluency	.25

15 LOWEST CORRELATIONS

Opposite sex interest	−.07
Insecurity	−.04
Anxiety	−.04
Seeks advice	−.03
Relaxed	−.01
Interesting person	−.01
Conventional values	.01
Offers advice	.05
Wide interests	.06
Fearful	.06
Seeks assurance	.07
Power interests	.08
Emotionally warm	.12
Expresses guilt	.12
Sexualizes situations	.13

ations tended to be smaller in magnitude than the cross comparisons between the three lab sessions. This is understandable and expected because the "real-world raters" knew the participants in much greater detail and were free to include a wide variety of data in the formation of their ratings. In contrast the "lab raters" were restricted to the material in a brief video as the sole source of information to form their BQ. The use of friends and acquaintances to obtain "real-world" data is a good example of the use of an approach to establish external validity. Remember that Session 3, the capital punishment debate, was more scripted, and still produced BQ scores that correlated well to Sessions 1 and 2, as well as the CQ scores. Finding consistency across the three lab sessions is another major important outcome. This research leads us to conclude that traits are quite consistent across situations. These findings provide very favorable evidence for the operation of traits as a unifying model for understanding the operation of personality.

REFERENCES

Allport, G. W. (1937). *Personality: A psychological interpretation*. New York: Holt, Rinehart.

Funder, D. C., & Colvin, C. R. (1991). Explorations in behavioral consistency: Properties of persons, situations, and behaviors. *Journal of Personality and Social Psychology, 60*, 773–794.

Latané, B., & Darley, J. M. (1970). *The unresponsive bystander: Why doesn't he help?* New York: Appleton-Century-Crofts.

Milgram, S. (1973). *Obedience to authority*. New York: Harper.

Mischel, W. (1968). *Personality and assessment*. New York: Wiley.

Nisbett, R. (1980). The trait construct in lay and professional psychology. In L. Festinger (Ed.), *Retrospections on social psychology* (pp. 109–130). New York: Oxford University Press.

CHAPTER 23

I WAS JUST
FOLLOWING ORDERS

The research presented in this chapter was begun in the early 1960s, about 15 years after the end of World War II and the defeat of Nazi Germany. Unlike other chapters of this book, this is not contemporary research. Why, then, is it included? Over the years since its publication Milgram's research on obedience has been arguably the most often discussed piece of research in psychology. Because his research strategy cannot be replicated by contemporary researchers due to ethical issues, we have elected to present this classic research here so that you will gain an appreciation for the power of laboratory research in psychology to explore issues that generalize to broader human and social topics. We will also examine the ethical questions raised by the treatment of participants. Indeed, Milgram's research on obedience demonstrates the power of situations to overwhelm our individual moral and ethical codes so that people act in ways contrary to their values and upbringing. Remember that in Funder and Colvin's research, described in the previous chapter, seemingly stable individual personality traits emerged when situations were not highly scripted. Milgram's research on obedience was highly scripted, in order to replicate the culture of Nazi Germany; a culture in which millions of innocent infants, children, and adults were killed "on orders." The Holocaust occurred in a sophisticated, educated Christian society whose ethics and values were contrary to the inhumane policies and practices of the Nazis. Milgram understood that obedience could operate as a positive process to facilitate many productive, prosocial activities. Civilization depends heavily on the concept and practice of obedience. Yet, how is it possible for so many people to commit heinous crimes in the name of obedience? Milgram sought to understand what situational factors could have facilitated obedience to malevolent authority. C. P. Snow (1961) stated:

> when you think of the long and gloomy history of man, you will find more hideous crimes have been committed in the name of obedience than have been committed in the name of rebellion . . . in the name of obedience they [German Officer Corps] were party to, and assisted in, the most wicked large scale actions in the history of the world. (p. 24)

Incorporating the research of S. Milgram, "Behavioral Study of Obedience," 1963, *Journal of Abnormal and Social Psychology, 67*, pp. 371–378.

Milgram's research emphasizes how a powerful situation can be instrumental in getting individuals to conform and engage in acts that might not be carried out in less-powerful or scripted contexts. This is in sharp contrast to the view that certain individuals are by nature highly obedient and others are defiant, with most of us in the great middle ground. This trait view would suggest that there are people who have the *evil-obedient* personality trait that would lead them to act as sadistic, brutal monsters. Milgram's research suggests quite the opposite, that is, that ordinary people placed in powerful situations are likely to conform to the expectations of authority figures, even if such obedience violates long-held personal values and principles.

THE MILGRAM OBEDIENCE SETUP

The participants were 40 males between the ages of 20 and 50 who responded to a newspaper advertisement or a mail solicitation. They agreed to come to Yale University to be part of a study of memory and learning. The participants represented a wide range of occupations and had a similarly wide range of educational levels. Milgram employed two confederates in this research. One represented an experimenter who was somewhat stern and dressed in a gray lab coat. The other confederate was a friendly 47-year male who played the role of an actual participant who arrived to take part in the research.

The procedure involved an actual participant and the confederate participant arriving at the same time to take part in the research. They were informed that the purpose of the research project was to evaluate the relationship between learning and punishment. They were told that one of them would be a learner and the other a teacher to assess the effect of punishment on the learning process. The participants blindly selected slips of paper from a hat to determine who would be the learner and who the teacher. The drawing was "fixed" so that the actual participant was always the teacher, while Milgram's confederate participant was always the learner. The learning task consisted of a list of word pairs in which the learner had to select the correctly paired alternative from a group of four after hearing the list read through once. The learner was placed in a separate adjacent room to the teacher and had an electrode attached to his wrist so a shock could be delivered from a shock generator placed in front of the teacher. The teacher communicated to the learner over an intercom in which the paired words were presented and the learner responses were evaluated as correct or incorrect. The learner was informed by the teacher of the shock level when punishment was administered for an incorrect response.

The shock generator was a realistic-looking apparatus that had all the trappings of a genuine piece of laboratory equipment. There were 30 on-off lever-type switches that appeared as if they could deliver a "shock" from 15 to 450 volts, in 15-volt increments. The switches on the apparatus were qualitatively labeled *Slight, Moderate, Strong, Very Strong, Intense, Extreme Intense Shock, Danger: Severe Shock,* and two further switches marked *XXX.* Each actual participant (the teacher) was administered a sample shock of 45 volts, to enhance the authenticity of the shock generator and to let them experience a level of shock described as *Slight.* The teachers were informed that their task was to administer a shock to the learner every time the learner gave an incorrect answer. In addition, the teacher was told to increase the shock level by 15 volts each time the learner gave an incorrect response.

During the paired-word learning process, the learner, at predetermined times, for all participants, would pound on the wall of his room and later fail to respond to the learning task. On those occasions the teacher (actual participant) would look to the experimenter for guidance on how to proceed. The experimenter used a series of increasingly stronger verbal statements to encourage the teacher to proceed with the learning task. Following are the experimenter's verbal remarks in increasing levels of strength:

"Please continue" or "Please go on."

"The experiment requires that you continue."

"It is absolutely essential that you continue"

"You have no other choice, you *must* go on."

"Although the shocks may be painful, there is no permanent tissue damage, so please go on."

"Whether the learner likes it or not, you must go on until he has learned all the word pairs correctly. So please go on." (Milgram, 1963)

The response measure in this research was the final amount of shock, in terms of voltage marked under the switch on the shock generator, that a participant administered before refusing the final request of the experimenter to proceed with the learning task. Milgram operationally defined an *obedient* participant as one who administered a shock at the 450-volt level. Participants who did not attain this level of compliance with experimenter requests, even if they administered shocks at, for example, the 435-volt level, were operationally defined as *defiant*.

As you have probably guessed, having read many of the research stories in this book, no shocks were ever administered to the confederate learner. The learner responses were predetermined and were exactly the same for all 40 participant teachers. All of the learner's protests and failures to respond were also predetermined and scripted to occur when the same shock levels were reached. At the completion of the "learning-punishment task" the participants were debriefed, reconciled with the learner (who they formerly believed was shocked), interviewed, and given some questionnaires. Milgram asserts that procedures "were undertaken to assure that the subject [participant] would leave the laboratory in a state of well being . . . and an effort was made to reduce any tensions that arose as a result of the experiment [you will recognize that this is not really an experiment]" (Milgram, 1963, p. 169).

RESEARCH FINDINGS

The distribution of participant's compliance levels, the voltage point at which they refused to administer any more shocks, is displayed in Table 23.1. Sixty-five percent of

TABLE 23.1   Voltage Levels at Which Participants Refused to Administer Further Shock

VOLTAGE LEVEL	NUMBER OF PARTICIPANTS WHO REFUSED TO GO BEYOND THIS VOLTAGE LEVEL
15	0
30	0
45	0
60	0
75	0
90	0
105	0
120	0
135	0
150	0
165	0
180	0
195	0
210	0
225	0
240	0
255	0
270	0
285	0
300	5
315	4
330	2
345	1
360	1
375	1
390	0
405	0
420	0
435	0
450	26

Source: From Milgram, 1963.

the participants worked their way to the end of the shock apparatus. They believed they had administered a shock of 450 volts and were operationally defined as *obedient.* It should be noted that the participants did not proceed gleefully from 15 to 450 volts. On the contrary, a large number of participants showed signs of extreme tension and nervousness, including sweating, trembling, biting their lips, groaning, and fits of nervous laughter. When the experimenter finally ended the learning task, many participants were notably relieved, wiped their brows, nervously smoked cigarettes, and some even shook their heads regretfully. The high percentage of participants who were obedient to an authority figure, the experimenter, and inflicted painful shocks on another person, was as surprising to Milgram as it might be to any normal person. He asked a group of Yale University psychology majors, who were unaware of the results, to predict the percent of obedience. They estimated that only a very small percent, perhaps 0 to 3 percent, would go all the way to the last switch on the shock apparatus. Milgram's colleagues were also polled and made predictions similar to the Yale students. What actually happens in the "real world" may be quite different from commonsense speculation. There is no substitute for data.

The high percentage of obedience observed among the participants indicated that long-held values (e.g., don't inflict pain on someone else) can be dispensed with quite easily if an authority figure orders you to do so. What would have happened to a participant if he said, "No, I refuse to go on, I won't give the learner any more shocks"? He would not have encountered any negative circumstances, and he would have been upholding a system of ethical values endorsed by our culture. It was surprising to Milgram how easy it was to get participants to engage in acts harmful to another person. Milgram was also unprepared for the level of emotional distress caused by the learning-punishment situation. Milgram reports that an observer related:

> I observed a mature and initially poised businessman enter the laboratory smiling and confident. Within 20 minutes he was reduced to a twitching, stuttering wreck, who was rapidly approaching the point of nervous collapse. He constantly pulled on his earlobe, and twisted his hands. . . . And yet he continued to respond to every word of the experimenter, and obeyed to the end. (Milgram, 1963, p. 171)

Milgram offers the following to explain the high levels of obedience:

- The research took place at Yale University, which has high prestige and is not likely to engage in questionable research.
- The research project was explained to the participant and had a significant goal and purpose.
- The learner and the teacher voluntarily agreed to be in the research and both had an obligation to see it to a conclusion.
- Participants were paid for coming to the laboratory and this may have increased their tendency to obey and complete the project.
- The fact that the learner ended up experiencing some pain was the seeming luck of the draw, a chance consequence that might have led him to be in the learner's position.
- The participants were told that the shocks were not dangerous and that the research had scientific importance.
- The participants were put in a situation in which they must choose between meeting the demands of the experimenter or the learner. The experimenter's demands come from the sphere of science, whereas the learner's demands are of a personal nature.
- The research task moved along at a rapid pace and did not allow the participants time to consider or reflect on how to handle the situation.

ETHICAL CONCERNS

Diana Baumrind (1964) raised ethical issues concerning the treatment of participants in Milgram's obedience research. She stated that the experimenters must balance professional and scientific interests against the welfare of participants. She believed that participants are sometimes coerced to be in research studies by virtue of being in a college course that requires research participation, to earn extra course credit, or even to earn money. Even if the participant just volunteered because of interest, without any coercion or pressure, the experimenter owes a debt to all participants. Baumrind states that Milgram's treatment of participants was unethical because participants were exposed to circumstances that obviously, by Milgram's own report, caused significant emotional disturbance. Baumrind noted that Milgram's detached, objective report of the emotional reactions of his participants, along with his casual statements that the anxiety and tension were eliminated before the participants left the laboratory were improbable. Baumrind asserted that Milgram was willing to trade off the stress of the participants for the findings of his research. Baumrind stated that the rationale of using a harsh means to achieve a desirable end goal might be justifiable if the goal had very high value for society. Baumrind states, "Unlike the Sabin vaccine, for example, the concrete benefit to humanity of this particular piece of work, no matter how competently handled, cannot justify the risk that real harm will be done to the subjects" (Baumrind, 1964, p. 422).

In response to Baumrind's (1964) sharp criticism, Milgram (1964) noted that the obedience research procedures dealt with the participant's emotional upset and also had positive benefits for those who served as participants. Milgram reported that every participant was given an extensive postresearch debriefing that included the fact that no shocks were ever administered to the learner. They also had a friendly reconciliation with the learner and an extensive discussion with the experimenter about the research. After the research was complete, participants received a written report of the research and its findings as well as a questionnaire regarding their own participation in the study. On this questionnaire, 84 percent of participants stated they were *glad* or *very glad* to have been in the study. Eighty percent of participants stated that more research of this type should be conducted, and 74 percent stated that they gained important personal knowledge from being a participant. In contrast to Baumrind's view that participants derived no benefit, Milgram (1964) cites the following statements made by participants 1 year after the obedience study:

> This experiment has strengthened my belief that man should avoid harm to his fellow man even at the risk of violating authority. (p. 850)

> To me the experiment pointed up . . . the extent to which each individual should have or discover firm ground on which to base his decisions, no matter how trivial they appear to be. I think people should think more deeply about themselves and their relation to their world and to other people. If this experiment serves to jar people out of complacency, it will have served its end. (p. 850)

One year after the completion of the obedience research Milgram hired an impartial psychiatrist to interview all 40 participants and to focus on any residual consequences from research participation. The psychiatrist found no signs that any of the participants was negatively affected by the obedience research experience. No signs of stress or trauma were found.

Milgram's future research in obedience to authority revealed that college students and women exhibited the same high rates of obedience, and that moving the research program from Yale University to a rundown office building in Bridgeport, Connecticut, had no impact on the results.

By contemporary ethical standards, which evolved because of the obedience studies, this research methodology would be considered highly unethical, even if the findings were of high social value. Therefore, it has been impossible to replicate or further investigate this issue with the same research design.

The obedience to authority research has shown us that it doesn't take highly sadistic monsters to engage in extremely cruel acts. Under the right situations, ordinary men and women from all socioeconomic levels can engage in barbarous acts. We have only to turn on the nightly news and see the events in Kosovo to realize the significance of Milgram's findings.

REFERENCES

Baumrind, D. (1964). Some thoughts on ethics of research: After reading Milgram's "Behavioral study of obedience." *American Psychologist, 19,* 421–423.

Milgram, S. (1963). Behavioral study of obedience. *Journal of Abnormal and Social Psychology, 67,* 371–378.

Milgram, S. (1964). Issues in the study of obedience: A reply to Baumrind. *American Psychologist, 19,* 448–452.

Milgram, S. (1974). *Obedience to authority: An experimental view.* New York: Harper and Row.

Snow, C. P. (1961, February). Either-or. *Progressive,* 24–25.

CHAPTER 24

GOING TO POT

Jonathan Shedler and Jack Block (1990) studied personality traits in an extensive longitudinal study of adolescent drug use. As described in Chapter 15, "Golden Oldies," a *longitudinal study* follows the same individuals over a period of time, collecting data on them at regular intervals. Usually this time period is no more than a few years because these studies can become expensive as they get longer. As a longitudinal study stretches out over time, it becomes more difficult to relocate the members of the original study. People move away and fail to keep in touch with the researchers. Others simply get tired of being studied and refuse to continue cooperating. Nevertheless, longitudinal studies are a powerful way of studying psychological factors across some portion of the life span.

Another research method, the *cross-sectional study*, overcomes some of the difficulties of the longitudinal study, but introduces a new problem. The cross-sectional study is of short duration. It selects people from different age groups and presumes these people are representative of those who have been, and will be, this age. Cross-sectional studies have been very useful in plotting the development of characteristics over a few years, usually the years of early childhood. A problem develops when cross-sectional studies are used to investigate changes occurring over large time periods across the life span. For example, imagine a study in which mathematical ability is being assessed. A cross-sectional approach might sample and test people who are currently 20 years old, 40 years old, 60 years old, and 80 years old. If the 80-year-olds perform less well than the others, it is not clear if this is because mathematical ability declines in old age or because this group had less formal schooling than the others. The 80-year-olds of today grew up during the Great Depression when many people did not have the money to finish school or go to college.

This problem is called a *cohort effect*. A cohort is group of people who are about the same age. There is a cohort effect when one group has lived through unique circumstances that have affected human development in some special way. In the example above, the particular history of these 80-year-olds means that they may be substantially different in years of education from people who will become 80 in the future. They cannot be considered representative of the next few generations of 80-year-olds in some types of research because of their unique experience during the Depression.

Incorporating the research of J. Shedler and J. Block, "Adolescent Drug Use and Psychological Health: A Longitudinal Inquiry," 1990, *American Psychologist*, *45*, pp. 612–630.

A LONGITUDINAL STUDY OF PERSONALITY AND DRUG USE

Before the work of Shedler and Block, a few longitudinal studies of personality and drug use had been undertaken. These tended to follow adolescents for a few years, at best (Brook, Whiteman, Gordon, & Cohen, 1986; Smith & Fogg, 1978). A more typical approach to personality and drug use has been to assess the personalities of groups of adolescents who report drug use, comparing them to groups who say they do not use drugs (see Cox, 1985, for a review).

A question raised by other cross-sectional or short-term studies is that even if personality traits are found to be correlates of drug use, it is still not clear which came first. As we have seen before, this is the perennial problem with studies that are correlational: they cannot determine if one variable is the cause and one is the effect. Determination of cause and effect can only come from an experiment, and even with an experiment one should be cautious. No experiment perfectly excludes every single imaginable variable except the independent variable, so we believe that even cause-and-effect conclusions from experiments should be considered tentative. As is often the case with human issues, the experiment to study the effects of drug use can be designed, but it could not be conducted. To determine if drug use causes certain personality traits, we would have to randomly assign one large group of kids to use drugs and another to abstain from drug use. This would be the independent variable. The dependent variable would be some subsequent measure of personality. Although this study could give us some important information, from a practical standpoint it is not going to be performed, and we believe that you can figure out why.

Although a solution to the cause-and-effect question just went up in smoke for practical reasons, some information about this question can be gained by a thorough longitudinal study. A longitudinal study might demonstrate that stable personality traits develop early in life, well before drug use was an issue. If kids who already had a particular cluster of traits became drug users as teenagers, the case would be strengthened that personality might cause drug use, not the other way around. This would be a very valuable step: one possible causal direction could be eliminated. However, even this longitudinal study could not tell us for sure that some third variables—for example, parenting style or genes—were not a major cause of both personality and drug use.

Participants

The data reported by Shedler and Block regarding personality and drug use come from a broad longitudinal study of personality. The participants in this study were 101 eighteen-year-olds. There were 49 males and 52 females. These kids were part of a group of 130 kids who were first studied when they were 3 years old. At that time, they were in one of two nursery schools in the San Francisco Bay area that cooperated in recruitment of participants for a longitudinal personality study. The kids lived primarily in urban settings and were from a variety of socioeconomic groups. Their parents had differing levels of education. The group was about two-thirds white, one-quarter

African American, and one-twelfth Asian American. The kids were given wide-ranging assessments of personality at ages 3, 4, 5, 7, 11, 14, and 18.

Procedure

At age 18, each participant had an individual interview with a skilled interviewer who questioned them about many aspects of their lives, including drug use. The interviews lasted approximately 4 hours and were videotaped. In the questions regarding drug use, the 18-year-olds were asked about their own frequency of using marijuana and other drugs. Were the kids honest in talking about their drug use? Shedler and Block argue that, at worst, drug use might be underreported in interview situations because kids might be reluctant to admit to using drugs. Shedler and Block further argue that there was every reason to believe that these kids answered honestly. The interviewers were skilled at gaining the confidence of kids. Moreover, it is important to remember these kids had been in this study since they were 3 years old. Over the years, they had always been assured anything they said would be kept confidential. Unlike participants in most studies, these kids knew from a lifetime of experience that the researchers would keep their promise.

The personality assessment that was done at age 18 was monumental. It was consistent with the painstaking and thorough nature of the rest of this study. Each participant had a session with each of four psychologists who administered different sets of procedures designed to facilitate the observation of personality. These procedures included performances on perceptual tasks and puzzle solving. These sessions were designed to be situations in which personality characteristics would be displayed. These psychologists who conducted the personality assessments were not the interviewers who had collected the earlier information about drug use. The psychologists were purposely not informed about the drug habits of the participants. When the sessions with the psychologists were over, each psychologist described the personality traits of each participant using the California Adult Q-sort or CQ, which has been previously described in Chapter 22, "Personality: Traits or Situations?"

As you will remember, the CQ is a device for turning observations of personality into numbers that can then be treated as quantitative data. One of the problems in the study of personality is the difficulty of turning qualitative observations—the ongoing stream of behavior—into valid quantitative data that are representations of the personality itself. Observations could be recorded merely by writing descriptions of personality, but these descriptions could not be handled statistically. Statistics are useful because they enable good summaries to be made describing behavior of the whole group. The CQ has been frequently used to measure personality, and its validity has been demonstrated. The CQ consists of 100 cards, each with a personality description printed on it. Table 24.1 shows 10 of the CQ items to serve as examples of what was on the cards.

Typically, CQ cards are sorted by the participant. However, in this study, when a psychologist was finished interacting with a participant, the psychologist would sort each card into one of nine piles, based on how well the description or trait on the card

TABLE 24.1   Sample Items from the California Adult Q-Sort

Is critical, skeptical, not easily impressed
Favors conservative values in a variety of areas
Seeks reassurance from others
Gives up and withdraws in the face of adversity
Is moralistic
Is unpredictable and changeable in behavior, attitudes
Tends to be rebellious and nonconforming
Is sensitive to anything that can be construed as a demand
Feels cheated and victimized by life; self-pitying
Expresses hostile feelings directly

matched the personality of the participants. The number one pile was for descriptions that did not match the personality at all. The number nine pile was for descriptions that perfectly matched the individual. The piles between one and nine were used to make intermediate ratings. Each trait was given the numerical score of the pile it landed in, so that for each participant, each of the 100 personality characteristics received a score between 1 and 9 indicating its appropriateness as a description of that participant.

The scores for each trait, from each participant, contributed by all four psychologists were averaged to give a final score for that individual. This helped to minimize the extent to which any one psychologist's ratings might affect the overall scoring. Even though the psychologists met with each participant at a different time, doing a different task, the CQ sort ratings of the psychologists were fairly similar, agreeing between 70 percent to 90 percent of the time. You will recognize that this agreement is a direct measure of the reliability of the evaluation. In this instance, but not always, reliability may well indicate validity, which, you will recall, is accuracy in measurement. It is possible, but unlikely, for all the psychologists to make similar ratings of a kid's personality and for all of them to be wrong. As discussed in Chapter 14, reliability is not always an indication of validity. Imagine that your bathroom scale is a seized-up ball of rust that looks like the ship's scale from the Titanic. It is rusted tight at 126 pounds. It will be highly reliable in weighing you, but it will not be valid, unless, of course, you really weigh 126 pounds.

For the purposes of longitudinal comparison, these CQ personality rating scores were compared with scores obtained from the same kids, back when they were ages 7 and 11, using the California Child Q-sort, or CCQ. This was a version of the adult Q-sort that was designed to assess the personality of children. The Q-sorts were conducted by entirely different sets of psychologists for each age group. This is very important because any bias that a psychologist developed about a participant could not have a repeated influence on the data over successive years. The same procedures were used as have been described for the Q-sort administration at age 18; except that at age 7 there were three psychologists and at age 11 there were five. As with the 18-year-olds, the ratings of the psychologists were reliable, and so by implication in this particular case, probably valid.

When the participants were 5 years old, they were brought to the lab and observed in a play session with their mothers and in a separate play session with their fathers. They were observed through a two-way mirror by a trained observer. They were also videotaped. They were given a variety of puzzles to solve that included arranging blocks and cutout colored pieces as well as finding their way through pencil-and-paper mazes. These tasks were constructed to be easy for the parents but challenging for the child. Observers used yet another Q-sort that contained descriptions of ways parents might interact with kids. This Q-sort was completed by the trained observer and by a second observer who watched the videotape. This was a method of checking the reliability of the observations. The exact same events were observed and the Q-sort outcomes that followed should have been similar. The Q-sort ratings of these two observers were combined to produce scores for parent interactions.

Assignment to Groups

Among the 18-year-olds, 68 percent had tried marijuana, having increased from 51 percent when the sample was interviewed at age 14. Thirty-nine percent used it once a month or more, and 21 percent used it weekly or more than weekly. When compared to other national studies of drug use, these results seemed about typical. Because of the relatively high numbers of participants who had tried marijuana, Shedler and Block decided to focus on marijuana use in this study. Only one participant reported heroin use, so Shedler and Block's sample could not, for example, have yielded anything worth knowing about the use of this drug.

Shedler and Block made some additional decisions that affected the way in which the results would be presented. They decided to divide the participants into three groups. The requirements for assignment to these groups operationally defined drug use for the study. *Abstainers* were those who had never tried any drug. *Experimenters* were those who had used marijuana "once or twice," "a few times," or "once a month" *and* had used no more than one other drug. *Frequent users* used marijuana once a week or more *and*, in addition, had tried at least one other drug. Table 24.2 shows the number of teenagers in each group.

You can see from these data that even though the initial group was quite large, breaking them up into three or six groups quickly reduced the number of people in

TABLE 24.2   Number of 18-Year-Old Males and Females in Each Drug Use Group

	MALES	FEMALES
Abstainers	14	15
Experimenters	16	20
Frequent Users	11	9

each group. Sixteen of the kids in the original longitudinal study could not be fit into any of the three groups and had to be dropped from the drug-use study. These might be kids who had used marijuana once or twice but had also tried several other drugs. In most cases when participants are assigned to groups based on complex criteria, certain participants will not fit into any of the groups. Because so much other information was available about the kids from the ongoing longitudinal study of personality development, we can assume that every effort was made to include as many of them as possible in the study of drug use. Indeed, Shedler and Block stated that "broader and narrower definitions for the various groups" were considered. They were able to convince themselves that mere changes in the definitions of the groups did not affect the overall findings of the study.

Results

In presenting the results of the study, Shedler and Block chose to use the *experimenters* as the group to which the other groups would be compared. This was done because experimenting was most typical in national samples of adolescents. It is important to have one group as the comparison group because it allows us to better assess the outcomes in the other two groups. For example, the psychologists rated the Q-sort card that said "*Undercontrols needs and impulses; unable to delay gratification*" an average score of 3.7 on the one to nine scale for the *experimenters*. That does not tell us very much until we compare it to the 2.9, which was the rating for *abstainers* and the 4.4 for *frequent users*. Each of these differences is statistically significant and suggests that the *frequent users* are more impulsive.

At age 18, the personalities of the *abstainers* and the *frequent users* were strikingly different. Compared to *experimenters*, *frequent users* did not have close friends and did not show emotions. It was obvious to those who interviewed them that they were unhappy. They did not seem to be able to control their behavior. They were described as "brittle," meaning that their feelings about themselves were fragile, and they were not confident about their abilities. They were unable to delay gratification: to put off the fun things in their lives until the unpleasant or tedious things were done. They were not reliable or ethically consistent and were prone to express hostile feelings in a direct way. Compared to the *experimenters*, 18-year-old *abstainers* were able to delay gratification better and were more rational, fastidious, and conservative. Like the *frequent users*, they did not have close friends and lacked social skills. Unlike the *frequent users*, they were anxious, tense, and predictable.

Shedler and Block were able to look back at the data that had been collected when these kids were younger to examine the extent to which these personality differences were recent developments. As at age 18, each group was compared to the group who would later be labeled *experimenters*. In speaking of the three groups of kids in early childhood, we will use the labels that were given to them later, at age 18, based on drug use. Of course this is not meant to imply that drug use had already started at age 7. Even in childhood, the kids who later became *frequent users* showed signs of maladjustment. At age 7 the descriptions of them include not likely to think ahead, not trustworthy, unlikely to develop close relationships, not curious, and unable to identify with admired adults. Shedler and Block summarized the observations from ages 7 and 11 by saying "the picture that emerges is of a child unable to form good relationships, who is insecure, and who shows numerous signs of emotional distress."

There were some similarities and some differences when the childhood personality of the *abstainers* was examined. At age 7 their descriptions included: eager to please, inhibited, conventional in thought, neat and orderly, likely to think ahead, obedient and noncreative. These traits showed considerable stability when the kids were observed again at age 11. Shedler and Block summarized by noting that *abstainers* presented a picture of children who were overcontrolled, timid, fearful, and morose. We can also see what they were not: they were not warm and responsive, not curious and open to new experience, not active, not vital, and not cheerful.

At ages 7 and 11 we can see some of the central personality differences that are also found at age 18. Both *abstainers* and *frequent users* were not stars when it came to personal relationships. Both seemed to be emotionally withdrawn compared to the *experimenters*. At early ages, the *abstainers* already appeared to be tense and overcontrolled, whereas the *frequent users* already seemed unable to adequately control their impulses. Patterns of drug use are associated with personality differences, and these differences have deep roots in childhood.

The differences found at age 18 may not have been a big surprise to you. Probably most people would guess that there might be personality differences among *experimenters*, *abstainers*, and *frequent users*. Many people believe that personality changes occur when kids are thrown into a drug-using peer culture. The story goes that some teenagers begin to hang out with the "wrong people" and become drug users. The teenage combination of peers and drugs is thought to account for teenage personality. The data presented by Shedler and Block suggest that this is a false picture.

THE ROOTS OF PERSONALITY

If personality has deep roots, where did the seed get planted? Probably this wording can be taken literally: there is considerable evidence that individual babies are different in the way they react to the world from the time they are born. For example, some newborns react to small amounts of stimulation, some react to stimuli for a brief period of time, and some are more likely to react over and over in quick succession (Lewis, 1992). A baby might not show any of these reactions, show a few of them, or show all of them. These differences are called *temperament*. Temperament is different from personality. It is a general early pattern of reacting to surroundings. Biological factors, such as the unique mix of neurochemicals in an individual infant's brain, are probably one major component of temperament. The amounts of various neurochemicals available can contribute to a consistent style of behavior and mood. Temperamental differences such as those found between inhibited and uninhibited kids have been shown to persist from the first year of infancy to the end of the second year and, in another study, from 2 to 8 years of age (Kagan & Snidman, 1991).

These early generalized temperaments interact with their environments and grow into personality. It is important to understand that this is a true interaction. It is a two-way street. Personality changes can be a result of events such as conditioning, rewards, punishments, and social learning opportunities. In other words, personality can change as a result of the environment. Personality can also change the environment. We can change existing environments or choose new ones.

From the viewpoint of a child, the parent is usually the most important person in the environment. It seems likely that the parent is an important influence in shaping the child's temperament into personality. Shedler and Block observed the kids in this study interacting with their parents when the kids were 5 years old. There were interesting similarities between the mothers of the *abstainers* and *frequent users.* Both groups of mothers were seen as being cold and unresponsive. Solving the puzzles that were provided in the lab could have been a fun activity; however, both sets of cold "momsicles" made it a grim and unpleasant task. They did not give their kids much encouragement while trying to solve the puzzles. At the same time, they pressured them to successfully complete the puzzles. This situation is called a *double bind.* The kids are expected to do well, but are not given the encouragement necessary for success. This double bind says to the child, "I want you to be successful, but don't bother me for help."

The fathers of the *frequent users* were similar to the fathers of the *experimenters* when they interacted with their 5-year-olds. The fathers of the *abstainers* were different; they wanted things done their way. They were domineering and critical of their children and rejected their children's ideas and suggestions. They did not enjoy being with their kids and arranged the situation so that the children did not enjoy being with them. These fathers would not be able to rent a house in *Mister Rogers' Neighborhood.*

It is important to carefully consider the results presented here in order to appreciate the findings of this remarkable study. It is equally important to avoid jumping to conclusions. Although the behavior of these kids varied from one day-to-day situation to the next, extensive personality screening over a long period of time shows considerable stability of personality characteristics. This argues against an extreme situational view of personality in which personality varies from context to context and has no underlying stability. Someone might say, "Wait a minute, all these kids were assessed in a highly artificial situation. This situation must have played a major role in determining personality while it was being assessed. That is why personalities were so reliable from year to year." Although this might be true, it would not account for the stable personality *differences* that were found when *abstainers* and *frequent users* were compared to *experimenters.* A naïve situational view would, instead, predict that all kids interacting with psychologists in a lab would have similar personalities in that situation. This is not what was found. Instead, these kids seem to have relatively enduring personality traits.

It might be tempting to go tearing off with the assumption that the parents were the cause of the maladjusted personality of 18-year-old *abstainers* and *frequent users.* In doing so, one would be confusing correlation with cause. The study has found a correlation between parenting style and later drug use. As we have discussed before, the parenting style may well be a cause of the behavior but the mere correlation of the two does not permit this conclusion to be confirmed. Indeed, the opposite may be operating: it is possible that the cold parental style was a response to an unsocial, withdrawn child's personality. Either way, the correlation does indicate that a cold and unresponsive parenting style, which puts kids in a double bind, allows one to *predict* later malad-justment in personality. With a characteristic as complex as personality the chances are remote that any single factor, even one as important as parenting style, is the sole cause. It is much more likely that parenting accounts for some part of the differences we observe.

Because parenting styles were observed well before the kids started to frequently use or consciously abstain from drugs, we can rule out the notion that the parenting style was a reaction to the children's pattern of drug use. Although this may sound silly, it is sometimes alleged that parents become cold and unresponsive as a reaction to drug-using kids. The findings here suggested that this is a false conclusion. Parental coldness preceded the formation of drug-related behavior.

Given that at age 18 the *abstainers* and the *frequent users* were more maladjusted, does the finding here suggest that the way to overcome maladjustment is to be like the *experimenters* and smoke a little weed every now and again? To draw this conclusion would be to confuse correlation with cause again. There is a correlation between per-sonality and drug-use patterns but this does not suggest that changing drug-use pat-terns will result in personality changes. On the contrary, the longitudinal grasp of this study suggests that personality traits are stable and resistant to change.

A few years ago the United States Government spent a great deal of money on a campaign to teach kids to "Just say no" to drugs. It may be too early to judge the effec-tiveness of this program, but the findings of Shedler and Block's study suggest that drug use is correlated with enduring personality traits, and therefore a small situational training program may have little effect. Perhaps this money would have been better spent in training people to be supportive parents. As educated taxpayers, we should learn to "Just say no" to programs that fly in the face of carefully conducted scientific studies.

REFERENCES

Brook, J. S., Whiteman, M., Gordon, A. S., & Cohen, P. (1986). Dynamics of childhood and adoles-cent personality traits and adolescent drug use. *Developmental Psychology, 22,* 403–414.

Cox, W. M. (1985). Personality correlates of substance abuse. In M. Galizio & S. A. Maisto (Eds.), *Determinants of substance abuse: Biological, psychological, and environmental factors* (pp. 209–246). New York: Plenum.

Kagan, J., & Snidman, N. (1991). Temperamental factors in human development. *American Psycholo-gist, 46,* 856–862.

Lewis, M. (1992). Individual differences in response to stress. *Pediatrics, 90,* 487–490.

Shedler, J., & Block, J. (1990). Adolescent drug use and psychological health: A longitudinal inquiry. *American Psychologist, 45,* 612–630.

Smith, G. M., & Fogg, C. P. (1978) Psychological predictors of early use, late use and nonuse of marijuana among teenage students. In D. B. Kandel (Ed.), *Longitudinal research on drug use* (pp. 101–113). New York: Wiley.

CHAPTER 25

TO CATCH A COLD

There is an increasing belief that stress in life may lead to the development of organic illness. The field of psychoneuroimmunology, a branch of behavioral medicine, deals with life and environmental stress, as well as psychological events that increase susceptibility to disease. Until recently it was largely assumed that organic disease could only have organic origins. Current thinking is that excessive environmental stress, which exceeds the person's coping ability, can have negative physical consequences, such as disease (Lazarus & Folkman, 1984). It is thought that high stress may lead to negative cognitive and emotional reactions that, in turn, may alter the effectiveness of the immune system. The immune system can be adversely affected by autonomic and central nervous system activation (Felten & Olshchowka, 1987), release of hormones (Shavit, Lewis, Terman, Gale, & Liebeskind, 1984), and maladaptive lifestyle changes such as drug usage, smoking, or alcohol (Cohen & Williamson, 1991).

Although there is a belief that stress leads to illness, the research findings are not clear as to whether immune system breakdowns could be of such magnitude as to increase susceptibility to infection (Jemmott & Locke, 1984). Research on the current topic, catching a cold, is also unclear on the relationship between stress and the development of illness. The research reported in this chapter focuses on this question—Can stress increase the likelihood of catching a cold? In the research described in this chapter healthy participants were assessed on their level of stress, personality features, and health practices. They were then intentionally exposed to a cold virus or a placebo. Placebos groups are commonly used in research in order to create a control condition in which participants receive exactly the same treatment as the experimental condition, but do not receive the active ingredient under study. In a drug study a placebo pill mimics the actual medication under investigation in size, color, taste, and even side effects, but the pill does not have the active therapeutic ingredient. In this study the placebo group was treated identically to the viral exposure group except that the solution the placebo groups received contained no cold virus, but rather

Incorporating the research of S. Cohen, D. A. J. Tyrell, and A. P. Smith, "Negative Life Events, Perceived Stress, Negative Affect, and Susceptibility to the Common Cold," 1993, *Journal of Personality and Social Psychology, 64*, pp. 131–140.

a saline solution. The importance of having a placebo group is to determine if factors other than the variable under study, in this case cold viruses, had any impact on viral infection and disease. We are likely to respond to placebos due to prior learning. For example, if we have a history of going to a physician and getting medication that relieves pain and symptoms, it is probable that we may develop pain and symptom relief by being exposed to talking to your physician. If this occurs, it is an example of classical conditioning in which the medication was the unconditioned stimulus and relief of pain and symptoms was the unconditioned response. Talking to your physician, without treatment, was the conditioned stimulus for the conditioned response of symptom relief. You can review the classical conditioning paradigm in Chapter 9.

PARTICIPANTS

The participants were 154 male and 266 female volunteers, with 394 randomly assigned to the virus infection group and 26 randomly assigned to the saline control group. The study was conducted at a medical research center in Salisbury, England. According to clinical evaluation and laboratory findings, all participants were judged to be in good health at the start of the investigation. Participants ranged in age from 18 to 54, with a mean age of 33.

PROCEDURE

The initial phase of the study consisted of a complete medical exam, administration of self-reported instruments including psychological stress, personality, and health practices questionnaires. Blood samples were obtained for immunity measurement and to check nicotine intake. Following these initial assessments participants were exposed to cold viruses using nasal drops. The placebo group was administered a saline solution. All participants were randomly assigned to either virus or saline control groups.

The viral infection resulted in illness rates ranging from 20 percent to 60 percent. For 2 days preceding the administration of nose drops and continuing for 6 days after exposure the participants were evaluated each day using a standard medical protocol. Protocol items included frequency of sneezing, eye tearing, nasal congestion, nasal blockage, postnasal discharge, sinus pain, sore throat, and coughing. In addition an objective count of number of paper tissues (e.g., Kleenex) used by the participants and twice-daily report of body temperature were made. Twenty-eight days after the viral exposure another blood sample was obtained. In all phases of this study, the researchers were purposely kept unaware as to the psychological status (based on the three measures used in the study) of participants and also whether or not they received a virus or were in the saline control group.

MEASURING PSYCHOLOGICAL STRESS

Psychological stress was assessed by the these measures:

- Selected items from the *List of Recent Experiences* (Henderson, Byrne, & Duncan-Jones, 1981). The number of major stressful life events rated by the participants as having a negative impact.
- *10-item Perceived Stress Scale* (Cohen & Williamson, 1988). This scale was used to measure the extent to which life circumstances are seen to be stressful. Items measured anxiety, sadness, anger, guilt, irritation, and related concepts.
- *Affect Intensity Measure.* A 5-point scale was used to assess affect (emotional) intensity experienced during the past week.

Previous research by Cohen, Tyrell, and Smith (1991) using the same measures suggested that the three scales were assessing a common underlying concept. Because these three measures are focusing on a single dimension, the researchers combined them into a single composite measure that was also used to assess stress.

HOW WE CATCH A COLD

The growth and action of microorganisms is responsible for the development of the common cold. Infection results in the intensification of the attacking microorganism. It is possible for a person to be infected with the invading cold virus without developing clinical symptoms. In this investigation the researchers operationally defined whether a person was infected with a cold virus and also whether a person demonstrated clinical symptoms of a cold. Infection was determined by the presence of a virus found in fluid samples (cultures of nasal secretions) or a rise in cold virus specific antibodies found in blood samples. The presence of cold symptoms was determined by clinical rating on a four-point scale ranging from complete absence of symptoms (0) to severe symptoms (3). A rating of a mild cold (2) or higher was operationally defined as a positive diagnosis of a clinical cold. In this study clinical diagnosis of colds agreed with participants' self-diagnosis in 94 percent of cases. Participants were operationally defined as having a cold if *both* infection and symptoms were detected. Thirty-eight percent (148 participants) of the total infected sample ($N = 394$) developed colds. In the saline control group no participants became infected.

MEASURING BODY TEMPERATURE
AND MUCUS WEIGHTS

In order to obtain additional, objective measures of a cold, the investigators measured body temperature and mucus weights. These additional measurements provided objective assessments not influenced by how an individual participant presented symptoms or how a clinician completed a rating scale. Mucus weights were calculated by weighing the paper tissues used by participants. Body temperatures and mucus weights were taken on the day before "infection" and on each succeeding day.

HEALTH PRACTICES OF PARTICIPANTS

Participants' health practices are important to evaluate because they may serve as important connections between stress and susceptibility to infection. Therefore smoking, alcohol consumption, exercise activity, sleep quality, and dietary habits were considered part of this study. Smoking was assessed objectively by reviewing cotinine levels in participants' blood samples. Cotinine is a biochemical indicator of nicotine intake that avoids the subjectivity of participants' self-report. However, in this study the correlation of self-reported smoking and cotinine levels was found to be +.96, indicating that both measures were assessing smoking behavior accurately. Alcohol consumption was measured by self-reports of the number of drinks per day with each drink (bottle of beer, glass of wine, shot of liquor) counting equally. Exercise was assessed by tabulating the frequency of engaging in walking, running, swimming, and other aerobic activities. Sleep was measured by a questionnaire tapping the various sleep qualities (e.g., feeling rested, difficulty falling asleep). Diet was measured by self-report items assessing participants' eating habits (e.g., dietary balance, eating vegetables and fruits).

PERSONALITY ASSESSMENT

Three personality dimensions were measured because the investigators thought it likely that psychological stress might be a result of more fundamental aspects of personality. Therefore they assessed self-esteem, personal control, and introversion-extroversion by using a variety of established scales. Self-esteem refers to the views that you hold about your own competencies. Personal control focuses on whether or not you believe that you control and are in charge of your life and can determine outcomes. An internal personal control orientation would represent the belief that you feel in charge of your own destiny, whereas an external personal control would represent the view that you feel things in life are a matter of chance and that you have little control of how things turn out. Introversion represents a need for privacy and a lack of need for interpersonal relationships; extraverts are outgoing and social.

FINDINGS

None of the saline control participants, the placebo group, became infected or developed colds and, therefore, the following data presented represents only the participants who were exposed to the genuine virus. For each of the four stress measure participants above the median score (a type of average) were considered high stress; those below the median were considered low stress. Table 25.1 presents the percentages of virally exposed participants in low and high groups on the four stress measures who became infected and of those who developed clinical colds.

As can be seen in Table 25.1, the rates of actual infection resulting from exposure are significantly higher for participants in the high groups for stress index (an overall composite score), perceived stress, and negative affect. The high stress group in the life events measure had greater levels of infection, but it was not statistically significant. In reviewing the data on those who actually developed a cold, the life events measure was the only assessment instrument to attain statistical significance between high- and low-stress participants. Therefore, while the life events measure did not differ significantly between high and low groups in determining infection, it did sig-

TABLE 25.1   Percentages of Virally Exposed Participants in Low- and High-Stress Groups Who Became Infected and Developed Clinical Colds Symptoms

	% INFECTED ($n = 394$)	% DEVELOPING COLD SYMPTOMS AMONG THOSE INFECTED ($n = 325$)
STRESS INDEX		
Low	78.7	43.2
High	86.3*	47.7
LIFE EVENTS		
Low	80.9	40.1
High	84.6	52.5*
PERCEIVED STRESS		
Low	78.4	44.2
High	86.7*	46.8
NEGATIVE AFFECT		
Low	76.9	45.8
High	88.2*	45.4

*$p < .05$ between low and high Groups.

nificantly differ for participants who actually became ill with a cold. Participants with high numbers of negative life events had higher percentages of clinical colds than participants with low life events scores. This finding does suggest that the life events assessment is measuring something different from the other two measures (i.e., perceived stress and negative affect). The diagnosis of clinical cold in the data presented in Table 25.1 was made by clinical judgment. The data from the two other more objective sources of the presence of a cold, mucus weight in paper tissues and body temperature, provided mixed findings. Life events were not found to be associated with mucus weight changes in paper tissues (a good attempt at objective measurement that did not work). Participants with high numbers of life events did have correspondingly higher body temperature after infection than those participants with low numbers of life events. Figure 25.1 presents the average body temperature of high (more than 2 stressful events) and low (2 or less stressful events) groups over the initial 5 days after being infected.

As you can see by the vertical axis scaling, the displayed centigrade temperature ranges from 36.4 to 36.55. The differences between high and low groups are quite small, but in all daily comparisons the high group always has a significantly higher body temperature than the low group ($p < .02$).

In analyzing the data among the three measured personality variables (self-esteem, personal control, and introversion-extroversion) and development of the common cold, no significant relationships were found. This suggests that these three broad personality measures had little to do with the development of the common cold. In addition the data analysis did not find that the many health practices investigated played a major role in the development of colds.

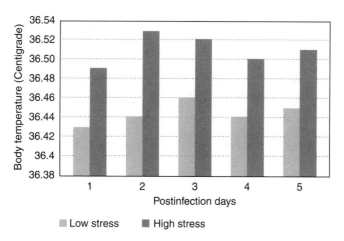

FIGURE 25.1   Postinfection Body Temperature for High- and Low-Stress Groups (Life Events Measure)

WHAT'S IT ALL MEAN?

It is important to distinguish between being infected and the development of clinical illness. Infection and the development of illness as indicated by clinical symptoms may be the result of different processes. Cohen and his research team note that infection is linked to viral replication, whereas becoming ill with a cold may be due to an inflammation in the immune response system, which leads to the release of chemicals (e.g., histamines, prostaglandins) that produce cold symptoms. Cohen's research program showed that high-stress participants have significantly higher rates of infection compared to low-stress participants in three of the four major measures. However, when it comes to the development of clinical symptoms of a cold it is only with the life events measures that we see a significant difference between high- and low-stress groups. On this measure, high-stress people developed cold symptoms at significantly higher rates than their low-stress counterparts.

This investigation provides evidence for a link between the psychological and environmental factors that play an important role in understanding a disease process. Simply focusing on organic, biochemical origins in understanding the development of illness may just reveal part of the picture. This research suggests that clinical medicine should focus attention on stress factors in understanding patient illness.

REFERENCES

Cohen, S., Tyrrell, D. A. J., & Smith, A. P. (1991). Psychological stress and susceptibility to the common cold. *New England Journal of Medicine, 325,* 606–612.

Cohen, S., Tyrrell, D. A. J., & Smith, A. P. (1993). Negative life events, perceived stress, negative affect, and susceptibility to the common cold. *Journal of Personality and Social Psychology, 64,* 131–140.

Cohen, S., & Williamson, G. (1988). Perceived stress in a probability sample of the United States. In S. Spacapan & S. Oskamp (Eds.), *The social psychology of health* (pp. 31–67). Newbury Park, CA: Sage.

Cohen, S., & Williamson, G. (1991). Stress and infectious disease in humans. *Psychological Bulletin, 109,* 5–24.

Felten, S. Y., & Olschowka, J. A. (1987). Noradrenergic sympathetic innervation of the spleen: II. Tyrosine hydroxylase (TH)-positive nerve terminals from synaptic-like contacts on lymphocytes in the splenic white pulp. *Journal of Neuroscience Research, 18,* 37–48.

Henderson, S., Byrne, D. G., & Duncan-Jones, P. (1981). *Neurosis and the social environment.* San Diego, CA: Academic Press.

Jemmott, J. B., III, & Locke, S. E. (1984). Psychosocial factors, immunologic mediation, and human susceptibility to infectious diseases: How much do we know? *Psychological Bulletin, 95,* 78–108.

Lazarus, R. S., & Folkman, S. (1984). *Stress, appraisal, and coping.* New York: Springer.

Shavit, Y., Lewis, J. W., Terman, G. S., Gale, R. P., & Liebeskind, J. C. (1984). Opioid peptides mediated the suppressive effect of stress on natural killer cell cytotoxicity. *Science, 223,* 188–190.

CHAPTER 26

SPACED OUT

Crowding. For most of us, living situations are likely to involve some crowding, now and in the future. Estimates vary, but it seems likely that the population of the world will double by the year 2040. Most of this increase is happening in less-developed countries, but its effects will be felt everywhere. In more developed countries, the most noticeable increase in population density has been in the shift from rural areas to urban areas. However, even with population increases, you can still be by yourself if you wish. In the United States, for example, there are 132 counties with fewer than two people per square mile. If that population density were applied to the five boroughs of New York City, only 600 people would live there, instead of 7.5 million (Duncan, 1993).

Psychologists who study population demographics make a distinction between the concepts of density and crowding. *Density* is an objective headcount; *crowding* is a subjective feeling. *Density* is the actual number of people living within a certain space. *Crowding* refers to the largely negative psychological feelings that can accompany living at high density. These feelings can range from generalized stress to specific feelings that other people are always in the way; that one never has a quiet moment to oneself. In some situations, architecture may be planned so that people can live at very high densities, yet not feel crowded. Nevertheless, some people feel crowded at very low densities.

This is one of the many areas in which it can be challenging to conduct meaningful studies on humans. One of the best-known early studies in this area involved laboratory rats (Calhoun, 1962). In this study, John Calhoun created a caged environment in which some rats ended up living at higher than usual densities. Calhoun observed a number of behaviors that appeared to be pathological when compared to the ordinary behavior of caged rats. There was more aggression among the rats at high density as well as failure to care for offspring. McCain, Cox, and Paulus (1976) studied prisons in which inmates lived at different densities. In the more dense living situations, there were higher rates of disciplinary problems, illness, suicide, and homicide. Making fair comparisons of different prisons might be quite difficult because factors other than density probably play a role in the experience of crowding. It would be easy to imagine that through force of necessity corrections officers might act differently in more dense prisons than in less-dense ones. If there were more prisoners per staff member in dense prisons, difficulties observed might be partially a result of staff ratios.

Incorporating the research of A. Baum and G. E. Davis, "Reducing the Stress of High-Density Living: An Architectural Intervention," 1980, *Journal of Personality and Social Psychology, 38*, pp. 471–481.

This situation in prison research is called a *confound*. A confound is some factor other than the independent variable that may make a difference in the dependent outcomes. In this situation, the outcomes—disciplinary problems, illness, suicide, and homicide—may be the result of density. However density is also linked to, or confounded with, other factors, such as staff ratios. For example, assume that high density and poor staff ratios in prisons always occur together. If so, a study could not determine the individual influences of density and staffing because there would be no way to hold one constant while varying the other. In a real prison situation, this study would probably be too costly to undertake. As a general point, research has the most clear cut findings when one factor is varied and the others that might be important are held constant, or otherwise controlled. More complex research designs may have more than one independent variable. Even with these designs, a few things are systematically varied and everything else that is believed to be important is held as constant as possible.

An additional problem with prisons is that the people who are incarcerated are not representative of the rest of the population. It may be easy to study density and crowding in prisons where living situations are assigned, but this situation may not generalize to nonincarcerated groups. The question becomes, where can we find groups of nonincarcerated people living at high density and assigned to rooms . . . hmmmm . . . what about college students?

ALTERED STATES OF LIVING

Andrew Baum and Glenn Davis (1980) conducted an experiment in which the architecture of several college dormitories was manipulated in order to study the effects of crowding. As elsewhere in this book, we are being careful to use the word *experiment* to refer to a very specific kind of investigation. Three different kinds of living situations were compared, and they were the independent variable in this study. An older type of long-corridor dorm that housed 40 students was compared to a different building in which groups of 20 students lived in short-corridor arrangements. A third group of students lived on another floor of the long-corridor dorm, but this floor had undergone some architectural alterations. In the middle of the long corridor, three rooms that had been bedrooms were turned into lounges. Two sets of unlocked doors were installed adjacent to the lounges (see Figure 26.1).

This arrangement had the effect of dividing the long corridor into two small corridors. The residency was reduced from 43 to 39 because two of the rooms that became lounges had been single occupancy and one had been double occupancy. Aside from this, the density on the floor was not changed. The doors and lounges tended to create two separate living units where once there had been only one. During the course of the study, the lounge rooms were rarely used, and they were not fully furnished until later. The location of the lounges and the central doors divided the corridor in such a way that each of the new, somewhat isolated, housing units included access to its own bathroom. Each of the three dormitory floors had been refurbished during the summer preceding the study, but only one had been modified to divide it in half. The residents formed the impression that all the housing areas included in the study had been substantially improved.

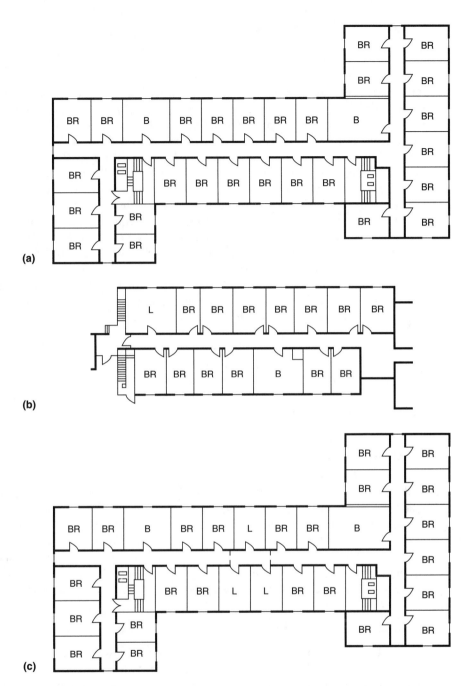

FIGURE 26.1 Floor Plans of Dormitory Corridors. (a) is the long-corridor arrangement, (b) is the short corridor, and (c) is the intervention floor—note lounge rooms and central doors in (c).

From "Reducing the Stress of High-Density Living: An Architectural Intervention," by A. Baum and G. Davis, 1980, *Journal of Personality and Social Psychology, 38*, p. 475. Copyright © 1980 by the American Psychological Association. Reprinted with permission.

The Participants

The participants in this study were first-year students, and they were all women who were randomly assigned to living areas. Limiting the study to women was probably a practical consideration because, depending on living arrangements, including men might have necessitated the inclusion of a number of additional floors. In some colleges, men and women share long corridors, but it is quite typical that long corridor dorms only have two bathrooms in each corridor. To divide such a mixed corridor in half would require many of the residents to leave their immediate housing unit to use the bathroom, seriously confounding the point of the study. However desirable it might have been to include men in the study, practical limitations prevented this.

Over the course of the study there was an attrition rate for participants of approximately 20 percent. Most of this was accounted for by illness and scheduling problems. A few of the students did not complete successive versions of a data-collection questionnaire and were dropped for that reason. There is no particular reason to think that the attrition introduced any particular bias into the study sample. This can sometimes be a problem in research, as was described in Chapter 3. In contrast to what did happen, if most of the dropouts in this study had come from one floor, the remaining individuals might no longer be considered a representative group of students. It is not possible to control attrition, and it is often an issue in longitudinal studies. Usually, the best that can be done is to have some assurance that groups are still comparable and that dropouts have not created a confound by making one group different from another in some important way.

Surveys

Students were surveyed during the first day of the orientation program at the beginning of the semester and again after 5 and 12 weeks. They were given a questionnaire that asked about their feelings concerning college and dormitory life. These surveys were administered in their dorm rooms. There were a number of questions on the surveys, but the primary focus of this study was the ratings about how crowded, hectic, and predictable students found dorm life. Students were also asked about expectations and success in maintaining control over social life and group formation. These survey responses served as operational definitions of the feeling of students about their living environments.

Naturalistic Observations

This study was unusual because it included some naturalistic observations among its dependent variables. Each floor was observed by a trained college-age male observer who was unaware of the hypothesis in the study. Three observations were made each week except for a few weeks that were abnormal (i.e., exam weeks or holidays). The observer moved through the three study sites recording the nature and location of social and nonsocial behavior, spending 5 minutes standing around in one end of the corridor then moving slowly to the other end and spending 5 minutes there. The observer also noted how many doors were open. Number of open doors was an operational definition of one type of sociability. The data were recorded covertly, and the success of this was illustrated by the fact that none of the residents were able to identify the observer when asked at the end of the semester.

Initial Laboratory Procedures

Eighteen students from each of the three groups were randomly selected for participation in the laboratory measures. Each of them arrived at the lab having been told that they were going to be in a study of "impression formation." Upon arrival, each participant was told that the study was running a few minutes late and was asked to wait in a waiting area. There were five chairs lined up against the wall, and a person was sitting in the first chair in the row. The participant was told that this was another participant for the lab study, but, in fact, this other person was a confederate of the experimenter. You will remember from previous chapters that a *confederate* in a psychological experiment is a person who is working for the experimenter and who behaves in some particular way as part of the setting of the experiment. The confederate in this study remained ready to respond, but did not make eye contact or initiate conversation.

The participant and the confederate were observed through a two-way mirror across from the chairs. The seat position of the participant was noted and the number of seconds that the participant looked at the face of the confederate was recorded. The point of this was to assess the social behavior of the participants using the operational definition of visual attention to another person. It would have been possible to do this with some kind of questionnaire asking how each participant would interact with a stranger in a waiting-room situation. Yet, what people say they would do and what they really do are sometimes different things. When people describe what they might do or think on a questionnaire, this is called a *soft measure* of behavior. When the actual behavior is observed, it is called a *hard measure*. This study had other hard measures that were taken in the naturalistic observation described above. It would have been possible to ask residents how often they left their room door open—a soft measure, but in this case an observer recorded the door positions—a hard measure. Although it can be fairly easy to criticize the validity of soft measures, it is more difficult to do so for hard measures: the doors were open or they were not; faulty recollections or opinions could not corrupt the data.

A Measure of Persistence

After 5 minutes in the waiting room, the participant was given a questionnaire that asked, among other things, how comfortable the participant felt while waiting with the confederate in the laboratory. Next, the participant was ushered into a separate room and presented with 12 difficult, but solvable, anagrams. Each of these scrambled words was presented on a separate card. The participant was told that 20 seconds would be allowed to work on each one and that the work had to be done mentally, with no writing allowed. The participant was told that she could come back to any unsolved anagrams for additional trials as often as she wished. This may seem a somewhat odd procedure, but it was really another hard measure, this time a behavioral measure of persistence. When the participant had either completed all the anagrams, or indicated that she did not wish to continue, she was debriefed and thanked.

Survey Results

The dependent variables from the surveys showed some longitudinal trends on the floors. As the semester progressed, long-corridor residents reported more difficulty in being able to control their lives in the dormitories ($p < .001$). They reported that their lives were more hectic ($p < .01$). Another measure of this lack of control was the extent to which residents felt they could regulate their social contact. Over time, this measurement also indicated social problems on the long-corridor floor ($p < .001$), while the intervention floor residents appeared to have social attitudes similar to those on the short corridor. Figure 26.2 shows these results.

The actual numbers on the *y*-axis refer to a 5-point scale on which residents rated their agreement with statements about control and regulation of social contact.

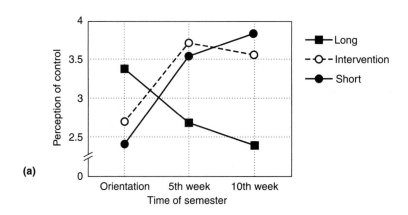

(a)

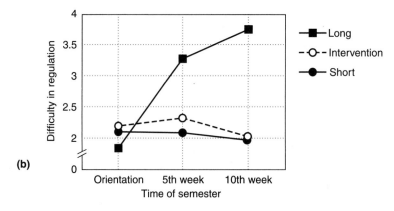

(b)

FIGURE 26.2   (a) Survey Results—Perceived Control (b) Survey Results—Regulating Social Contact. Survey results collected across the semester from residents in their dormitory rooms concerning control of living situation (a) and ability to regulate their social contact (b).

Life on the long corridor also affected the friendships formed by residents. Survey data indicated that these students felt less successful at making friends and, as weeks went by, they felt they knew fewer other residents as friends. Although there were no differences in feelings of crowding among the three floors at orientation, by the 5th and 12th weeks the long-corridor residents felt more crowded than the others did.

A sinister trend toward learned helplessness also appeared among the long-corridor residents. In the psychological literature, learned helplessness refers to a pattern of behavior in which an individual no longer attempts to find remedies for aversive circumstances (Seligman, 1991; Seligman & Maier, 1967). Figure 26.3 contains survey responses that showed that long-corridor residents reported lower levels of motivation to gain some control over their housing situation ($p < .001$). In particular, they felt that

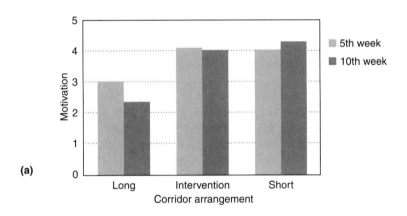

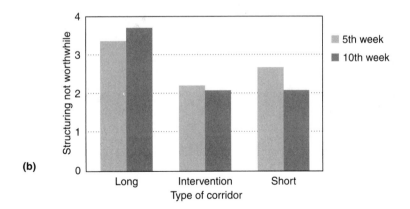

FIGURE 26.3   (a) Survey Results—Motivation to Achieve Control   (b) Survey Results—Not Worth Structuring Sociality. Survey results collected across the semester from residents in their dormitory rooms concerning motivation to achieve control over social interactions in the dormitory (a) and the worth of trying to structure situations to improve social interactions (b).

it was not worth trying to structure social situations to improve social interactions with others ($p < .001$).

Naturalistic Observational Findings

The observational dependent measures tended to support the general impression that social activity decreased over the semester for the long-corridor residents when compared to the others. These data are presented in Figure 26.4.

The gaps in the data in Figure 26.4 are the weeks during which observations were not made. There are two measures displayed in this figure—the percentage of activity that was rated as social and the number of open doors. Open doors were chosen because Baum and Davis believed that they represented an aspect of social life: an indication

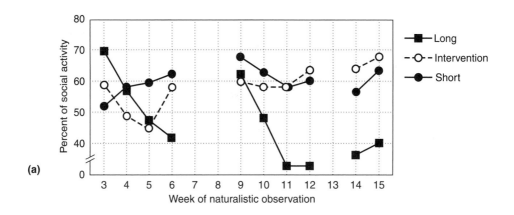

(a)

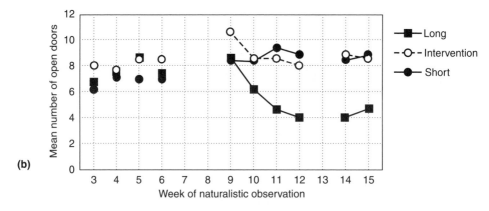

(b)

FIGURE 26.4   (a) Observed Percentage of Activity Rated as Social   (b) Mean Open Doors during Observations. Data from covert observations in dormitories of percentage of activity that could be considered social (a) and number of open doors (b).

that the residents of the room were open to social interaction. Although two different measures are shown in Figure 26.4, they both support the contention of decreased social activity in the long corridor. It is noteworthy that all groups appear to be similar at the beginning of the semester but not at the end. A statistical analysis of the data confirmed this. There were no significant differences among groups from the 3rd to the 9th week, but significant differences appeared in weeks 10 through 15 ($p < .001$).

In Figure 26.4, week 9 seems to show an increase in social activity on each of the floors. Baum and Davis believe that this was because week 8 was an open week, used by many students as a vacation. Upon returning in week 9, residents were more socially active as they reinvolved themselves in dormitory life. Although not expressed as a correlation coefficient, this point is based on correlational thinking. If you wish to extrapolate this finding, you should be sure to tell your college administrators that dormitory life can be improved by having a vacation every week or two. We only make this suggestion to illustrate the care that should be exercised when correlational findings are assumed to be causal and applied to real situations.

Laboratory Findings

The laboratory findings in this study consisted of both hard and soft measures. The hard measures were the number of seats left open between participant and confederate, the amount of time the participant spent looking at the confederate's face, and anagram performance. The soft measures included questionnaire ratings of discomfort, rated on a 7-point scale, while waiting for the anagram task to begin. The results of these assessments are presented in Table 26.1.

As with the other measures, the data presented in Table 26.1 support the hypothesis that long-corridor living has a detrimental effect on social behavior. Long-corridor residents chose to sit farther away from the confederate in the lab waiting area ($p < .05$), they spent less time looking at the confederate's face ($p < .05$), and they were more

TABLE 26.1 Mean Responses in Laboratory Measures

	SEATS AWAY FROM CONFEDERATE	FACIAL REGARD FOR CONFEDERATE (SECS)	DISCOMFORT AFTER WAITING	NUMBER OF ANAGRAMS ATTEMPTED
Long corridor	2.6	18.2	4.3	15.8
Intervention corridor	1.9	50.3	2.8	21.8
Short corridor	2.0	52.2	2.7	20.6

Note: In each column, the long corridor score is statistically significantly different ($p < .05$) from the scores of residents from the other two corridors.

uncomfortable waiting for the lab procedure to begin ($p < .05$) (although, of course, for them it had already begun, but they did not know it). They also attempted fewer anagrams ($p < .01$). The first three of these measures quite clearly suggested differences in social behavior. The last may seem a bit beside the point. Who cares about anagrams? The point here is not the anagrams, but the persistence of the students at a task—any task. The survey data from the students showed that among the long-corridor residents, motivation to enact change is low. As we have noted, this sounds like learned helplessness. The massive literature on learned helplessness suggests that it involves more than just reluctance to take new actions to solve problems, it also involves giving up easily, or failing to persist, in repeated actions that might lead to problem solutions (see, for example, Heyman, Dweck, & Cain, 1992, and Jones, Slate, Marini, & DeWater, 1993). It is noteworthy that being good or bad at the anagram task did not influence persistence on the task. Some students from each floor were good at anagrams and some were not. Good, bad, or indifferent, long-corridor residents gave up easily.

DISCUSSION

It is likely that this study had high internal validity. The independent variable was the living arrangement: long corridor, intervention corridor or short corridor. The hypothesis was that living arrangement would make a difference in social behavior. Part of the claim to internal validity in this study came from the variety of dependent measures: hard and soft, laboratory and real world. This would have been a much less convincing study if, for example, only questionnaires had been used to assess social behavior. A variety of measures at different times that pointed to the same conclusions suggested solid support for the general hypothesis. In addition, it is likely that this study had a good claim to external validity. It is not known if men or upper-level students would have reacted differently but, otherwise, there are many reasons to believe that subdivisions of long corridors would have positive social effects.

Baum and Davis pointed out that this kind of architectural intervention does not have to be very expensive. The actual changes to the building were minimal, and the largest cost to the college was the lost revenue from the three rooms that became lounges. The lounges themselves did not seem to be a necessary part of the intervention, but having them there as unoccupied space may have increased the perception that the intervention corridor was smaller.

For us, the most striking thing about the findings of this study was the extent to which a seemingly small intervention had persistent effects on the lives of the individuals involved. The real value of an experiment is that the results can be cautiously interpreted in cause-and-effect terms. The students were randomly assigned to the three floors, and there is no indication that the groups were different at the beginning of the study. Indeed, the data that were collected during orientation showed no significant differences among groups. The differences appeared as the semester unfolded. The effect of housing on social behavior in the dormitories was robustly demonstrated in this study. Perhaps the biggest surprise was the extent to which the influence of the housing unit seemed to permeate the lives of these students beyond the living unit. We might not have guessed that the social behavior of the long-corridor dwellers would be different in the laboratory setting.

The suggestions of helplessness that accompany crowding in this study imply that college housing should not be taken lightly. The beginning year of college is a time when it is very important for students to begin to take charge of their own lives. The frightening conclusion that might be drawn from this study is that those students who live in crowded environments become less likely to try to do something about situations that have made them unhappy. If this becomes a lifestyle trend, there is likely to be more unhappiness for them in the future.

REFERENCES

Baum, A., & Davis, G. E. (1980). Reducing the stress of high-density living: An architectural intervention. *Journal of Personality and Social Psychology, 38*, 471–481.

Calhoun, J. B. (1962). Population density and social pathology. *Scientific American, 206*, 139–148.

Duncan, D. (1993). *Miles from nowhere*. New York: Penguin.

Heyman, G., Dweck, C., & Cain, K. (1992). Young children's vulnerability to self-blame and helplessness: Relationship to beliefs about goodness. *Child Development, 63*, 401–415.

Jones, C., Slate, J., Marini, I., & DeWater, B. (1993). Academic skills and attitudes towards intelligence. *Journal of College Student Development, 34*, 422–424.

McCain, G., Cox, V., & Paulus, P. (1976). The relationship between illness, complaints, and degree of crowding in a prison environment. *Environment and Behavior, 8*, 283–290.

Seligman, M., & Maier, S. (1967). Failure to escape traumatic shock. *Journal of Experimental Psychology, 37B*, 1–21.

Seligman, M. E. P. (1991). *Learned optimism*. New York: Knopf.

CHAPTER 27

WEIGHT LOSS THAT WORKS

Obesity affects one-third of the adult U.S. population and represents a serious public health problem with consequences for physical and psychological health (Kuczmarski, Flegal, Campbell, & Johnson, 1994). Obesity is a medical condition that refers to being severely overweight and is directly linked to diabetes, high blood pressure, and coronary heart diseases (Pi-Sunyer, 1994). Obesity also affects how other people perceive and treat each other and even how you may view yourself. Ryckman, Robbins, Kaczor, and Gold (1989) reported that obese people are often stereotyped as slow, sloppy, and lazy.

Over the past several years behavioral approaches to weight management have become the principal modes of treatments (Sbrocco, Nedergaard, Stone, & Lewis, 1998). Such programs, however, have been criticized for high relapse rates and for promoting a mentality of dieting (Brownell & Rodin, 1994; Garner & Wooley, 1991; Glenny, O'Meara, Melville, Sheldon, & Wilson, 1997).

In recent years some newer treatments have emerged that do not stress dieting as the dominant strategy to permanent weight loss (Ciliska, 1990; Omichinski & Harrison, 1995). The idea behind these strategies is that discontinuing the diet orientation to food may be psychologically beneficial and may in the long term result in more stable weight loss. Regrettably, there have only been a few real empirical tests of these newer approaches to permanent weight management. The present research is designed to empirically examine the efficacy of cognitive-behavioral approach emphasizing individual choices and minimizing *dieting* (Behavioral Choice Therapy; BCT) in comparison to a traditional behavior therapy (TBT).

PRESENT STUDY

The BCT approach relates eating behavior in certain situations to outcomes and goals using decision theory (Sbrocco & Schlundt, 1998). A person's goals regarding food choices go well beyond the need to satisfy hunger and extend to factors such as self-

Incorporating the research of T. Sbrocco, R. C. Nedegaard, J. M. Stone, and E. L. Lewis, "Behavioral Choice Treatment Promotes Continuing Weight Loss: Preliminary Results of a Cognitive-Behavioral Decision-Based Treatment for Obesity," 1999, *Journal of Consulting and Clinical Psychology, 67*, pp. 260–266.

esteem and social acceptance. Research has shown that obese women were not aware of the positive reinforcers that served to maintain their maladaptive eating behaviors. Other research by Sbrocco and colleagues (Sbrocco et al., 1998; Sbrocco & Schlundt, 1998) indicate that in traditional dieting programs obese women failed to learn to eat in moderation and often overate or underate. In contrast, women with normal weight generally were moderate eaters. This research suggests that obese women would benefit from learning to eat in moderation and learning that they had choices and could make decisions about what to eat. It was hypothesized that a treatment plan centered on (1) learning to eat moderately, (2) learning to exercise moderately, and (3) disconnecting eating and self-evaluation (i.e., how you feel about yourself) might prove effective in promoting more permanent weight loss.

In the present study, comparing TBT and BCT in weight management, it was expected that the TBT participants would achieve greater weight loss in the active treatment phase, but would gain back weight after the cessation of treatment. In contrast, it was thought that the BCT participants would lose weight more gradually than the TBT participants would during the active treatment phase, but would continue a gradual steady weight loss into the nontreatment follow-up phases. This assumption was based on the hypothesis that the BCT groups had learned a pattern of moderate eating and moderate exercise, whereas the primary focus of TBT group was dieting and reduced caloric intake. It would also be expected that the BCT participants would experience an increase in self-esteem compared to the TBT group, because they chose to eat in moderation, gained an understanding of their eating behavior, and had success in controlling their weight.

METHOD

The participants in this study were women between the ages of 18 and 55 who were 30 percent to 60 percent above established body weight chart limits and responded to newspaper advertisements. They were in good health, were nonsmokers, and had medical clearance for participation. Participants paid a $150 fee to participate in the study, which was refunded at the end of the program. It is likely that the researchers imposed a fee to increase participant commitment to the program. Several participants had a reduced fee based on their financial situation. All participants completed a two-week pretreatment phase during which they recorded eating, weight, and other information. There were 24 women in the final participant pool, with half randomly assigned to either the BCT or the TBT group.

Measures

Physical—Weight and Body Mass Index (BMI) were calculated at pretreatment, at weekly meetings, posttreatment, and at follow-up sessions. Height, part of the BMI calculation, was determined at pretreatment.

Behavioral Commitment—The number of sessions attended and the number of self-monitored records were used as indices of adherence and dedication to the treatment program.

Eating Records—Participants were trained to use a Psion palmtop computer to record self-monitored behavior. The Comcard Computer-A-Diet Nutrient Balance System (1993) software facilitated the standardized recording of foods eaten and situational factors associated with eating behavior. The Comcard software contained a list of almost 4,000 foods. Participants were instructed to weigh all foods on a scale and to respond to six computer generated questions regarding the context of their eating. Specifically, the participants were asked to record the following data about their eating: date, time, location, level of hunger, level of stress, and with whom they ate. From this data, individualized goals including immediate and weekly feedback was provided to participants. The researchers monitored caloric intake as a measure of adherence to the caloric prescription set for the participant.

Psychological Self-Report Measures—The following self-report measures were completed at pretreatment, midtreatment, posttreatment, 3-month follow-up, and 6-month follow-up:

Eating Inventory-Restraint Scale (Stunkard & Messick, 1988). This scale was employed to assess changes in dietary restraint.

Eating Disorders Inventory-2 (EDI-2; Garner, 1991). This scale was used to measure behavioral and cognitive characteristics observed clinically in eating disorders. The following three subscales of the EDI-2 were used in the present research: Drive for Thinness, Bulimia, and Body Dissatisfaction.

State Self-Esteem Scale (SSES; Heatherton & Polivy, 1991). Designed to assess clinical changes in self-esteem.

Beck Depression Inventory (BDI; Beck, Ward, Mendelson, Mock, & Erbaugh, 1961). Designed to assess symptoms of depression.

Participants were scheduled to attend 13 weekly 1½ hour treatment sessions. Leaders experienced in behavioral treatment of weight management led the sessions. The same leaders facilitated both the TBT and BCT groups. Participants in both groups were given 2-week meal plans including recipe booklets. The only difference between the two groups was the amount of food. The TBT participants were given a 1,200 kcal/day (5,023 kJ) diet. The BCT participants were given a 1,800 kcal/day (7,534 kJ) diet. Both groups of participants were told to abide by the specific requirements of their plan and were offered encouragement. At weekly meetings each participant's Psion-diary data was downloaded and immediate feedback was provided including graphic presentations of caloric intake, fat intake, a list of their highest fat foods, and alternative low-fat food options. Participants were instructed to eat at a constant caloric rate to avoid overeating or overrestricting food intake. Both groups were matched according to meeting topic, length of sessions, homework, contact with treatment leaders, self-monitoring of eating behavior, and exercise instructions. The prescribed exercise for both groups was home-based walking for 30 min/day, in a single session, 3 days/week. Participants maintained exercise records.

Traditional Behavior Therapy (TBT) Plan

Schlundt's (1987) treatment model, consisting of 12 weeks of active treatment, has shown to produce a short-term weight loss of approximately 12 lb. (5.45 kg). The participants were informed that the goal of the program was to promote significant weight loss and to help them to maintain the loss through behavioral approaches. Participants were taught self-monitoring, stimulus control, and behavioral substitution techniques. Self-monitoring involves the systematic observation and recording of one's own behavior(s). Because people may have inaccurate ideas about how they behave, self-monitoring provides them (and their therapist) an objective profile of observed behavior(s). Learning about stimulus control of behavior teaches people about how behaviors may be associated with stimulus or environmental events in their lives. This allows people to analyze, understand, and begin to modify their own behavior(s). Behavioral substitution is the replacement of a maladaptive or problematic behavior (e.g., overeating) with a more adaptive behavior. Participants were encouraged to avoid high-calorie, high-fat foods and to keep their daily caloric intake to 1,200 kcal (5,023 kJ). Participants were instructed to explore their reasons for eating, and if stress was a factor, to use means other than eating as an adaptive response.

Behavioral Choice Treatment (BCT) Plan

The participants were informed that their treatment plan for weight loss was not based on dieting. In fact, they were instructed *not* to diet. Part of their treatment was to view eating as a choice. They were also told that their weight loss would be slower than under traditional plans but that permanent weight loss was the ultimate treatment goal. Concepts of healthy behavioral choices, appropriate food selection, exercise options, and developing healthy patterns of eating were stressed. Participants learned to identify their own choices and the consequences that controlled these decisions. Participants were helped to modify and restructure their thinking in order to enable them to attain positive outcomes with respect to food choices. If a participant felt badly about eating a high-calorie or high-fat food, cognitive restructuring and behavioral modeling were utilized to enable the participant to eat a small amount of the "taboo" food and thereby develop the cognitive belief that she could handle such foods in moderation. Not being able to eat in moderation and not being able to eat small quantities of high-caloric or high-fat foods were seen as deficits in skills that could be learned through cognitive restructuring, modeling, and homework assignments. Cognitive restructuring is the process of helping clients identify self-defeating or irrational thoughts and replacing them with more appropriate ones. Modeling is the learning strategy discussed in Chapter 11, "I Do!" This form of learning is based on observing how others act and imitating their behavior. Homework assignments are often used to take behaviors learned in treatment and apply or practice them in the "real world." Participants in the BCT groups were told to eliminate the word *dieting* from their language and thinking as well as the associated concepts of food restriction and rigid rules. They were encouraged to engage in pleasurable, positive activities not associated with eating and to participate in regular exercise. Finally, they were encouraged to accept themselves for who they were and to lessen their concern about body weight and eating behavior. They were instructed to focus on the future and look toward their ultimate goal weight rather than on dieting, which usually focuses on how to lose the most amount of weight in the shortest amount of time.

RESULTS AND DISCUSSION

Demographic data collected from the participants in the TBT and BCT groups showed that they did not differ significantly in age (M = 43.1, M = 39.6); weight (M = 89.54 kg, M = 89.56 kg); or caloric intake (M = 9,964 kJ, M = 10,654 kJ). A kilocalorie (kcal), what most of us call a calorie, can be converted to kilojoules (kJ) by multiplying by 4.184. Therefore, a person on a 2,000 kcal diet is on an 8,368 kJ diet.

Figure 27.1 shows the weight changes (in kilograms; 1 lb. = .454 kg) for all treatment and follow-up assessments. The data analysis showed that the TBT groups had greater weight loss at the midtreatment assessment. The groups did not differ at the 3-month follow-up. There was, however, a difference between the groups at both the 6- and 12-month follow-up, with the BCT having achieved a significantly greater weight loss.

Participants's commitment to treatment and the honesty of the data collected was reviewed by checking participants' self-reported diet adherence and exercise commitment. Caloric consumption differed significantly between the two groups, with the TBT group consuming, on average, approximately 1,363 kcal, whereas the BCT group consumed, on average, approximately 1,674 kcal. This was not unexpected because the TBT was instructed to consume 1,200kcal/day, and the BCT was instructed to consume 1,800 kcal/day. The data indicated that the TBT group was consuming more than instructed, and the BCT group was consuming less than instructed.

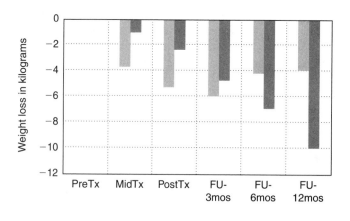

FIGURE 27.1   Weight Changes (in Kilograms) from Pretreatment to 12-Month Follow-Up

Figures 27.2 and 27.3 present the frequency (days/week) and duration (minutes per week) of exercise from pretreatment through the 12-month follow-up for both groups. Both groups significantly increased their frequency of exercise during the treatment phase of the study, with greater increases observed in the TBT group. The frequency of exercise for the BCT group tended to be constant from midtreatment to posttreatment. The TBT group tended to decrease exercise frequency from posttreatment to 12-month follow-up. Despite the reported differences at some points of assessment, there were no overall significant differences between groups in their exercise frequency at any of the three follow-ups.

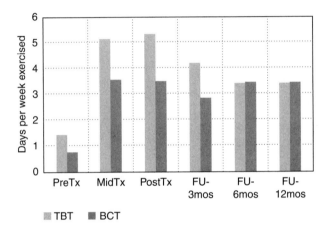

FIGURE 27.2   Number of Days per Week Exercised from Pretreatment to 12-Month Follow-Up

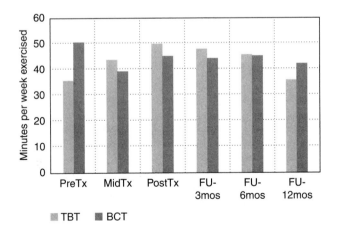

FIGURE 27.3   Number of Minutes per Week Exercised from Pretreatment to 12-Month Follow-Up

The self-report measures recorded by participants in both groups are displayed in Figures 27.4 through 27.9. The Restraint subscale of the Eating Inventory showed no significant differences between the BCT and TBT groups during active treatment. However, they did differ significantly in posttreatment follow-up, with the BCT group indicating lower Restraint scores. On the Drive for Thinness subscale of the EDI-2 there was no significant difference seen between BCT and TBT groups. There was a

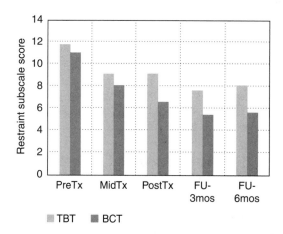

FIGURE 27.4   Restraint Subscale (Eating Inventory) from Pretreatment to 12-Month Follow-Up

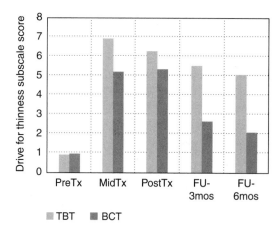

FIGURE 27.5   Drive for Thinness Subscale (Eating Inventory) from Pretreatment to 12-Month Follow-Up

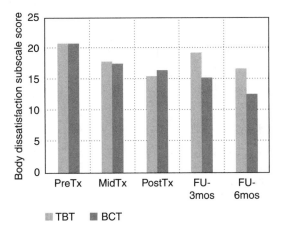

FIGURE 27.6   Body Dissatisfaction Subscale (Eating Disorders Inventory-2) from Pretreatment to 12-Month Follow-Up

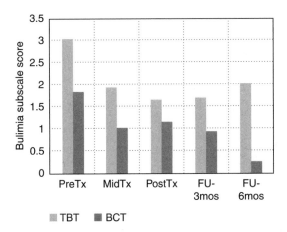

FIGURE 27.7   Bulimia Subscale (Eating Inventory) from Pretreatment to 12-Month Follow-Up

trend on the EDI-2 Body Dissatisfaction subscale in which the BCT group showed less body dissatisfaction over time, whereas the TBT group showed just the opposite, more body dissatisfaction in follow-up. The EDI-2 Bulimia scale did not suggest that either group evidenced clinical scores of bulimia, an eating disorder, nor were there any differences noted between BCT and TBT groups. There was a trend, however, for the TBT groups to have higher scores at all assessment checkpoints than the BCT group. The State Self-Esteem Scales showed no differences between groups at pretreatment,

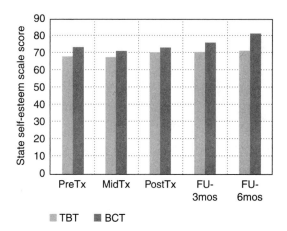

FIGURE 27.8   State Self-Esteem Scale from Pretreatment to 12-Month Follow-Up

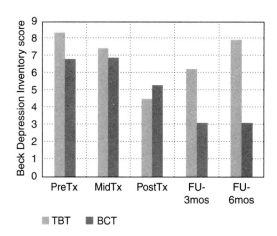

FIGURE 27.9   Beck Depression Inventory from Pretreatment to 12-Month Follow-Up

with both BCT and TBT participants showing favorable levels of self-esteem. In both the BCT and TBT groups there was a trend of increased self-esteem during the course of treatment and follow-up. The Beck Depression Inventory showed no differences between groups at pretreatment and no significant differences over the course of treatment. Neither group evidenced significant levels of depression. The Depression scores of the BCT group continued to drop (i.e., lower levels of depression) in follow-up whereas the TBT group the Beck scores increased to pretreatment levels over time.

This research is notable for the maintenance of weight loss by the BCT group up to 1 year after active treatment. Typically, traditional behavioral weight-reduction programs have a pattern of weight regain after the cessation of ongoing treatment (Glenny et al., 1997). The exercise findings for the BCT participants was also encouraging because they maintained exercise levels in the follow-up. In contrast, the exercise pattern for the TBT participants started out with a bang and then tapered off. According to the guidelines of the National Heart, Lung, and Blood Institute (NHLBI, 1998), the typical BCT participant went from a BMI of 32.82 to a BMI of 29.13 after 15 months. This represents a diagnostic change from Obese to Overweight. The typical weight loss in the BCT was 11 percent. To calculate your own BMI visit the www.phys.com site on the Internet and click on the calculator section. This will enable you to determine your BMI status.

This investigation had some limitations. Self-report data were used extensively, with overreporting exercise and underreporting eating a possibility. The sample size of 12 in each group was smaller than was desirable. It also might have been advantageous to have a control group that met during the 13-week active program, but received no active weight-reduction treatment. Finally moderately obese women may not be representative of all groups of overweight persons. In spite of these drawbacks, however, this is an excellent example of how newer, cognitive-behavioral, health-focused treatment can be used to manage an important public health problem.

REFERENCES

Beck, A. T., Ward, C. H., Mendelson, M., Mock, J., & Erbaugh, J. (1961). An inventory for measuring depression. *Archives of General Psychiatry, 4*, 53–63.

Brownell, K. D., & Rodin J. (1994). The dieting maelstrom: Is it possible and advisable to lose weight? *American Psychologist, 49*, 781–791.

Ciliska, D. (1990). Beyond dieting: Psychoeducational interventions for chronically obese women. A non-dieting approach. In P. E. Garfinkel & D. M. Garner (Eds.), *Eating disorders* (Monograph Series No. 5). New York: Brunner/Mazel.

Compute-A-Diet Nutrient Balance System [Computer software]. (1993). Worcestershire, England: Comcard.

Garner, D. M. (1991). *The Eating Disorder Inventory—2 professional manual.* Odessa, FL: Psychological Assessment Resources.

Garner, D. M., & Wooley, S. C. (1991). Confronting the failure of behavioral and dietary treatments for obesity. *Clinical Psychology Review, 11*, 729–780.

Glenny, A. M., O'Meara, S., Melville, A., Sheldon, T. A., & Wilson, C. (1997). The treatment and prevention of obesity: A systematic review of the literature. *International Journal of Obesity, 21*, 715–737.

Heatherton, T. F., & Polivy, J. (1991). Development and validation of a scale for measuring state self-esteem. *Journal of Personality and Social Psychology, 60*, 895–910.

Kuczmarski, R. J., Flegal, K. M., Campbell, S. M., & Johnson, C. L. (1994). Increasing prevalence of overweight among U.S. adults. *JAMA: Journal of the American Medical Association, 266*, 1535–1542.

National Heart, Lung, and Blood Institute. (1998). *Clinical guidelines of the identification, evaluation, and treatment of overweight and obesity in adults.* Washington, DC: Author.

Omichinski, L., & Harrison, K. (1995). Reduction of dieting attitudes and practices after participation in a nondiet lifestyle program. *Journal of the Canadian Dietetic Association, 56,* 81–85.

Pi-Sunyer, F. X. (1994). The fattening of America. *Journal of the American Medical Association, 272*(3), 238–239.

Ryckman, R. M., Robbins, M. A., Kaczor, L. M., & Gold, J. A. (1989). Male and female raters' stereotyping of male and female physiques. *Personality and Social Psychology Bulletin, 15,* 244–251.

Sbrocco, T., Nedegaard, R. C., Stone, J. M., & Lewis, E. L. (1998). *Differences in decision making patterns among obese and normal weight women.* Unpublished manuscript.

Sbrocco, T., Nedegaard, R. C., Stone, J. M., & Lewis, E. L. (1999). Behavioral choice treatment promotes continuing weight loss: Preliminary results of a cognitive-behavioral decision-based treatment for obesity. *Journal of Consulting and Clinical Psychology, 67,* 260–266.

Sbrocco, T., & Schlundt, D. G. (1998). *Applying decision theory to understand cognitive regulation in dieting: "Dysregulation" makes sense.* Manuscript submitted for publication.

Schlundt, D. G. (1987). *Helping others lose weight: A step-by-step program.* Nashville, TN: Author.

Stunkard, A. J., & Messick, S. (1988). *The eating inventory.* San Antonio, TX: Psychological Corporation.

CHAPTER 28

I THINK I CAN, I THINK I CAN

The way we think about our own abilities can have a serious impact on our performance. *Ability* is an interesting concept because it is often contrasted with another concept, *performance*. *Ability*, by definition, is supposed to refer to potential for behavior, whereas *performance* more often refers to the observed level of behavior. *Ability* is a somewhat slippery concept, because it cannot be directly observed. Some psychologists believe that there are tests that can measure ability, but not all scientists agree (Cohen, 1998). Research in psychology has identified two different views that people might take concerning ability. The first of these, the *entity* view, is most in line with the standard definition: it treats ability as a fixed quantity that will not change. In this view one possesses a certain amount of ability and that is all there is ever going to be. A person may not perform up to potential, but whether or not full potential is reached, it is limited. In contrast, the *incremental* view suggests that if a person wants more ability, it can be gained through hard work. These are the positions taken, respectively, by American and Japanese cultures described in Chapter 14, ". . . And All of the Children are Above Average." American schoolchildren were likely to be entity theorists, believing that native ability was important. Japanese children were incremental thinkers who believed that the key to success was to work hard.

These two views of ability are closely related to another concept: *self-efficacy*. Self-efficacy refers to the judgments individuals make about their capabilities to mobilize the motivation, cognitive resources, and courses of action needed to enable future performance on a specific task. If you have self-efficacy about some particular behavior, it means you believe you can perform the behavior, and, probably, you also believe that you are quite good at it. Just as with *The Little Engine That Could* in the children's story, research has shown that self-efficacious beliefs can lead to actual differences in performance.

SELF-EFFICACY IN JOB TRAINING

In contrast to the situation of earlier generations, it is now unrealistic to expect to enter the workforce and find lifetime employment with one company. The website of the

Incorporating the research of J. J. Martocchio, "Effects of Conceptions of Ability on Anxiety, Self-efficacy, and Learning in Training," 1994, *Journal of Applied Psychology, 79*, pp. 819–825.

California Trade and Commerce Agency sounds a contemporary warning: the average worker can expect to change jobs about six times, often as a result of factors that go beyond personal dissatisfaction. Companies are frequently rearranged, moved, and downsized. Jobs within organizations can quickly cease to exist, being replaced by other positions requiring different skills. Because of financial pressures, workplaces are being transformed into high-performance sites where cost can be the single most important factor in personnel decisions. New jobs typically require rapidly changing skill sets that will require lifelong learning for all workers.

The federal government is spending considerable amounts of money on job-training programs in an attempt to train or retrain workers of all ages. Most of this money is being distributed in the form of grants to states for the establishment of vocational training programs. Much of the research about job training has focused on learning specific skills (Gagne, 1962). However, as long ago as the 1940s, a program called Job Instruction Training (JIT) recognized that putting the trainee "at ease" was an important part of job-training programs (Gold, 1981). Unlike other approaches that merely gave instruction and manipulated rewards, this component of JIT recognized that workers' attitudes were an important part of learning. It may seem obvious that positive attitudes toward learning can result in better learning, but many job-training programs have neglected cognitive states. Although putting a person at ease may involve physical arrangements such as having adequate light and sufficiently comfortable work surroundings, it could also include a variety of attitudes (Kraiger, Ford, & Salas, 1993). Some of the attitudes that have been found to increase the probability that an individual will benefit from training are: realistic expectations about learning (Hicks & Klimoski, 1987), self-confidence (Tannenbaum, Cannon-Bowers, Salas, & Mathieu, 1993), and self-efficacy (Mitchell, Hopper, Daniels, George-Falvy, & James, 1994).

Joseph Marticchio (1994) studied the extent to which beliefs about self-efficacy and ability affected the performance of an adult population who were learning to use computers for the first time. If you have ever tried to teach computer skills to someone who has never used a computer at all, you will appreciate the complexity of this task. Many small routines are learned as part of computer literacy. Frequent computer users take these routines for granted. They are so commonplace to users that they may not be mentioned by instruction manuals. Consider the difference between the location of the cursor on a screen of word-processed material and of the mouse pointer on the screen. Anyone who has word processed very much will not confuse these two. Further, people skilled in word processing will know that clicking the mouse will move the cursor to the mouse pointer's location on the screen, but that the mouse pointer will be "left behind" in that location by the cursor as soon as keyboarding starts adding new lines to the text. This is a difficult concept to fully describe in print. Instruction manuals are inclined to leave this out, assuming that people know it. If people are not aware of this convention, it may take a long time to learn. There are hundreds of other little procedures that enable experienced users to quickly figure out new software.

Adults who use computers for the first time may experience substantial fear of the machine. They have probably heard stories of computers "crashing" or "locking up," and they fear that some accidental combination of keystrokes will destroy the machine or, at least, result in loss of software or data. Nevertheless, adults who are looking for good jobs will probably have to learn some computer skills. Marticchio thought that individuals who had incremental ideas about ability, seeing ability as acquirable, might see computer training as an opportunity, not a threat. Marticchio designed a field study to examine this. This field study was probably an experiment, but it was conducted in a real setting with real job trainees. These real-world setting factors probably give this study a greater claim to external validity than if the experiment had been conducted in a lab with college students pretending to be job trainees. The study offered three related hypotheses containing the following propositions:

> Hypothesis 1. People who were trained to believe that computer skills were an acquirable ability would experience lower levels of computer anxiety following training than they experienced before training. In contrast, trainees who experienced entity information about computer skills during training would have more computer anxiety after training than before it.

> Hypothesis 2. Trainees given the acquirable skill, or incremental, condition would show greater computer efficacy beliefs after training, compared to before. Trainees in the entity condition would report less computer efficacy following training.

> Hypothesis 3. Trainees' acquisition of declarative knowledge about computers would be influenced by computer anxiety and efficacy, as assessed by posttraining measures.

Participants

Seventy-six service and administrative employees of a large public university participated. Almost half of them were men, and the average age of the entire group was 42.2 years. A little over 80 percent of these people had never used a microcomputer before. The others indicated that coworkers had written down specific instructions about which keys to press but the implication was that they had virtually no knowledge of the machine beyond a few specific instructions.

Procedure

Each participant was provided with an identification number that researchers used to link the measures of behavior taken before and after training. Participants were told, in advance, that this number would not be used to connect their performance in training with their name. This was a strategy for protecting these participants from thinking that their employer might have monitored their training. The goal was to avoid job-related threats of adverse outcomes for insufficient progress. Issuance of identification numbers to link various measures is a procedure often used when it is desirable that participants remain anonymous. Some voluntary medical tests, such as tests for HIV infection, use this as a way of linking blood samples to test results, allowing the identification of different pieces of data from the same person without the use of names.

The training program involved a 3-hour course that constituted an introduction to microcomputing. A lecture was delivered, after which trainees used microcomputers to practice the routines that were covered in the lecture. In the lecture, the researcher, who served as the instructor for the training, began the session with introductory remarks. Next, participants introduced themselves and each stated the personal goal he or she had for the session. After this, each trainee filled out a questionnaire. At the end of the training session another questionnaire was administered followed by a short multiple-choice test of computer knowledge. Finally, they were debriefed.

A number of measures were taken before any training began. The purpose of these was to provide assurance that the groups, which received different research manipulations, were equivalent at the beginning of the study. Demographic measures were collected to assess the equivalence of experimental groups before they received the training that included the independent variable. Age, sex, education, length of service with the university, occupation, and computer experience were recorded. Participants' expectations for training were also assessed. Participants rated the likelihood that using a computer would result in some "gain" and "benefits" in their work. They rated this on a 7-point scale ranging from 1 = *highly unlikely* to 7 = *highly likely*.

Participants were assigned to one of two conditions, or training manipulations: (a) information that computer ability is a fixed entity and (b) information that computer ability is a skill that can be acquired in increments. This information was integrated into the instructions for the computer skill learning exercises that trainees used. To avoid experimenter expectancy effects, defined in Chapter 1, instructions that contained the entity or incremental manipulation were all printed, and the researcher working with the participants was purposely kept unaware of the content. The following is an example of an incremental instruction from the study:

> [You should] Remember the old saying 'Practice makes perfect,' which holds true for computer skills. In acquiring your DOS [computer] skills, you will probably make some mistakes. That's normal. People who learn how to use microcomputers do not begin with faultless performance. Again, it is important to remember that the more practice you have, the more capable you will become.

In contrast, the following is an example of an entity instruction from the study:

> [You should] Remember the old saying 'Work smart, not hard,' which holds true for learning microcomputer skills. You will probably make mistakes during this DOS [computer] exercise. Such mistakes should serve as a useful reminder to work smart, not hard. Again, learning how to use microcomputers is based on skills that you already possess. Thus, I encourage you to work smart.

The differences seen in statements presented above were typical of the other passages found in the instructions, and this informational difference was the independent variable in this experiment.

There were a number of measures used as dependent outcomes in this study. Computer anxiety was measured on a 10-item self-report questionnaire, The Computer Anxiety Rating Scale (Heinssen, Glass, & Knight, 1987). This contained items such as "I feel apprehensive about using computers," which were rated by participants on a 7-point scale where 1 = *strongly disagree* and 7 = *strongly agree*. Total scores on this instrument could range from 10 to 70, high scores indicating greater reported anxiety about computers. Computer efficacy was measured using a 6-item scale adapted from Hollenbeck and Brief (1987). Items such as "Using microcomputers is probably something I will be good at" were rated on a 7-point scale from *strongly disagree* to *strongly agree*. Higher total scores represented higher computer efficacy. In addition, following the training session, participants took a test of what is called declarative knowledge. This test was the type of multiple-choice test that is often used in college classes to test knowledge of material that has been covered in a course. In this study, the test of declarative knowledge was a 10-question multiple-choice test that was designed to be fairly difficult so that it could *discriminate*, meaning show the difference, between those who learned the material and those who did not. If a test is too easy, everyone scores well and the test does not discriminate. This is called a *ceiling effect*, meaning that every-one scores at or near the top. If a test is too difficult, the reverse happens in scores: no one does well. This is called a *floor effect*. In both of these situations a test does not iden-tify those who have learned and those who have not. About half of the participants cor-rectly answered each of the items on this test, showing that ceiling and floor effects had been avoided.

Two other questions were asked following the training session. These were included as a check to see if the manipulation in the study, the attempt to create par-ticular attitudes about computer ability, was actually successful in changing attitudes. The two statements that formed the manipulation check were: "I can learn from the mistakes I make when learning how to use a microcomputer" and "Making errors reflects limits to my ability to learn microcomputers." These were rated on a 7-point scale from 1 = *strongly disagree* to 7 = *strongly agree*. Once participants had rated these, the answers to the second question were transposed, or reverse-scored, so that high scores indicated the conception of ability as an acquirable skill on both questions. The scores on these two statements were added together to give a final score assessing the effectiveness of the manipulation.

Results

No differences were found between the participants in the two experimental condi-tions on the pretraining measures of age, education, computer experience, length of service, computer efficacy, computer anxiety expectations, sex, or occupation. This is important because if there had been preexisting differences between groups in these variables it would have been difficult to interpret the outcomes of the study. If, for example, one group had been higher in computer efficacy before training, it would not have been clear that the independent variable, the information about ability in the training session, had been responsible for differences in the dependent measures.

Following the training sessions, the two questions that were proposed as a check for the effectiveness of the manipulation yielded significant differences in the expected direction, as can be seen in Figure 28.1.

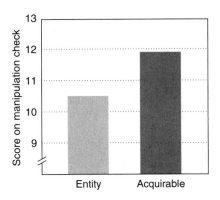

FIGURE 28.1 Scores on Manipulation Check for Both Groups. Scores from the manipulation check in which participants were asked two questions that assessed the extent to which mistakes indicated a permanent lack of ability. The scores for the two questions were combined in this figure. Higher scores indicated more self-efficacy.

The mean for the entity group on this manipulation check was 10.49 and the mean for the acquirable skill group was 11.88. These means were statistically significantly different ($p < .05$).

Part of Hypothesis 1, that trainees in the acquirable condition would be less anxious about computers after training, was supported by the scores on the Computer Anxiety Rating Scale. The difference shown for the acquirable group before training compared to after training was statistically significant ($p < .001$). These data are shown in Figure 28.2.

The other part of the hypothesis, that trainees in the entity condition would experience more anxiety as a result of training, was not supported. Apparently being reminded that ability is an unchanging quantity does not alter the amount of anxiety these people felt. As can be seen from Figure 28.2, the entity group seemed to be starting at a lower level of anxiety than the acquirable group, even though this difference was not statistically significant.

Hypothesis 2 stated that trainees receiving incremental instructions would experience an increase in computer efficacy beliefs as a result of training and that the opposite would be true for entity instructions. This hypothesis was supported. The data are shown in Figure 28.3.

Thinking critically about these numbers, you can see that the differences were not very large. In producing Figure 28.3, we have truncated the scale and stretched it, which has the effect of seeming to magnify the difference. Although this makes it easier for you to see what is going on, it is important to remember to pay attention to the

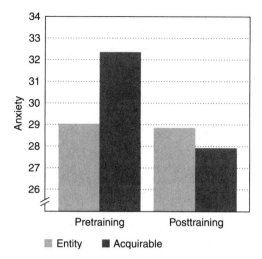

FIGURE 28.2   Computer Anxiety before and after Training

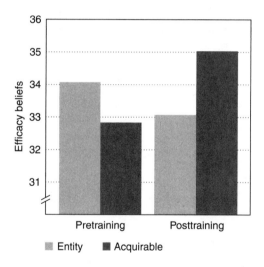

FIGURE 28.3   Self-Efficacy Beliefs before and after Training

scale along the left side, called the *y-axis*. In this case, the magnitude of the differences amounts to a few points on a 42-point scale. These differences were significantly different statistically, $p < .001$ for the acquirable skill condition and $p < .05$ for the entity condition. Nevertheless, the differences were small in magnitude. If you look back at Figure 28.2, you will notice that the situation was similar for those data: differences were small, considering that the scale could range from 10 to 70. We purposely did not mention this in our description of Figure 28.2 because we wanted to give you a chance to notice it for yourself. In order to critically evaluate data, it is important to pay attention to the size of the differences, no matter how they are graphed and no matter what the statistics say about them. We do not want you to think that scientific reports are purposely untruthful; they are not. Scientists assume that their readers will pay attention to the data and arrive at their own assessment of the importance of the findings.

Perhaps surprisingly, the third hypothesis asserting that differences in declarative knowledge would result from differences in conception of ability, did not receive support in this study. However, computer efficacy and computer ability had some effects on declarative knowledge when data from all participants were combined, without regard to the experimental manipulation they had received. Participants were considered as new quasi-experimental groups of people high in computer anxiety or low in computer anxiety using the median, the middle score in the group, as a dividing point. The same was done for groups of people with high and low computer efficacy. Both of the variables used in this new group assignment, anxiety and efficacy, were measured *before* the experimental manipulation. Regardless of the experimental manipulation, people low in anxiety and people high in efficacy did better on the test of computer knowledge. The data for this quasi-experimental rearrangement of the participants can be seen in Figure 28.4.

The cautions we suggest for the other figures apply to this one as well. The knowledge test scores could range from 0 to 10 correct and although the differences are statistically significant (*Anxiety: p* < .05; *Efficacy: p* < .001) the magnitudes of the differences found were somewhat small. Subsequent analyses of the data suggested that

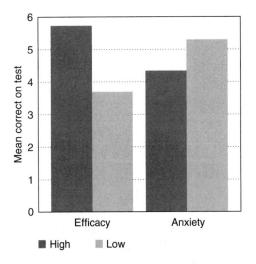

FIGURE 28.4   Declarative Knowledge Test Scores. Outcomes of the test of computer knowledge, which was given immediately following the training session.

age of the participants was important, particularly in predicting performance on the knowledge test. Age accounted for almost two thirds of the variance in test performance. The variance is a measure of the variability within a set of scores. Therefore, a considerable amount of that variability—people scoring high or people scoring low on a test—was attributable to their age. The relationship was inverse in that the younger people did better on the test. Additional analysis also showed that in the acquirable ability condition, decreases in anxiety were greater among the older trainees. Within the entity condition, younger trainees did not experience any change in efficacy. They may have been sufficiently secure in their beliefs about what they could do so that a few instructions did not threaten them. However, among older trainees, the entity condition decreased computer efficacy. Among these older trainees, efficacy with computers was not very high before the training and it was even lower after training. The instructions had undermined some of their beliefs about how successful they were likely to be in using computers. In summary, the primary outcomes on older people were that the acquirable condition had good effects in lowering anxiety, but the entity condition had adverse effects, decreasing self-efficacy.

DISCUSSION

We have said that the size of the outcomes in this study tended to be statistically significant but small. Yet these findings are important because the manipulation was small, simple, and inexpensive. The treatment only involved inserting instructions of one sort or another into a training program. Given the simplicity of the manipulation, it may seem surprising that there were any differences in the outcome. These differences illustrate the power of a few words to change attitudes or behavior. It is likely that attitudes are easier to change in domains where the individual is uncertain about performance.

Age was found to be a very important variable in this study. Recently there has been quite a bit of research on learning styles in adults. Probably some of this has been prompted by the large number of adult baby boomers in a rapidly changing workforce. Several studies have suggested that anxiety can interfere with memory in adults (Stigsdotter, Neely, & Backman, 1993; Yesavage, Lapp, & Sheikh, 1989). Martocchio's research demonstrated the effectiveness of cheap and easy incremental reminders in lowering anxiety in adults. The goal of applied psychological research is to help people function better in daily life, and this field experiment can be seen as a modest attempt to fulfill this goal. Attitudes about change are important in adult education programs, and creation of proper attitudes can be one step toward successful training.

REFERENCES

Cohen, M. N. (1998). *Culture of intolerance: Chauvinism, class and racism in the United States.* New Haven, CT: Yale University Press.

Gagne, R. M. (1962). Military training and principles of learning. *American Psychologist, 17,* 83–91.

Gold, L. (1981). Job instruction: Four steps to success. *Training and Development Journal, 35,* 28–32.

Heinssen, R., Glass, C., & Knight, L. (1987). Assessing computer anxiety: Developmental validation of the computer anxiety rating scale. *Computers in Human Behavior, 3,* 49–59.

Hicks, W. D., & Klimoski, R. J. (1987). Entry into training programs and its effects on training outcomes: A field experiment. *Academy of Management Journal, 30,* 542–552.

Hollenbeck, J. R., & Brief, A. P. (1987). The effects of individual differences and goal origin on goal setting and performance. *Organizational Behavior and Human Decision Processes, 40,* 392–414.

Kraiger, K., Ford, J. K., & Salas, E. (1993). Application of cognitive, skill-based and affective theories of learning to new methods of training evaluation. *Journal of Applied Psychology, 78,* 311–328.

Martocchio, J. J. (1994). Effects of conceptions of ability on anxiety, self-efficacy, and learning in training. *Journal of Applied Psychology, 79,* 819–825.

Mitchell, T. R., Hopper, H., Daniels, D., George-Falvy, J., & James, L. R. (1994). Predicting self-efficacy and performance during skill acquisition. *Journal of Applied Psychology, 79,* 506–517.

Stigsdotter, A., Neely, A., & Backman, L. (1993). Maintenance of gains following multifactorial and unifactorial memory training in late adulthood. *Educational Gerontology, 19,* 105–117.

Tannenbaum, S. I., Cannon-Bowers, J. A., Salas, E., & Mathieu, J. E. (1993). Factors that influence training effectiveness: A conceptual model and longitudinal analysis. *U.S. Naval Training Systems Center Technical Reports,* Technical Report 93-011.

Yesavage, J., Lapp, D., & Sheikh, J. A. (1989). Mnemonics as modified for use by the elderly. In L. W. Poon, D. Wilson, & B. Wilson (Eds.), *Everyday cognition in adulthood and late life* (pp. 598–611). Cambridge, England: Cambridge University Press.

CHAPTER 29

BETTING ON THE WINNERS

GAMBLING AS A PSYCHOLOGICAL DISORDER

Probably most of us, many times a week, offer to bet on something: "I bet it rains this afternoon; I bet we get a quiz in psychology today; I bet we end up being late for lunch. . . ." Most of our little wagers are not taken up by those around us and are forgotten. However, for some people, placing bets and other forms of gambling are a recognized psychological disorder. Starting in 1980, the *Diagnostic and Statistical Manual*, 3rd edition (*DSM-III*) (American Psychiatric Association, 1980) recognized a set of symptoms that defined pathological gambling. This manual is updated regularly, and it is taken by many to be the definitive list of disorders and symptoms within psychology, as well as in the medical specialty called psychiatry. This manual listed pathological gambling as "a chronic and progressive failure to resist impulses to gamble and gambling behavior that compromises, disrupts or damages personal, family or vocational pursuits." It is a preoccupation and urge that increases when people are stressed. The financial problems it creates lead to even more intense gambling. The debts incurred can also lead to various types of crime, such as embezzlement, theft, and knowingly writing bad checks. It includes the attitude that money causes, yet is the solution for, all one's problems. People who have this disorder often lie to obtain more money. They are overconfident and energetic, but at times show signs of anxiety and depression. In males, it typically begins in adolescence whereas in females it appears later in life. It is estimated to be a problem for at least 2 to 3 percent of the adult population.

Notice that within the symptoms listed previously there are two different kinds of things: cognitive patterns and behavioral patterns. Concepts such as *urge, preoccupation*, and *attitude* refer to thoughts or cognitions, whereas *telling lies to obtain money* and *intense gambling* are behaviors. Often symptoms of psychological disorders include both thoughts and behaviors because disordered thinking is likely to be accompanied by problem actions.

Incorporating the research of C. Sylvain, R. Ladouceur, and J. M. Boisvert, "Cognitive and Behavioral Treatment of Pathological Gambling: A Controlled Study," 1997, *Journal of Consulting and Clinical Psychology*, 65, pp. 727–732.

APPROACHES TO TREATMENT OF PATHOLOGICAL GAMBLING

Various approaches have been tried as means of treating pathological gambling. For example, Dickerson and Weeks (1979) described a case study of a program that included *controlled gambling* in which an individual was allowed to make only small bets once a week. This manipulation was coupled with additional behavioral management and therapy. Behavior changes persisted over 15 months. This was a single-participant case study, and there was no control individual or group. Although it may serve as a pilot study suggesting treatment, caution should be exercised in generalizing the findings to other individuals. As we noted in Chapter 4, "Half and Half," the case study is a weak research method for generalizing to large populations. Although psychological therapy is a common treatment, unfortunately it is fairly rare that some types of psychological therapies are evaluated to see if they are effective. One reason for this is that not all psychotherapists value science or have scientific training. Without an understanding of the power that the scientific method has to evaluate new knowledge, assessment of therapeutic outcomes can be a matter of opinion. If treatment programs are to be evaluated successfully, they must be designed from the beginning with evaluation in mind. In order to be evaluated, treatment programs must make the assumption that psychological problems can be operationalized into measurable behavior. Participants should be randomly assigned into treatment and no-treatment control groups. Behavior problems should be assessed before treatment begins, after it has ended, and again after a longer period of time has passed.

A great deal of work and planning is required to design good research on efficacy of psychological treatment programs. Often the numbers of people being treated are small, and the treatment is not sufficiently standardized or quantified to permit numerical data to be collected. Probably one reason for this is that an individual therapist is unlikely to have a large number of clients with a single disorder, such as pathological gambling. Additionally, unless the therapist is interested in scientific data collection, treatment of individuals is likely to be the only goal. To make matters more difficult, following treatment, people can be hard to find, disrupting assessment of long-term outcomes. In most studies of gambling previous to the one discussed in this chapter, the only outcome measured was the frequency of gambling behavior. This seems narrow, given the multiple symptoms described in the *DSM-III.*

CONTROL GROUPS IN THERAPY EVALUATION

It is usual, but poor practice, to have no control groups in studies of treatment for pathological gambling (Lesieur & Blume, 1987). Having a control group that receives no treatment is very important in studies of therapy because it is the only way to know that the treatment itself, and not mere passage of time, is making a difference. To do a scientific evaluation, ideally, a group of pathological gamblers would be randomly assigned either to the treatment group or to a no-treatment group. Following treatment, the two groups could be compared to determine the efficacy of the program. You may have some concern about the ethics of purposely withholding treatment from people identified as having a psychological disorder. One of the solutions to this ethical dilemma has been to put the no-treatment control group on a wait list, so that they are promised therapy eventually. They do not get it while the study is in progress but it is given to them, at no charge, as soon as possible after the study has ended. Although this may help to answer the ethical dilemma, it means that researchers have to assure themselves that wait-listed control participants do not seek therapy elsewhere while they are waiting.

THE GAMBLER'S FALLACY

Carolyn Sylvain, Robert Ladouceur, and Jean-Marie Boisvert (1997) conducted a controlled study of a treatment program for compulsive gamblers. Sylvain and her colleagues argued that treatment should be based on both cognitions and behaviors specific to gambling. These have been specified in the *DSM-III* and were the target of treatment. Ladouceur and Walker (1996) found that erroneous ideas about the concept of randomness were a primary cognitive component of the mistaken beliefs of gamblers. Gamblers believe and act as if they could predict, and maybe control, events that are not predictable or controllable. According to Ladouceur and Walker (1996), even though gamblers may not expect to win any particular gamble, they have mistaken beliefs that lead to continued gambling. They believe that they have found, or can find, ways to predict events that are governed by chance. These researchers also noted that gambling is frequently associated with superstitious behaviors. Within psychology, this term refers to a mistaken belief that there is a real causal link, called a *contingency*, between two events, when, in reality, there is no contingency at all. Gamblers are likely to think their chance of winning is increased if they use their lucky dice, bet their birthday as a lottery number, or hold a gold coin in one hand while betting with the other. In actuality, of course, there is no contingency between any of these specific behaviors and winning. One of these erroneous ways of thinking is so common that it has become a technical term: *the gambler's fallacy*. One version of the gambler's fallacy is the idea that independent or random events are linked: if you lose a game of chance 30 times in a row, this means your number is about to come up, and you will win. In fact, your chances do not change. If you repeatedly toss an unbiased coin and, by chance, happen to toss 10 heads in a row, the probability of a head on the 11th toss is still 50 percent. The string of head tosses does not affect the next independent random event.

Participants

The participants in this study were gamblers who were seeking help for gambling problems. There were 56 men and 2 women among them. They were evaluated by a clinical psychologist who was experienced in working with people diagnosed as pathological gamblers. All of the participants met the criteria for pathological gambling found in the *DSM-III-R* (American Psychiatric Association, 1987), which was the current edition of the *DSM* at the time the study commenced. Their most common mode of gambling was playing video poker, but others bet on horse races or played casino games. Some were recruited for the study either through advertisements in the newspaper or announcements on radio or TV. Others were referred by a professional care provider such as a physician, psychologist, or social worker. The study was conducted in the Province of Quebec in Canada. All 58 potential participants underwent a preliminary evaluation and 18 of them refused treatment following this evaluation. The remaining 40 individuals were randomly assigned to the treatment group or control group. Eight participants subsequently dropped out from the treatment group and 3 from the control group, leaving 29 individuals. These were reassigned so that 14 received treatment and 15 were left in the control group. Other studies of addictive behavior have shown similar proportions of participant attrition (Stark, 1992). This number of refusals and dropouts is high, but you should remember that these people are adults with complicated lives who were about to be involved in a rigorous program aimed at changing a problem behavior. They could not be required or coerced to remain in the study. The participants who completed treatment were significantly different from the dropouts and refusers on two variables: those completing the program began gambling at an older age ($p < .05$) and their *problem* gambling appeared later in life ($p < .05$). Does this invalidate the study as a whole? We do not believe so. Clearly part of your skill in thinking critically about scientific studies includes careful consideration of problems such as the characteristics of participants who drop out. In this case, at worst, these differences might limit our ability to apply these study findings to problem gamblers who had gambling problems early in life. People who do not understand science may be more likely to categorically dismiss an entire study because of a limitation such as this. In contrast, an educated critical thinker knows that there will always be some imperfections in studies. The important thing is to evaluate their effect on whatever conclusions may be drawn. Scientific researchers do not try to hide the problems that appear in the course of research; they point out problems that can be seen in the design of the study or in the data and discuss them in their publications. If the problem is sufficiently large, the study will not be published. With smaller blemishes, researchers expect the reader to be critical. Researchers give their readers the information required to make a cautious, realistic interpretation of the results.

In the treatment group the mean age was 37.6 years and in the control group it was 42.6 years. Half of the participants in each group were evaluated by a second clinician to check the reliability of the diagnosis. There was a 100 percent agreement between the evaluators. In other types of studies, the reliability of one rater is often checked by another observer who is unaware of the original ratings. You can appreciate that this was probably not possible here; clients who see a clinical psychologist do not expect the psychologist to be unaware of the problems they are having. In this case the participants described these problems, and the nature of the reliability check was to see if the second clinician agreed that the symptoms indicated the same diagnosis.

Procedure

At the beginning of the study, all participants were made aware that because of random assignment to groups, some individuals would not be receiving treatment immediately.

Once random assignment had taken place, participants in the control group were contacted and told that they would be on a waiting list. They were assured that they would receive treatment as soon as possible and that it was expected that all participants would receive treatment within 4 months. During this wait, they were phoned monthly as a way of keeping in contact with them. Two control participants felt that they could not wait any longer and were immediately assigned to the treatment group. None of the wait-listed patients reported receiving other therapy for this problem while they were waiting for treatment.

Cognitive-behavioral therapy was administered by two female psychologists who had, respectively, 4 and 5 years of clinical experience. They were supervised by Robert Ladouceur, a psychologist with 20 years of experience in cognitive-behavioral therapy. In the first session, treatment group participants were asked the question, "Are you willing to make an effort to reduce or stop gambling?" In order to continue in the study they had to answer in the affirmative. They also rated, on a scale of 1 to 10, their motivation to change the problem behavior.

The experience and training of the therapist are very important to the success of cognitive-behavioral therapy, but we would like to be clear that nothing magical or mystical is involved. By "nothing magical or mystical," we mean that the entire therapeutic process can be understood by ordinary people. It is a concrete teaching process in which a client learns to do new things and to think different thoughts. Unfortunately, popular media often depict psychological therapy as being a version of psychoanalysis, the approach developed 100 years ago by Sigmund Freud (see, for example, Freud, 1935). Freud believed that problems were rooted in unconscious desires and childhood problems. His therapy was supposed to dig deep into an unconscious mind using arcane and symbolic interpretations of the patient's verbal responses. Classically, the patient would lie on a couch and say anything that came into his or her head, while the therapist listened and attached florid interpretations to what was said. It was believed that as the contents of the unconscious came into the conscious mind, people could become aware of urges, often socially unacceptable urges, with sexual overtones. The patient's growing awareness of the unconscious was thought to be part of the cure. This kind of therapy was an art, not a science.

We took this little aside to illustrate what cognitive-behavioral therapy is *not:* it is not psychoanalysis or anything particularly like it. It does require a therapist with sharp clinical skills, but the skills are used to discuss the client's conscious thoughts and viewpoints about the world. The client is made aware that changing patterns of thinking can help to change behavior. The reverse is also important: changing one's behavior can change thinking. It is a rational and empirical approach that has no use for unconscious childhood trauma, hidden sexual urges, or couches. In some kinds of therapy, empirical evaluation is impossible, or nearly so. In contrast, the ultimate goal of cognitive-behavioral therapy is behavior change that can be observed and measured. As a result, cognitive-behavioral therapy can be evaluated through scientific means.

Cognitive-behavioral therapy was administered to the treatment group participants, or *clients*, in individual sessions. Sessions occurred once or twice a week and lasted between 60 and 90 minutes. This group received an average of 16.7 hours of treatment, with the maximum being 30 hours. They did not receive any additional therapy for this or other problems during the course of the study.

The cognitive-behavioral therapy had four main components. We describe these in some detail because we want you to understand the direct and sensible nature of this therapeutic approach. It has a strong empirical basis as well as a singular and determined goal to change behavior.

1. Cognitive correction. This component was aimed at correcting the misunderstanding of randomness. It included direct teaching about the concept. Random, by definition, means *not predictable*. Control is impossible. Erroneous beliefs commonly held by gamblers, including the gambler's fallacy, were exposed as misconstruals and explained. A recording was made of the participant pretending to gamble. The participant reviewed this with the therapist, and the therapist offered detailed corrections of the faulty beliefs indicated by the participant's verbalizations. An example of one of these was "if I lose four times in a row, I will win for sure the next time."

2. Problem-solving training. Participants were taught some specific strategies for dealing with problems in their lives. Obviously, the primary application of these tactics was to deal with some of the symptoms of gambling. They were taught to define the problems in unambiguous terms, collect information about the problems, generate alternative solutions listing the advantages and disadvantages of each, and to implement the solution, subsequently evaluating their effectiveness. These are the same processes that most of us use daily in a somewhat haphazard way, but the participants were taught to go through the steps in a careful and rational way. An example of one of the problems that was approached in this way was the need to get better control over spending to pay off debts incurred from past gambling. This was designed to help break the cycle of gambling to pay off debts.

3. Social skills training. Some of the individuals in the program suffered from links between poor social skills and gambling. For example, some of them needed assertiveness training because even if they did not want to gamble, friends would persuade them to do so. These people needed to be taught how to resist social pressure from people they liked. Role-playing was an important part of this training. Through role-play, gamblers could practice and learn the communication skills necessary to steer them through social situations that might, otherwise, lead to gambling.

4. Relapse prevention. As part of the therapy, participants discussed the possibility of relapsing and described their past relapses. Risk factors for relapse were identified, and participants were taught specific ways to avoid the creation of high relapse-risk situations. For the gamblers, these included events such as carrying cash, loneliness, stress, and lack of alternate social activities.

Dependent Variables

The dependent variables, or outcome measures, included the number of *DSM-III-R* criteria for pathological gambling that still described the participant. If the program was successful, there would be a decrease in this variable. Another dependent variable, or *D.V.*, was the outcome of the South Oaks Gambling Screen (SOGS), a valid self-report instrument. A total score of 5 or more on SOGS interview questions has been found to be indicative of pathological gambling (Lesieur & Blume, 1987). Beyond this threshold, higher scores indicate more problems with gambling. As an additional measure, participants rated their perception of their own control over gambling on a scale from 1—*no control*, to 10—*all control.* They also rated their desire to gamble on a 1 to 10 scale. Several measures were taken of self-reported frequency of gambling including the number of gambling sessions, the number of hours spent gambling, and the total amount of money spent on gambling during the previous week.

Pretreatment Scores

In order to assure themselves that the treatment and wait list control groups were not different with respect to some dimension of gambling, the dependent measures described above were assessed on both groups before treatment began in order to obtain a pretreatment baseline. Because participants had been randomly assigned to the groups, there was no reason to think groups would be different, but, of course, by chance, it is possible for random assignment to produce groups that are different with respect to the primary characteristic under investigation: in this case, gambling. For example, if, by chance, all the heaviest gamblers had ended up in the wait list control group, and no pretreatment measure had been taken, differences in dependent measures at the end of the study might suggest program success, when, in fact, the program had made little difference in changing behavior. For this reason, baseline measures were taken before any treatment began. No statistically significant differences were found between the groups in any of those measures of gambling.

Results

The changes between pretreatment and posttreatment for the treatment group and the same period of time for the wait list control group are found in Table 29.1. The control group received no treatment between these measures, so any changes in their scores must be a result of other things that were happening in their lives. Statistical analysis showed that the treatment group and the control group were statistically significantly different at the posttreatment measure for each of the five dependent variables, all at $p < .01$. As a result of the therapy, the treatment group had fewer of the pathological gambling diagnostic criteria from *DSM-III-R*, reported less desire to gamble, and had a lower South Oaks Gambling Screen score (SOGS). They reported a higher perception of control over gambling and a higher belief that they could refrain from gambling.

Table 29.2 shows the data for self-report frequency-of-gambling variables during pretreatment, posttreatment, and 6-month follow-up. Initially, it might seem that some of the numbers reported in Table 29.2 are going to make it difficult to interpret the findings of the study with respect to frequency of gambling. A glance at the means

TABLE 29.1 Means of the Main Variables at Pretreatment, Posttreatment, and 6-Month Follow-Up Measurements for the Treatment Group and the (Wait List) Control Group

	PRETREATMENT	POSTTREATMENT	6-MONTH FOLLOW-UP*
DSM-III-R			
Treatment	7.3	1.1	1.3
Control	7.1	5.7	
PERCEPTION OF CONTROL			
Treatment	1.4	8.0	8.6
Control	2.7	3.6	
DESIRE TO GAMBLE			
Treatment	5.7	2.0	0.5
Control	6.3	6.1	
BELIEVE CAN RESIST GAMBLING			
Treatment	2.8	8.4	8.8
Control	3.4	3.7	
SOGS			
Treatment	12.6	2.7	2.7
Control	13.1	13.0	

Note: *DSM-III-R* refers to the number of diagnostic criteria found in the Diagnostic and Statistical Manual that were met and SOGS refers to the scores obtained on the questionnaire.

*At 6-month follow-up only 10 participants were included.

might suggest that, even though the groups were formed by random assignment, the unusual has happened: frequency of gambling appears to be quite a bit lower in the treatment group compared to the control group, even in the pretreatment measures. Arithmetic means can be misleading. There was a great deal of variability in these data, with a few individuals gambling either a great deal more than the mean or a great deal less. In this particular case, the mean is an inadequate one-number summary of the entire data set because there is so much variability. Probably the median, which is the middle score in the distribution, would be a better summary, but when scores are widely variable, no single number is likely to represent them very well. Remember, when the treatment and control group means for frequency of gambling were compared statistically before treatment began, there were no statistically significant differences.

TABLE 29.2   Means of the Three Frequency-of-Gambling Variables at Pretreatment, Posttreatment, and 6-Month Follow-Up Measurements for the Treatment Group and the (Wait List) Control Group

	PRETREATMENT	POSTTREATMENT	6-MONTH FOLLOW-UP*
NO. OF GAMBLING SESSIONS			
Treatment	0.8	0.2	0
Control	1.5	1.7	
NO. HOURS SPENT GAMBLING			
Treatment	1.4	0.9	0
Control	3.3	4.6	
MONEY SPENT ON GAMBLING			
Treatment	23.29	8.57	0
Control	99.67	188.00	

*At 6-month follow-up only 10 participants were included.

As you think critically about this issue you also need to see that the treatment groups and the control groups should be compared with themselves. The magnitude of group means is less important than the amount of change in them. If the program was effective we should see a statistically significant decrease between pretreatment and posttreatment in the treatment group. We do. If we want to conclude that this change is a result of the therapy, not just time passing by, we should not see a significant decrease between pretreatment and posttreatment in the control group, as, indeed, we do not.

Six months after the end of therapy, measures were taken again on the 10 participants from the treatment group who were available. Four of the original participants were not included in the 6-month follow-up data. Three of them could not be located despite numerous attempts, and the other participant had probably relapsed. As can be seen from Table 29.1 and Table 29.2, 6 months later, the changes in gambling persisted among the 10 remaining participants. All pretreatment measures shown in Table 29.1 for the treatment group were significantly different from their 6-month follow-up scores ($p < .01$). Table 29.2 shows that at 6 months, those remaining in the study had no gambling activity.

Twelve months after the end of therapy, it was possible to reach nine of the participants from the original treatment group either by telephone or in interview. For eight of the nine, therapeutic gains persisted, and they were no longer considered pathological gamblers according to *DSM-III-R* criteria. One of these nine had relapsed and was still considered a pathological gambler.

DISCUSSION

The results of this study suggest that cognitive-behavioral therapy can effectively treat pathological gambling for some individuals. Their attitudes changed and so did their behavior. The success of this program has to be evaluated in the light of the initial dropouts and refusals. At this point, there is no evidence that this approach would work for everyone, even though it may have been successful for those who completed the program. In addition, it was a requirement that participants be willing to consider behavior change. There are probably many people who are classifiable under *DSM* criteria who are not willing to change their behavior. There is no therapy that is likely to be effective for people who make hard-line refusals.

Part of the success of this program may have been a result of its multifaceted approach to the problem. These individuals received help in changing erroneous beliefs about gambling. This cognitive component was linked to problem solving and relapse prevention in this program, helping people to develop the skills required to decrease or eliminate problem behavior. As we noted at the beginning of this chapter, the approach here was based on learning and, as you have seen, the therapy consisted of a variety of efforts to teach new skills, cognitive and behavioral. There was no hidden magic here. The therapy involved a skilled teacher, the therapist, working with a willing learner to change behavior. The process was not basically different from what might happen in learning to play tennis from an expert coach: behavior is changed. This is an important study because, although the final numbers were small, it was a careful and concerted attempt to evaluate the outcome of psychotherapy. If therapy had been seen as a probing of the unconscious in an attempt to repair primal forces, rather than an attempt to change behavior, there would be no outcome to measure. Psychoanalytic adjustments to some supposed unconscious mind cannot be observed or counted, so the type of controlled study presented in this chapter cannot be used to evaluate psychoanalysis. It is difficult for us to understand how a therapeutic approach can have any claim to success in the absence of observable and measurable outcomes.

REFERENCES

American Psychiatric Association (1980). *Diagnostic and statistical manual of mental disorders* (3rd ed.). Washington, DC: Author.

Dickerson, M. G., & Weeks, D. (1979). Controlled gambling as a therapeutic technique for compulsive gamblers. *Journal of Behavior Therapy and Experimental Psychiatry, 10*, 139–141.

Freud, S. (1935). *An autobiographical study.* New York: Norton.

Ladouceur, R., & Walker, M. (1996). A cognitive perspective on gambling. In P. M. Salkovskis (Ed.), *Trends in cognitive and behavioral therapies* (pp. 89–120). New York: Wiley.

Lesieur, H. R., & Blume, S. B. (1987). The South Oaks Gambling Screen (The SOGS): A new instrument for the identification of pathological gamblers. *American Journal of Psychiatry, 144*, 1184–1188.

Stark, M. J. (1992). Dropping out of substance abuse treatment: A clinically oriented review. *Clinical Psychology Review, 12*, 93–116.

Sylvain, C., Ladouceur, R., & Boisvert, J. M. (1997). Cognitive and behavioral treatment of pathological gambling: A controlled study. *Journal of Consulting and Clinical Psychology, 65*, 727–732.

CHAPTER 30

BEHAVIORAL TREATMENT FOR DENTAL FEAR IN AUTISTIC CHILDREN

Autism is a baffling and disabling disorder that impacts a child's language, motor, social, cognitive, and perceptual development. The disorder occurs in approximately 4 children in 10,000, and prevalence estimates suggest much higher occurrence in boys (Ritvo et al., 1989). Autism is typically suspected in infancy and diagnosed early in childhood. Autism has *not* been shown to be related to socioeconomic level of parents, ethnic or racial heritage of parents, religious affiliation of families, or parental educational background (Ritvo et al., 1989). The *Diagnostic and Statistical Manual of the American Psychiatric Association (DSM)* was described in Chapter 29 and *DSM* typically focuses on the behavioral characteristics of the individual being assessed and has attempted to reduce ambiguity (i.e., increase validity and reliability) in the diagnostic process. The following major characteristics from the *DSM* will serve to give you a synopsis of the profound impact that autism has on the developing child. Not all diagnosed autistic children have all of the following symptoms. However, diagnosed autistics have many problematic behaviors across the categories listed below.

- **Impairments in social interaction and difficulty in using nonverbal behaviors**
    Eye contact
    Facial expressions
    Body postures and gestures
    Lack of peer relationships
    Does not seek to share enjoyment, interests, or achievements with others
    Deficit in emotional responsivity
- **Impairments in communication**
    Delay or total lack of spoken language
    Marked impairment in conversing with others
    Stereotyped and repetitive language
    Deficit in spontaneous play activity

Incorporating the research of D. M. Luscre and D. B. Center, "Procedures for Reducing Dental Fear in Children with Autism," 1996, *Journal of Autism and Developmental Disorders, 26*(5), pp. 547–556.

■ **Behavior is repetitive, restricted, and stereotyped**
   Preoccupation with one or more stereotyped interests
   Inflexible adherence to specific, nonfunctional rituals
   Stereotyped and repetitive motor behaviors
   Persistent focus on parts of objects

Autistic children are not warm and fuzzy, cuddly babies who respond to affection and attention. They don't smile, they appear to ignore social and interpersonal interactions, and they do not display much emotion. Their language is significantly impaired and, if present, is often marked by the repetition of a limited number of words. They often engage in self-stimulatory behavior, which may consist of repetitive motor movements such as rocking, moving their hands quickly in front of their eyes, or hitting their head. Autism is not a disorder that you "outgrow," and as adults autistic individuals encounter significant problems in adaptation. Many of you may have initially encountered the disorder of autism in the film *Rain Man*. In this film we see Dustin Hoffman play a character who is an "autistic-savant," capable of extraordinary mathematical and memory skills. This subtype of autism is the not the usual autistic case; typically, people with autism have cognitive deficits that fall within the range of mental retardation.

The research presented in this chapter does not seek to treat the major symptoms of autism but rather deals with a specific, serious problem that results from the autistic child's inability to cope in the world. Autistic children are frequently unable to tolerate dental examinations because of their fears generated by entering the dentist's office, sitting in the examination chair, and allowing the dentist to poke around the mouth with various instruments (Burkhart, 1984; Kopel, 1977). For this reason parents of autistic children do not take them for routine dental care. As a consequence the children have poor dental health with high rates of cavities and high incidence of periodontal disease (Butts, 1967; Starks, Market, Miller, & Greenbaum, 1985). When dental care is absolutely required because of serious disease, the treatment may involve hospitalization and anesthesia because their cases are more complicated, and routine office treatment is impossible to undertake (Braff & Nealon, 1979; Kamen & Skier, 1985; Lowe & Lindemann, 1985). The general plan of intervention in this treatment was to use three forms of behavior therapy—desensitization, modeling, and positive reinforcement. All behavior therapy shares a common origin in the learning models of classical conditioning, operant learning, and observational learning. These forms of therapy consider that behavior change is acquiring adaptive new behaviors to replace patterns of behavior that were maladaptive. In this case, the autistic children will be acquiring adaptive, nonphobic behaviors to the process of being examined by a dentist. Prior to the advent of behavioral therapies in the 1960s there was very little in the way of beneficial treatment for many of the difficult patterns of behavior seen in autism.

TREATMENT PROCEDURES

In consultation with teachers and parents, six autistic children were studied to evaluate intensity of dental fear. A single *in vivo* dental test session was performed to determine extent of dental fear. The term *in vivo* refers to a procedure or treatment that takes place in the natural environment in which it is likely to occur. This is in contrast to a laboratory or a therapist's office, which are artificial settings. *In vivo*, in this investigation, means that the treatment is taking place in an actual dental office setting. The three children selected for further treatment were chosen because they could not sit in the dentist's chair for more than a minute, and two of the three initiated aggressive patterns of behavior. Two of the three participants were boys age 9 and a third boy who was age 6. The participants were nonverbal and all had developmental, educational, and adaptive behavior profiles indicative of functioning in the severely mentally retarded range. The three children with lesser problems were not part of this study. The investigators selected the three children with the most maladaptive behaviors in order to demonstrate that the behavioral techniques were applicable to the most challenging cases.

A dental fear hierarchy consisting of 13 steps was devised to take the children from outside the dental office building (low fear) to being able to tolerate new procedures by a dentist during an exam (high fear). Hierarchies used in this type of treatment contain a continuum of levels of fear beginning with the mildest level and ranging to the highest levels. The strategy is that the child achieves success in accomplishing nonfear responses in a slow systematic manner always beginning at low levels and working toward the high end of the fear continuum. Think of it as climbing a high ladder. The initial steps are easy, but as you move toward the top it can become more anxiety provoking. Climbing the ladder slowly, step-by-step, helps to give you a sense of success and accomplishment, without fear. The dental fear hierarchy is found in Table 30.1. A video was produced with same age peer models serving as actors who go through the 13 steps of the dental exam in the *in vivo* situation. An analog dental office was constructed in the children's school so that treatment sessions could be conducted more conveniently and without transporting the children. This analog "dental office" was quite realistic and had all the equipment, trappings, and paraphernalia to convey authenticity.

TABLE 30.1   The 13-Step Fear of Dental Examination Hierarchy

1. Leaving the car or classroom to go to the examination.
2. Entering the building or the hallway in which the examination takes place.
3. Entering the dentist's waiting room.
4. Sitting or playing in the dentist's waiting room.
5. Entering the dentist's examination room.
6. Sitting in the dentist's examination chair.
7. Leaning back in the dentist's chair.
8. Wearing a protective apron.
9. Being able to tolerate the overhead dental light.
10. Opening mouth for the dental mirror.
11. Opening mouth for dental explorer.
12. Opening mouth for dental evacuator.
13. Being able to tolerate new procedures by dentist.

The likely reason for creating an analog office was so that the study could proceed without disrupting the normal routines of an actual dental office. The analog office was designed to be similar to the actual dental office in equipment, tools, and physical space. In addition, the analog office was constructed in the children's school so it was quite convenient to conduct the treatment program. However, the actual *in vivo* dentist's office was used for half the baseline sessions and once a week when the treatment sessions began. In addition, the actual office was used in the final step of the hierarchy (i.e., being able to tolerate new procedures by dentist). In summary, most treatment sessions were conducted in the analog dental office with weekly and final step sessions conducted in the actual dentist's office. The use of the actual dental office was necessary to be assured that the behavior changes seen in analog treatment were generalizable to the actual office.

The treatment for all three children consisted of collecting baseline data on accomplishment of the 13 steps in the dental fear hierarchy. The children were all initially quite resistant with aggressive and noncooperative behavior patterns dominating. Figure 30.1 shows the data for the three children, in terms of steps accomplished.

As you can see from Figure 30.1, two of the three children completed six steps in baseline and one child completed nine steps. The treatment began at one step above the final step completed in baseline. Progress was assessed by the accomplishment of steps in the hierarchy.

The following three different behavioral treatment modalities were all used at the same time to combat the children's dental fear.

Desensitization—In the desensitization procedure antianxiety stimuli were selectively used based on children's preferences to combat the dental fear. Examples of

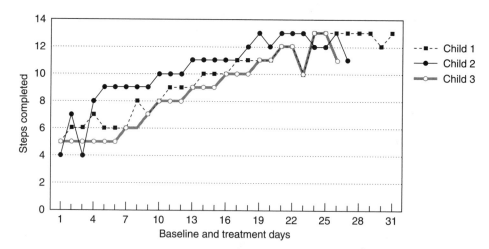

FIGURE 30.1 Baseline and Treatment Sessions. The initial baseline days for Child 1, 2, and 3 were Days 1 and 2, Days 1 through 4, and Days 1 through 6, respectively. The days following baseline represented active treatment using systematic densensitization, modeling, and positive reinforcement.

some of the stimuli were country music, rhymes, a mirror, and Play-Doh. When presented, these stimuli served to relax the children and therefore served to oppose the development of fear and anxiety. In Chapter 9, "Being Sick of the Hospital," you learned about the Pavlovian classical conditioning paradigm. The technique of desensitization is based on counterconditioning; a strategy that takes a behavior that is already learned and seeks to replace it with an alternative behavior. In this case, the researchers are seeking to replace the fear response to dental examination with a neutral, or even better yet, a positive response. In classical conditioning terms, the treatment of counterconditioning or desensitization seeks, in the context of the CS (i.e., dental examination) to replace the CR of fear with a new CR of neutral or happy feelings.

Video Modeling of a Peer—During treatment sessions a video showing normal children modeling the steps in the hierarchy was shown to the autistic children. The video presentation shown to the child was at the step being worked on during the specific treatment session planned for that day. Observation of a model similar to you who encounters an experience you are going through without pain is likely to make the experience more positive for you. In Chapter 11, "I Do!," a complete discussion of the social learning (the terms *modeling* and *imitative learning* are also used to mean the same thing) is presented.

Positive Reinforcement—Following each child's successful accomplishment of each step in the hierarchy a positive reinforcement selected specifically for the child was given. Providing a positive reinforcer contingent on a desirable response, in this case participating in the dental exam, will increase the rate of dental examination participation. In Chapter 10, "Yoking Smoking," you can review the operant conditioning paradigm and see how powerful positive reinforcement can be in building behaviors.

FINDINGS

Figure 30.1 presents the data on each child during analog and *in vivo* sessions. A global analysis of the data shows a steady rate of accomplishment of steps in the hierarchy toward elimination of dental fear. This treatment program is a case study of three autistic children being treated for dental fear. Although it has the trappings of some more sophisticated research designs (e.g., objective descriptions of treatment interventions and quantitative measurement) the study does not meet criteria for being considered an experiment. The investigators in this project base their conclusions and summary findings on clinical significance rather than on statistical significance. Clinical significance is a judgment call based on whether the autistic children, in this case, have accomplished sufficient skills to make a difference in their lives.

The data suggested that the reduction in fear learned in the analog sessions generalized to the *in vivo* environment. The researchers view this as an important clinical finding because it means that changes accomplished in analog settings are transferable to the real world. Analog treatment is much more easily conducted, and confirmation of its value is significant for future interventions. Upon initiation of treatment all aggressive acts directed toward the dentist ceased. The findings obtained in this sample of autistic children indicate that treatment with a behavioral intervention package consisting of desensitization, modeling, and reinforcement can be clinically effective in eliminating dental fears. The three participants in this study were all able to participate in an analog dental examination within less than a month of the initiation of treatment. In addition, after a small number of *in vivo* sessions, the participants were able to take part in an actual dental examination. The positive findings of this study do not represent a treatment for the widespread devastating effects of autism. However the results do indicate that autistic children respond positively to behavioral forms of intervention to improve the quality of their lives. The researchers noted that Child 2 needed to be strapped to a papoose board in order to be treated on past dental visits. Certainly the treatment strategies presented in this research offer a more humane and positive approach that can be accomplished relatively efficiently. These findings also suggest that behavioral interventions to other maladaptive patterns of behavior in autistic children would be recommended.

REFERENCES

American Psychiatric Association. (1994). *Diagnostic and statistical manual of mental disorders* (4th ed.). Washington, DC: Author.

Braff, M., & Nealon, L. (1979). Sedation of autistic dental patient for dental procedures. *Journal of Dentistry for Children, 46,* 404–407.

Burkhart, N. (1984). Understanding and managing the autistic children in the dental office. *Dental Hygiene,* 59–64.

Butts, J. (1967). I. Dental status of mentally retarded children; II. A survey of the prevalence of certain dental conditions in mentally retarded children of Georgia. *Journal of Public Health Dentistry, 27*(4), 195–211.

Kamen, S., & Skier, J. (1985). Dental management of the autistic child. *Special Care in Dentistry, 5*(1), 20–23.

Kopel, H. (1977). The autistic child in dental practice. *Journal of Dentistry for Children, 44,* 302–309.

Lowe, O., & Lindemann, R. (1985). Assessment of the autistic patient's dental needs and ability to undergo dental examination. *Journal of Dentistry for Children, 52,* 29–35.

Luscre, D. M., & Center, D. B. (1996). Procedures for reducing dental fear in children with autism. *Journal of Autism and Developmental Disorders, 26*(5), 547–556.

Ritvo, E. R., Freeman, B. J., Pingree, C., Mason-Brothers, A., Jorde, L., Jenson, W. R., McMahon, W. M., Peterson, P. B., Mo, A., & Ritvo, A. (1989). The UCLA-University of Utah epidemiologic survey of autism: Prevalence. *American Journal of Psychiatry, 146,* 194–199.

Starks, D., Market, G., Miller, C., & Greenbaum, J. (1985, July). Day to day dental care: A parent's guide. *Exceptional Parent,* 13–17.

CHAPTER 31

I CONFESS

We have all watched the police dramas in film and on TV in which the suspect is sitting in a small dimly lit room with bare walls. A few detectives who are eager to get him to confess to a crime are interrogating the suspect. In real criminal cases, as well as in popular media, a confession is viewed as powerful evidence in the prosecution of a case. The criminal justice system has constructed a number of safeguards to protect suspects from confessing to criminal acts that they did not commit. For example, suspects are read their Miranda rights and are given the opportunity to meet with an attorney. In addition, physical violence or threats into agreeing to confess to a crime may not coerce suspects. Of course, police officers may attempt to utilize a variety of methods to gain confessions from suspects they believe were responsible for a crime. Saul Kassin and Katherine Kiechel, in introducing their research, refer to a popular police manual (Inbau, Reid, & Buckley, 1986), now in its third edition, which guides police officers in a detailed nine-step strategy of techniques to elicit confessions. The approaches suggested use either a ploy of *minimization* or *maximization*. Minimization is a strategy that creates trust between the interrogator and the suspect by having the interrogator downplay the legal charges, place blame on the victim, state some reasons to soften the consequences of the crime, or provide the suspect with some excuses for the criminal behavior. On the other hand, maximization refers to the use of procedures to frighten the suspect by magnifying and exaggerating the gravity of the crime and the strength of the evidence. Minimization can be typified as "good cop," whereas maximization can be typified as "bad cop" in the stereotype of detective stories. Kassin and Kiechel (1996) point out that although the American criminal justice system excludes confessions based on threats and false promises; courts have admitted coerced evidence under certain conditions.

However, research has continually shown that people believe it is unlikely that an individual would ever confess to a crime that they did not commit (Sukel & Kassin, 1994). Kassin and Wrightsman (1985) outline three categories of false confessions. Remember, in each category the person is admitting to a crime that he or she had not committed.

Voluntary: This is the case in which a person confesses without external pressure. This may seem a little farfetched, but it does occur.

Incorporating the research of S. M. Kassin and K. L. Kiechel, "The Social Psychology of False Confessions: Compliance, Internalization, and Confabulation," 1996, *Psychological Science*, 7, pp. 125–128.

Coerced-Compliant: This is the case in which a person admits to a crime in order to avoid a harsh interrogation, eliminate potential physical harm, or obtain a positive benefit.

Coerced-Internalized: This is the case in which a person develops the belief that they actually did commit the crime as a function of the process of interrogation.

It is this third type of false confession that is the focus of Kassin and Kiechel's research discussed in this chapter. It may seem like a very odd or unusual event for a person to come to believe they actually did commit a crime. However, there have been reported cases where police have used phony evidence to convince a vulnerable suspect that they actually committed a crime. Although not under study in the present research, it would be interesting to explore the factors that relate to vulnerability to this type of false confession. Kassin and Kiechel allude to participant's personality, level of stress, age, and mental status as potential factors related to vulnerability. Wright (1994) related the case of Paul Ingram, who was charged with satanic murders of newborn infants and rape. Although he initially denied the charges, while being interrogated under police custody for 6 months he was exposed to many crime scene details, including photographs. He was also informed that he was likely to be repressing (i.e., unconsciously forgetting) his criminal involvement. A clergyman as well as the police pressured him into making a confession. Eventually he began to "remember" how he came to commit the crime, and he entered a plea of guilty and was imprisoned. In this case there never was any physical evidence linking Ingram to the crime. A later review of this case indicated that Ingram was "brainwashed" into confessing to a crime he never committed.

Another line of contemporary research that tied directly to this sort of false confession is the work in memory. It is apparent that information occurring after an event has happened can significantly alter the recall of the event. The research reported in Chapter 16, "Kids Say the Darndest Things," is a very good case in point. The research described in that chapter suggests that young children were particularly at risk for "false memory." Loftus (1993) indicated that it is even possible to implant false memories of trauma, including child abuse, that presumably were long buried in the unconscious mind. This has raised an enormous amount of controversy, especially by questioning the authenticity of adults remembering "repressed" incidents of child abuse. All of this leads us to the present research questions: Is it possible for crime suspects to accept guilt for crimes that they never committed? Can the memories of these suspects become altered so that they believe and substantiate their guilt?

THE CRIME

The best way to investigate this issue would be to set up an experimental procedure and use actual suspects, real police officers, and other practices and procedures of the criminal justice process. However, this is not possible because the experimental procedures would place suspects in potential jeopardy by not offering them the best defense. They would have to conform to the experimental procedures that would likely relegate their own particular needs to a secondary status. This is, of course, unethical and cannot be done. It is important for you to know that many important issues cannot be investigated in the environment in which they occur because of ethical concerns. In this study, like many others, the question was explored by setting up a laboratory simulation of the issue we want to investigate. Observations in labs are not automatically equivalent to what happens in the actual setting. However, through careful laboratory experiments, a great deal can be learned that has significant implications for real-world events.

The participants in this experiment were 79 male and female undergraduate college students. The students participated for extra course credit and were drawn from a student body with a mean SAT of 1300 (a very bright group). The students believed they were going to be involved in an investigation of reaction time. The students were randomly assigned to one of the four following groups:

High vulnerability—False witness present
High vulnerability—False witness absent
Low vulnerability—False witness present
Low vulnerability—False witness absent

The specifics of the above groups' characteristics will be defined as we go along in the procedures. The procedure involved having two people (one was a participant and the other a female confederate) engage in a keyboarding assignment. The task involved the confederate reading a list of letters and the participant typing the letter on a computer keyboard. The roles were to be reversed after 3 minutes, but this never occurred because of the emergence of "the crime." Before the typing began, participants were informed specifically not to press the "ALT" key. If they pressed this key it would induce the experimental program to terminate and data collected would be lost. It would end the experimental session. After a minute of the experimental procedure, while the confederate was reading letters and the participant was typing, the computer stopped functioning and an agitated, upset experimenter accused the participant of having pressed the "ALT" key against specific directives not to do so. Participants in all four groups initially denied the accusation. After the experimenter fiddled with the keyboard and told the participant that data had been lost, he again asked if the participant touched the ALT key.

The first independent variable manipulated by the experimenters was vulnerability. Vulnerability referred to how certain each participant was concerning his or her own status regarding "the crime." *High Vulnerability* means that you are not very certain about whether or not you committed the crime, whereas *Low Vulnerability* means that you are pretty certain you are innocent. Vulnerability was manipulated by varying the pace of the key-typing task. High rates of key typing (67 letters per minute) are equated to high vulnerability; low rates (43 letters per minute) of key typing are equated to low vulnerability. The assumption is that at low relaxed speeds you are very aware of your behavior and keying and are less likely to make errors due to rushing. At high-keying speeds, you are moving at a feverish pace and are likely to mis-key and not be aware of even making a mistake. The task for the participant was to key type letters that were read by the confederate at either high or low speeds.

The second independent variable was whether or not there was falsely incriminating evidence available, in this case, the presence of a witness to "the crime." In this experiment, after the participant initially denied involvement in pressing the ALT key, the experimenter asked the confederate if she saw anything. In the *False Witness Present* condition, she confirmed that the participant did, indeed, press the ALT key. In the *False Witness Absent* condition, the confederate stated she did not see what happened.

The experimenters used three dependent variables to assess different levels of the participant's response to being falsely accused. Remember that no participant in any of the four conditions ever touched the ALT key; all were falsely accused. The first dependent measure was *Compliance*, which was measured by whether or not participants agreed to sign the following "confession note" drafted by the experimenter:

I hit the 'ALT' key and caused the program to crash. Data was lost.

To assess the participant's *Internalization*, the second dependent measure, recordings were made of the participant's behavior immediately upon leaving the laboratory room. In a reception room, a confederate pretending to be the next participant, who overheard what transpired in the laboratory room, met the participant leaving the lab. The confederate asked the participant, "What happened?" The recording of participants' responses was coded for internalized guilt presence or absence by independent raters who did not know which of the four experimental conditions participants were in. The raters were "blind" as to the participant's group so that this would not impact on their ratings. The agreement between raters was 96 percent indicating excellent consensus on what was meant by the presence or absence of internalized guilt. An example of an internalized guilt present response was "I hit the wrong button and ruined the program"; an example of the absence of internalized guilt was denial of any involvement in the "crime."

To determine the presence or absence of *Confabulation*, the third dependent variable, the experimenter brought the participant back into the lab room and reread the list of letters used in the experiment. The participant was asked to remember details of how or when they hit the ALT key. This investigation sought to determine if the participants would create specific details or evidence, in police terms, to account for the "crime" they were accused of committing. A positive confabulation response might be "I hit it with my hand after you asked me to type a Z." An absence of confabulation would be any failure to come up with a description of how they committed the "crime" of hitting the ALT key. Inter-rater assessment judging the presence or absence of confabulations achieved 100 percent agreement. In accordance with good research procedure, all participants were completely debriefed at the conclusion of the session.

THE FINDINGS

Across all four groups, almost 70 percent of the participants signed the confession, 28 percent showed internalization, and 9 percent confabulated to include details of their

TABLE 31.1   Percentage of Participants Showing Compliance, Internalization, and Confabulation

GROUP	PERCENTAGE		
	Compliance	*Internalization*	*Confabulation*
High vulnerability— witness present	100	65	35
High vulnerability— witness absent	65	12	0
Low vulnerability— witness present	89	44	6
Low vulnerability— witness absent	35	0	0

research experience to show how they committed the "crime." The detailed results, broken down by groups, are shown in Table 31.1.

The major hypothesis in this study was that high vulnerability with a witness would most likely lead to higher levels in the three dependent measures, and low vulnerability without a witness would favor lower levels in the dependent measures. The data confirm this hypothesis. Differences between these groups in statistical analyses were significant at $p < .001$ for compliance and internalization, and $p < .005$ for confabulation. As we have seen in other chapters, such levels of probability make it exceedingly unlikely (1 in a 1,000 or 5 in a 1,000) the results were a result of chance alone. In looking further at the data, you can see that 35 percent of participants in the low vulnerability—witness absent group indicated compliance by signing the confession. However, none of these participants showed any signs of internalization or confabulation. If you look at the groups that included the presence of a witness and had high vulnerability (i.e., the two independent variables) you see how powerful these were, especially when combined, to affect all three dependent variables. This investigation provides strong support for the idea that increasing a suspect's vulnerability and providing a false witness can influence people to take the responsibility for acts they did not commit. These independent variables, vulnerability and witness present, are not unusual practices, but rather are common strategies used in the investigative process. The findings in this study suggest that caution should be employed by those in the criminal justice system because it is very possible, even likely, that a suspect may sign a confession, internalize blame, and even confabulate details, when, in fact, they are completely innocent. Keep in mind that the outcomes seen in this study were obtained on participants who were intelligent, self-assured college students who were under minimal stress. If you compare these participants to actual crime suspects who are under high stress, often in jail, and separated from family and friends, you can imagine the effect obtained in this study may be magnified greatly in the "real world."

REFERENCES

Inbau, F. E., Reid, J. E., & Buckley, J. P. (1986). *Criminal interrogation and confessions* (3rd ed.). Baltimore, MD: Williams & Wilkins.

Kassin, S. M., & Keichel, K. L. (1996). The social psychology of false confessions: compliance, internalization, and confabulation. *Psychological Science, 7,* 125–128.

Kassin, S. M., & Wrightsman, L. S. (1985). Confession evidence. In S. M. Kassin and L. S. Wrightsman (Eds.), *The psychology of evidence and trial procedure* (pp. 67–94). Beverly Hills, CA: Sage.

Loftus, E. (1993). The reality of repressed memories. *American Psychologist, 48,* 518–537.

Sukel, H. L., & Kassin, S. M. (1994, March). *Coerced confessions and the jury: An experimental test of the "harmless error" rule.* Paper presented at the biennial meeting of the American Psychology-Law Society, Sante Fe, NM.

Wright, L. (1994). *Remembering Satan.* New York: Alfred A. Knopf.

CHAPTER 32

I'M OK, YOU'RE NOT

Prejudice, as the word is usually used, is an irrational attitude of hostility directed against an individual, group, or race. It is an ugly thing. It is also very common. When this irrational attitude is directed against the supposed characteristics of a group, it is a kind of prejudice called *stereotyping*. Prejudice has been studied for a long time in psychology (see, for example, Miller & Bugelski, 1948), and during the past decade there have been many studies on this important issue (see Hilton & von Hippel, 1996, for a review).

It takes some courage to do these studies because in order to study prejudice and stereotypes, we have to admit that they exist. Moreover, the study of these attitudes often involves exposure to the distasteful details of prejudicial beliefs that may be held by those around us, maybe even by people we like, or love. This can make us uncomfortable, and rightly so. One reason why the study of prejudice is undertaken in psychology is because researchers are horrified by it. They believe that achieving understanding of prejudice may be one pathway to eliminating it. Sometimes the researchers themselves are members of the stereotyped group under study. You can imagine it is not easy for them to receive constant reminders of negative stereotypes about their own group.

We take the time to introduce this topic in this way because the study to be reviewed in this chapter examines stereotyping and other prejudice against two groups: young Jewish women and gay men. Some students are members of one of these groups, and many of you will have friends or family members included in these groups. It may upset you to read aspects of the stereotypes that are held about these people. It upsets us. Psychologists study many topics that are deeply and personally upsetting to some people including such things as racism, sexuality, religious practices, social class, and child abuse. We believe it is better to study sensitive topics than to ignore them. Ignorance has always been a poor solution to human problems.

Steven Fein and Steven Spencer (1997) did three related experiments to test different aspects of a hypothesis that prejudice is linked to a person's own self-image. As we have seen in previous chapters, it is not unusual that several small studies are reported in one journal article. If the studies are closely related, there is some economy for the reader. The introduction to the topic is likely to be the same for all of them, and the conclusions can summarize all the study findings at once. Fein and Spencer

Incorporating the research of S. Fein and S. J. Spencer, "Prejudice as Self-Image Maintenance: Affirming the Self through Derogating Others," 1997, *Journal of Personality and Social Psychology*, 73, pp. 31–44.

believed that, ironically, prejudice results from inherent attempts of people to maintain their own feelings of self-worth and self-integrity. People like to feel good about themselves. When something threatens positive feelings about the self, probably the best way to deal with the resulting discomfort is to confront the source. We do not always do that. If, for example, you have done something that later does not appear very smart—such as sitting on the plate of pizza (with extra toppings) that you left on a kitchen stool—you might rationalize it by saying that you were tired and not thinking too clearly. This permits you to remove the threatening idea that you were stupid, replacing it with the idea that you were merely tired. Your sense of self-worth and self-integrity has been maintained or restored.

Steel, Spencer, and Lynch (1993) pointed out that threats to self-worth do not always have to be addressed directly. Sometimes people will accept one set of negative implications about themselves and turn elsewhere to bolster some other aspect of their self-image, increasing their overall total sense of self-adequacy. For example, a person who feels that he is not particularly intelligent might accept and ignore that feeling, while taking particular pride in some other sort of personal achievement.

Unfortunately, making negative assessments of others is another tactic people use to feel better about themselves. Threats to a person's self-image can result in that person becoming more prejudiced. When people make disparagements in order to feel better, they avoid having to do anything about the sources of threat that lowered their self-image in the first place. The ability of prejudice to restore positive feelings about the self in prejudiced people has been called the *self-affirming* nature of prejudice. Self-affirmation is the name given to our own reassurance that we have overall personal worth and integrity.

STUDY 1

Fein and Spencer (1997) believed that increased self-affirmation ought to lead to decreased prejudice. A good way to think about this proposition is to imagine that each person needs to maintain a certain pool or supply of feelings of self-worth. Unfortunately, prejudice has been shown to boost self-worth and adds to this supply. If the self-worth supply is increased by having people do other, nonprejudicial, self-affirming things, self-worth levels will be high, and prejudice will be less necessary. Fein and Spencer set up a situation in which one group of people had the opportunity to review some aspect of their lives that they particularly valued and to remind themselves of the reasons why this value was important. This was the self-affirmation manipulation. Another group performed a task involving similar amounts of time, but did not engage in self-affirmation. The opportunity to self-affirm or not was an independent variable in this study.

Participants and Procedure for Study 1

The participants in Study 1 were 54 students from an introductory psychology course at the University of Michigan who received course credit for being in the study.

They were told that they were going to be in two experiments. The first was described as a study of values and the second was supposed to be an investigation of how people evaluate job applicants. Really, the "values study" was a manipulation, or set of created conditions, within the experiment designed to create or boost self-affirmation in half the participants. *Self-affirmation* and *no-affirmation* were operationally defined by the manipulation in the so-called values study. Half of the participants received the self-affirmation manipulation. The participants in the self-affirmation group were given a list of words such as *social life, business, pursuit of knowledge*, and *art*. They were asked to choose the topic from the list that had the most value to them and write a paragraph about why it was important. This was considered self-affirmation because it gave the participants a chance to feel good about their beliefs. In contrast, the participants in the no-affirmation control group were asked to choose a value that was least important to them and write a paragraph about why this value might be important to someone else. This no-affirmation procedure was conducted so both groups would have a somewhat parallel lab experience with the exception that one group was self-affirmed and one was not.

For the second part of Study 1, the participants were told their task was to evaluate a woman who was applying for a job as personnel manager in an organization. They were told to assess the fit between this individual and the job as accurately as possible. They were given a job description and a fictitious job application. The application was constructed by the experimenters to make the candidate appear fairly well qualified for the position, but not an excellent match. There was a photograph on the application. After examining the application, the participants were asked to view an 8-minute videotape that showed an interview with the applicant. The woman playing the applicant put on an adequate performance, but was not outstandingly positive or negative.

All research participants saw the same videotape. The application materials shown to all participants were the same except a few modifications had been made to imply that the woman belonged to one of two different ethnic groups: Jewish or Italian. These groups were chosen because at that time on the Michigan campus there was a prejudicial stereotype that was widely held among the student body about young Jewish women. These women were the target of racist jokes about what was called the Jewish American Princess, or JAP, stereotype. This particular prejudice was chosen for study because many students openly believed it and seemed to see nothing racist in its endorsement. Italian ethnicity was chosen for comparison because pilot testing indicated that there was no widely held stereotype of any sort associated with Italian ethnicity on this campus.

In order to manipulate the ethnicity of the woman who was supposed to be the job candidate, some applications had different details than others. Half of the applications had the name Julie Goldberg, but on the others the name was Maria D'Agostino. Julie's application showed her volunteering for a Jewish organization and Maria's listed volunteer work for a Catholic organization. On the application, Julie belonged to a sorority that consisted predominantly of Jewish women, whereas Maria belonged to a sorority that had mainly non-Jewish women as members. All the other printed material was identical. The photograph was varied slightly so that Julie was wearing a Star of David necklace and Maria was wearing a cross. Julie had her hair clipped up with what was known on the campus as a "JAP clip," whereas Maria had her hair down. Because the participants viewed the same video, a sweater was arranged to cover the necklace and the woman's hair was arranged to be intermediate between clipped up and let down.

Dependent Measures for Study 1

Participants rated the job applicants in terms of overall personality on a 7-point scale. Twenty-one specific traits were rated including *intelligent, friendly, trustworthy, arrogant, materialistic, cliquish, happy, warm, superficial,* and *vain.* The extent to which applicants were qualified for the job was also rated. *Prejudice* was operationally defined as high scores given on negative personality traits in this procedure.

Results of Study 1

Fein and Spencer predicted that participants who had not been self-affirmed and who thought the job applicant was Jewish would be more negative towards her. The data are presented in Figure 32.1.

The prediction was supported; although there were no significant differences among the personality ratings from the two self-affirmed groups and the non–self-affirmed group who believed the candidate was ethnically Italian, the nonaffirmed people who thought she was Jewish rated her personality significantly more negatively ($p < .05$). As you can see in Figure 32.1, the same pattern was found for evaluation of the candidate's qualifications for the job. The data presented in Figure 32.1 consist of the total ratings given by each participant, averaged with the total ratings for all other participants. Because there were 21 traits rated, it appears that, most typically, participants rated traits around 3 or 4, using the middle of the 7-point rating scale. Ratings of about 3 or 4 on each of 21 traits would result in the kinds of totals found in Figure 32.1. We mention this because as part of your critical thinking, you should always try to discover what is being scaled when interpreting graphic material.

The nonaffirmed participants rated the Jewish woman as significantly less qualified ($p < .001$). The data shown for qualifications consisted of the average of the total ratings given by each participant on each of four statements, using a 7-point scale. An example of one these statements was "I feel this person would make an excellent candidate for the position in question."

STUDY 2

In Study 2, Fein and Spencer asked if posing a threat to self-image would make people more likely to use stereotypes to describe a member of a group. To return to the analogy of a pool or supply of self-worth discussed in Study 1, threatening self-worth ought to lower the supply, forcing people to behave in ways that would rebuild self-worth. In a way, this was the opposite question from that posed in Study 1: this second study set

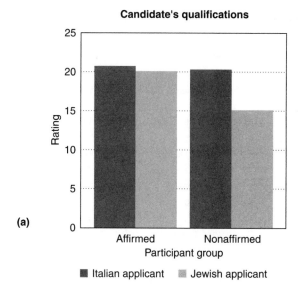

(a)

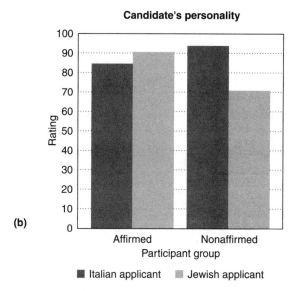

(b)

FIGURE 32.1   Ratings from Study 1. Affirmed and nonaffirmed participant's ratings of candidate's qualifications (a) and personality (b) for Italian and Jewish applicant conditions.

people up to feel negatively about themselves and predicted this would make them more likely to stereotype others. This was expected because, as was shown in Study 1, self-affirmation decreased prejudice. It would make sense, therefore, that a lowered self-affirmation would be associated with more prejudice, demonstrated in this case by increased stereotyping.

Participants and Procedure for Study 2

The participants were 61 male undergraduates from Williams College who were given either extra credit in their introductory psychology course or an opportunity to win money in a lottery. Allowing research participants to take part in a drawing for cash is one way to attract willing participants without having to spend as much money as would be required to pay each one of them a significant sum.

Half of the participants, the experimental group, received a bogus intelligence test given on a desktop computer. They were told that this was "a new form of intelligence test that is given on the computer. It measures both verbal and reasoning abilities." They were told it was a valid way to measure intelligence. In fact, the fake test had been constructed so there were no possible correct answers to some questions, and the time limits given were so short that some items could not possibly be done in the time allotted. At the end of the test, the computer gave these participants a fake score for each part of the test. These scores ranged from the 56th percentile down to the 33rd percentile. The percentile rating of a score tells what percent of scores are typically found below the score in question. At best, these students were being told that they were barely in the top half of the population of people who had taken this intelligence test. Williams College is a very selective college, and these scores were disappointing to the experimental group participants, who were accustomed to doing well on other standardized tests, such as the SAT. The other half of the participants, the control group, were given the same test, but were told that it was a fake intelligence test. They were also told they were in the control group of a study and that although they should do the test, they should not work too hard because some of the questions were impossible. They were told not to worry about the phony scores they would receive at the end. In short, they were told the truth about what was going on.

Following the testing experience, both groups were given what was described as a social judgment task. They were told they would be read some information about a man and then would make some judgments about him. The story they were told was of a man, Greg, who was trying to make it as an actor while living in the East Village in New York City. He got a part in a controversial play directed by a young director. He was eager to work with this particular director. The pronouns indicated that the director was a man. After some rehearsals, Greg asked the director if he wanted to get "a drink or something" so they could talk more about Greg's part in the play. There were more details in the story, but this was the substance. The intelligence test procedure had created two groups: those who were told the truth about the test (neutral self-image group) and those who thought the test was real (negative self-image group). These two groups were divided in half. Half of each group received an additional implication about Greg: that he was gay. The other half was led to believe that he was straight. This was accomplished by small changes to the story of Greg. In the *straight-implied condition*, participants were told that Greg had a girlfriend named Anne with whom he had been living for several years. She was mentioned several times in the story. In the *gay-implied condition*, participants were told Greg had "a partner," but no name or gender was specified. With these two independent variables: *IQ test feedback* and *Greg's implied sexual orientation*, four experimental groups could be constructed:

Neutral test feedback/Gay implied
Neutral test feedback/Straight implied
Negative test feedback/Gay implied
Negative test feedback/Straight implied

Dependent Measures in Study 2

Following the story about Greg, participants were asked to rate Greg's personality on a number of measures using an 11-point scale ranging from 0—*not at all like Greg*, to 11—*extremely like Greg*. Three of the dimensions rated were not considered to be part of a gay stereotype: intelligent, funny, and boring. The stereotype-relevant traits included sensitive, assertive/aggressive, considerate, feminine, strong, creative, and passive. If participants endorsed the gay stereotype they scored Greg high for some of these traits (e.g., sensitive, feminine) and low for others (e.g., assertive/aggressive, strong). This was done on purpose so that participants would pay attention to their ratings and not merely mark all traits high or low, without thinking about them.

Results for Study 2

The results of this study are shown in Figure 32.2. Remember that some individuals had been given a negative self-image through thinking that they had done poorly on a real intelligence test. Others had an experience that had little or no effect, called here

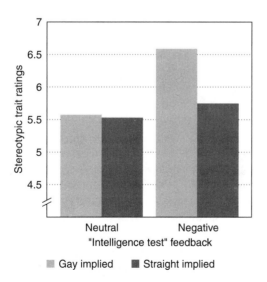

FIGURE 32.2   Findings from Study 2.
Amount of stereotypical gay trait ratings of Greg by neutral and negative feedback participants in the gay-implied and straight-implied groups.

a neutral effect, on self-image: they had taken a test that they had been told in advance was a fake.

As Fein and Spencer predicted, participants who had experienced an attack to their self-image on the intelligence test were significantly ($p < .001$) more likely to use stereotypically gay descriptions when their information implied that Greg was gay.

PARTICIPANTS AND PROCEDURE FOR STUDY 3

Study 3 combined some procedures of Study 1 and Study 2. Participants were 126 introductory psychology students from University of Michigan who participated as partial fulfillment of a requirement in an introductory psychology course. Seventeen students were excluded because they were Jewish and 7 because they were foreign students, unlikely to be familiar with the stereotype about Jewish American women. Two more were eliminated during participation because they refused to believe the false feedback about their supposed intelligence test.

All participants were given the bogus intelligence test used in Study 2. In this study, however, all participants were told that the intelligence test was real, but half of them were told they had done very well and half were told they had done poorly. Next they were given a scale developed by Heatherton and Polivy (1991) that measured their self-esteem. *Self-esteem* was operationally defined as the score on this instrument. On this scale, self-esteem scores could fall between 20 and 100. After completion of this scale, they were sent on to what they believed to be a second study in "social evaluation." This second study was the same procedure as in Study 1, requiring evaluation of a supposed job candidate who was either Jewish or Italian. Following this, self-esteem was measured again.

Results of Study 3

The personality ratings that participants gave the supposed job applicant are shown in Figure 32.3. When individuals received negative feedback on their intelligence test performance and the candidate was Jewish, the personality ratings were significantly lower ($p < .01$). Self-esteem was measured twice: after receiving information about their intelligence test scores and after rating the job applicant. After the second measurement, the change in self-esteem was calculated by subtracting the first measurement from the second for each candidate. Figure 32.4 shows the average self-esteem change in each group.

Participants who evaluated the Jewish candidate and who received low scores on the fake intelligence test had a significantly greater increase in self-esteem ($p < .05$). There is a statistically significant difference, but it is not as dramatic as it may appear if you consider the scale on the y-axis of Figure 32.4. In this study, self-esteem could range from 20 to 100, and the maximum change seen here is a bit more than 3 points. In evaluating graphic presentations of data, there is no substitute for being a careful consumer. It is important to look at the graph to discern the overall trends in the data,

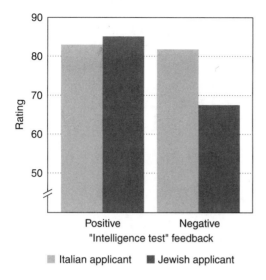

FIGURE 32.3   Results from Study 3. Ratings of candidate's personality from positive and negative feedback participants for Italian and Jewish applicant conditions.

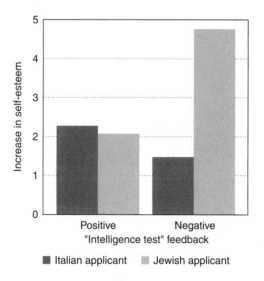

FIGURE 32.4   Increases in Reported Self-Esteem following Ratings of Italian-Appearing or Jewish-Appearing Applicant for Negative and Positive Feedback Applicants

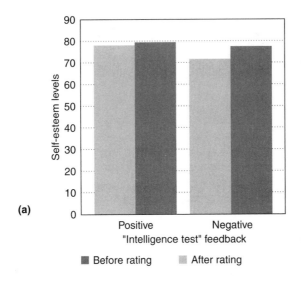

(a)

Self-esteem levels

"Intelligence test" feedback

■ Before rating   ■ After rating

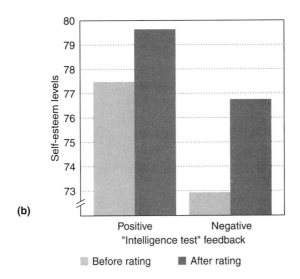

(b)

Self-esteem levels

"Intelligence test" feedback

■ Before rating   ■ After rating

FIGURE 32.5   What a Difference a Scale Makes. The top (a) and bottom (b) graph both show the same data taken from the Fein & Spencer study: the self-esteem levels before and after rating the Jewish applicant. Although the numbers are the same in both graphs, on the *y*-axis of graph (b) a small section of the range was selected and stretched to make the differences appear to be bigger.

but it is also important to look carefully at the *y*-axis. Differences between groups can be made to appear striking if the data range is stretched out or if only part of the whole data range is shown. This is illustrated in Figure 32.5, using the self-esteem data from Figure 32.4 plotted in two different ways.

When part of the range is shown, the graph should indicate this with a "break line" that is either two little hash marks or a little squiggle in the otherwise straight vertical axis. The break line is there to help alert you that part of the data range is missing. In sources other than scientific journals, for example in advertising, the *y*-axis is often distorted and break lines are missing in a deliberate attempt to mislead. Within scientific publications, the data presented in graphs are also described in the results, where you can find statistical tests that should support the graphic depictions of data. For example, even though the self-esteem differences in the study were small in absolute terms, the results indicated that the differences were statistically significant. Of course, Fein and Spencer pointed out the small but significant nature of these differences. As we have mentioned before, we would not want you to think that reputable scientists purposely misrepresent data. Exaggeration of data is, however, common practice in the realm beyond reputable science. As a consumer of information, you should protect yourself by paying attention to important details, such as the ways in which data are presented.

DISCUSSION

The results of this study supported the overall hypotheses of Fein and Spencer. Study 1 showed that participants who were self-affirmed were less likely to be prejudiced than those who were in a neutral state. Study 2 showed that participants who had been given negative feedback were more likely to stereotype an individual than those in a neutral state. Study 3 showed that negative self-esteem not only leads to prejudice but that prejudiced ratings, in turn, raised the self-esteem of the raters.

Aside from its important main findings, this study also illustrates the shallowness of stereotyping and other prejudice. Although prejudicial beliefs may be considered by bigots to be great truths and may be deeply held, it is noteworthy that this study showed how little was required in order for prejudice to be invoked resulting in negative ratings of other people. A necklace, hairstyle, and social group activities were enough to decrease ratings of job suitability for Julie. A residence in the East Village, living with a partner, as well as a few other nonspecific descriptors were adequate to make college men apply existing gay stereotypes to Greg. Clearly it does not take anything substantial to unleash the mechanisms of prejudice.

It is important to notice that the prejudice displayed here, particularly following a lowering of self-esteem, was not broadly aimed, shotgun fashion, at anybody and everybody. If that were so, in Study 3 Maria would also have been rated lower in personality and job-suitability by individuals who received negative feedback from the fake intelligence test. The prejudice seen here seems to be turned on in response to an attack to self-esteem, but only when participants thought that the applicant belonged to a group for which there was a preexisting negative stereotype. This research also casts doubt on the view that bigotry is a personality characteristic that is stable over time and across conditions. At least in this study, students were not as likely to act in a biased manner until their own self-esteem was threatened. Are there students who would not act prejudiced even in the face of severe threats to self-esteem? This is a question for future research.

This study is part of a traditional view within social psychology that sees behavior largely as the outcome of a particular context, rather than viewing it as a result of ingrained and stable personality traits as we have seen in other chapters. These two views are not really contradictory, and there is some evidence that both of them operate together. Situations can be powerful determinants of behavior but probably only within the limits set by more stable traits. The cautionary tale is that given a sufficiently powerful setting, many of us might become bigots. An understanding of what is going on here might help to decrease prejudice. We hope most people would feel worse, not better, if they realized that they had disparaged another person only to raise their own feelings of self-worth. It is an empirical question.

REFERENCES

Fein, S., & Spencer, S. J. (1997). Prejudice as self-image maintenance: Affirming the self through derogating others. *Journal of Personality and Social Psychology, 73*, 31–44.

Heatherton, T. F., & Polivy, J. (1991). Development and validation of a scale for measuring state self-esteem. *Journal of Personality and Social Psychology, 60*, 895–910.

Hilton, J. L., & von Hippel, W. H. (1996). Stereotypes. *Annual Review of Psychology, 47*, 237–271.

Miller, N. E., & Bugelski, R. (1948). The influence of frustrations imposed by the in-group on attitude expressed toward the out-group. *Journal of Psychology, 25*, 437–442.

Steel, C. M., Spencer, S. J., & Lynch, M. (1993). Self-image resilience and dissonance: the role of affirmational resources. *Journal of Personality and Social Psychology, 64*, 885–896.

CHAPTER 33

IT'S IN THE BAG

COGNITIVE DISSONANCE

Cognitive dissonance, sometimes shortened to *dissonance*, is the name given to the unpleasant feelings that are experienced when there is a difference between our attitudes and our behavior (Festinger, 1957). In one of the classic research demonstrations of dissonance, Festinger and Carlsmith (1959) assigned college student participants to a couple of tasks designed to be boring and pointless. One of these involved a tray with 12 spools on it. Participants were told that their goal was to remove and replace the spools in the tray, over and over, for 30 minutes while being watched and timed by an experimenter. Next, they were presented with a board that had 48 square pegs in it. The task with these was to lift each peg out and give it a quarter of a turn clockwise before replacing it. This was continued one after another, over and over, for an additional 30 minutes. Next, they were told that another student was usually employed to describe the research as "enjoyable," "interesting," "intriguing," and "exciting" to a subsequent participant who was already waiting in another room to be in the study. The experimenter explained that the student who usually did this could not show up that day and asked if these participants who had just completed the task would be willing to help out by saying these positive things to the next participant. In short, they were asked to lie. Participants received one of two levels of payment for telling this lie. Half of them were told that the usual payment was $1 and half were told it was $20—a considerable sum of money in 1959, when the study was done.

Once they had completed the task and told their lies, they were interviewed about their real feelings concerning the spool placing and peg turning. In this interview, the group that had been paid $1 rated the tasks as being more enjoyable than the group that had been paid $20. The people who were paid $1 had been put in a situation where dissonance was created. They had lied about these boring tasks and only received $1 in payment. The easiest way to remove the dissonance was to change their opinions. That is exactly what happened: they begin to think that the tasks were really

Incorporating the research of J. Stone, E. Aronson, A. L. Crain, M. P. Winslow, and C. B. Fried, "Inducing Hypocrisy as a Means of Encouraging Young Adults to Use Condoms," 1994, *Personality and Social Psychology Bulletin, 20*, pp. 116–128.

quite interesting and enjoyable. It seems that they might have been thinking something like "It was boring. I said it was fun. Why did I say that for only $1? Wait a minute, I guess it wasn't so boring after all, it was kind of interesting." The $20 group showed no comparable shift in attitude. They knew the task was boring, but they had a reason why they would lie about it to someone else: they were well paid.

This study illustrated one of the more interesting aspects of cognitive dissonance: people were uncomfortable and something had to be changed in order to reduce dissonance—attitudes or behavior. Dissonance motivated a change because of the discomfort associated with it. Particularly when attitudes and behavior are in conflict, it is often easier to change the attitude than to change the behavior. In Festinger and Carlsmith's study, it was not possible to change the behavior because it was in the past—the spools had been placed and the pegs had been turned.

Even when the behavior can be changed, it is sometimes easier to change the attitudes. For example, it is likely that smokers are aware of the health risks associated with this addiction. This should create dissonance between the attitude, *smoking is dangerous*, and the behavior, *I smoke*. There are two ways a person could reduce dissonance. The behavior could be changed; that is, the individual could quit smoking. However, it is more likely that the attitude will be modified. The smoker might say, "smoking is dangerous, but not for *me*. I feel fine. Anyway, I know someone who lived to be 96 and smoked two packs a day. . . ." Thinking critically about behavior includes being cautious about generalizing from anecdotes which begin "I know a person who. . . ."

There have been hundreds of studies of cognitive dissonance; some of them examined this concept from a theoretical standpoint. It was not unusual for studies of dissonance to suggest practical applications as well (Petty, Wegener, & Fabrigar, 1997). A research project by Stone, Aronson, Crain, Winslow, and Fried (1994) illustrated this point. Their original motivation was to apply the cognitive dissonance theory to the problem of HIV and AIDS prevention among sexually active young adults. According to the United States Center for Disease Control, the HIV epidemic, with its end-stage illness known as AIDS, is the leading cause of death of Americans aged 25 to 44. From the beginning, the HIV infection spread quickly: the first 100,000 cases of AIDS in the United States were diagnosed within the first 9 years of the epidemic. The next 100,000 cases were diagnosed within the following 18 months. More than 300,000 Americans have died of AIDS-related complications. It is estimated that between 800,000 and 1 million Americans are infected with HIV.

Stone et al. (1994) wanted to explore the extent to which cognitive dissonance could be used to encourage condom use in young adults, who comprise the population most at risk for HIV infection. Hypocrisy is a form of cognitive dissonance, and Stone and his colleagues felt that many college students had a prevailing hypocrisy about condom use. Hypocrites are people who have contradictions in their lives. They may say one thing and do another. They might be people who make themselves appear, through words or actions, to be better than they really are. Many people believe that they should systematically use condoms to prevent HIV infection, yet they do not behave according to this belief. On the surface it might seem that this dissonant situation would be a motive for change with the result being more frequent use of condoms. There are, however, numerous studies on this topic showing that students are more likely to change their attitudes than their behavior (Hays & Hays, 1992; Netting, 1992; Roche & Ramsbey, 1993).

PARTICIPANTS

The participants were recruited from a pool of students in psychology classes. Extra course credit was available to reward them for participation in research. The study was advertised as being about "health and persuasion" and sought students 18 to 25 years old who had been heterosexually active within the previous 3 months. These criteria were used in order to include people who might be at risk for HIV infection and who might have some use for condoms. Students who were married were screened out, as were those who had taken a blood test for HIV. This latter group was excluded because part of the experimental manipulation included raising awareness of HIV, and it was believed that people who had been tested for HIV had probably already had their awareness raised by the circumstances of the test. The final ethnically diverse sample consisted of 32 males and 40 females between the ages of 18 and 25 ($M = 19.20$). In addition to course credit for 1 hour of participation, they were paid $4 and told that this was because the experiment "sometimes runs a little more than an hour."

PROCEDURE

When the participants arrived, a sign on the door led them to believe they were at the AIDS Research Program Office. They were told that they would be helping to develop an AIDS prevention and education program for high schools. They were further told that a goal of this program was to teach sexually active teenagers that "condoms are the easiest and most reliable way to prevent the transmission of AIDS during intercourse." The variables that defined the experimental groups in this study were *commitment/no-commitment* and *mindful/unmindful*.

Commitment Manipulation

To operationally define *commitment*, participants were asked to develop a little persuasive speech about the role of sex in HIV and to deliver it to a video camera. They were told that the researcher thought college students would be highly effective in communicating to high school kids because the college students were older and more experienced, yet otherwise not so different that they would lose credibility. They were given some fact sheets about HIV and asked to outline their speech on paper. Next, they were allowed to rehearse, and their speech was taped. After this, they filled out a short HIV/AIDS knowledge questionnaire. The researchers believed that giving the speech and having it taped would result in commitment. In the noncommitment condition participants were told to develop a persuasive speech about HIV and AIDS. They did not have to give the speech and so no taping took place. They were told that the purpose of developing the speech was to see if there was a relationship between developing persuasive material and memory for material of similar content. After outlining the speech, the participants completed the HIV/AIDS knowledge questionnaire, ostensibly to test their memories for facts.

Mindfulness Manipulation

The other independent variable was mindfulness. Half of each group described above received the *mindful* condition. The *mindful* participants were told that their task was to try to figure out why condoms are difficult for most people to use. They were told this information was going to be included in the prevention program for high school students to help them "deal more effectively with these situations." Participants were given a list of circumstances that might make it difficult to use condoms. The items on this list had come from an earlier study (Aronson, Fried, & Stone, 1991), but participants were not told this. Participants were asked to read the list and then to make a separate list of circumstances surrounding their own past failures to use condoms, including personal examples missing from the list they had been given. In this way researchers believed that participants would become mindful of the problems they had experienced and, in addition, of their own failure to use condoms. As you can see, mindfulness was operationally defined as asking participants to reflect about problems with condoms. The other half of the participants received the *unmindful* condition. They went directly from the commitment or noncommitment procedure to the dependent measures, without any reference to their own past condom use.

Experimental Groups

Although they did not know it, all participants had been assigned randomly to one of four experimental groups before they arrived in the lab. The combination of the two manipulations described above created four different groups: (1) mindful and committed, also called the *hypocrisy* group, (2) commitment and unmindful, (3) mindful and noncommitted, and (4) unmindful and noncommitted, an *information-only* control group. This is a standard procedure for dealing with two independent variables. Four groups, arranged in this way, are adequate to assess the effects of each of the variables. It is common in psychological research that two pairs of variables are used to create four groups. Indeed, we have seen this before in Chapter 16, "Kids Say the Darndest Things." The design of this study is diagrammed in Figure 33.1.

Dependent Variables

Stone and his colleagues used two sorts of dependent variables in this study: self-report and behavioral. In general, self-report measures are easier to collect. They are usually questionnaires, surveys, or interviews. As we have noted in previous chapters, the problem is that what people *say* may not be a good representation of what they *do*. Even in a carefully constructed study, if all the outcomes were self-reports about behavior, we might have reason to be cautious about the validity of the findings. This is not to say that questionnaires and interviews are necessarily lacking in validity, we are only

FIGURE 33.1 Design of this Study Showing Creation of Four Groups from Two Pairs of Variables

		Commitment	
		Yes	No
		Prepare talk	Prepare talk
		Make video	No video
Mindfulness			
	Yes	Hypocrisy	Mindful only
Think about own past			
Difficulties with condoms			
	No	Commitment only	Information only
No opportunity given to			
think about own past			
Difficulties with condoms			

suggesting that one might have a little less confidence in the validity of findings if they were entirely based on self-reports. In contrast, although behavioral measures may have more validity, they can be very difficult to construct.

In the study by Stone et al. (1994) the self-report dependent measures were two interview questions: one about frequency of past condom use and one about predicted future condom use. Both questions were answered by having participants rate the percentage of use on a scale from 0 percent to 100 percent. This scale consisted of a 17 cm horizontal line like this with 0 percent printed at one end and 100 percent at the other:

0% _____ 100%

The students were asked to make a mark somewhere along the line to represent the likelihood of condom use. For example, if their estimate was 50 percent, the mark would be made in the middle.

Given that the topic of the study was condom use, the construction of a behavioral measure presented more of a challenge. As Stone and associates pointed out "we cannot crawl into bed with our subjects [participants] during their lovemaking." As an admittedly less-direct behavioral measure, the participants were given the opportunity to purchase condoms. The researchers were aware that purchasing condoms and using them are not the same thing. Nevertheless, taking condoms is a behavioral indication of intent to use them. The condom purchase was engineered to make it seem confidential because the researchers believed that, otherwise, factors such as social pressure to buy condoms might influence condom-purchasing behavior more than personal convictions.

One of the reasons why participants were paid $4—ostensibly for their time— was to be sure that each of them had money to buy condoms when the opportunity was presented. After they were given the money, they were asked to fill out a receipt for the social science business office. But before they could begin the receipt they were given the following story:

> ...the AIDS educators from the Health Center sent over some condoms and pamphlets on AIDS when they heard about our prevention program. They wanted us to give our subjects [participants] the opportunity to buy condoms for the same price they are sold at the health center—10 cents—and this way you don't have to go across campus and stand in a long line. I need to go next door and prepare for the next subject, so go ahead and finish this receipt; you can leave it here on the table. And if you want to buy some condoms, just help yourself to anything on that desk; that dish has some spare coins so you can make change. OK? Thanks again for coming in today. (Stone et al., 1994)

Next, the experimenter left the participant alone, closing the office door. There were 140 condoms, 10 each of 14 different brands, in a clear plastic container. A sign said that they were 10 cents each and change was available in a bowl next to the condoms. To assess the number of condoms taken by each participant, the container was recounted and refilled after each person left.

More Questions

As the participants were leaving, the experimenter appeared in the hallway, claiming to have forgotten to ask them to complete a questionnaire about their recent sexual behavior. Although this might have seemed a bit contrived, no one refused. The questionnaire asked the frequency of sexual intercourse during the past month and the past year, as well as the number of sexual partners during these time frames. Participants were also asked about frequency of condom use. Following this, they were debriefed.

As an attempt to measure the long-term effectiveness of the experimental treatments on subsequent sexual behavior, telephone interviews were conducted with the participants approximately 90 days after the experiment. The interviews were conducted by research assistants who were unaware of the experimental condition to which the participants had belonged. In the phone calls, researchers introduced themselves, reminded participants about the study, and asked if they could obtain some follow-up information about the participant's sexual behavior since the study ended. No participant refused to help with this request. The questions concerned frequency of sexual intercourse and condom use and were similar to those that had been asked at the end of the lab study.

Results and Discussion

The researchers believed having participants make their speeches for the video camera followed by a reminder of their own problems with condoms and hit-or-miss condom use would induce classic cognitive dissonance, or hypocrisy. Attitudes about condom use would be at variance with behavior, and this would produce stronger dissonance in this group than in any of the other groups. The question was, would this dissonance provoke behavior changes? The primary measure of this was the condom-purchasing behavior of participants in each of the four groups. Figure 33.2 shows that hypocrisy, or dissonance, represented by the commitment/mindful group did result in more people obtaining condoms when compared to the commitment-only group ($p < .003$), the mindful-only group ($p < .04$), and the information-only group ($p < .01$).

Although a higher percentage of the participants who were experiencing dissonance purchased condoms, the number of condoms purchased did not show this as clearly. Figure 33.3 presents these data.

Both commitment-only and mindful-only groups purchased significantly fewer condoms than the dissonant hypocrisy group ($p < .04$ and $p < .05$, respectively). The information-only group was not significantly different than the hypocrisy group

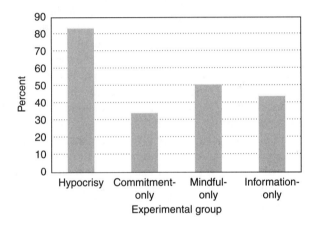

FIGURE 33.2   **Percentage of Participants Who Obtained Condoms**

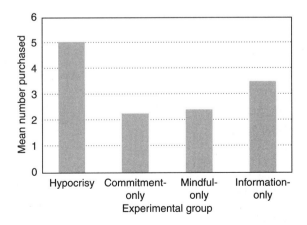

FIGURE 33.3   **Number of Condoms Obtained**

($p < .23$). There is no particular explanation for this nor does it support any particular hypotheses. The data concerning number of condoms purchased were, as researchers sometimes say, a bit fuzzy. The outcome was not as clear and obvious as it was for the percent of purchasers shown in Figure 33.2. The researchers presented the findings shown in Figure 33.3 so as to be completely honest about the outcomes and because it is possible that future research will uncover an explanation of why the number of condoms purchased did not present a clearer picture. Perhaps, surprisingly, there were no gender differences on these measures: the purchasing behavior of males and females were not significantly different.

Self-Report Data

You will remember that participants were asked to estimate their past condom use and to predict their future condom use. The data for *past* condom use did not present clear trends. This was expected because participants were randomly assigned to groups. There would be no particular reason to think that any group ought to be any different from any other group in past behavior. The participants' predictions of future condom use resulting from the experimental conditions are depicted in Figure 33.4.

The trend seen in this figure is in the expected direction. Students who had experienced hypocrisy were more likely to think that they would use condoms in the future. Commitment seems to be an important part of this and, indeed, the level seen for commitment-only was not significantly different from that found for hypocrisy. The levels for participants in the hypocrisy condition were higher than those in the mindful-only ($p < .03$) and information-only ($p < .01$) conditions. You will remember that the data here were collected by asking students to respond to a scale line 17 cm long running from 0 percent to 100 percent.

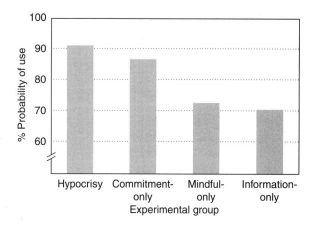

FIGURE 33.4 **Percent Probability of Future Condom Use**

Follow-up Interviews

In telephone interviews conducted 3 months after the original study, researchers were able to reach 64 (89 percent) of the original 72 participants, and 52 (81 percent) of them reported having been sexually active since the study. Three of these participants were dropped from the interview data because they reported levels of sexual activity and condom use that were so high as to seem unlikely. Each of these individuals claimed to have had sexual intercourse over 90 times since the study and reported using condoms over 90 times. In comparison, the highest group mean among other participants was 24 instances of sexual intercourse with an average of nine condoms used. It seems likely that the three participants who were dropped from the study had decided to have a bit of fun with the researchers in giving their answers. If this is what happened, it is fortunate that they exaggerated to the extent that they were easy to detect. This incident raises a serious issue for interview and survey research in general. Setting aside the problems of faulty memory, discussed earlier in Chapter 16, "Kids Say the Darndest Things," and Chapter 17, "Flash in the Pan," if people willfully wish to mislead researchers, it is sometimes fairly easy to do so. This further illustrates the value of behavioral measures that, depending on the research design, can be more difficult to falsify than mere verbal responses on surveys or interviews. If these three participants had wanted to disrupt the behavioral measure in this study, they could have taken handfuls of condoms, paying for them or not. They did not do this. Nevertheless, when they were phoned at home, with some distance between them and the researcher, they felt comfortable in seemingly exaggerating their levels of sexual activity. This has been a common problem in self-report studies of sexuality (Catania, Gibson, Chitwood, & Cotes, 1990).

Table 33.1 presents some of the data from the follow-up phone interview. Although, for example, the percentage of participants reporting condom use was higher in the hypocrisy group than in the commitment-only group, it was not significantly different from the mindful-only and information-only group. A perusal of this table suggests that the 3 month follow-up interviews provided, in the words of Stone and associates, "very little indication that the subjects [participants] in the hypocrisy condition were using condoms more regularly than subjects in the control conditions. . . ."

Does this study have a practical application? It is certainly a contribution to our understanding of behavior. Although long-term effects were muted, the creation of dissonance had some immediate effects on condom purchasing. It is probably unrealistic to hope that one short experience with dissonance would create permanent changes in behavior. Although it is a topic for future research, it is possible that a program that increased commitment and raised mindfulness at regular intervals would have more staying power. It is not easy to make permanent changes in behavior. Psychologists sometimes talk about a *behavior trajectory* in which behavior continues to develop in a single direction over quite long periods of time. We have seen these before in the elderly "Termites" of Chapter 15, "Golden Oldies," and the personality development in Chapter 24, "Going to Pot." As we saw in Chapter 6, "Zipping Up the Genes," our genetic endowment may also contribute to the creation of stable modes of behavior. In contrast, some programs have been shown to result in behavior change, at

TABLE 33.1   Self-Reports of Sexual Behavior Collected 3 Months after Participation in the Study

	HYPOCRISY	COMMITMENT ONLY	MINDFUL ONLY	INFORMATION ONLY
Percentage reporting condom use	92%	55%	71%	75%
Average amount of intercourse	13.6	9.1	24.2	18.4
Average number of sexual partners	1.2	1.5	1.1	1.4
Frequency of condom use	2.75	1.82	2.00	2.08
Number of condoms used	5.83	3.91	9.00	7.41
Percentage of times condoms used	63%	46%	44%	65%

least for selected groups of people. We have discussed this in several earlier chapters. The discovery of ways to achieve positive, lasting behavior change has been an elusive goal, but it continues to be a major focus of some psychological research. We consider this to be a highly important endeavor.

REFERENCES

Aronson, E., Fried, C. B., & Stone, J. (1991). Overcoming denial and increasing the intention to use condoms through the induction of hypocrisy. *American Journal of Public Health, 81*, 1636–1638.

Catania, J. A., Gibson, D. R., Chitwood, D. D., & Cotes, T. J. (1990). Methodological problems in AIDS behavioral research: Influences on measurement error and participation bias in studies of sexual behavior. *Psychological Bulletin, 108*, 339–362.

Festinger, L. (1957). *A theory of cognitive dissonance.* Evanston, IL: Row, Peterson.

Festinger, L., & Carlsmith, J. M. (1959). Cognitive consequences of forced compliance. *Journal of Abnormal and Social Psychology, 58*, 203–210.

Hays, H., & Hays, J. (1992). Students knowledge of AIDS and sexual risk behavior. *Psychological Reports, 71*, 649–650.

Netting, N. (1992). Sexuality in youth culture: Identity and change. *Adolescence, 27*, 961–976.

Petty, R. E., Wegener, D. T., & Fabrigar, L. R. (1997). Attitudes and attitude change. *Annual Review of Psychology, 48*, 609–647.

Roche, J., & Ramsbey, T. (1993). Premarital sexuality: A five year follow-up study of attitudes and behavior by dating stage. *Adolescence, 28*, 67–80.

Stone, J., Aronson, E., Crain, A. L., Winslow, M. P., & Fried, C. B. (1994). Inducing hypocrisy as a means of encouraging young adults to use condoms. *Personality and Social Psychology Bulletin, 20*, 116–128.

CHAPTER 34

WHO'S AFRAID OF
THE BIG BAD AD?

In this book we have tried to stress the side of psychological research that has some relevance to the real world. In doing so, we have avoided articles that are almost purely theoretical. If you were to go look in psychology journals, you would find some articles that seem to have no practical application. This basic research sometimes contributes to theories that have applications to daily life, sometimes not. We are not saying that basic research is without value, but it is our opinion that purely theoretical science may not be the best way to introduce psychology. At the other end of the continuum, there are studies whose applications were the main reason for their existence. The study of behavior to address practical questions is often called *applied psychology* because it applies psychology to the real world. This is a large field that includes advertising and marketing, as well as many other types of research aimed at solving problems in daily life.

A great deal of applied research is found in the area of consumer psychology. Consumer psychology is a large field that includes all aspects of consumer behavior including topics such as the effects of brand names, efficiency of distribution systems, preference for times of shopping, convenience of store locations, and responses to advertising. Vast sums of money are spent on attempts to persuade people to buy things. A minute-long TV advertisement during the Super Bowl can cost more than a million dollars. The purchase of goods is a type of behavior and, as you might expect, psychologists have long had an interest in understanding the power of advertising to convince people to buy products. One of the founders of the psychological viewpoint called *behaviorism*, John B. Watson, spent the last half of his career as an advertising executive. Psychologists who were behaviorists believed that the goal of psychology should be to measure and predict behavior, without any reference to mental states. Advertising welcomed Watson's practical approach to behavior. Ironically, in contrast to his views about the uselessness of considering internal states, Watson sometimes blatantly used the internal state *fear* in his attempts to sell products. One of his advertisement campaigns featured a dramatic photograph of a surgical team at work in a hospital operating room with the caption "And the trouble began with harsh toilet tissue . . ." (Hothersall, 1990).

Incorporating the research of M. S. LaTour, R. L. Snipes, and S. J. Bliss, "Don't Be Afraid to Use Fear Appeals: An Experimental Study," 1996, *Journal of Advertising Research*, 36, pp. 59–67.

LaTour, Snipes, and Bliss (1996) conducted research into the use of fear appeals in advertising. Their research considered not only the effectiveness of fear, but also the ethics of using fear to persuade people to buy a product. One source of inspiration for their study came from a short-lived, but well-known, example of an ethical problem in fear advertising that stemmed from a commercial for a popular brand of athletic shoe. In this commercial two individuals were bungee jumping. Only one of them was wearing shoes made by the advertiser. The jumper wearing the other brand of shoes plunged to his death as his feet came out of his shoes. As the camera focused on the loose shoes dangling in the bungee cords, the voice-over stated that the advertised brand "fits a little better than your ordinary athletic shoe" (Garfield, 1990). This joke about violent death was felt to be in bad taste by many consumers and was quickly discontinued in response to complaints. Many people would regard this ad as an obvious example of poor ethical judgment on the part of the shoe manufacturer and the advertising agency. It could be argued, in contrast, that this was a joke in bad taste, not a serious attempt to invoke fear. Nevertheless, there are many advertisements that do seriously attempt the induction of fear to motivate buying. Many health and hygiene products use this approach, ranging from pills that are depicted as keeping elderly people alive, to threats concerning bad breath. The advertisement is often gentle, but the threat is there: elderly people who use this medication *will* be around to play with their grandchildren. Those who do not use it are taking their chances.

Advertisers are aware that stepping over the boundary in fear appeals can backfire. As Treise, Weigold, Conna, and Garrison (as cited in LaTour et al., 1996) noted: "Consumer opinion that a specific advertising practice is unethical or immoral can lead to a number of unwanted outcomes, ranging from consumer indifference toward the advertised product to more serious actions such as boycotts or demands for government regulation."

Research on the effects of differing levels of fear in advertising has led to somewhat contradictory overall results. Some studies found that most persuasion takes place at low to moderate amounts of fear. However, other studies suggested that the relationship between fear and persuasion is linear: more fear resulted in more persuasion. One reason for this variability may be that the thought processes involved in fear are different for some people (Rotfeld, 1989). Although some people may respond strongly to a particular fear stimulus, others may not. Some people may be kept awake for many nights by the notion that seeing one insect in a house means that there are more, many more, crawling around in the walls. Other people might not be bothered by this idea. If most of the participants in a research study about an ad campaign for insecticide were from one or the other of these groups, they might react quite differently to fear messages threatening teeming hoards of household insects.

LaTour and colleagues (1996) conducted an experiment using advertisements with strong and mild fear appeals in order to answer two questions:

1. Do consumers perceive the strong fear appeal as less ethical than the weak fear appeal?
2. How effective is a strong fear appeal compared to a weak fear appeal when it comes to positive consumer attitudes toward the ad itself, the brand of item being advertised, and the intent to purchase?

PARTICIPANTS

The participants in this study consisted of 305 women who were shopping in a large shopping mall in the southeastern United States. Their mean age was 28 years. Sixty percent of them were single, 34 percent were married, and the rest were divorced or widowed. Their median household income was between $30,000 and $40,000, and they had an average of 14 years of education. Seventy nine percent of them were white, 17.4 percent were African American, and 3.6 percent belonged to other races or ethnicities. They were randomly chosen from shoppers in the mall by female doctoral candidates who served as researchers. The researchers stopped people and asked if they would be willing to take part in a study. Some mall traffic was allowed to pass between each attempt to recruit participants. About half of those who were selected for inclusion in the study agreed to participate. To help ensure a representative sample, the selection of participants was done in a way to eventually include people from across the hours of operation of the mall. The data collection for the entire study required 9 weeks of work in the mall.

PROCEDURE

The technique used was an example of what is called the *mall intercept technique*. This has become a popular method of testing advertisements in the past few years because it has been shown to produce quality data (Bush & Hair, 1985). In this study, a strong and a mild version of a videotaped advertisement was constructed by editing an actual television infomercial for a "stun-gun" device. The stun gun was targeted for sales to women as prevention against assault and rape. A stun gun is a small handheld device that, through small prongs on one end, is able to deliver an attention-getting 200,000-volt shock to an attacker. Focus groups were conducted before the study to assist in choosing material from the infomercial that would send a strong and a mild fear message. A focus group is a group organized to discuss a particular issue. In this instance, a focus group was used to collect opinions about research procedures. In the end, the *mild* advertisement consisted of testimonies from actual police officers talking about the utility of the stun gun in preventing assaults. The *strong* fear appeal consisted of the same set of testimonies followed by a written statement on the screen saying that the material to follow was a recording from an actual 911 call to police made by a woman from a suburban neighborhood who had discovered a prowler in her house. In her case, the police arrived too late, and she was brutally attacked and raped. This notice was followed by scenes of a housing suburb at night with a voice-over of an actual emergency call. To make sure she could be understood, the victim's words appeared on the screen as subtitles. She became progressively more frantic in her pleas on the phone. Finally, as the assailant broke into her bedroom, the woman's last frantic and desperate words are heard: "Why are you here?! Why?! Why?! . . ."

Because the advertisements involved the stun gun, any women who already owned a firearm or a stun gun, as well as any who had seen or heard about the original infomercial on TV, were screened out and did not participate in the study. The researchers used three different locations in the mall to set up a small television and videotape player that had headphones for listening to the sound. The researchers also set up movable partitions that allowed sufficient privacy so that only one participant at a time would be exposed to a stimulus videotape. People who agreed to participate were asked to sign consent forms. They were assured that their responses to the stimulus tapes would be anonymous, confidential, and used only for academic research. Next, they were taken to one of the partitioned areas to view either the strong or the mild version of the advertisement for the stun gun.

Dependent Measures

The dependent measures were questions on a questionnaire that asked about the participants' (1) perceptions of the ethical nature of the ad, (2) other attitudes toward the ad, (3) attitudes toward the particular brand of the product, and (4) intention to buy the product. Perceived ethicality of the ad was measured with a scale called the Reidenbach and Robin Multidimensional Ethics Scale. This instrument was reported to have a high level of validity when checked against other accepted measures (Reidenbach & Robin, 1990). It measured two kinds of ethical thought: a *moral* dimension and a *relativistic* dimension. Participants were asked to make ratings on a 7-point scale anchored at the ends by adjectives of opposite meanings. The moral dimension was measured using adjectives reflecting absolute moral standards, such as: *fair/unfair, just/unjust, morally right/not morally right*, and *acceptable to my family/not acceptable to my family*. The relativistic dimension assessed ethical judgments made with reference to the society or the culture such as: *culturally acceptable/not culturally acceptable* and *traditionally acceptable/traditionally unacceptable*. A direct single item, which asked the participants to rate the ad as *ethical/unethical*, completed the measures of ethics.

Other attitudes toward the advertisement were measured by asking participants to rate ad characteristics on a 6-point scale running from *no, definitely not* to *yes, definitely*. The ad characteristics that were rated in this way were *Good, Distinctive, Appropriate, Easy to Understand*, and *Objective*. Attitudes to the particular brand of stun gun featured in the ad were collected on the same kind of 6-point scale. The brand characteristics were: *High quality, Interesting, Appealing, Desirable, Good*, and *Useful*.

Researchers also assessed intent to purchase the product. Participants were told that the stun gun was typically sold in the local area for between $60 and $80. Purchase intention was measured by asking participants to respond to a single 6-point item that read *I plan to purchase [brand name]*. This statement was rated with a 6-point scale anchored at the ends by *no, definitely not* and *yes, definitely*.

As a check to see that people were paying attention and that the experimental manipulation was doing what it was supposed to, two additional items were asked. On a 6-point scale from *no, definitely not* to *yes, definitely* participants were asked to rate whether the ad clearly featured an actual violent crime. As a further manipulation check, they were asked to rate how tense the ad made them feel on a 4-point scale from *definitely do not feel* to *definitely feel*. Lastly, participants were asked to rate, on a 6-point scale, how confident they felt of their own ability to use a stun gun to stop an assailant.

Results

Participants were randomly assigned to one of two different groups and, as would be expected with random participant assignment, there were no significant demographic differences between the group that saw the mild ad and the group that saw the strong version. There were also no significant differences between the groups in their reported confidence in their ability to use a stun gun to stop an attack on themselves. Preexisting attitude differences between groups on this question would have constituted an important confound. Ideally the groups should be similar in every way except in exposure to the independent variable or variables.

Manipulation Check

The data in the manipulation checks (having noticed the violent crime or not and having experienced tension) should be different for the two groups if the advertisements were doing what they were supposed to do. These data are presented in Figure 34.1.

The differences seen in Figure 34.1 are in the predicted direction. The *strong* group had noticed the violent crime and experienced more tension. If this manipulation check had failed to produce these differences, it would have been difficult to interpret other results from the study. This would have indicated that participants had not

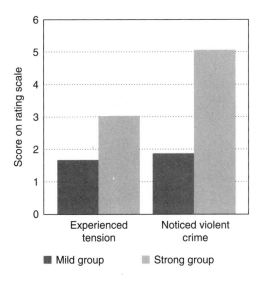

FIGURE 34.1   Manipulation Check.
Participants' mean ratings on a 4-point scale of the amount of tension they experienced watching the advertisement and their recollection, on a 6-point scale, that the advertisement featured a violent crime.

responded to the different levels of the independent variable. As can be seen, the manipulation check was successful and differences between groups on both manipulation check questions were statistically significant ($p < .001$).

Attitude about Ad and Brand

The independent variable did make some difference to attitudes toward the advertisement and to the brand of product. The data are presented in Figure 34.2.

These data are the result of adding together the scores on the six different 6-point scales that were used to assess attitudes to ad and to brand. These scales were scored in such a way that higher numbers reflect more positive attitudes on the descriptors that were words such as: *Good, Appealing,* and *Appropriate*. The attitudes toward the advertisement are significantly different ($p = .005$). The attitudes toward the brand just missed the usual standard for statistical significance. Ordinarily, psychological science considers that results have to meet a criterion of $p < .05$ in order to be considered significant. As we have described in other chapters, $p < .05$ means that the probability that the difference is the result of chance factors (rather than the independent variable) is 5 percent, or 1 in 20. The statistical test on the data for *attitude to brand* found a significance level for this difference of $p = .065$. Sometimes researchers will say that a finding like this "approaches significance" or that there is "a trend toward sig-

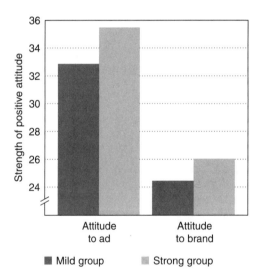

FIGURE 34.2   Attitudes to Ad and Brand by Group. Mean ratings on six different 6-point scales (summed), each reflecting the extent of positive attitudes toward the advertisement and the brand of the product.

nificance in the data." Strictly speaking, however, this outcome is not significant. It has not met the accepted criterion, no matter how close it is. LaTour et al. (1996) avoid this issue by simply supplying the data and letting the reader decide. If this were a life-and-death matter, as it might be in the test of a new drug, one might absolutely insist on high levels of statistical significance in order to be persuaded. In this case, we agree with the way the researchers have handled their finding. They have given us the numbers and allowed us to decide if we wish to consider a significance level of $p = .065$ to be adequate in a questionnaire study of advertising. Although the research question about attitudes to brands is interesting, it is not so important that calling this significant or not will have earth-shattering consequences. This is a reason why replications of studies can be useful. If this study were to be replicated a few times, we might gain a more clear picture of the significance, or lack thereof, for these data.

Purchase Intention

Probably the data that would be of most interest to a product manufacturer would be the purchase intention resulting from the mild or strong version of the advertisement. Responses to this item are shown in Figure 34.3.

The data here show a significantly greater purchase intention in the strong group ($p < .001$), suggesting that the advertisement that produced the most tension, or even fear, was the most effective. This study was not done to sell stun guns. These researchers had backgrounds in the areas of marketing and management. They were interested in understanding how advertisements work. If product sales had been part of the goal, it might have been possible to go beyond purchase intention to actual purchase. It would have been interesting to know if, given the chance, the *strong* group

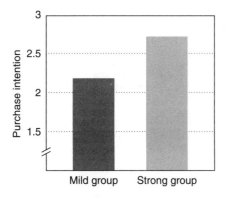

FIGURE 34.3   Purchase Intention by Group. Purchase intention ratings of the statement "I plan to purchase [brand name]" from *no, definitely not* to *yes, definitely* on a 6-point scale.

would have actually purchased stun guns more frequently than the *mild* group. This difference was significant, but small. It was less than 1 point on a 6-point scale. We can only speculate about what this difference would mean in terms of numbers of stun guns that would be sold if the mild and strong advertisements were actually used. There is no way to determine this from the data presented. Even though the difference was small, it might reflect millions in sales, or it might reflect nothing.

Ethics

The last major question asked by this research was if the mild or strong version of the advertisement would be rated as different from an ethical standpoint. The data are presented in Figure 34.4.

Outcomes were not significantly different for either the multidimensional ethics scale or the single item about ethics. At least in this study, it would seem that people did not perceive a frightening advertisement to pose an ethical problem. Responses to the two ethical dimensions measured by the Reidenbach and Robin Multidimensional Ethics Scale (1990), moral and relativistic, were similar so the two types of scales were combined in data analysis. The scores on both this scale and the single ethical question presented in Figure 34.4 were quite high, suggesting that people in both the strong and the mild condition were rating the advertisement as being: *fair, just, morally right, culturally acceptable,* and *ethical.* These outcomes lead the authors to the conclusion that fear appeals are not seen as an ethical problem. The title of their original research article is "Don't be afraid to use fear appeals: An experimental study." In the context of this study, that conclusion seems to be warranted. However, we might see it differently if the advertisement in question had featured a fear appeal to sell some unnecessary, or even dangerous, product to impoverished elderly people. The abstract of the original research study says that the "results help to blunt 'blanket' criticism of fear appeals and

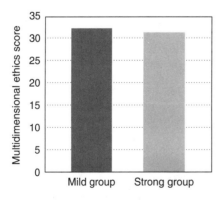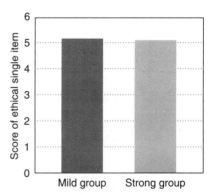

FIGURE 34.4   Dependent Measures That Were Ratings of the Ethics of the Mild and the Strong Advertisement. Differences between groups were not significant on either measure.

provide evidence for advertising executives who wish to argue for serious consideration of fear appeal use." We might also want to consider this message carefully. The fear appeal can be useful. There are some things about which people should be afraid. People who engage in high-risk behaviors should be afraid of HIV infection and subsequent AIDS. People who drink alcohol should be afraid to drive a car or operate other machinery. Perhaps fear appeals in advertisements should be used when fear is appropriate. It is a matter of personal judgment whether fear should be considered as just one more ordinary tactic to make people buy things.

One reason why we chose to include this study is because it illustrates an area of applied psychology that offers employment opportunities for people with backgrounds in psychology. Popular culture sometimes seems to think that psychology is the same thing as counseling or that its main mission is to treat mental illness. Probably this image is formed by television portrayals of psychologists on talk shows or situation comedies. On talk shows, psychologists are seen as those people who analyze problems on stage, dealing out simple and glib solutions. Sometimes these people have degrees in psychology, sometimes they do not. The other TV depiction of the psychologist comes from situation comedies in which people with funny problems come to be treated by a clinical psychologist who lives a luxurious and humorous life. Real mental illness is not funny. Life as a clinical psychologist is not as affluent, carefree, and comic as television programs suggest. The television characterization of psychology is misleading. As you have seen in many of the chapters in this book, not all psychologists work with people who have personal problems. Many psychologists are scientific researchers trying to understand behavior.

There is employment potential for people with knowledge of psychology. Virtually all organizations need to evaluate themselves. Businesses need to assess whether or not they are effective. Government agencies have to convince elected officials that they should continue to receive funding. There are good jobs in these domains for people who are curious about behavior, creative in their thinking, and skilled in scientific psychology. Psychology is more than a collection of facts; it is also a set of skills. People with good sets of skills are likely to find good careers. That is what we want to happen to you.

REFERENCES

Bush, A. J., & Hair, J. F. (1985). An assessment of the mall intercept as a data collection method. *Journal of Marketing Research, 22,* 158–167.

Garfield, B. (1990). Good taste takes deep dive in bungee ad for Reebok pump. *Advertising Age, 61,* 51–52.

Hothersall, D. (1990). *History of psychology* (2nd ed.). New York: McGraw-Hill.

LaTour, M. S., Snipes, R. L., & Bliss, S. J. (1996). Don't be afraid to use fear appeals: An experimental study. *Journal of Advertising Research, 36,* 59–67.

Reidenbach, R. E., & Robin, D. P. (1990). Toward the development of a multidimensional scale for improving evaluations of business ethics. *Journal of Business Ethics, 9,* 639–653.

Rotfeld, H. (1989). Fear appeals and persuasion: Assumptions and errors in advertising research. *Current Issues and Research in Advertising, 11,* 21–40.

CHAPTER 35

I'M WARNING YOU

The research topic in this chapter focuses on important variables that influence people to follow warnings. For example, every time we travel by plane the flight attendants warn us about what to do in the event the aircraft loses pressure and we need to use the emergency oxygen system. Our own travel experiences suggest that passengers largely ignore the attendant's demonstration in favor of reading their newspapers, adjusting their luggage, or taking a snooze. On a recent flight the warnings were given over the television monitors. It appeared that even fewer passengers were paying attention to the monitors, but that could be checked out in a formal research program. We are constantly receiving warnings: warnings about our diet, exercise, driving, parenting, relationships, medications, and so on. We are often noncompliant, and the warning has little impact in modifying our behaviors. It is important to note that most people would agree that the warnings given are useful and beneficial. Certainly it would be helpful to know what to do if the aircraft lost pressure and oxygen was not readily available. Health-care professionals often warn their patients about weight control, exercise, and medications, and these warnings are ignored even though they are vital for a person's health. What are the variables that impact the adherence or neglect of warnings? The series of experiments in this chapter investigate how *cost* and *social influence* impact our decision regarding acceptance or rejection of warnings. *Cost*, as defined in this research program and generally in psychological investigations, refers to the effort an individual has to expend or the convenience to the individual, whereas *social influence* refers to the impact that other people have on our behavior.

Previous research in this area suggests that warnings have largely not been shown to be effective (McCarthy, Finnegan, Krumm-Scott, & McCarthy, 1984). In 1987, Wogalter and associates confirmed that the location or placement of a warning affected compliance. They found that if a warning was given early in the instructions, it resulted in the highest degree of compliance. In addition, the prominence of the warning was also related to compliance. Cunitz (1981) and Peters (1984) noted that warnings have both an informational and behavioral role. The informational function informs the

Incorporating the research of M. S. Wogalter, S. T. Allison, and N. A. McKenna, "Effects of Cost and Social Influence on Warning Compliance," 1989, *Human Factors, 31*, pp. 133–141.

consumer about the correct manner of usage of the product so as to avoid danger, whereas the behavioral role attempts to persuade the consumer to focus on the warnings and modify the consumer's actions in the direction of safety.

Cialdini (1993) stated that people are exposed to thousands of social influence attempts each day, largely from advertisers. In order to make sense of this bombardment of influence, Cialdini argued that we resort to heuristics to help us to make decisions about how to respond to the barrage of social influence. Heuristics are simple "rules of thumb" that we employ to clarify tasks in order to come up with an effective decision in a speedy manner. For example, suppose you just moved into an apartment in an unfamiliar community and you were very hungry and wanted to find a fast-food burger restaurant. How would you go about the task? Using a heuristic that fast-food restaurants are located near interstate highway exits might well be a "rule of thumb" that would be successful. This is called a "rule of thumb" because it is usually successful, but not always. Eagly and Chaiken (1984) propose the following heuristic strategies that have been successful in getting people to comply with warnings:

- Expertise of the source: Warnings from a well-known cardiologist about diet and exercise affecting blood pressure would likely have greater impact than similar opinions from your plumber.
- Positive value of the source: Warnings from a person you know will likely have greater influence. Advertisers have capitalized on this by providing endorsements by famous entertainment and sports figures.
- Warning quality: The quality is often inferred from the quantity of specific reasons cited in the message. The more specific reasons suggested, the higher the perception of message quality, and therefore warning value.
- Statistical arguments: Warnings tend to be perceived as more effective if they are upheld by statistics. If a person is told that 80 percent of dentists use Blah-Blah mouthwash, and it is further supported with figures and charts, it is likely to be an impressive warning.
- Behavior of others, social influence: People model the behavior and experience of others, and their experience becomes a guide for how to respond.

The research described in this chapter targets this final heuristic—social influence—as an independent variable that was examined in reference to its potential effect on compliance to warnings. In addition, the cost to the individual, often in terms of effort and time commitment, was studied in conjunction with social influence. The procedure for the initial three experiments focused on a chemistry laboratory project in which participants mixed chemicals according to specific instructions. In the first experiment, the independent variable was cost and the dependent variable was compliance with warnings. The second and third experiments studied how social influence, in both low- and high-cost situations, effected compliance with warnings. The fourth and final investigation took the lessons learned from the chemistry laboratory experiments into a real-world setting to determine how the lab findings hold up. This final study provided genuine external validation of the laboratory findings and made the results much more meaningful and applicable.

RESEARCH STUDY 1

The objective of this initial study was to evaluate the effect of two levels of cost (low and high) on compliance with a warning in a chemistry laboratory. The participants in this experiment were 23 introductory psychology students. The research was conducted in a traditional chemistry laboratory with the typical assortment of beakers, flasks, measuring devices, solutions, and so forth that conveyed a sense of authenticity to participants. The lab situation was designed to portray an environment in which the participants were being asked to handle chemicals that could possibly be dangerous. In performing the chemistry assignment, participants were given their directions in written form and were told to complete the task as quickly and precisely as possible. They were also told that their work would be evaluated for correctness. After the above instructions, participants were given the following printed caution:

> WARNING: Wear gloves and masks while performing the task to avoid irritating fumes and possible irritation of the skin. (Wogalter et al., 1989, p.135)

After the warning statement the participants were given the specific written directions necessary to measure and mix the solutions and complete the assignment. The procedure for participants consisted of signing of consent documents in a room where safety equipment—gloves and masks—were obviously placed on a table. They were then led to an adjacent room where the chemistry project was conducted. Next they were given verbal directions to be precise, to produce high-quality work, and to complete the work in 5 minutes. The participants were randomly assigned to one of two conditions: low cost (masks and gloves in the consent signing room as well as in the chemistry room) and high cost (masks and gloves were only accessible in the consent signing room). The independent variable, therefore, was cost (high or low) and the dependent variable was participant compliance with the safety warning (wearing both mask and gloves). The low-cost condition required little effort for the participants to comply because the safety equipment was in the chemistry laboratory. The participants in the high-cost condition would have had to exert some effort and leave the laboratory to obtain the safety gear. The results of this experiment are presented in Table 35.1.

The findings provide clear evidence that low-cost conditions enhance compliance with safety directives. A statistical analysis of the results confirmed that the cost variable was indeed statistically significant at $p < .01$. This means that luck or other extraneous variables were not likely to be responsible for the effect on the dependent variable and that readers can place confidence in the findings. The findings from this study, that is, low cost facilitating warning compliance, were seen in the previous research of Wogalter et al. (1987) as well as in other studies of compliance in the field of social psychology (Piliavin, Piliavin, & Rodin, 1976).

TABLE 35.1   Percentage of Compliance with Safety Warning in Three Experimental Studies

WEARING GLOVES & MASK WHILE CONDUCTING CHEMISTRY PROJECT	PERCENT OF COMPLIANCE BY PARTICIPANTS
Experiment 1	
Low cost (N = 11)	62%
High cost (N = 12)	17%
Experiment 2	
Low cost	
Compliant confederate (N = 8)	100%
Noncompliant confederate (N = 9)	33%
Experiment 3	
High cost	
Compliant confederate (N = 10)	70%
Noncompliant confederate (N = 10)	0%

EXPERIMENT 2

In this experiment the independent variable was the social influence of being exposed to a compliant or noncompliant confederate. The participants in the study are unaware of the confederate's role and are led to believe the confederate was another participant in the experiment. The general finding in the social psychology literature (Cialdini, 1993) is that people who are exposed to others who comply tend to comply in similar situations. In the same way, being exposed to noncompliant examples leads to noncompliance in participants. This second experiment sought to determine if the general findings stated above occurred in a warning compliance situation. The 17 students in this experiment were introductory psychology students. The chemistry laboratory setup was similar to the first study, except that more equipment was required to accomplish the task. The necessary safety equipment was in the same room as the participant and near the chemistry laboratory setup. It was therefore low cost for all participants. Experimental procedures were the same as the first study with one exception—the confederate, who acted like another student, worked near the participant and demonstrated compliance (i.e., wore safety mask and gloves) or did not comply (i.e., did not wear safety equipment). Table 35.1 (Experiment 2) shows that participants were highly influenced by the extent of confederate compliance in a low-cost situation. A statistical analysis of the results confirmed that the cost variable was indeed statistically significant at $p < .001$. Simply put, when a confederate complied, the participants always complied, and when a confederate did not comply, two-thirds of the participants followed the confederate's lead and did not wear safety equipment.

EXPERIMENT 3

This third experiment followed the same pattern as the second study with one change—high cost was substituted for low cost. Would participants comply with the social influence of a confederate in a high-cost context where safety equipment was located in a room adjacent to the chemistry laboratory? The participants were 20 introductory psychology students. The results can be seen in Table 35.1 (Experiment 3). The findings clearly show that warning compliance is significantly (p <.001) impacted by the influence of a confederate, under conditions of high cost to the participant. Under the high-cost conditions 70 percent of participants complied with warnings when working beside a compliant confederate. In contrast, if the confederate was noncompliant, not one single participant followed the warnings.

In summarizing the data from the three experiments, the following major conclusions can be drawn:

- Low cost is much more effective than high cost in getting individuals to comply with warnings when there is no model for the behavior.
- Social influence is a powerful factor, and individuals tend to follow the lead of others under both low- and high-cost conditions.

Experiments in laboratories are an excellent method of obtaining useful data in understanding such issues as the variables affecting warning compliance. It is vitally important however to determine whether the results obtained in the experimental lab operate outside the lab in the real world. It is laudable that the research described in this chapter chose to provide an out-of-lab field experiment to investigate the generalizability of the findings discovered in the three laboratory experiments

The field study was done in a women's dorm at a university. The three-story dorm had an elevator that traveled from the basement to the third story. On the ground floor a handwritten sign was affixed to the wall adjacent to the elevator controls. The sign stated:

CAUTION: Elevator may stick between floors. Use the stairs. (Wolgalter et al., 1989)

A stairwell was located about 10 feet from the elevator. The study collected data on elevator and stair usage, with warning sign posted, under three conditions:

- No confederate (essentially a baseline condition to ascertain typical usage)
- Compliant confederate
- Noncompliant confederate

The actual procedure for conducting this study involved a confederate who either (1) chooses to use the stairs after reading the warning sign or (2) a confederate who reads the sign and chooses to use the elevator. In each condition a single participant observed the confederate's actions. The data recorded, the dependent variable, was the

TABLE 35.2   Percentage of Compliance with Elevator Warnings in Three Conditions

EXPERIMENTAL CONDITION	COMPLIANCE WITH ELEVATOR WARNING SIGN
No confederate ($N = 18$)	33%
Compliant confederate ($N = 18$)	89%
Noncompliant confederate ($N = 18$)	28%

frequency of warning sign compliance in the three conditions. Table 35.2 presents the percentage of compliance in the three conditions.

In both the baseline condition (no confederate) and in the noncompliant confederate condition, the percentage of participant compliance was approximately the same, 28 to 32 percent. However, when a participant was confronted with a confederate who was compliant with warning messages, it was very likely (89 percent of the time) that the participant also complied. This study confirms the findings of the laboratory research and shows the powerful impact of social influence to comply. Probably noncompliant confederates had little impact on participants largely because the baseline response was quite low and likely could not be further decreased even through social influence.

IMPLICATIONS

The outcomes of this series of studies can be usefully applied in many nonlab situations. For example, the research suggests that it is desirable for organizations, manufacturers, and institutions to make warnings as easy and convenient to follow as possible. Reducing the cost (i.e., effort) for an individual is an issue for designers and engineers to implement so that the product or service is used in the safest manner. If a product requires considerable effort to operate in the safest manner, individuals will likely have low rates of compliance. For example if a paint and vanish remover requires plastic gloves for safety, this research would recommend that the gloves be included with the product in order to lower the effort of compliance and ultimately enhance safety. Wogalter et al. (1989) noted that hair coloring products typically include protective plastic gloves with the product to enhance consumer compliance with the safety instructions. It is also likely that organizations that use strategies requiring low effort to gain compliance will benefit by having their products used in a safe manner and therefore avoid possible legal issues. Our students have informed us that condoms are conveniently available in dorm bathrooms. The ready availability certainly meets the test of low cost and would likely increase usage to avoid the potential dangers of unsafe sex.

The research described in this chapter certainly supports the view that observing a single person complying with a safety warning facilitates compliance in others. The converse, observing a person who fails to comply with warnings, also has a powerful influence in inhibiting compliance among observers. These findings argue that employers should not allow a single example of noncompliance in safety situations because it can serve as an effective model for increasing noncompliance in other workers.

The impact of cost and social influence can operate and can be seen in a wide range of human interactions. If you are interested in seeing how these variables and others operate, the work of Latane (1981) and Cialdini (1993) are excellent resources.

REFERENCES

Chaiken, S. (1980). Heuristic versus systematic information processing and the use of source versus message cues in persuasion. *Journal of Personality and Social Psychology, 39*, 752–766.

Cialdini, R. B. (1993). *Influence: Science and practice* (3rd ed.). New York: HarperCollins.

Cunitz, R. J. (1981). Psychologically effective warnings. *Hazard Prevention, 17*, 5–7.

Eagly, A. H., & Chaiken, S. (1984). Cognitive theories of persuasion. In L. Berkowitz (Ed.), *Advances in experimental social psychology* (Vol. 17, pp. 268–359). New York: Academic Press.

Latané, B. (1981). The psychology of social impact. *American Psychologist, 36*, 343–356.

McCarthy, R. L., Finnegan, J. P., Krumm-Scott, S., & McCarthy, G. E. (1984). Product information presentation, user behavior, and safety. In *Proceedings of the Human Factors Society 28th Annual Meeting* (pp. 81–85). Santa Monica, CA: Human Factors Society.

Peters, G. A. (1984). A challenge to the safety profession. *Professional Safety, 29*, 46–50.

Piliavin, I. M., Piliavin, J. A., & Rodin, J. (1976). Costs, diffusion, and the stigmatized victim. *Journal of Personality and Social Psychology, 32*, 429–438.

Wogalter, M. S., Allison, S. T., & McKenna, N. A. (1989). Effects of cost and social influence on warning compliance. *Human Factors, 31*, 133–141.

Wogalter, M. S., Gofrey, S. S., Fontenelle, G. A., Desaulniers, D. R., Rothstein, P. R., & Laughery, K. R. (1987). Effectiveness of warnings. *Human Factors, 29*, 599–612.

Wogalter, M. S., McKenna, N. A., & Allison, S. T. (1988). Warning compliance: Behavioral effects of cost and consensus. In *Proceedings of the Human Factors Society 32nd Annual meeting* (pp. 901–904). Santa Monica, CA: Human Factors Society.

CHAPTER 36

DOES TV VIOLENCE SELL?

In the United States the television is a basic feature of the home, with greater than 98 percent of households having one or more sets (American Psychological Association, 1993). It is also the dominant force for commercial advertising according to Bushman (1998). Data from Huston and associates (1992) indicate that adults spend more time in front of the television that any other single activity outside of working and sleeping. And children spend more time watching TV than they do in school. Television clearly is a dominant activity for American family life.

TELEVISION IS VIOLENT

Comprehensive research on television programming (National Television Violence Study, 1996, 1997) found that approximately 60 percent of programming on cable and network television consisted of violent content. Before children become teenagers they are likely to be exposed on television to over 8,000 murders and more than 100,000 various incidents of violence on television (Huston et al., 1992). Surveys indicate that the American public is consistent in its belief that violent programming should be reduced or eliminated (Fischer, 1994; Zipperer, 1994). The television industry, in response, appears to believe that television just mirrors our culture and is not exaggerating or overemphasizing violence. However, research (Oliver, 1994) suggests that television violence far overestimates the violence that can be found in the real world. It is possible that television executives believe that violence is an effective way to capture greater numbers of viewers and, therefore, will be more attractive to commercial advertisers. However, as Bushman (1998) related, increasing violence does not necessarily increase the viewership of a program (Diener & Defour, 1978; Diener & Woody, 1981; Sprafkin, Rubinstein, & Stone, 1977).

BUSHMAN'S THINKING

The research described in this chapter explores the effectiveness of commercials during both violent and nonviolent programs. Does a viewer remember the content of a

Incorporating the research of B. J. Bushman, "Effects of Television Violence on Memory for Commercial Messages," 1998, *Journal of Experimental Psychology: Applied, 4*, pp. 1–17.

commercial better if it is placed in a program of violent content or nonviolent content? Bear in mind that the content of a commercial must be remembered in order to sell the product. Although Bushman's research does not assess whether actual purchase decisions are altered by placement during violent/nonviolent programs, memory for commercial details is certainly a very desirable characteristic.

WHY VIOLENCE MAY AFFECT MEMORY

Two suggestions have been made about why commercials might be ineffective in violent programs:

- Violent programs put viewers in a bad mood and may make them angry (Anderson, 1997; Bushman, 1995). Anger generated by watching violence may activate other anger-related concepts and inhibit the information from the commercial, therefore decreasing the value of the information contained in the commercial (Bower, 1981; Isen, Clark, Shalker, & Karp, 1978).
- Mood management theory (Isen, 1984; Parrott, 1993) suggests that violence might put viewers in a negative mood. Viewers placed in a negative mood by programming engage in an active process to improve their negative mood. In contrast, viewers in a program-initiated positive mood seek to continue their positive mood without the need for an active cognitive process to make changes. The mood change or mood repair process, demands that individuals devote more cognitive energy toward themselves rather than directing this energy outward. Therefore, in repairing a mood, individuals would be less focused outwardly on commercial messages, thereby minimizing the impact of the commercials. This is probably not something that advertisers would want to happen.

BUSHMAN'S RESEARCH

The above theoretical explanations are interesting, but Bushman's research does not test them directly. The first two experiments focus on the impact of television violence on memory for commercial information. The third experiment examined whether or not anger induced by a violent program impairs a person's memory for details of a commercial.

EXPERIMENT 1

This experiment was designed to examine the impact of television violence on participants' memory for brand name of the product and specifics of the commercial. The participants were 200 volunteers who were undergraduate psychology students (100 males and 100 females). They received additional course credit for being in the experiment. The participants were randomly assigned to watch either a 15-minute violent or nonviolent video movie segment. The movie segments were determined by previous research not to differ on participants' self-reported arousal or on objective measures of physiological arousal (e.g., blood pressure, heart rate). The videos used were determined to be equally arousing and exciting, but different in violence. The 15-minute videos used in this experiment were taken from the films *Karate Kid III* (violent) and *Gorillas in the Mist* (nonviolent). The violent video showed a karate tournament in which an arrogant opponent repeatedly broke the rules and fought in a dirty manner. The nonviolent video depicted a scientist observing and interacting with gorillas. Each 15-minute video was interrupted at the 5-minute and 10-minute point for a 30 second commercial. The commercials used were for Krazy Glue and Wisk detergent. The order of the commercials was counterbalanced and therefore half the participants watched the Wisk commercial first, and half saw the Krazy Glue commercial first. At the 5-minute point and the 10-minute point the commercials interrupted the video. To make the 15-minute video and commercial sequence even more realistic, a network station identification logo and message were also made part of the video. After watching the video the participants:

1. Listed the brand names of the products shown in the commercials.
2. Listed all the details they could recall about the commercials.
3. Reported the number of television hours in various categories that they watched per week.
4. Reported whether they had seen the film or commercials shown.

After collecting the above data, participants were debriefed.

RESULTS OF EXPERIMENT 1

The presentation order of the commercials, the sex of participant, habitual exposure to television violence, previous exposure to the film segments, and previous exposure to the commercial used were *not* related to the dependent variables. The results of this experiment are presented in Table 36.1. In terms of brand name recall, participants who watched the nonviolent video had significantly higher rates of recall than those who watched the violent video film segment did. When asked to recall commercial details, participants in the nonviolent situation had higher scores than the group that watched the violent film segments. The findings indicate that watching commercials in a context of violence impairs memory for commercials

EXPERIMENT 2

Bushman conducted this second experiment to replicate the initial study and to investigate another dependent measure, visual brand recognition. The decision to purchase a product may not require a person to remember the brand name, but only to be able to recognize it on the store shelf. This acknowledges the fact that shoppers frequently make choices between brands in the store at the time of purchase (Bettman, 1979). In

TABLE 36.1   Experiment 1—The Impact of Television Violence on Recall of Commercial Brand Names and Commercial Details*

DEPENDENT MEASURE	VIOLENT FILM (MEAN SCORE)	NONVIOLENT FILM (MEAN SCORE)
Brand name recall**	1.22	1.50
Commercial details***	6.69	8.61

*Differences between violent and nonviolent groups for both dependent measures were significant at $p < .05$.

**Scores on brand name recall ranged from 0 (no brands recalled) to 2 (both brands recalled).

***Scores on commercial details ranged from 0 to 22.

this situation, consumers are faced with many competing brands, and if prior advertising is effective they need only to recognize the product. This is different than having the product name stored in memory and seeking it out while shopping.

The participants and general procedure for this second experiment were similar to the first experiment with the addition of the visual brand recognition test. Participants were shown the videos and commercials and given the same brand name recall and commercial message recall as in Experiment 1. In addition, the third dependent measure, visual brand recognition, was accomplished in the following manner. Participants were informed that the video segment they watched had two commercials, one for a laundry detergent and the other for a glue product. The participants then watched slides of six different glue products (Krazy Glue and five other glue products) and six different laundry detergents (Wisk and five other detergents). The task for the participants was to write the brand name seen in the video segment. This measure did not require that they recall the brand name because it was presented along with five other competitors. They only needed to be able to recognize it.

RESULTS OF EXPERIMENT 2

The results of this second experiment are presented in Table 36.2. Participants who watched the nonviolent video segment *recognized* more brands than participants who watched violent videos ($p < .05$) and also *recalled* more brand names ($p < .05$). In this study the differences between violent and nonviolent groups on the commercial message recall dependent measure were in the predicted direction (i.e., the nonviolent group recalled more details), but were not significant ($p > .05$).

This second experiment replicated the findings of the initial study and provided some new findings. The added recognition measure in particular provided an even

TABLE 36.2   Experiment 2—The Impact of Television Violence on Brand Name Recognition, Recall of Commercial Brand Names, and Commercial Details*

DEPENDENT MEASURE	VIOLENT FILM (MEAN SCORE)	NONVIOLENT FILM (MEAN SCORE)
Brand name recognition**	1.66	1.85
Brand name recall**	1.21	1.56
Commercial details***	7.10	8.01

*Differences between violent and nonviolent groups for brand name recognition and recall were significant at $p < .05$.

**Scores on brand name recognition and brand name recall ranged from 0 (no brands recalled) to 2 (both brands recalled).

***Scores on commercial details ranged from 0 to 17.

more realistic appraisal of how consumers make decisions, giving the research greater ecological validity.

EXPERIMENT 3

The goal of Experiment 3 was to see whether or not anger mediates how television violence influences memory for commercials. In other words, does anger resulting from watching violence impair memory? Bushman also explored how positive affect (the opposite of anger) served as a possible intermediary variable affecting memory. The advantage of exploring polar-opposite emotions was that information could be gathered on whether or not anger impairs memory and conversely on whether or not positive affect facilitates memory. In this experiment, the researchers used the same general procedures except that four video segments of violence and nonviolent films were used. Violent video segments included the films *Cobra, Die Hard, Single White Female,* and *The Hand That Rocks the Cradle.* Nonviolent video segments included *Awakenings, Chariots of Fire, Field of Dreams,* and *Never Cry Wolf.* Participants were randomly assigned to watch one of the possible eight videos. After watching the video segment participants filled out a rating form to assess anger and positive affect. Anger was determined by the number of adjectives endorsed on subscale of the Multiple Affect Adjective Checklist (Zuckerman & Lubin, 1985). Some of the anger items were *angry, annoyed, furious.* Positive affect was assessed on participants' endorsement of adjectives (e.g., *alert, ethusiastic*) from the Positive and Negative Affect Schedule (Watson, Clark, & Tellegen, 1988). Based on the results of the first two experiments, the researchers expected higher brand recognition, brand recall, and commercial message memory scores for participants watching nonviolent videos than the group who observed the violent video segments. The researchers used a complex statistical analysis to determine whether or not television violence increases viewer anger and thus decreases a viewer's ability to retain information about commercials. This line of reasoning was based on the views discussed earlier suggesting that anger interferes with the commercial information presented and that the viewer has to use his or her cognitive resources to cope and "repair" their negative mood (mood management). Participant's arousal and positive affect were not hypothesized to have negative effects on the participants' mood and therefore would not decrease commercial recall.

RESULTS OF EXPERIMENT 3

As you can see in Table 36.3, the participants watching nonviolent video segments had significantly higher rates of brand recognition, recalled more brand names, and recalled more details of the commercials than the participants who watched violent video segments. This is consistent with the results of the previous experiments and provides a valuable replication. The complex data analysis from this third experiment discovered that anger was a very important mediator of the effect of television violence on a participant's memory for commercials. General arousal and positive affect did not have the significant impact that anger had. This finding provides insight into why television violence diminishes participants' ability to recall important details of a commercial. It looks as if television violence makes a person angry, and that anger decreases the ability of the person to remember commercial details. This research suggested that television advertisers should be aware that if they present commercials during violent programming, viewers may actually have to focus on mending and repairing their own emotional and cognitive states. They may have

TABLE 36.3   Experiment 3—The Impact of Television Violence on Brand Name Recognition, Recall of Commercial Brand Names, and Commercial Details*

DEPENDENT MEASURE	VIOLENT FILM (MEAN SCORE)	NONVIOLENT FILM (MEAN SCORE)
Brand name recognition**	1.65	1.79
Brand name recall**	1.14	1.31
Commercial details***	5.10	6.28

*Differences between violent and nonviolent groups for all three dependent measures were significant at $p < .05$.

**Scores on brand name recognition and brand name recall ranged from 0 (no brands recalled) to 2 (both brands recalled).

***Scores on commercial details ranged from 0 to 18.

to calm down from the anger generated and therefore have less available time to focus on the commercials. This research should send a cautionary note to advertisers—placing commercials in a violent context might not pay off in sales. Bushman points out that this series of experiments does not directly examine whether or not television violence impacts the actual purchasing behavior of viewers. However, because the decision to purchase is often based on information from commercials, lack of memory for important commercial details added to arousal of anger is likely to have a negative effect on purchasing.

In summing up this research, Bushman states the following three reasons why advertisers might want to avoid placing commercials for their products in violent programming:

1. Most viewers voice upset toward the amount of violence presented on television (TV Guide, 1992; Zipperer, 1994).
2. Film and television violence increases violence in viewers through observational learning and therefore contributes negatively to our society (National Institute of Mental Health, 1982; Paik & Comstock, 1994).
3. Based on the research conducted by Bushman, placing commercials in the context of violent programs makes no economic sense for advertisers. Viewers of such commercials get angry and have decreased memories for many important aspects of the commercial message.

REFERENCES

American Psychological Association. (1993). *Violence and youth: Psychology's response*. Washington, DC: Author.

Anderson, C. A. (1977). Effects of violent movies and trait hostility on hostile feelings and aggressive thoughts. *Aggressive Behavior, 23*, 161–178.

Bettman, J. R. (1979). Memory factors in consumer choices: A review. *Journal of Marketing, 43*, 37–53.

Bower, G. (1981). Mood and memory. *American Psychologist, 36*, 129–148.

Bushman, B. J. (1995). Moderating role of trait aggressiveness in the effects of violent media on aggression. *Journal of Personality and Social Psychology, 69*, 950–960.

Bushman, B. J. (1998). Effects of television violence on memory for commercial messages. *Journal of Experimental Psychology: Applied, 4*, 1–17.

Diener, E., & DeFour, D. (1978). Does television violence enhance program popularity? *Journal of Personality and Social Psychology, 36*, 333–341.

Diener, E., & Woody, L. W. (1981). Television violence, conflict, realism, and action: A study in viewer liking. *Communication Research, 8*, 281–306.

Huston, A. C., Donnerstein, E., Fairchild, H., Feshbach, N. D., Katz, P. A., Murray, J. P., Rubinstein, E. A., Wilcox, B. L., & Zuckerman, D. (1992). *Big world, small screen: The role of television in American society*. Lincoln: University of Nebraska Press.

Isen, A. M. (1984). Toward understanding the role of affect in cognition. In R. Wyer, Jr., & T. Srull (Eds.), *Handbook of social cognition* (pp. 179–236). Hillsdale, NJ: Erlbaum.

Isen, A. M., Clark, M., Shalker, T. E., & Karp, L. (1978). Affect, accessibility of material in memory and behavior: A cognitive loop? *Journal of Personality and Social Psychology, 36*, 1–12.

National Institute of Mental Health. (1982). *Television and behavior: Ten years of scientific progress and implications for the Eighties (Vol. 1), Summary Report*. Washington, DC: U.S. Government Printing Office.

National Television Violence Study. (1996). *National television violence study* (Vol. 1). Thousand Oaks, CA: Sage.

National Television Violence Study. (1997). *National television violence study* (Vol. 2). Studio City, CA: Mediascope.

Oliver, M. B. (1994). Portrayals of crime, race, and aggression in "reality-based" police shows: A content analysis. *Journal of Broadcasting and Electronic Media, 38*, 179–192.

Paik, H., & Comstock, G. (1994). The effects of television violence on antisocial behavior: A meta-analysis. *Communication Research, 21*, 516–546.

Parrott, G. W. (1993). Beyond hedonism: Motives for inhibiting good moods and for maintaining bad moods. In D. M. Wegner & J. W. Pennebaker (Eds.), *Handbook of mental control* (pp. 278–305). Upper Saddle River, NJ: Prentice Hall.

Sprafkin, J. N., Rubinstein, E. A., & Stone, A. (1977). *The content analysis of four television diets* (Occasional Paper 77-3). Stony Brook, NY: Brookdale International Institute.

TV Guide. (1992, October 10–16). TV Guide poll: Would you give up TV for a million bucks? *TV Guide, 40*, 10–13, 15, 17.

Watson, D., Clark, L. A., & Tellegen, A. (1988). Development and validation of brief measures of positive and negative affect: The PANAS scales. *Journal of Personality and Social Psychology, 54*, 1063–1070.

Zipperer, J. (1994, February 7). Violence foes take aim: Advertisers and affiliates caught in the crossfire. *Christianity Today*, pp. 40–42.

Zuckerman, M., & Lubin, B. (1985*). Manual for the MAACL-R: The Multiple Adjective Checklist Revised.* San Diego, CA: Educational and Industrial Testing Service.

SUBJECT INDEX